The Governator

ALSO BY IAN HALPERIN

Unmasked: The Final Years of Michael Jackson

Who Killed Kurt Cobain?

Love & Death: The Murder of Kurt Cobain

Fire and Rain: The James Taylor Story

Shut Up and Smile: Supermodels, the Dark Side

Bad and Beautiful: Inside the Dazzling and
Deadly World of Supermodels

Best CEOs: How the Wild, Wild Web Was Won

Céline Dion: Behind the Fairytale

Miss Supermodel America

Guy Liberté: The Fabulous Story of the
Creator of the Cirque du Soleil

Brangelina: Angelina Jolie and Brad Pitt

The Governator

*From Muscle Beach to His Quest for
the White House, the Improbable Rise of
Arnold Schwarzenegger*

Ian Halperin

HARPER LUXE

An Imprint of HarperCollins*Publishers*

HarperCollins books may be purchased for educational, business, or sales promotional use. For information please write: Special Markets Department, HarperCollins Publishers, 10 East 53rd Street, New York, NY 10022.

FIRST HARPERLUXE EDITION

HarperLuxe™ is a trademark of HarperCollins Publishers

Library of Congress Cataloging-in-Publication Data is available upon request.

ISBN: 978-0-06-200223-5

10 11 12 13 14 ID/OPM 10 9 8 7 6 5 4 3 2 1

Dedicated to Ben Weider (1923–2008),
the incredible visionary whose lifelong
pursuit was spent bringing bodybuilding
into the international spotlight

Contents

Introduction

As the convoy of limousines drove toward Vienna's Schönbrunn Palace on June 4, 1961, thousands of Austrian citizens thronged the streets. They cheered till they were hoarse, jubilant that their country had been chosen to play a part in what many were predicting to be the end of the cold war. It was the most exciting thing to happen to their country since the Anschluss.

But it wasn't their peripheral role in hosting the potentially history-changing Vienna Summit between the United States and the Soviet Union that had attracted most of the screaming onlookers that afternoon. It was a chance to glimpse the exciting new American president, John F. Kennedy, and his glamorous wife, Jackie.

Like most of the rest of the world, Austrians were captivated by the charisma and youthful hopefulness of the handsome president, who promised a new era in international relations.

As the thirteen-year-old Arnold Schwarzenegger listened with his family to news of the meetings 125 miles away and the adulation being poured on Kennedy, he was swept up by the excitement. Even his normally reserved mother, Aurelia, could barely contain her enthusiasm for the youthful president.

For days leading up to the summit, the Austrian media had gushed with stories about Kennedy and his exciting background, portraying him as the American equivalent of royalty and describing his aristocratic upbringing, his world travels, his beautiful and accomplished wife, his rapid ascension to power.

To many a young boy in a similar situation, raised in a small provincial town, under the thumb of an overbearing father, with no apparent way out, Kennedy's life might seem like a fairy tale.

But as a young Arnold Schwarzenegger took in the scene that day, he vowed to himself that one day his countrymen would cheer for him the way they did for Kennedy.

1.
Rough Start

Almost half a century after John F. Kennedy's starring role at the Vienna Summit, I landed in the Austrian capital searching for clues to help explain how Schwarzenegger achieved a dream that at the time seemed impossible.

My guidebook was his 1977 autobiography *Arnold: Education of a Bodybuilder*. This was written long before most of the world had ever heard of him; still, reading the book—which is closer to a weight-training manual than a memoir—makes it obvious that he was confident even then.

It is a two-hour drive to Thal, the pastoral village where Schwarzenegger was born in July 1947 to Gustav and Aurelia Schwarzenegger.

Thal, it turns out, is a suburb of Graz, the capital of the Styrian region. In advance of my trip, I had been told by an Austrian friend that Styrians are considered the hicks of Austria, though this may reflect the snobbishness of the cosmopolitan Viennese more than a fair assessment of Styria's people. Still, the region is often mocked for its lack of sophistication, its conservative moral values, and its lack of worldliness. And while I had always assumed that Schwarzenegger's much-parodied thick accent is simply a product of his foreign upbringing, it seems that it is in fact a characteristic of the Styrian way of talking—a dialect commonly known as High German.

In this tiny village of about 2,000 inhabitants— unlike Vienna, where many people spoke English—it was very difficult to find anybody who could speak more than a few English words. And when people did speak English, their thick accent made it difficult to understand what they were saying. My first destination was Schwarzenegger's birthplace at Thal Linak 145. After asking directions of three people who spoke only German, I finally said to a woman on a bike, "Schwarzenegger house." She smiled and pointed the way.

When I reached the large two-story house, there was nobody at home. A sign indicated that the Anderwalt family lived here now, and I remembered that Frau Anderwalt had given a newspaper interview a few years earlier, explaining that she and her husband had bought the house in 1979. She mentioned that whenever Schwarzenegger visited the village, he always brought a camera crew to accompany him to his boyhood home. Whenever the cameras were rolling, she recalled, he was very jovial. But as soon as they were switched off, he was "cold and unfriendly."

His attitude may stem from the fact that he did not have very fond memories of growing up here. Although Thal now brags about the origins of its most famous resident, whose formative years were spent in the postcard-pretty village, Arnold Schwarzenegger's childhood was anything but idyllic.

There is an old saying about Schwarzenegger's homeland: "The Austrians are brilliant. They have managed to persuade the world that Beethoven was Austrian and Hitler was German." The fact is that Hitler was born in Austria and his countrymen welcomed him with open arms upon his ascension to power. It is the country's dirty little secret, one that the Austrians are often reluctant to discuss. In the months immediately following World War II, when Gustav Schwarzenegger settled in Thal, nobody in Austria asked what anybody else had done in the war, because nobody really wanted to know the answer.

And so when Gustav moved to Thal in 1946 and applied for the position of police chief, the job was his, despite an official prohibition against hiring former Nazis for police work. Then again, despite the title, the job wasn't very desirable. It paid a mere pittance and most often consisted of directing hikers from nearby Graz who ventured to the village for a picnic or rowboat ride on its picturesque lake.

Gustav grew up in a working-class family in the nearby Styrian industrial city of Neuberg. His father, Karl, was a mountain of a man whose genes are often credited with influencing Arnold's own muscular build. Like Karl, who died in his forties because of a work-related accident, Gustav worked in the Neuberg steel factory before joining the Austrian army for his compulsory military service. He was a talented musician who could play six different instruments, specializing in the flügelhorn. Following his discharge from the army, he worked for many years as a postal inspector and then as a policeman. His life was rather routine, but Karl always dreamed of something bigger, for himself and for Austria.

The answer lay in the nation over the hills.

In 1933, after Hitler took power in neighboring Germany, membership in the Nazi Party was made illegal by the Austrian government, nervous that

Hitler's brand of National Socialism would catch on. With a common language and culture, many Austrians considered themselves German and, as the Depression ravaged the Austrian economy, resulting in high unemployment and widespread poverty, many looked longingly at Germany's economic gains and at the fierce national pride that the Führer, an Austrian, had instilled.

By 1938, Hitler had made it clear that he considered Austria part of the German Reich and it was only a matter of time before Germany annexed Austria, by force if necessary. As early as 1934, the German leader had signaled his designs when Chancellor Engelbert Dollfuss of Austria was assassinated by Nazis in a failed coup.

The Austrian National Socialist Party was still in principle an underground movement, though it had been operating out in the open for months, by the time Gustav Schwarzenegger visited one of its offices in early 1938 and filled out a membership form.

Not long afterward, in March 1938, German troops marched into Austria, to be openly greeted by thousands of cheering Austrians waving Nazi flags and giving Hitler's salute. The overwhelming majority of Austrians enthusiastically voted to ratify the Anschluss (annexation) a month later, and Austria officially became part of the Third Reich.

A year later, in April 1939, Gustav Schwarzenegger enrolled in the German army. It was long believed that he served there simply as a military policeman. Decades later, a more sinister set of facts would emerge to shed light on Gustav's real wartime record—a record of complicity with evil that would later haunt Arnold as he climbed the ladder of success. Gustav was discharged from the army in February 1944, suffering from malaria. In October 1945, a few months after the war came to an end, he married twenty-three-year-old Aurelia Jadrny. She had been born in a suburb of Vienna and had previously been married to a man named Heinrich Muller, who had been killed during the war. At the time she met Gustav, she was working in a wartime relief office dispensing food stamps as part of the government's strictly controlled rationing program.

Although not a lot is known about Aurelia's past, Arnold once confided to a girlfriend that his mother had been in the crowd when Hitler rode triumphantly through the streets of Vienna following the Anschluss. And, like Gustav, she was taken in by the power and charisma of the Führer, to the point where she "almost swooned."

In 1946, Gustav and Aurelia moved from Mürzsteg to Thal, where he was to assume his new position as police chief. By then, she had given birth to one son, Meinhard, a year earlier and had another one on the way. Arnold was born in Thal on July 30, 1947.

After I leave the old Schwarzenegger house, I run into a student who speaks passable English walking his bike. I ask him where I might locate people who knew Arnold Schwarzenegger and he tells me my best possibility would be at the Café Thalersee, next to Lake Thal, a few minutes to the south. With a spectacular view of the lake and mountains, the inn has apparently been the center of life at Thal for decades as well as a tourist magnet for hikers from Graz who rent the colorful rowboats and pedal boats. The person who greets me, a young man in his twenties, speaks surprisingly good English and I tell him I am researching a documentary about the childhood of Arnold Schwarzenegger. He tells me that his parents and grandparents knew the family but that he has met Arnold only twice, briefly, when Arnold visited. He tells me I should speak to the proprietor, Karl Kling, whose family has owned the establishment since Schwarzenegger started to frequent the place and who knew the young Arnold quite well. Kling is due back in half an hour, so I have a bowl of goulash and a coffee while I'm waiting. I later discover that Arnold's favorite dish is the wild mushroom soup that he used to eat in this very dining room. Indeed, there are signs of Schwarzenegger everywhere: photos, handwritten notes, and even postcards of Arnold available for sale at the counter.

When Kling arrives, he is happy to talk to me, but his English is very poor. His employee is far too busy to translate for me, so I do my best to elicit his story. "I knew the family well," he tells me. "Frau Schwarzenegger was very nice. She worked here, sometimes, in the kitchen, making pastries. I was friends with Arnold, but he was older than me. We were neighbors." Kling tells me he was born in 1955, so he is about eight years younger than Arnold.

Arnold, he tells me, was very "funny," but it was the brother, Meinhard Schwarzenegger, whom everybody knew. "They were always playing jokes on people," he says, laughing.

Indeed, a number of accounts of Schwarzenegger's childhood portray him and his brother as pranksters, constantly playing practical jokes on other children. "He was a rascal, surely, but that's very normal," his classmate Franz Hormann told the biographer Laurence Leamer. "He played a few great pranks. He was part of every great prank." These are usually depicted as good, harmless fun, but the British writer Wendy Leigh, who is fluent in German, discovered something far darker when she conducted her own investigation in the late 1980s, journeying to Thal and talking to the townspeople who knew Arnold best.

One of those townspeople told her that the "Schwarzeneggers were hated in Thal. Today everyone loves them, but forty years ago no one wanted to have anything to do with them."

As Leigh discovered, Arnold and his brother weren't in fact known as the town pranksters. They were known as bullies, the terror of the village. It didn't take much investigation to discover who influenced this behavior.

During my conversation with Karl Kling, he didn't have anything unflattering to say about Arnold or the Schwarzenegger family, though he conspicuously refrained from saying anything positive about Gustav. Once I did the math, however, I soon realized that Kling couldn't have known Schwarzenegger as well as he claims, for he was only eleven years old when Arnold left Thal for good.

However, the English-speaking café employee I had met when I first arrived provided considerably greater insight when I spoke to him on a break later. Despite the fact that he did not know Arnold Schwarzenegger at all well, he had access to someone who did: his grandmother, who died several years ago, and who had been active for years in the local Catholic church with Aurelia Schwarzenegger.

"My grandma always told me that Arnold's mother was a wonderful woman; she called her a very dear lady. They were both very devout, very religious, and I think what they both had in common was that they were married to bad men."

He told me that Gustav had a reputation in the village as a very jolly man, filled with life, when he was sober, but that he was a very mean drunk. And as the years passed, and his drinking got worse, he was known to be violent. "My grandma never knew whether he beat up Aurelia but she suspected he did. She never saw any signs, never any marks, but she said she witnessed terrible fights. He would yell at her many times; he kept her under his control."

She didn't know the boys very well, he recalls, but she always described Arnold's older brother, Meinhard, as "very handsome" and said that the Schwarzenegger brothers were "a lot of trouble." She claimed that Aurelia "protected" them from their father.

The employee says he never met Gustav, because the family had moved away from Thal before he was born, but there is considerable evidence to back up the grandmother's description of Gustav as an ugly drunk.

Others have described him as extremely possessive and jealous, keeping Aurelia on a tight leash. He was said to favor his firstborn son, Meinhard, over Arnold. This preference is often explained by the fact that he suspected Arnold wasn't his; he was known to rant about this to his fellow villagers when he got drunk enough, though there is no evidence that he ever shared his suspicion with Arnold.

For years, Arnold described his father as a strict disciplinarian, without much further elaboration. But in the early 1990s, he finally opened up about the abuse he had suffered at the hands of his father.

"My hair was pulled. I was hit with belts," he recalled. "So was the kid next door. It was just the way it was. Many of the children I've seen were broken by their parents, which was the German-Austrian mentality . . . I have seen one kid almost get his ear ripped off right in front of me because he was fighting with someone else. I think it was a very much more brutal time. Break the will. They didn't want to create an individual. It was all about conforming."

When Gustav's drinking and violent fits became too much, Aurelia often sent Arnold to stay with his uncle Alois in the nearby town of Mürzzuschlag.

Perhaps inspired by Gustav's example, Meinhard—the golden boy, favored by both his father and his

mother—was also known to frequently pick on Arnold, hazing and tormenting him with great relish. But perhaps this could be simply put down to normal sibling rivalry, as Arnold never mentioned it publicly. His father was known to pit the boys against each other at any opportunity, even forcing them to box on occasion.

Arnold would later credit the cruel treatment at the hands of his father with toughening him up and causing him to empathize with other people's suffering. But at the time, there wasn't a lot of empathy on display, as Arnold and his brother showed their own cruel streak in front of their peers.

"Gustav had taught him to hate and humiliate rather than love," writes Leigh. "Now Arnold, incited by his brother, began to terrorize other people."

Leigh interviewed one source who witnessed Meinhard and Arnold whipping a group of girls with stinging nettles. Another time, the two boys stood in the middle of the road, refusing to let the local milkman pass. Then they hit him until he bled; and when he complained to the chief of police, he received no justice, because the chief happened to be the father of the assailants. Another villager described to Leigh standing at a bus stop and watching a young Arnold approach a twelve-year-old girl, pull her book-filled schoolbag out of her hand, and throw it into the river.

She quotes the headmaster of the boys' school, Herr Stanzer, as praying to be rid of the Schwarzenegger brothers. Meinhard was, in fact, eventually expelled and sent to reform school.

Despite his father's lofty position, the Schwarzeneggers were actually living a very austere life.

"Where I started was a little farm community outside the Austrian town of Graz," Schwarzenegger would later recall of his childhood. "Now, that may make you think of sunny hillsides with buttercups dancing in the breeze, and happy children with rosy cheeks, eating strudel. But that's not what I think of. First of all, strudel was a luxury. It was right after World War II, and the country was absolutely devastated and destroyed. We had no flushing toilet in the house. No refrigerator. No television. What we did have was food rations— and we did have British tanks around to give us kids an occasional lift to the elementary school."

Most young Austrians—even those facing a life of poverty, an abusive alcoholic parent, and crushing boredom—would have looked at their life as the natural order of things with no way out. But Arnold Schwarzenegger was already planning his escape.

2.

Developing the Look of Power

As with much of the mythology surrounding Arnold Schwarzenegger's meteoric rise, there are many different versions, some conflicting, of how the young Austrian boy decided to take up bodybuilding as his life's pursuit. Each version was furnished by Schwarzenegger himself at some point in his career to conform with the public persona he was crafting at the time. In that respect, he is probably not much different from any other celebrity.

In his 1977 autobiography, he pinpoints his epiphany as the first time he put his fingers around a barbell, when he was fifteen years old. At that moment, he writes, "I felt the challenge and exhilaration of hoisting the heavy steel plates above my head."

In his teens he played a variety of sports and had achieved a reputation as a competent athlete, though not a superb one like his older brother, Meinhard, who excelled in every sport he played. Their father, Gustav, had been a champion ice curler and was determined that both his sons would distinguish themselves in sports. Like most Austrian boys, Arnold had been playing soccer from an early age and had played on competitive local teams since he was ten. But his heart wasn't really in it. Since the age of thirteen, Arnold knew team sports weren't for him. His reasons were revealing. "I was already off on an individual trip," he recalled. "I disliked it when we won a game and I didn't get personal recognition. The only time I really felt rewarded was when I was singled out as being best."

To keep his father happy, he continued to play soccer, but he also tried a number of individual sports to determine which he liked best. He ran, he swam, he boxed. He entered javelin and shot put competitions. But none of these sports "felt right." Then his soccer coach decided that the team could get into better shape by lifting weights for an hour a week.

The first time he entered a bodybuilding gym, he knew he had found his calling.

"Those guys were huge and brutal," he wrote. "I found myself walking around them, staring at muscles I couldn't even name, muscles I'd never even seen before. The weightlifters shone with sweat; they were powerful looking, Herculean. And there it was before me—my life, the answer I'd been seeking. It clicked."

Soccer players needed strong legs, not the kind of muscles typical of serious bodybuilders. So Arnold threw himself into leg weights. As often as he could, far more often than his teammates, he went to the gym. One hour a week couldn't satisfy his passion for the heavy steel. Soon the other weightlifters noticed how seriously he took his pursuit. They encouraged him to pursue bodybuilding, adopting him as their protégé. "These weightlifters became my new heroes," he wrote.

Before long, Arnold had become a fixture on the shore of Lake Thal, where he could often be spotted doing chin-ups on the branches of trees or handstand push-ups. His physique expanded rapidly, but the townspeople couldn't understand why he would throw himself into such a strange pursuit.

"I could not have chosen a less popular sport," he recalled. "My school friends thought I was crazy. But I didn't care. My only thoughts were of going ahead, building muscles and more muscles."

While most of the hormone-charged boys in Thal were girl crazy by the age of fifteen, Arnold had never shown the slightest interest in the opposite sex. This concerned Gustav considerably. For a time, he openly speculated about whether his youngest son was gay. That began to change as Arnold's muscles took on a life of their own and the local girls began to take notice. Not of all them were favorably impressed, however.

"The strangest thing was how my new body struck girls," he recalled. "There were a certain number of girls who were knocked out by it and a certain number who found it repulsive. There was absolutely no in-between. It seemed cut and dried."

The reactions, positive and negative, gave him added motivation to get bigger. It was attention he craved, and he was getting that everywhere he went. Whenever he caught a girl looking at his ever-expanding frame, he would casually raise his arm and flex his biceps to elicit a reaction.

Soon Arnold had more girls than he could handle, more even than his handsome brother Meinhard, who had been dating regularly since age twelve. "I had no difficulty getting girls," Arnold recalled. "I'd been introduced to sex with almost no hangups. The older bodybuilders at the gym had started including me in their parties. It was easy for me. These guys always saw to it that I had a girl. 'Here, Arnold, this one's for you.'"

When he could tell that a girl was repulsed by his muscles, he admitted, this made him want her all the more. One girl who claimed she wasn't the least turned on by his body was named Herta. He was desperate to make her change her mind. After weeks of flirting, he finally got up the nerve to ask her out on a date.

"I wouldn't go out with you in a million years," she said. "You're in love with yourself. You're in love with your own body. You look at yourself all the time. You pose in front of the mirror."

Her reaction came as a slap in the face, he recalls. Nor was it the first time that Schwarzenegger would be accused of narcissistic behavior—a syndrome that had long been associated with bodybuilders and was first defined at the beginning of the twentieth century, when Sigmund Freud wrote of the phenomenon as a psychological syndrome in his paper "On Narcissism."

The father of psychoanalysis argued that a certain amount of narcissism is necessary for normal development. But when the narcissist starts to sublimate his libido and direct it to his own ego, Freud concluded, a pathological form of megalomania begins to emerge. In recent years, the syndrome has been recognized in the mental health field as a full-blown condition, narcissistic personality disorder, affecting less than 1 percent of the population. More tellingly, given Schwarzenegger's history, the onset of the condition is thought to come most often in early adolescence and is commonly attributed to childhood abuse and trauma inflicted by parents, authority figures, or even peers.

Decades after Freud first documented the condition, an American psychologist, Alan Klein, decided to apply his theories to bodybuilding, studying a cross section of weightlifters at gyms in California to determine the connection between narcissism and bodybuilding culture. Klein found significant links, discovering that most bodybuilders he came across had started with a feeling of insignificance.

"The construction of large and imposing looking physiques," he writes in his 1993 study, *Little Big Men*, "is somehow (directly or indirectly) an attempt to overcome such feelings. For the bodybuilder suffering from such feelings, the shocked reaction of the public is almost as good as looks of admiration. That look of shock or approval ricochets between his needs for confirmation and sense of self, and others' perception. In the look of incredulity the bodybuilder sees reflected a self that resembles the look of power and which earns the acknowledgment he so badly needs; and this constitutes a dimension of narcissism that is central to bodybuilding."

Schwarzenegger, however, firmly denied that his preening was linked to narcissism, rejecting such accusations as misguided.

"Nobody seemed to understand what was involved in bodybuilding," he argued. "You do look at your body in a mirror, not because you are narcissistic, but because you are trying to check your progress. It has nothing to do with being in love with yourself. Herta would never have told one of the track stars that he was in love with himself because he had someone check his speed with a stopwatch. It just happens that the mirror, the scales and the tape measure are the only tools a bodybuilder has for determining his progress."

His father's suspicions about Arnold's sexuality had long since passed, given the steady stream of girls into and out of his bedroom. However, Gustav and Aurelia soon noticed that their son never actually dated any of these girls. In fact, it was rare for Arnold to be seen with the same girl twice. As he would later confess, girls were merely "sex objects"—a confession that would come back to haunt him years later.

"I saw the other bodybuilders using them in this way and I thought it was all right. We talked about the pitfalls of romantic situations, serious ones, how it could take away from your training. . . . I couldn't be bothered with girls as companions. My mind was totally locked into working out, and I was annoyed if anything took me away from it. Without making a conscious decision to do so, I closed a door on that aspect of growing up, that vulnerability, and became very protective of my emotions. I didn't allow myself to get involved—period. It wasn't a reasoned choice; it just happened out of necessity."

Arnold would later reveal that he crossed girls off his list, except as "tools for my sexual needs."

He was interested in only one thing. He started to devour American bodybuilding magazines such as *Bodybuilder* and *Mr. America,* dreaming that one day he would appear in their pages. It was in one of these magazines that he saw the first photo of the man he wanted to become—the South African champion, Reg Park.

"I responded immediately to Reg Park's rough, massive look," he recalled. "The man was an animal. That's the way I wanted to be—ultimately: big. I wanted to be a big guy. I didn't want to be delicate. I dreamed of big deltoids, big pecs, big thighs, big calves; I wanted every muscle to explode and be huge. I dreamed about being gigantic. Reg Park was the epitome of that dream, the biggest, most powerful person in bodybuilding."

Girls weren't the only item he crossed off his list in pursuit of his new obsession. "I eliminated my parents too," he admits.

Neither Gustav nor Aurelia could understand his obsession with bodybuilding. This was not a sport for

Austrian boys. "My god!" Gustav told his wife at one point. "I think we better go to the doctor with this one, he's sick in the head." Aurelia was worried for Arnold and nagged him almost daily to give up lifting weights and take up a more normal pursuit.

"I couldn't be bothered with what my mother felt," he recalls. As for his father's misgivings, Arnold was even less concerned. "Reg Park had become my new father image," he reveals.

Although there are accounts of weight-lifting contests in ancient Greece, Rome, and even Egypt, the sport of aesthetic bodybuilding is said to date back to eleventh-century India, where the first gyms were established and athletes lifted *nals,* carved stone weights. By the sixteenth century, bodybuilding was considered one of India's national pastimes, essential for achieving the health and stamina men needed to endure the rigors of daily life.

Before long, however, the goal was not merely to achieve good health but to display the body for aesthetic purposes. Men tried to outdo each other in pursuit of large muscles, which soon became prized by the women of Indian and other Asian societies.

By the time of the Renaissance, the aesthetic ideal also caught on in Europe, where Michelangelo's celebrated statue of David and other acclaimed artworks provide a prime example of the way society prized the ideal male physique.

By the nineteenth century, European circuses and carnivals would often feature a strongman, though these men were often displayed alongside bearded ladies, sword swallowers, two-headed animals, and other so-called freaks—an indication of how bulging muscles were still viewed by most people.

Although there were a number of celebrated strongmen during that era, the father of modern bodybuilding is usually said to be a Prussian, Friedrich Wilhelm Müller, better known as Eugene Sandow.

Sandow left Prussia in 1885 to avoid military conscription and started to travel with a number of carnival sideshows, where his powerful build and huge muscles were a popular draw.

When the first modern Olympic games were held in Athens in 1896, they featured two weight lifting events, an indication that the sport had achieved mainstream acceptance around the time when Sandow was beginning to make a name for himself. Unlike his contemporaries, who displayed their bodies as a spectacle, Sandow had come to view a bodybuilder's physique as a work of art. His predecessors had always been overweight and unsightly, whereas Sandow valued symmetry and aesthetics. He was soon discovered by the legendary impresario Florenz Ziegfeld, who featured Sandow at the Chicago World's Fair, billing his show as "muscle display performances."

Ziegfeld encouraged Sandow to show off his muscles in a variety of poses, aware that the public was more fascinated by his physique than by the amount of weight he could lift. To his act, Sandow added such colorful feats as breaking a chain with his chest, and before long he had emerged as Ziegfeld's first major star. He was soon touring the vaudeville circuit, performing in most of America's great variety theaters and becoming a household name throughout the country, especially after Ziegfeld encouraged him to perform extra feats that kept him in the public eye, such as fighting a lion or performing in a strip show for a women-only audience.

In 1894, the fledgling Edison Studios filmed Sandow flexing his muscles and preening for the camera, and this motion picture soon became the most popular in the new medium. But it wasn't Sandow's physique or showmanship that was to be his lasting legacy. It was his pioneering role as an entrepreneur, turning bodybuilding into a lucrative industry.

Sandow had decided that his life pursuit would be to reform the dietary and exercise habits of the whole world. To this end, in 1898 he began publishing a magazine replete with tips about fitness and diet. Its circulation grew by the week and before long, fitness became a national craze. To capitalize on this success, he published a book, *Strength and How to Obtain It;* this book was a bestseller, and a few years later he wrote another book, which would give its name to a new sport: *Bodybuilding, or Man in the Making.*

He became an evangelist for his well-thought-out ideas about the relationship between health and exercise. In his magazine, he was one of the first, and certainly one of the most influential, advocates of compulsory physical education in public schools, arguing that a weak child could not learn properly. He was the first to develop exercises for pregnant mothers to lessen the pain of childbirth, and he recommended that employers should offer their workers a regular break for daily exercises.

Through his magazine, *Physical Culture,* Sandow marketed a line of exercise equipment, featuring muscle-building and endurance devices that he had invented; variations of these can still be found in modern gyms.

In the first edition of *Physical Culture,* published in 1898, Sandow advertised the first major bodybuilding contest ever staged in the modern era, to be held three years hence at London's Royal Albert Hall "to afford encouragement to those who are anxious to perfect their physiques." What stood out for most readers was the prize money being offered: 1,000 guineas, an enormous sum equivalent to more than $5,000 at the time. The money offered an incentive for a new generation of bodybuilders to devote themselves to developing a prizewinning physique.

One of the distinguished judges asked by Sandow to pick a winner was none other than the creator of Sherlock Holmes, the author Sir Arthur Conan Doyle.

The contestants were judged not just on size, but on symmetrically even development and form. The criteria and the format of the tournament would later form the basis of modern bodybuilding contests; as a result, the winner of the present-day Mr. Olympia contest is awarded "the Sandow"—a golden statuette in the image of the sport's pioneering founder. A few years after the contest at Royal Albert Hall, Sandow was actually hired as a personal fitness trainer by King George V, who had also caught the exercise craze.

His numerous bodybuilding ventures made Sandow a rich man, but he continued to tour, unable to give up the spotlight and attention that bodybuilders crave. When he died in 1925, his influence had already spawned a new generation of imitators and entrepreneurs, eager to cash in on the popularity of the sport.

One of these imitators was an American, Bernarr Macfadden, who founded a magazine called *Physical Development* shortly after Sandow's own magazine first appeared. Macfadden had invented a chest expander that he was eager to promote, capitalizing on Sandow's popularization of bodybuilding. Observing the success of the Royal Albert Hall contest, Macfadden staged a physique contest of his own two years later at New York's Madison Square Garden; this was the first such contest to take place in America, and it became an annual event, searching for "The Most Perfectly Developed Man in America." The posing techniques used in these contests, in fact, became the recognized standard for today's bodybuilding competitions.

In 1921, the winner of Macfadden's contest was an Italian immigrant, Angelo Siciliano, who claimed the top prize of $1,000.

Siciliano had arrived at Ellis Island with his parents at the age of ten and settled in Brooklyn. Not speaking a word of English and skinny to the point of emaciation, young Angelo was constantly being taunted and beaten up by neighborhood bullies. One day at Coney Island Beach, a lifeguard kicked sand into the face of the ninety-seven-pound youngster, humiliating him in front of a girl he was trying to date.

Not long after that, Siciliano visited the Brooklyn Museum, where he saw statues depicting Apollo, Hercules, and Zeus. Inspired, he pasted a photo of Eugene Sandow on his dresser mirror for inspiration and started working out with dumbbells, ropes, and elastic grips, intent on achieving the physique of those Greek gods. After months of sweating, he had still not managed to put on very much muscle until one day, on a visit to the Bronx Zoo, he had his epiphany, as he would later recall in his memoirs.

Watching a lion stretch in a cage, he thought to himself, "Does this old gentleman have any barbells, any exercisers? . . . And it came over me. . . . He's been pitting one muscle against another!"

Siciliano went home, tossed out his old exercise equipment, and developed a technique pitting one muscle group against another, tensing his hands behind his back and pushing them against his legs. He would later coin a new term to describe the technique, "isometrics." Within a few months, his skinny physique began to expand dramatically, causing his friends and family to take notice. One day, he claims, a schoolmate looked at his new muscles, and said, "You look like that statue of Atlas on top of the Atlas Hotel!"

In 1922, Siciliano legally changed his name to Charles Atlas and developed a twelve-lesson course, which he called "Dynamic Tension." He became famous when he marketed it on the back cover of comic books with an ad featuring a bully kicking sand into the face of a "97-pound weakling" named Mac, in front of the weakling's girlfriend. After taking the course and building up his muscles, Mac later returns to the beach and beats up the bully, winning back the girlfriend and the admiration of those around him.

Arnold Schwarzenegger may never have had sand kicked in his face, but he was determined to be the best.

3.

The Marnul Rule

My next stop was the Graz Athletic Union, better known as Marnul's gym, home of the former Mr. Austria and Arnold Schwarzenegger's first trainer. I knew I was in the right place when I saw photos of Arnold all over the walls. But by my calculations, its proprietor would have been an old man by now and surely semiretired at the very least. However, to my surprise, I locate Kurt Marnul right away, giving advice to a burly weightlifter. Wearing a T-shirt and still displaying a solid physique, Marnul looks much younger than his seventy-nine years, thanks in part to his bushy eyebrows and mustache.

Given his long association with celebrities and with many international athletes, including the Austrian Olympic weight lifting team, I assumed that Marnul could speak at least functional English. But I soon discover that he can barely understand a word.

The language barrier, however, was the least of my worries. I was already well aware how difficult it was to get any of Schwarzenegger's friends or associates to speak about him on the record without first obtaining his formal permission. I decided to pose as a travel writer doing a tourist piece about Graz, a city little known except by its association with the Governator, even though it is the second-largest city in Austria.

When I arrived at the gym on a weekday afternoon, there was a man in his thirties doing biceps curls who spoke a little broken English, but not enough to function as a competent translator. Two hours later, I had found someone who could translate for me—a Swiss street musician named Hansueli, who had studied art in London for two years and who agreed to accompany me back to the gym for 50 euros.

Marnul was all too happy to talk to me about his role in developing the teenage Schwarzenegger into the most famous bodybuilder the world has ever known. In fact, it soon became evident that he was used to talking to journalists, not to mention anybody else who would listen, about his claim to fame. Marnul was a shameless self-promoter who had evidently developed the narrative very carefully over the years for maximum impact and maximum credit to himself and his subject. And the first anecdote made me wonder how reliable his account was.

"The first time I talked to the boy, Arnold, he told me he would one day be Mr. Universe," Marnul recalled. "He knew exactly what he wanted and he expected me to help him make it a reality."

"Did you believe him?" I asked.

"I didn't think he would be Mr. Universe, of course, but I admired his confidence. That's one thing Arnold always had. I didn't think he was built to be a champion. His brother Meinhard, who I also knew, I thought had the potential. He was a natural. He had a better shape. But I was of course willing to train him. That is what I did, I turned boys into men, I developed a program for him to get bigger."

In those days, the Athletic Union was nothing more than a basement room in the corner of the athletic stadium, featuring crude weight lifting and workout equipment crafted by Marnul himself. Only a couple of years before my visit, I learned, the equipment that had turned Schwarzenegger into a superman had been sold to a gym in eastern Europe and replaced with modern gear. Still, it was hard to believe that Marnul's gym, reeking of sweat and muscle linament, had ever turned out a champion. Yet in talking to Marnul, even through a translator, I soon realized that he was not a run-of-the-mill gym proprietor.

One of the few things I knew about Marnul before I arrived was that it was he who introduced a teenage Arnold to steroids. In his 1977 autobiography, Schwarzenegger had still not acknowledged the role performance-enhancing drugs played in his development.

Years later, Schwarzenegger was forced to admit that he had in fact been training on steroids for years. And in the years since this admission, Marnul publicly outted himself as having first introduced the boy to the performance-enhancing drugs. Yet, in the context of a travel piece, I wasn't quite sure how to broach the question without arousing his suspicion. I finally raised the subject in a roundabout way.

I told him I once belonged to a gym in Canada where bodybuilders sold anabolic steroids in the locker room. I asked whether that ever happens in his gym. "I try to stop it," he replied.

I told him that I thought I had read an article in which he claimed to have given Arnold Schwarzenegger steroids.

He nods.

"Yes, they were legal then. Everybody took them."

He leads me over to a wall and points to a photo from the 1970s of Schwarzenegger flexing, his entire body bulging with muscles.

"You can't look like that just by lifting weights," he says matter-of-factly. "It's impossible."

Since the beginning of sports, athletes have always sought an artificial edge—something to make them run faster, jump higher, or lift more weight than the competition. According to Scandinavian mythology, the Norse warriors known as berserks would drink a mixture called butotens, prepared from a hallucinogenic mushroom, and increase their physical power by a dozen times. But drinking the mixture also carried a significant risk of going crazy; hence the modern term "berserk." As far back as 776 B.C., there were reports of sportsmen consuming sheep testicles, which were rumored to enhance athleticism—to give what modern athletes would call a testosterone boost.

In 1889 the Mauritian physiologist Charles-Édouard Brown-Séquard developed and injected into himself the first artificially produced substance containing testosterone: a concoction of testicular extracts from dogs and guinea pigs that he said improved physical strength, intellectual abilities, and even appetite. Appearing before the Société de Biologie in Paris that year, he claimed that his concoction actually reversed the aging process, though his colleagues were skeptical. Still, it was only a matter of time before the discovery led to the first anabolic steroids, especially since the athletic world was already proving itself desperate to use and experiment with performance-enhancing drugs.

Such drugs had long been a fixture in endurance sports by the beginning of the nineteenth century. Abraham Woo—the winner of a particularly grueling walking race held in 1807—bragged that he had used opium to keep himself awake for twenty-four hours while competing against Robert Allardyce. There were also numerous accounts of swimmers and bicyclists drinking cocaine tonics before and during races.

The first recorded death from the use of doping in sport came in 1886 when a cyclist died from an overdose of trimethyl.

By 1895, the use of artificial stimulants in sports was so pervasive that the *New York Times* wrote an editorial condemning the practice: "We feel sure that all true athletes would disdain any such injurious and adventitious aids. There are no drugs which will help one to win a game that could not be won without them, and the general effect of drug taking . . . is distinctly bad."

Five years later, in 1900, the word "dope" was used to describe the widespread practice of drugging race-horses to improve their performance; this later led to the term "doping" to describe using performance-enhancing drugs.

But it was an incident in 1904 that proved just how far athletes were willing to go for an extra boost.

During the running of the marathon at the 1904 Saint Louis Olympics, a Cambridge medical student, Thomas Hicks, was struggling along at the nineteen-mile point and had slowed to a walk. His handler, Charles Lucas, was following along in a car, providing sponges and water. When he saw Hicks's state, he administered one milligram of strychnine, the active ingredient in rat poison, inside egg whites. The elixir gave Hicks an instant boost, and he ran for another mile before Lucas saw him slowing down again. Lucas decided one more dose would do it, this time washed down with some French brandy. Hicks barely made it to the finish line before collapsing, his face ashen. But he won the race and later bragged about the method, causing a bit of a stir.

It wasn't his use of strychnine, however, that had the public and other runners upset. It was the fact that he didn't share his magic formula with the other competitors.

"The marathon race, from a medical standpoint, demonstrated that drugs are of much benefit to athletes along the road," Hicks later wrote, defending the practice.

In 1928, the International Amateur Athletic Federation officially banned the use of any performance-enhancing stimulants. But because there were no drug-testing methods yet available, athletes could easily violate the ban with impunity.

In the 1930s, scientists—funded by competing drug companies—raced to become the first to synthesize testosterone. In 1934, a Swiss chemist, Leopold Ružička, became the first to do so. He was later awarded a Nobel Prize for his discovery.

During World War II, German soldiers were rumored to have received anabolic steroid treatments to increase their aggression and improve their stamina, though these reports may be apocryphal. Hitler's physician claimed that the Führer himself was injected with testosterone derivatives to treat a number of ailments.

In 1945, just after the war ended, Paul de Kruif wrote *The Male Hormone*, summarizing the positive findings of Swiss and German chemists about the strength benefits of synthetic testosterone, which had begun widespread commercial production that year. Almost immediately came the first reports from California bodybuilding gyms about the prevalence of testosterone supplements.

At the 1952 Winter Olympics in Oslo, Norway, a number of speed skaters required medical attention because of their use of amphetamines, which had become the drug of choice in many sports by the early 1950s. Two years later, at the World Weight-lifting Championships in Vienna, the Soviet Union's team dominated the competition for the first time, winning most of the weight classes with ease. Some athletes had noticed syringes strewn around the locker room and reported this discovery to the American team physician, John Ziegler, who had himself administered amphetamines to his athletes but knew the Soviet Union must be onto something else. When he questioned his Soviet counterpart over drinks after the medals ceremony, the Russian doctor admitted that his athletes had received injections of testosterone.

When Ziegler returned home and reported on the miraculous results of the Soviet Union's training regi-men, he was determined that the Americans needed to catch up or risk continual defeat. He immediately tried injecting weak doses of testosterone into himself, into the American trainer, and into three of his star weightlifters, each of whom gained more weight and muscle than any training program had ever produced. But Ziegler also noticed significant side effects associated with the treatment. His goal was to develop a substance that could produce the same results but with less risk to health.

Ziegler approached the pharmaceutical giant Ciba, offering to develop such a drug. The company was especially suited to the task because it had been given access to the records of the Nazis' drug experiments, including research on testosterone, which had been seized by the U.S. government after the war.

The result of Ziegler's research was the first anabolic steroid, methandrostenolone (Dianabol), which was patented and released by Ciba in 1958.

Ziegler immediately set out to use it to full advantage as a muscle aid for bodybuilders, administering the new drug to the U.S. weight lifting champion Bill March in 1959 at the York Athletic Club.

Ziegler later turned against the use of steroids in sport after he discovered significant adverse health effects associated with their use. He also came to regard the use of steroids as a form of cheating, a conclusion later echoed by most international sports federations, which banned their use. Ziegler would end up suffering from serious heart disease, which he attributed to his own experimentation with steroids; he died of heart failure in 1983.

By the time Kurt Marnul first met Arnold Schwarzenegger in 1961, only three years after anabolic steroids became commercially available, he had become a firm believer in the power of drugs to provide a meaningful edge in competition. Marnul was himself a former Mr. Austria, and he claimed that he had been introduced to steroids by Steve Reeves, the American bodybuilder best known for his portrayal of Hercules in a number of B-list "sword and sandal" movies in the early 1960s. Reeves, who befriended Marnul in France in 1952, never publicly acknowledged his own alleged steroid use and would later become a crusader for drug-free bodybuilding.

By 1961, the adverse health effects of steroid use were already fairly well known. John Ziegler himself had begun to notice heart and liver distress in his athletes after the 1960 Olympics, discovering that many of them had taken as much as twenty times more steroids than he recommended in his training regimen. Coaches everywhere were beginning to see the prevalence of abuse, especially among weightlifters and bodybuilders who were determined to build up as much muscle as fast as possible. The more steroids, the faster results were achieved—damn the health consequences.

When I asked Kurt Marnul whether he knew at the time that steroids were potentially dangerous, he said, "Of course I knew. Everybody knew. People were taking crazy amounts; they didn't care what it did to them, as long as they built up and built up. Their hearts could explode. That's why I made sure my boys were careful. I made sure they took only low doses. Arnold never took anything without my supervision. He was smart about it; all my boys were."

Wendy Leigh, however, interviewed one Austrian bodybuilder who trained with Schwarzenegger who tells a different story.

"Arnold took steroids in doses that terrified the other bodybuilders. I saw him swallow eight or nine Dianabols at a time. Then he would take a gulp of milk, a handful of protein tablets, and while he was still swallowing and could hardly talk, say, 'Right now I'm ready,' and start training."

The former Mr. Universe Rick Wayne claims that it was Schwarzenegger who in turn introduced him to steroids.

"I was in Munich in the 1960s, and Arnold gave me my first bottle of Dianabol," he recalled. "He was nineteen at the time and said he had been taking them for several years."

Steroids alone, however, couldn't produce the monster physiques that were beginning to dominate bodybuilding competitions. By the time he got to Hollywood, Steve Reeves had transformed himself from a relatively streamlined body to a Herculean figure in only a few short months, leading many to conclude that drugs were responsible for his greatly expanded figure, as Marnul has long claimed. But Reeves was also known for his intensity in the gym; he spent far longer on his workouts than other bodybuilders. He claims that this work ethic gave him his edge and his superior physique.

But Marnul explains that hard work and steroids go hand in hand: "The drugs themselves don't make you bigger. They make your muscles expand faster from your workouts than lifting weights alone will. That's their secret."

Nobody, he tells me, ever worked harder than Arnold Schwarzenegger.

"The reason he became the best is that he was willing to put the most work in. I never saw anybody before or to this very day who worked as hard at becoming a champion. He trained and trained and trained, through the pain; nothing could stop him. His father didn't approve of this sport, bodybuilding. He wanted Arnold to become a curler. He started to forbid him to come to my gym, but I think the mother helped convince him that it was good for the boy."

Marnul never mentioned it to me, but there are reports, possibly apocryphal, that Schwarzenegger would occasionally slip out of his house at night and on weekends, bike to Graz, and break into the gym through a window so he could work out.

Whether or not he took it to that extreme, he later confessed that he had become "literally addicted to bodybuilding."

Using crudely fashioned equipment, he even built himself a gym in the basement of his home where he could train whenever the mood struck him.

His only thought, Schwarzenegger explained, was to build up more and more muscles. His friends thought he was nuts; his father made no secret of his disapproval, frequently lamenting that his son wasn't "normal"; but nothing could dissuade him from his goal.

"I remember certain people trying to put negative thoughts into my mind, trying to persuade me to slow down," he later wrote. "But I had found the thing to which I wanted to devote my total energies and there was no stopping me. My drive was unusual, I talked differently than my friends; I was hungrier for success than anyone I knew."

Part of the appeal, he explained, was the camaraderie among his fellow bodybuilders, who took him on as a protégé. At the time, he claims, there were no more than twenty or thirty bodybuilders in all of Austria, and these were the only people who could relate to Schwarzenegger's new obsession, who could understand his drive.

But, just as in Thal, where his cockiness and bullying had alienated him from most of the town, the brash newcomer was unpopular almost from the beginning.

"From the first night when he walked into the Union, we all thought Arnold had a big mouth," the Athletic Union's former trainer, Helmut Cerncic, told Wendy Leigh.

According to Cerncic, Schwarzenegger turned to a bodybuilder named Johnny Schnetz soon after starting training there, and said, "Well, I give myself about five years and I will be Mr. Universe."

"We all looked at each other as if to say, 'This boy is crazy,'" recalled Cerncic. "If you add to that the fact that every so often he would make a derogatory remark about one of the other bodybuilders, the result was that no one had much respect for him. In fact, he got on our nerves."

Clearly, not all the bodybuilders shared Cerncic's negative opinion, however. There was at least one regular at the Graz Athletic Union, a twenty-year-old medical student, Karl Gerstl, who took to the teenage Schwarzenegger immediately and whose friendship would shape Schwarzenegger's life and career. And for a boy who had never before had any close friends, whose father was a former Nazi, and who had gown up in a region known particularly for its deep strain of anti-Semitism, there was one thing especially notable about Schwarzenegger's instant bond with the young student. Karl Gerstl was Jewish.

4.

Fascinated by Gerstl

Before I even sit down to meet Karl Gerstl at a café in Graz, near the clinic where he still practices medicine, he tells me that I am wasting my time. "It is my father you should be talking to, not me," he tells me. "I have not much to offer."

I would soon discover that it was indeed Karl's father, Alfred—now almost ninety and not healthy enough to sit down for an interview—who had played a more important role in the life of my subject. But a passage about Karl in Schwarzenegger's autobiography convinced me that he could offer some valuable insight into what made his friend tick.

For, while it was Kurt Marnul who had the most profound impact on Arnold Schwarzenegger's early physical development, it was Karl Gerstl, according to Schwarzenegger, who "helped lay the foundation for my later thinking." By his own admission, young Arnold had not given thought to much beyond girls and bodybuilding while growing up in Thal. School bored him. He just didn't see the point. He had been forced to enroll in a vocational school, studying carpentry, because he was unable to grasp basic academic subjects and most of the people in Graz, including his own father, had dismissed him as a musclebound simpleton. But Karl Gerstl immediately saw beyond the exterior and recognized an untapped intelligence that nobody else had bothered to discern. Studying medicine at the local university and raised by an intellectual, Gerstl believed that intelligence and bodybuilding were not at all incompatible. On the contrary, just as a generation of writers had long recognized boxing as a sweet science in which every great practitioner used his head as much as his fists, so too was bodybuilding a sport requiring a good deal of mind power.

Before and after workouts, Gerstl—who was also a karate champion—would wax philosophical to his friend, whom he came to regard as a younger brother.

"He was much younger than me, but he was already far better than me as a bodybuilder," recalls Gerstl. "He was better than everybody. He dominated the gym. At first I think he had something to prove—he bragged a lot—but after a time, everybody knew he was the leader, he didn't have anything to prove, and he changed. He was a very nice guy when he wasn't shouting about how good he was. We had some very good conversation."

Before the Nazis annexed Austria in 1938, there was a thriving Jewish community in Graz, notwithstanding the notorious anti-Semitism of the local populace. On the eve of Kristallnacht in November 1939, 1,600 Jews lived in the city—the second-largest Jewish population in Austria, after Vienna's. But on the night of November 9 and 10, the synagogue was dynamited and burned to the ground, the Jewish cemetery was desecrated, and 300 Jews were rounded up and sent to Dachau, many to their deaths. By the end of the war, only 110 Jews remained.

One of those remaining was Alfred Gerstl, who had managed to survive the war because his father, also named Alfred, had converted to Catholicism in the 1930s for the sake of survival, after being denied a position with the national railway because of his Jewish faith. Despite this experience, Alfred Sr. had always considered himself a German and was a great admirer of Frederick the Great, the German philosopher king, who was famously tolerant toward Prussian Jews.

When Hitler reared his head next door in Germany, Alfred was unconcerned, wrongly believing him to be a "transitional figure" and anti-Semitism a passing trend that would never be tolerated by German officers.

As a result of the elder Alfred's conversion, the family was spared being sent to a concentration camp with Graz's other Jews when the war began. But Alfred Jr. was classified as a "half-breed" and as such was forced to drop out of music school and then to abandon his apprenticeship as a gunsmith, because someone with Jewish blood was not allowed to handle weapons. Instead, he became an apprentice toolmaker; he was still too young for military service. At the age of seventeen, he spent a few days in jail after a street brawl with a member of the Hitler Youth. He knew the day was coming when he would receive his draft notice and would be forced to serve a regime that he despised. During his brief stint in custody, Alfred made his first contact with a small resistance group centered at the Graz opera house, and when he was drafted into the Wehrmacht in 1942, these resisters helped him go underground.

Concealed by a Catholic woman whom he later married, Gerstl spent the next two years wending his way back and forth between Graz and Slovenia, working as a courier for the resistance. In this capacity, he carried supplies, medicine, munitions, and information to Tito's partisans, who were fighting the Nazi puppet government of Yugoslavia. He also helped smuggle soldiers deserting from Hitler's army.

When the war ended and he returned to his home-town, Alfred believed it was safe to once again practice Judaism, though he soon discovered that the war had not done much to extinguish the rabid anti-Semitism in Austria or in Graz. This was made all too clear to him when he made the decision to get involved in politics. He later explained that he decided not to join the left-leaning Social Democratic Party because party officials were suspicious of his political leanings, implying that he had joined the resistance for religious rather than political reasons.

"To the Jews I'm a Christian, and to the Christians, a Jew," he later lamented.

Curiously, Gerstl decided instead to join the People's Party, a conservative political movement long associ-ated with the Catholic church and not a natural haven for an Austrian Jew. Yet many of his colleagues in the resistance were members, and they urged him to join, unconcerned by his religious beliefs. The deciding factor appeared to be the party's strong anti-Marxist stance at a time when Austrians were flirting with so-cialism, an ideology that left Gerstl cold.

An avid sportsman and weightlifter, Gerstl had encouraged his son to pursue bodybuilding as a complement to karate training. Every summer, Karl's father would host barbecues for the bodybuilders at the lake in Thal near where Arnold grew up. At one of these gatherings, Karl first introduced the elder Gerstl to Schwarzenegger. The unlikely pair hit it off immediately.

"He was a remarkable boy, even in those days," Gerstl later recalled. "Friendly, eager to learn, purposeful."

Soon he had invited Arnold to train with his son at his house, where his wife had installed a weight-training room because, he explained, "at the Graz Athletic Union the old hands didn't always let the boys use the equipment."

Despite his affiliation with the conservative People's Party, Gerstl always had an intellectual curiosity that caused him to reach out to Austrians of all political stripes as long as they had something important to say.

For years he had hosted a regular political salon at his home, where conservatives, anarchists, Jews, and Christians would gather to discuss the future of Austrian society and how to come to terms with their country's disgraceful flirtation with Nazism. At a time when most of his countrymen preferred to sweep this dark chapter under the rug, the salon made Alfred Gerstl nearly unique.

And when Arnold Schwarzenegger found himself invited by Alfred to attend these gatherings, he was immediately drawn to a world far removed from any he had known before.

At Gerstl's salons, nothing was off-limits. Intimidated by the far-ranging political and philosophical discussions, many of which he didn't understand, Arnold sat there quietly, simply taking it all in. Alfred was also an aficionado of classical music and would play symphonies and operas for his guests, exposing Arnold to the great tenors, sometimes even singing himself. But Gerstl's salons were about politics more than culture, and mostly the guests talked about lofty subjects.

Arnold rarely participated in the discussions, knowing he was out of his league, but he sat riveted, and it was soon clear that the new world of ideas he was exposed to on a weekly basis was having an influence on the teenager.

Alfred later claimed that Arnold's father knew and approved of his son's attendance at the home of a prominent Jew, saying he knew the boy was "in good hands." Gerstl met Gustav on a number of occasions and would later downplay Gustav's flirtation with Nazism.

"He only became a Nazi the way tens of thousands of other people did," Alfred later explained. "I think he did it under economic pressure. Anyway, I only heard about it later. I knew him well. He was a very strict father, who wasn't too happy at first about his son's bodybuilding, but he supported his friendship with Karl."

Arnold's mother approved of the friendship as well, but after a while she began to have reservations about the company her son was keeping. Aurelia Schwarzenegger was a devout Catholic and had dragged both her sons to the Catholic church in Thal every Sunday since Arnold was old enough to talk. He never had much use for the tedious sermons and pious morality, but he had never given much serious thought to religion in general.

Though the Gerstl salon gathered mostly conservatives, a sprinkling of radicals and freethinkers would also attend. One such regular was an older man, Helmut Knaur, who called himself an anarchist and had been imprisoned by the Nazis in a labor camp in North Africa. Knaur, who was known as a libertine and a free spirit, had been introduced to bodybuilding by the much younger Alfred Gerstl and would, during workouts, hold court, bellowing about whatever topic was on his mind that day.

Knaur attempted to teach the bodybuilders English by bringing copies of *Playboy* magazine, and though Arnold never got very far beyond the photos, he did absorb Knaur's advice that there was a world beyond Austria.

"He was a very important influence to inspire me to learn, to speak languages, to be more worldly," Schwarzenegger told the *Los Angeles Times* years later, about Knaur. "He said, 'Think big.'"

"Helmut was a wonderful character," Karl Gerstl tells me. "Arnold enjoyed his company. So did I—he was very entertaining and very knowledgeable. He was also very contrary; he loved to argue. He was one of the few people who would stand up to my father. They would have long fights about issues. They didn't see eye to eye about politics, you know."

The Gerstls were almost certainly the first Jews Schwarzenegger had ever met, and certainly the first he ever befriended. To this day, it is hard to ascertain how much he knew about his own father's Nazi past, a subject that would come back to haunt him decades later when he claimed he was oblivious of it. Still, it seems hard to believe that he didn't know his father had served the Nazis in some capacity during the war.

Yet this was a subject that nobody ever talked about in those days. Gerstl was determined to change that.

"A whole generation in Austria grew up without any historical background," explained Albert Kaufmann, the son of a Jewish resistance fighter from Graz and another of the boys who often trained with Schwarzenegger and Karl Gerstl and attended Alfred's salons. Karl Gerstl, in fact, told me that Kaufmann was "more Jewish" than his own family, who were "a little bit Jewish, a little bit Catholic." Schwarzenegger's time at the Gerstl house attending these political and social gatherings "influenced Arnold and provided him with a historical perspective," Kaufmann told the *Los Angeles Times* in 2003, explaining that Schwarzenegger "inhaled" the political atmosphere.

As Arnold sat listening intently, surrounded by the menorahs and other Jewish symbols around Gerstl's apartment, he heard for the first time stories of Hitler's atrocities, stories never mentioned at school and of course never discussed around his family's own dining room table: stories of the murders, the roundups, the atrocities; stories of the everyday anti-Semitism experienced by Alfred Gerstl before the war; stories of the hardships and the beatings Helmut Knaur had experienced at the hands of Nazi guards at Strafkolonie 999, the labor camp where he was imprisoned.

Years later, Gerstl explained to a reporter his reasoning for inviting young people like Arnold to those sessions.

"The condition was they had to listen," he said. "Arnold was very inquisitive. He always wanted to know why we were against the Nazis. He always understood the need to protect the weak."

Through the stories, Gerstl stressed time and time again his vision of a tolerant Austria. When I asked Karl Gerstl how much influence these gatherings had had on his friend's future political career, he simply shrugged. "It's hard to say," he finally said. "You never knew how much he was listening. Even I was sometimes bored, I hate to admit. Arnold stayed out of respect for my father, that was obvious."

Years later, as governor of California, Schwarzenegger would reflect back on those days and admit that during the sessions at the Gerstl home, he would often be daydreaming about his next workout rather than taking in the discussions.

"We paid very little attention," he told Laurence Leamer, "but as time goes on it has an impact. "[Gerstl] would be talking about classical composers, Beethoven and Mozart. And he would be talking about tolerance and about the Second World War. He was educating us in a way. He could reach me much better than my father."

Indeed, Schwarzenegger would often refer to Alfred Gerstl as his second father and mentor, and decades later he flew to attend the wedding as best man when Gerstl, after two decades as a widower, married a woman from Graz. By then, the old man had enjoyed a long and distinguished career in Austrian politics, serving as a senator and as the president of the upper house of the Austrian parliament.

As his old friend rose through the political ranks, Schwarzenegger would make it a point to visit Gerstl whenever he returned to Austria, immersing himself in the politics of the People's Party, in which Gerstl had become a very powerful figure. The politician would take his former protégé around and introduce Arnold to his political allies, regaling him with the gossip, the intrigue, and the machinations of the political system. Arnold couldn't get enough, and he began to cultivate friendships with many prominent Austrian politicians, notably Gerstl's friend Josef Krainer, the governor of Styria.

Schwarzenegger would return the favor after he became famous, introducing Gerstl to Hollywood celebrities whenever Gerstl visited America. Just as Schwarzenegger was becoming enamored of political power, it seemed, the old man was becoming starstruck. At one point, Gerstl confided to an interviewer his fondest dream—to have Schwarzenegger play a modern version of the golem in a major Hollywood movie, portraying the mythical Jewish superhuman figure, which had been a staple of Yiddish folklore for centuries. Gerstl had even developed a screenplay.

"I think you can say that my father in those years had a very strong influence on Arnold the later politician," explains Karl Gerstl, "much more so than when Arnold was young. I don't know enough about politics to tell you what exactly, but you can see many examples from his policies in California. People say it's a contradiction perhaps to be a conservative but also caring and tolerant. That is what Arnold gets from my father. That is much more the European way of conservative politics than what you usually see in America, no?"

On one of his visits to Austria to spend time with his mentor, Schwarzenegger would meet and befriend another rising politician in Gerstl's People's Party. It was a friendship that would later haunt him. The politician's name was Kurt Waldheim.

5.

Training Like a Spartan

By 1963, when he was sixteen, Arnold had no real friends his own age. When he wasn't working out, he spent most of his spare time with Kurt Marnul, Karl and Alfred Gerstl, or Helmut Knaur, all considerably older than himself.

"Each of them became a father image for me," he later recalled. "I listened less to my own father. [They] were my new heroes. I was in awe of them."

But by this time Arnold also had another hero. Like most of the boys his age, he spent every Saturday afternoon at the Graz cinema, which usually played B movies and serials from America. One Saturday the featured picture was *Hercules and the Vampires*, in which the hero was tasked with ridding the earth of thousands of bloodthirsty vampires. The plot and the special effects were inane, but Arnold didn't care. He sat "transfixed," staring up at the screen at the leading man.

"Reg Park looked so magnificent in the role of Hercules," he later wrote. "And, sitting there in the theater I knew that was going to be me. I would look like Reg Park. I studied every move he made, every gesture. . . . Suddenly I realized the house lights were on and everyone else had walked out."

From that moment, Schwarzenegger recalled, his life was utterly dominated by Reg Park, who had won the 1958 Mr. Universe contest before embarking on a Hollywood career. Arnold's bodybuilding friends were more impressed by Steve Reeves, another bodybuilder turned actor who had starred in the first Hercules production in 1957. But Arnold didn't care for Reeves, finding him too "elegant, smooth, polished." Park had a rougher, more powerful look, "everything a man should be." It was a look that Schwarzenegger would one day make his own.

"I knew in my mind that I was not geared for elegance," he would explain. "I wanted to be massive. It was the difference between cologne and sweat."

Up until this stage in his life, Arnold had trained simply for the joy of it. Now his bodybuilding had a mission.

"From that point on, my life was utterly dominated by Reg Park," he explained. "His image was my ideal. It was fixed indelibly in my mind."

He began to collect bodybuilding magazines that discussed Park's training program; posters; interviews—anything that might help him become like his new idol. He was desperate to know what Park ate, how he lived, how he did his workouts.

Park's photos adorned the walls of Arnold's bedroom. From the moment he woke up in the morning, he studied those photos religiously, noting the size of Park's chest, arms, thighs, back, and abdominals.

"I became obsessed with Reg Park," he reflected. "He was the image in front of me from the time I started training. The more I focused in on this image and worked and grew, the more I saw it was real and possible for me to be like him."

At the Athletic Union, in his basement, at the Gerstls' apartment, he trained and trained, constantly working to increase his size until the day he could stare in a mirror and see the body of Reg Park reflected back at him.

"The model was there in my mind, I only had to grow," he recalled.

Watching the intensity of Arnold's workouts and the amazing results—helped along by the steroid injections and tablets he was taking on a regular basis—Kurt Marnul and Karl Gerstl became convinced that Arnold's boast of becoming Mr. Universe was for the first time a very real possibility.

They predicted that Arnold could reach the top within five years. But he was too impatient to accept that time line.

"I had this insatiable drive to get there sooner," he recalled. "Whereas most people were satisfied to train two or three times a week, I quickly escalated my program to six workouts."

His parents were baffled. His father, also a champion athlete, believed Arnold was overtraining. "What will you do with all those muscles once you've got them?" he asked.

Arnold didn't hesitate. He wanted to be the "best built man in the world," he declared. When his father remained unconvinced, he finally revealed his true goal: "Then I want to go to America and be in movies. I want to be an actor."

Gustav was dumbfounded. He implored Aurelia to talk some sense into their foolish son. Arnold wasn't particularly concerned about his parents' objections. He believed they simply didn't understand. Still, to appease his father, he regularly joined Gustav at the curling club, participating in a pastime Gustav would tell him was a "real sport."

As a natural athlete, Arnold excelled at curling, even placing sixth in the Graz junior championship. But if he couldn't be the best, he just didn't see the point. He had set his sights on becoming the greatest bodybuilder in the world, and if he was going to start to reach that dream, he knew from Kurt Marnul and Karl Gerstl that the secret to improvement was competition. If he was to achieve his goal of becoming Mr. Universe, he would, Marnul informed him, need to first become Mr. Austria, as Marnul himself had done years earlier.

This initial goal inspired him to drastically increase his program, stretching his training sessions to a grueling two hours a day. Each week, he kept adding more and more weight, "bombing" his muscles furiously. He religiously studied Reg Park's regimen, working repeatedly on the "basic movements"—bench presses, chin-ups, squats, rowing, barbell curls, wrist curls, pullovers, leg extensions, and calf raises.

But before he could hope to be invited to compete for Mr. Austria, he knew he must first win the Mr. Styria bodybuilding championship, held every year at the elegant Steirer Hof Hotel in Graz. This was the contest that years before had launched Kurt Marnul's career.

Arnold had no doubt that he would emerge as the winner. He was far and away the biggest bodybuilder in all of Graz. How could he lose? However, he hadn't yet realized that the contest is about more than size; it is also about contour, definition, and the best sculpted physique.

The contestants took to the stage and strutted their stuff, but Arnold had placed only second, losing to a smaller but better-defined rival. He was crushed. He later put his defeat down to the "faults of poor early training" and "provincial thinking," which concentrated on mass and bulk above all else.

But there was one consolation in defeat. As the runner-up, he was presented with a trophy, the first Arnold had ever won.

Not long after his second-place showing in the Mr. Styria contest, he emerged triumphant for the first time in a bodybuilding competition—the Mr. Junior Austria contest, which he won handily. The trophy he carried home that day would prove handy.

Aurelia had never entirely approved of her son's newfound obsession. She had persuaded Gustav to let him continue his pursuit, arguing that at least he wasn't a criminal, but she constantly let it be known that she didn't approve of the time he was putting into his "crazy" hobby.

However, his mother's attitude changed, recalled Arnold, the day he came home with his championship trophy.

"She took it and ran from house to house in Thal, showing the neighbors what I had won," he wrote. "It was a turning point for her. She began to accept what

I was doing. Now, all of a sudden, some attention was focused on her. People singled her out. She too was treated as a champion. She was proud of me. And then (up to a certain point) she encouraged me to do what I wanted."

A year later, after competing and placing third in the Mr. Austria competition, Arnold finally became Mr. Styria, proudly claiming the trophy in the ballroom with Alfred Gerstl in attendance, beaming at the success of his protégé.

Aurelia Schwarzenegger wasn't the only one who began to look at Arnold differently after his early success. Before long, he recalls, he was being stopped on the street and singled out by townspeople who had never had much use for him before.

"People began looking at me as a special person," he writes. "Partly this was the result of my own changing attitude about myself. I was growing, getting bigger, gaining confidence. I was given consideration I had never received before; it was as though I were the son of a millionaire."

In a rare moment of introspection, Schwarzenegger confesses that his need for adulation may have stemmed from sibling rivalry, noting, "Perhaps it was because I had an older brother who'd received more than his share of attention from our father."

Whatever the reason, he added, he had a strong desire to be noticed, to be praised. He basked in the new flood of attention.

Still, despite the recognition, he believed that most of the villagers in his hometown looked at him as a "novelty, a freak." He admitted that he was never actually accepted by the people of Thal. There were certain social groups, he recalled, in which the people were "intimidated" by bodybuilding and, as a result, talked down to him. The dichotomy between Alfred Gerstl's sophisticated social circle in Graz, where Arnold was welcomed as an equal, and the condescending attitude of his backwater neighbors was somewhat ironic.

It was assumed by his parents and their friends that Arnold would eventually come to his senses and settle down to a sensible career. To his family and teachers, he recalls, the only acceptable way of life was "being a banker, secretary, doctor or salesman." They urged him to pursue something "legitimate," perhaps register with an employment agency.

But that was for normal people, and Schwarzenegger claims that even then he knew he was destined for something greater. He stopped bothering even responding to the advice of those around him and began listening to his "inner voice," his instinct.

"Normal people can be happy with a regular life," he declared. "I was different. I felt there was more to life than just plodding through an average existence. I'd always been impressed by stories of greatness and power. Caesar, Charlemagne, Napoléon were names I knew and remembered. I wanted to do something special, to be recognized as the best. I saw bodybuilding as the vehicle that would take me to the top, and I put all my energy into it."

Gustav had put his reservations aside and begun to accept his son's passion as a suitable pastime. No longer did he drag his son with him to the curling club or pressure Arnold to resume playing soccer. He was impressed by the girls and the trophies that Arnold was bringing home. But Gustav assumed that all this would never lead to anything, and as Arnold approached his eighteenth birthday, there was a drumbeat of questions. "What are you going to do with your life?" Gustav asked his son constantly. The reply was always the same: "I'm going to be a professional bodybuilder, I'm going to make it my life."

Pure foolishness, Gustav scoffed. Nobody can make a living doing such a thing. Arnold merely shrugged, vowing not to be drawn into an argument he couldn't win.

But as he continued to bulk up, day after day continuing the strict regimen he had set for himself, toward the goal of being like Reg Park, he too knew that the challenge of making a living as a bodybuilder was daunting.

Arnold knew that, like all Austrian boys, he would be required to perform one year of compulsory military service when he turned eighteen. Unlike most of his peers, he was actually looking forward to it.

The idea of uniforms and medals appealed to him immensely, and army discipline was not particularly objectionable. He likened it to the discipline required for successful bodybuilding and welcomed the regimentation—the firm, rigid structure. Given Gustav's military style, army life, he recalled, wasn't much different from being at home.

"My father always acted like a general, checking to see that I ate the proper way, that I did my studies," he wrote.

Arnold later claimed that Gustav's military connections enabled his son to get a plum assignment, as a driver in a tank unit, despite the fact that he was only eighteen and twenty-one was the minimum age required to drive the complicated tanks at the time.

But other sources claim that it was actually Alfred Gerstl who pulled strings, using his political connections. By this time, Gustav's reputation and influence were severely tarnished: he had drunkenly molested a woman on a bus, prompting a formal complaint. The incident had resulted in disciplinary action, and he had been transferred to a police station in Raaba. a suburb of Graz, where he was no longer the chief of police but a subordinate officer.

In August 1965, shortly after he turned eighteen, Private Arnold Schwarzenegger reported for basic training with Tank Battalion 4 at the Belgier Barracks at Graz. This Austrian army post had a rather notorious history, having been used as an SS barracks during the Nazi occupation of Austria. Near the end of the war, seventy-seven prisoners of war, Hungarian Jews, and resistance fighters were massacred and buried under the barracks, on orders from the local Nazi gauleiter, though the mass grave wasn't discovered until years after Schwarzenegger served there.

Though Arnold later claimed he wanted to drive tanks because they appealed to the part of him that "has always been moved by any show of strength and force," it is more likely that he chose the tank unit because it was the army unit nearest to Graz and enabled him to be close to his family and the bodybuilding community. Still, he loved feeling the powerful recoil of the M-47 tank guns when he fired, even though he never really mastered the complicated machines, which had been built by the U.S. military during the Korean War and given to Austria in the early 1960s, by which time they had become obsolete.

Once, during a night exercise, Arnold was driving his rusty old M-47 when he noticed a fellow tank driver rolling along in a brand-new American M-60, the newest tank in the Austrian arsenal and one he could never hope to drive, given his youth and inexperience. Over the radio, the two commanders began to debate who had the faster tank. Arnold was so cocky that he couldn't imagine being beaten by anyone, even by somebody in a state-of-the-art machine. He decided to put his counterpart to the test, slamming his machine into first gear and racing down the slope where they had both been coasting. The driver of the M-60 followed close behind.

"The other guy could have surely gone faster but he was afraid," Arnold recalled years later. "The hatch was open so my head was sticking out and I was convinced that I was braver than him and when I heard screams from behind—well—I thought he had probably soiled his pants. But when I stopped at the end of the slope, a guy grabbed me from behind and told me that he and seven other infantrymen had been sitting on my tank when I took off, and all except for him had fallen off the back as they couldn't hold on."

The same thing had happened to the other tank, so both commanders drove back up the slope, collecting the men sprawled on the ground, unharmed.

As punishment for his reckless antics, Arnold was forced to park his tank in the mud and crawl under the vehicle, up the rear, in through the hatch, out of the front driver's hatch, and back underneath the tank—fifty times.

"In the end each lap took four times as long because I had at least 10 kilos of mud on my uniform and I almost couldn't move," he recalled. "They could have also jailed me in a military prison for seven days but I still believe that this was a much more effective punishment."

After another incident, in which he failed to park his tank properly, letting it roll into the river, he was removed from tank driving and transferred to a more appropriate assignment—bodybuilding.

His mornings were still spent cleaning and oiling tanks, but after lunch, he was now ordered to head straight to the gym where he had deposited the dumbbells and weight machines he had brought with him from home to complement the army's flimsy equipment. Even though his bodybuilding regimen had always required strict discipline, it was nothing compared with the military discipline he encountered even in the gym.

"Every time an officer walked by the window and caught me sitting down, he'd threaten to have me put in jail," he recalled. "That was his duty. If you got caught goofing off when you were supposed to be oiling and greasing the tanks, you'd be put away. The army felt it was no different with what I was doing. I must train, they said, I must be lifting weights all the time."

He used the opportunity to continue building the foundation he had begun at the age of fifteen. He soon devised a way to train six hours at a stretch without exhausting himself. It helped that he had been given authorization to eat whenever he wanted in order to provide the protein necessary for such a grueling workout.

"The army became a luxury," Arnold would later claim approvingly of his new diet. "Before that, I only ate meat once a week or so because my family didn't have the money. In the army, you could have meat every day. And then, if you screwed up, they would put you in the kitchen at night to peel potatoes and do preparation work for the chef the next day. That was no punishment to me; it was the ideal situation, to go and eat everything you wanted. There was always meat left over, and there were eggs that you could make right there. So I worked out, then did my duty for two hours, and then I'm eating. I was actually gaining the most weight during that period."

In fact, he was now eating four or five times a day, including pounds and pounds of tasteless, overcooked army meat. Having consumed twice as much food at each sitting as he ever had before, he immediately returned to the gym to burn the extra calories and try to convert them to muscle.

At the behest of Kurt Marnul, he had for years been combining his bodybuilding training with a regimen of Olympic weight lifting, and he had won the Austrian heavyweight division weight lifting championship the year before. Even though bodybuilding and weight lifting can work against each other, developing the wrong respective muscles, Arnold claimed he lifted weights to prove a point. A bodybuilder didn't merely look strong; he *was* strong. A well-developed set of muscles was not merely for ornamentation. The combination of disciplines had soon put an additional twenty-five pounds on his 200-pound frame. He was determined not to waste this body development on impressing a bunch of army officers. He was itching to compete, determined to put his new muscles to the test. But there was one hitch, and it was due to last another nine months.

6.

Muscular Private

In his 1977 autobiography, Schwarzenegger recounts a story that has been repeated over and over by every subsequent biographer and has taken its place in his lore. He claims that one night during basic training, he went AWOL, crawling over the wall, with only the clothes on his back, and caught a train to Stuttgart, Germany, to accept an invitation to compete in Europe's elite junior bodybuilding competition, which he won handily.

"The Junior Mr. Europe contest meant so much to me that I didn't care what consequences I'd have to suffer," he recalled, claiming that he had barely enough money to buy a third-class train ticket, and that the train took an entire day and night to reach Stuttgart, 400 miles away.

But, like many other incidents in his chronology-challenged autobiography—undoubtedly composed by a ghostwriter relying on his subject's faulty memory—the story may not be entirely accurate. It appears that Schwarzenegger did go AWOL to sneak off and compete in Stuttgart that October, but it wasn't the Junior Mr. Europe pageant he entered. According to Albert Busek, coproducer of the competition, the title on the line that weekend was Best-Built Man in Europe. At the time, this was an amateurish contest sponsored by Busek's magazine, and it never attracted the continent's elite bodybuilders.

"Arnold didn't apply to enter the contest; he just showed up," recalled Busek years later. "In those days, you could do that."

According to Schwarzenegger's account, he arrived in Stuttgart nervous and exhausted from the long train trip, but also excited at the prospect of his first international contest, one that he had read about in the German muscle magazine published by Albert Busek.

"I had no idea what was going on. I tried to learn something by watching the short men's class, but they seemed as amateurish and confused as I was," he recalled of his arrival. "I had to borrow someone else's posing trunks, someone else's body oil."

He had spent the train trip mentally rehearsing a posing routine—a composite of all Reg Park's poses that he'd memorized from the magazine photos posted all over his wall at home.

But the instant he stepped before the judges at the Wulle Rooms where the contest took place, everything he had prepared suddenly vanished from his mind.

"Somehow I made it through the initial posing. Then they called me back for a pose-off. Again, my mind was blank and I wasn't sure how I'd done. Finally, the announcement came that I'd won."

Busek had heard stories coming out of Austria about the man people were referring to as the "Styrian Oak," but this was the first time he had seen Arnold in person.

"Immediately upon seeing him, I knew everything I had heard about him was true," he recalled. "He won the contest easily, beating the best German guy we'd had in years, Franz Dischinger."

As he received his trophy, Arnold could not believe that he had won and that he could now claim to be the best-built man in all of Europe even if it was not really true.

"I felt like King Kong," he said of the adulation from the crowd. "I loved the sudden attention. I strutted and flexed. I knew for certain that I was on the way to becoming the world's greatest bodybuilder. I felt I was already one of the best in the world. Obviously, I wasn't even in the top 5,000; but in my mind I was the best."

After the show, Busek—at twenty-two, only four years older than Arnold—took the Austrian prodigy to dinner. It was the beginning of a lifelong friendship. The whole time they were sitting in the restaurant, he claims, he was thinking to himself that he had just discovered a future superstar.

"I already knew that, physically, he had the greatest potential I'd ever seen," Busek told *Flex* magazine in 2005. "As we talked, his personality and sense of fun made a deep impression on me. He had a hunger for success and a drive for improvement I'd never experienced in anyone before or since. He told me he was looking to make the next step in his bodybuilding career. He told me his ambition was to eventually go to the United States, become the best bodybuilder in the world and be a movie star."

Unlike others who had heard the same boast from the brash teenager, Busek believed him.

The army was not as impressed, at least not at first. As Arnold climbed back over the wall two days later, he was caught by a patrol and immediately arrested. For the next seven days, he sat in a narrow cell, with only a blanket and a stone-cold bench, subsisting on soup, bread, and water. But nothing could dampen the thrill of his victory.

"I had my trophy and I didn't care if they locked me up for a whole year; it had been worth it."

By the time he was released from jail a week later, after proudly showing his trophy to anybody who entered the brig, word had spread through the entire camp about his victory in Germany. Declaring that it brought "prestige" to the unit, his commanding officer decided no further punishment was warranted. Instead, Arnold was given a two-day pass.

He had become something of a folk hero at the camp. Even in the field, he recalled, the drill instructors held him up as an example to the other men, urging them to follow the muscular private.

" 'You have to fight for your fatherland,' they said. 'You have to have courage. Look at what Schwarzenegger did just to win this title.' I became a hero, even though I had defied their rules."

Once he had completed basic training, Arnold was permitted to return to his parents' house on weekends. This was a convenient place to bring home the scores of women he was collecting, a different kind of trophy for the brash stud. The combination of muscles and

his army uniform had women fighting for his attention the moment he stepped into one of Graz's taverns.
He'd then whisk them home and out again the next
morning, past his parents—usually without so much
as an introduction. Aurelia, with her strict Catholic
morals, didn't approve. But Gustav seemed to gain a
newfound respect for his son's success with women.

"He felt it was perfectly all right to make out with
all the girls I could," Schwarzenegger later recalled.
"In fact, he was proud I was dating the fast girls. He
bragged about them to his friends. 'Jesus Christ, you
should see some of the women my son's coming up
with.'"

The tense relationship between father and son had
changed, he explained, "because I'd established myself
by winning a few trophies and now had some girls.
He was particularly excited about the girls. And he
liked the idea that I didn't get involved. 'That's right,
Arnold,' he'd say, as though he'd had endless experience, 'never be fooled by them.' That continued to be
an avenue of communication between us for a couple of
years."

Soon, Gustav would wait up for Arnold and his
latest conquest, bringing out a bottle of wine and some
glasses, getting a vicarious thrill from his son's promis-
cuity.

In July 1966, shortly before his discharge from the army, Arnold finally got a chance to compete for the title Junior Mr. Europe, this time with the army's blessing. The confusion about the dates in his auto-biography, contradicted by Albert Busek, may stem from the fact that this contest, like the Best-Built Man in Europe in October 1965, took place in Stuttgart. It may indeed be Busek whose recollection is faulty, but the German publisher and promoter insists that his chronology is correct because "1965 was a big year for me. I got married, our son was born, and I met Arnold."

Whether Junior Mr. Europe took place in October 1965 or June 1966, it was a milestone for Schwarzenegger, who again won the contest with little effort. The same venue also hosted the European powerlifting championship, which was won that year by a short but powerful Sardinian, Franco Columbu, who later recalled their first encounter.

"I met Arnold on a stage when he won Junior Mr. Europe and I won a powerlifting competition," he told CNN in 2003. "And he won—I won my powerlifting competition. And I say, 'Where are you from?' He said, 'I'm from Austria.' I was from Italy and this is in Germany. And at that moment, I said, 'Wow, you won. This is incredible, it's the first time I saw you.'

He says, 'Oh, yes. I'm finishing my military in Austria, I'm going to come back to Munich. And then if you want, we can train together, and I want to become Mr. Universe.'"

Columbu seems to confirm Busek's account—that Mr. Junior Europe occurred in the summer of 1966, not in the middle of Arnold's basic training in 1965 when he went AWOL. But, more important, this was the beginning of a lifelong friendship, an unbreakable bond, and a professional rivalry. Columbu, who at twenty-four was six years older than Arnold, stood only five feet five inches, but had an immensely powerful frame. The son of a shepherd, he had once been a jockey and had also captured the Italian lightweight boxing championship a few years earlier. He now lived in Munich, where he was working part-time as a trainer between workouts.

"Why don't you come to Germany?" he asked his new friend, speaking German with a thick Italian accent and probably sounding as foreign to the Germans as Schwarzenegger sounds when he speaks English today. "You'd do well there. Lots of beautiful women, lots of work. We can work out together in the day, and find plenty of girls at night."

The suggestion was seconded that evening when Albert Busek took Arnold and Columbu to a local tavern to celebrate their victories. He also brought along his partner, Rolf Putziger, who was the majority owner of the gym in Munich where Columbu worked as a trainer. Together, the three of them sang the virtues of the Bavarian capital. Each of them had a different motive for bringing the Styrian Oak to Germany. Busek wanted his muscle magazine, *Sports Revue*, to sponsor Arnold as he rose to the top of the bodybuilding world, perhaps even riding his coattails all the way to Mr. Universe. Putziger was gay and was instantly struck by the handsome young man; but he also thought Schwarzenegger would be good for business at his gym, bringing in members as his fame increased, as Busek assured him it would. Columbu fancied the sexual adventures he and Arnold could get up to, cutting a swath through the fräuleins of Munich. They all painted an appealing picture.

Putziger laid it on thick, Arnold recalled in his autobiography. "Schwarzenegger, you have a real talent for bodybuilding. You'll be the next great thing in Germany. As soon as you're out of the army, I'd like you to come to Munich and manage my health and bodybuilding club. You can train as much as you want."

He even offered to pay for Arnold's ticket to London the following fall to watch the Mr. Universe contest.

"What do you mean, *watch?*" Arnold asked. He had already made up his mind that he was going to compete in that contest and take the title.

Putziger was taken aback by his cockiness. "You don't think . . . ?" he started to ask.

"Yes," Arnold replied. "I'm going over there and compete, not to watch."

"No, no, no," responded the businessman, laughing. "You can't do that. Those guys are big bulls. They're big animals—so huge you wouldn't believe it. You don't want to compete against them. Not yet." His words were slightly intimidating, but not entirely convincing.

In less than three weeks, Arnold would be discharged from the army, and he still hadn't decided what to do with himself. Alfred Gerstl had arranged a city job working at the municipal swimming pool of Graz, which would enable him to continue training with Kurt Marnul at the Athletic Union in his spare time. But Arnold had decided long ago that his homeland was too small and "stifling" to contain his ambitions.

"I'd always had a claustrophobic feeling about Austria," he recalled. 'I've got to get out of here,' I kept thinking." That night, he made up his mind.

At the end of July 1966, Schwarzenegger received his discharge papers from the army. He immediately headed to his parents' house to break the news and say his good-byes. On August 1, he boarded a train at the Graz station for the four-hour journey to Munich.

"I was like a black trying to get out of Harlem," he told the *Atlanta Journal and Constitution* years later. "I knew when I left home that I'd never go back except as a visitor. On the train, leaving, I looked back and knew it wasn't home anymore."

7.

A Deafening Roar

Within minutes of stepping off the train at Munich's Hauptbahnhof station, Schwarzenegger recalls, he was "overwhelmed." Compared with sleepy Graz, Munich was a thriving cosmopolitan metropolis, with people arriving from all over Europe every day. He had never seen so many people, crowds, and cars everywhere. Had he made a mistake leaving Austria? he asked himself for a fleeting moment. Here he was, a big Austrian kid from a small country village—fresh, naive, and still relatively innocent.

After he found his way to Putziger's house, the gym owner drove Arnold around the city in his Mercedes, showing off the sights, as well as the fruits of his own growing empire, all linked to bodybuilding: the health club that Arnold would manage and the offices of his publishing company, which produced the popular muscle magazine *Kraft Sportrevue*, run by Albert Busek. Arnold was immediately impressed, though also a little wary of Putziger's attentions. Growing up, he had never met a *Schwuler*, the German pejorative term for a homosexual, at least not knowingly. Yet there was little doubt about the older man's orientation, which only two decades earlier would have condemned him to internment at Dachau, the Nazi death camp located in a Munich suburb, only a fifteen-minute drive from the house where Putziger now resided and where he offered to let Arnold stay.

Uncomfortable, Arnold stayed with Putziger for the first night as his new boss oriented him to the new job, managing the small health club on Schiller Strasse and providing personal fitness training to its members, who included a number of amateur bodybuilders but were mostly sedentary office workers trying to get into shape. While he looked for his own quarters, Arnold moved his belongings to a small storage room at the back of the gym. There, he slept fitfully on a cot with his legs hanging off, but safe at least from his boss's leering attention.

After a few days, Albert Busek helped him find a room in a boardinghouse, the only lodgings he could afford on the meager salary Putziger was paying him.

It wasn't exactly the life he described to his parents in his first letter home, "making a decent salary and making progress in every direction." But he couldn't let on that he was struggling; otherwise, they "would have gotten on my case to return home," he recalled.

Managing a health club, Arnold discovered for the first time that he had a flair for business, devising strategies for bringing in a new customer base and figuring out how to make Putziger's Gym the center of bodybuilding in Munich.

"He adjusted very quickly," recalled Busek years later. "In those days, weight training was not fashionable." Among the odd assortment of regulars were powerlifters, wrestlers, and some boxers. One of the wrestlers was Harold Sakata, who had become famous for playing "Odd Job" in the James Bond movie *Goldfinger* three years earlier.

But Arnold wasn't as keen about the other part of his job, acting as a personal trainer to the "disgusting, superficial" people who expected him to work magic on their out-of-shape physiques as they merely "went through the motions." He resented anybody who wasn't willing to put in the maximum effort, and he was frustrated by having to waste his time on people "who would never benefit" from what he taught them. But he realized that he had to do it in order to survive.

He was most concerned about what he called his "split life"—acting as an instructor half the time while trying to train himself for his ultimate goal, the Mr. Universe title. He never lost sight of why he had come to Munich in the first place.

To compensate for his work schedule, he devised a unique split routine, training twice a day six days a week. He worked out in the morning from 9 to 11 A.M. before attending to the club members and routine gym business. Then, after the last flabby client walked out the door, he would return at 7 P.M. for another two-hour lifting session. This grueling schedule was unheard of at the time and defied all conventional wisdom in exercise science. Fellow bodybuilders, even Albert Busek, believed he was "overtraining," and they worried that such a regimen would cause him to "lose size," that his muscles would start to deteriorate. Yet within two months, he had actually gained an additional five pounds of muscle. Nobody had ever seen somebody work as hard, or an athlete who was as determined to achieve his goal.

"He had to always train and always do the most," recalled his training partner, the future Mr. Universe Karl Kainrath, who was in awe of Arnold's sheer determination. "We knew he would do great things. He knew it, and we knew it."

Before long, rumors began to spread beyond Munich about the Austrian "monster." With little effort, he won the Mr. Germany contest, as spectators began to converge from all over the continent to see him in person, impelled by the laudatory coverage in Busek's magazine. Busek featured Schwarzenegger's physique prominently in every issue, and predicted in a January 1966 cover story that Arnold would be the world's greatest within three years. There were many, however, who believed he was already head and shoulders above any European competitor. His twenty-inch arms were undeniably the largest on the continent, as he discovered when he arrived to compete in the Mr. Europe contest and the spectators crowded around him to gape.

Even the judges were astounded at his powerful physique. In fact, he recalled, they almost "fainted" when he began to flex. "Oh my god, where did this guy come from?" he overheard one judge asking the others after he struck a double biceps pose onstage. Hearing that, he knew he already had the contest won and immediately went into overdrive, filling up with energy and going ten minutes over his allotted time, not wanting to leave the platform as he struck pose after pose for the appreciative audience.

Recalling the event years later, Schwarzenegger remarked about how the members of the audience couldn't believe what they were seeing. They touched his muscles and asked, "How did you do it?" They thought he "must be training under some special drug program or something," he recalled, implying that his supersize frame was simply the result of his unique training methods and his twice-a-day training routine. But, despite the fact that Kurt Marnul was no longer at his side, Schwarzenegger had brought with him from Austria enough steroids to help pump up his muscles to a size impossible to achieve by hard work alone. Still, there was nothing yet illegal about his pharmaceutical helpers, and he knew that the giant Americans he would soon encounter were also chemically enhanced.

When the winner was announced, the nineteen-year-old Arnold had won "in a cinch." But whereas a year earlier such an achievement would have been a thrill, it was no longer enough. There was only one title that counted. "In my own mind, I *was* Mr. Universe," he recalled. "I had this absolutely clear vision of myself up on the dais with the trophy. It was only a matter of time before the whole world would be able to see it too."

His victory at Mr. Europe automatically qualified him for an all-expenses-paid trip to Mr. Universe, scheduled to take place at the end of September in London. But, two weeks later, when he entered and won another contest sponsored by a rival federation, he learned that the offer was rescinded. It was his first taste of the divisive politics and competing interests that have racked the world of bodybuilding. Putziger too had reneged on his initial offer to finance Arnold's trip, and for several weeks it appeared that he would not have the means to travel. Hearing the news, one of Putziger's chief competitors, Reinhart Smolana, who had for months wanted to lure Arnold to work at his own gym, offered to help. Smolana was a respected bodybuilder who had won his weight class at Mr. Universe a year earlier but knew he didn't have the build to win the overall title. He knew of only one person who stood a chance to compete for the big prize, the nineteen-year-old colossus who was causing such a buzz among Munich's bodybuilding elite and who came in occasionally to train on the specialized equipment unavailable at Putziger's. Even so, Smolana expected it to take two or three years before Schwarzenegger could hope to compete with the likes of the British giant, Paul Nash—who, he warned Arnold, "is so big he'll wipe you off the stage." Still, he believed Schwarzenegger had to compete with the world's best to get a taste of what bodybuilders had to do to get to the top.

Smolana began to collect money from his friends and clients to sponsor Arnold's transportation and hotel expenses, loudly telling anybody who would listen that if Putziger was too cheap to support his own employee, he himself would take up the slack and get behind the young Austrian wunderkind. Within a month, the money had been collected and Arnold stepped up his training for the big event.

Meanwhile, as he got closer to what he believed was his date with destiny, Arnold had discovered that there was more to life than working out. He had hooked up with Franco Columbu, who was working as a trainer at a gym outside the city, and together the unusual duo formed the legendary, unbreakable friendship that persists to this day.

Schwarzenegger's description of his burgeoning relationship with the Sardinian bodybuilder portrays the buddies as a pair of sedate homebodies. "Franco would invite me over to his apartment and cook," he recalled in his autobiography. "He was already a good cook. So we had a terrific time."

But those who were around at the time paint a very different picture. Heinrich Schein, now living in New York, was a regular patron of Putziger's gym who frequently socialized with Arnold and Columbu during that period. Over a beer at the White Horse Tavern in Greenwich Village, Schein describes the two as a "pair of holy terrors."

"They were a funny duo, those guys," he recalls. "Arnold was just enormous; Franco was a short, odd-shaped guy. But they were both strong as shit. They would compete with each other to see who could lift the most. Arnold would be calling Franco a midget and then the little guy would lift a ton and everybody would be standing around in disbelief and they would make a little show of it, insulting each other the whole time. Then after they competed with each other in the gym, they would go out to the bars at night and compete to see who could pick up the most women. Most of the women would say no—they were very crude about it. In those days, women wouldn't necessarily be turned on by those kinds of muscles, at least in Munich. I wasn't built like either of them but I was a big guy and I remember women would get turned off by the big muscles. It changed later on, but this was the 1960s and that wasn't considered very attractive. But they would always persist and they would always score. They never gave up till they convinced a woman to go home with them. And they were not subtle about it; they'd walk right up to a woman and say, 'Want to fuck?'—the German equivalent. Eventually they'd find someone who would. It was a game with them. We would sometimes take bets to see who would succeed first. You hear me tell the story and you probably think they were drunk, no? But neither of them really drank a lot. That's just the way they were. They were very funny, though, so it wasn't as obnoxious as you probably imagine. It was more entertaining; even the women would often laugh. I wish I had a video camera to capture that time."

When the biographer Wendy Leigh returned to Munich two decades later to interview those who had been witness to Schwarzenegger's antics, she discovered much the same kind of stories about him. But she didn't describe his actions as "funny," painting instead a portrait of a brash, cruel, testosterone-fueled loud-mouth who alienated people wherever he went, leaving behind a stream of helpless victims.

The story she heard most frequently concerned Arnold's reputation as a legendary practical joker, though the objects of the jokes rarely found them funny. The most frequent victims, she discovered, were the novice bodybuilders who would apply to join the gym. Hearing about his reputation, they would almost always ask Arnold for advice, and he was always ready to oblige, dispensing "tips" to help them attain a physique like his in a short time.

Once he counseled a bodybuilder to eat a sugar cube on the first day, then increase the number to two cubes the second day, and so on until he was eating thirty cubes per day. He advised another that eating two pounds of ice cream would pack on the muscle. Another unwitting supplicant, Leigh writes, nearly choked to death after Arnold told him that instead of blending the usual concoction of egg whites and vitamins, he should knead the mixture together and eat it as if it were an apple.

Collecting one story after another about Arnold's cruel jokes, Leigh theorizes that because he was known for his ability to endure severe pain while training, he also knew how to inflict it and never hesitated to do so. She believes that the cruel jokes were a way of asserting his power, and that by playing his pranks in front of other bodybuilders, he was categorizing those he came into contact with as "victims and predators." Each practical joke, she writes, served to "cloak him in yet more impenetrably powerful armor, bringing him friends, admiration, and supremacy."

One of his training partners explained, "Arnold always made a fool of people he didn't respect." Kurt Marnul too recalled that Schwarzenegger was unrepentant about the consequences of his jokes, contemptuously dismissing his victims by saying, "They are so stupid. I would never do what they do."

Schein, however, told me he doesn't recall any examples of Arnold's cruelty from those days, although he remembers that Arnold had a definite reputation as a practical joker. "I don't remember any specific jokes, but he would make fun of people. He and Franco would say a lot of cruel things to each other, but that was a sport with them—they didn't mean it. He never did anything particularly mean to me, though he would insult me every day like he did everybody else. That was not mean-spirited, it was more like jock talk."

But if Schein can't recall a specific practical joke from that time, Schwarzenegger himself certainly could, as he demonstrated during the filming of the documentary *Pumping Iron,* when he described a particular favorite, explaining that he liked to pull pranks when he thought somebody was being particularly arrogant or "misusing the sport of bodybuilding." It seemed that there was a young German bodybuilder, "Power Mike," who was entered in the Mr. Munich contest and fancied himself quite an accomplished poser with, as he told Arnold, a "perfect body." Even so, he wanted to come up with a new posing routine, something "way out, which nobody expects."

Arnold explained that he was in correspondence with all the top U.S. athletes and that he had heard of a new routine: it was all the rage in American bodybuilding circles but hadn't yet reached Germany. It involved screaming at the top of one's lungs while posing.

In the complicated, tangled world of bodybuilding, various rival federations staged their own contests, some featuring professionals, some featuring amateurs, each purporting to crown the world's greatest with names like Mr. World, Mr. Universe, and Mr. Olympia. It was difficult for the casual observer to determine which contest could lay claim to the legitimate title, or if such a title existed. Eventually Schwarzenegger would win all that mattered, erasing any doubt about his being the best in the world. This contest was staged by the National Amateur Body-Builders' Association (NABBA), was actually known as Mr. Universe (Amateur), and was held every year in London. Another contest, staged by the same organization, took place in the United States and featured only professionals, also competing for the Mr. Universe title. It was Arnold's goal to eventually seize that title as well, but first things first. If he won this title, he could call himself Mr. Universe, and that had been his goal since the first time he lifted a barbell at the Graz Athletic Union four years earlier. He already had a number of titles under his belt, most recently winning the European powerlifting championship. But these laurels no longer meant anything to him; he referred to them as the "Mr. Thises and Mr. Thats." Knowing virtually no English, he had spent the entire flight practicing the phrase, "I would like to go to the Royal Hotel, please." Luckily, he was sitting across the aisle from two Munich businessmen who happened to also be staying at the Royal and offered to let him ride with them in their taxi. But when they arrived and Arnold saw no bodybuilders anywhere, he instantly knew something was amiss. Sure enough, he was at the wrong Royal Hotel. The desk clerk hailed a taxi and sent him to the correct address, near to where the contest was being held in London's West End.

This time when he arrived at his destination, there was no mistaking it. At least fifty hulking men congregated outside the doors. He had never seen anything like them. Even to Arnold, they seemed "monstrous," though he soon discovered that their size was an illusion, created by jackets padded out to twice the width of their shoulders. Actually, it was Arnold, they heard, who was the monster, and they had been waiting to see for themselves whether he truly had the twenty-inch arms that they had read about in *Kraftsportrevue* and other European bodybuilding magazines.

Though many Americans had arms of this size, it was unheard of for a European, especially one only nineteen years old; and as Arnold stepped out of the cab, the bodybuilders immediately crowded around him, feeling his arms and talking in at least ten different languages. He was flattered by the attention, but also a little taken aback by the "dudes with funny haircuts from India and Africa." He had never before seen a black man "with frizzy hair."

Among the people who witnessed Arnold's arrival that day was a British gym owner, Jim Charles, who was one of the Mr. Universe judges. Years later, Charles recalled that his first sight of Schwarzenegger was an eye-opener. "Someone said to me, 'You've got to come and see this kid. He's only nineteen years old and he's got twenty-inch arms.' Arnie whipped off his shirt and did some flexes while I took pictures. Later on, he put together a ninety-second routine to demonstrate how strong his muscles were."

After Arnold was through entertaining his new admirers, he brought his bag into the lobby to check in. There, he saw a few Americans he recognized from the muscle magazines; and after looking at them up close, he concluded that the photos he had seen had been deceiving. "I began to feel I could beat them all," he recalled. That idea vanished the first time he saw Chet Yorton stepping out of an elevator. Arnold stepped back with a sinking feeling, "almost in amazement." At that moment, he recalls, he accepted defeat.

Until the moment he laid eyes on Chet Yorton, the twenty-seven-year-old reigning Mr. America, Arnold firmly believed that 230 pounds of body weight and twenty-inch arms were a ticket to the top. But that idea changed after he took one look at Yorton, who had begun lifting weights just out of high school to recover from a serious car accident that nearly required a leg to be amputated. As Arnold sized him up from head to toe, concluding that he was like a "special creation of science," he realized that a true winner had to have a specific look, a winning look—and Yorton had the look. Yorton was golden brown, cut up, defined, each muscle "mapped with veins." European bodybuilders simply did not look like this, and the black-and-white photos in U.S. muscle magazines couldn't capture the magnificence. This was the first time Arnold realized the value of being able to see a bodybuilder's veins. It was an awe-inspiring sight and one that he instantly vowed to duplicate, even as he concluded that there was no way he would be going home with the winner's trophy that weekend.

When he awoke the next morning, now resigned to his fate in the coming competition, Arnold realized that he had barely enough money to cover his hotel bill and assorted expenses. As he watched his fellow body-builders wolf down the mammoth breakfasts that they needed to fuel their superhuman physiques, he knew that he could never afford the steep prices charged by the hotel dining room. Taking pity on him, Jim Charles treated him to breakfast at a neighboring café. "He was really hard-up, so I bought him a coffee and baked beans on toast," recalled Charles years later. "He still owes me the money for it. It must be all of a couple of bob!"

The most important part of an international body-building competition is not the pageant that takes place onstage before the spectators; it is the prejudging, which usually happens in the afternoon on the first day. In contrast to the pageantry of the stage contest, this is a somewhat sedate phase attended by a small group of media people, bodybuilders, and federation officials. One by one, the judges call out the competitors from each class—short, medium, and tall—and consider them in a group and individually. All the while, the judges make a series of notations on their individual score sheets, which are kept secret until the main event in front of an audience, when the winners of each class are announced and the overall victor out of all three classes is announced.

As the judges walked silently around the room during the prejudging phase—held in the ballroom of the Royal Hotel—on Saturday afternoon, Arnold attempted to assess their reactions. Considering the enthusiasm they showed when he was called forward, he felt he was doing well, much better than he expected. But even as he beamed at his showing, he noticed something that gave him pause. Arnold was the tallest competitor in the tall class, yet it was Chet Yorton who posed last, apparently because he had been late to register. Posing last was a definite advantage, leaving an enduring impression on the judges, and Arnold immediately concluded that this was a "trick, a typical American trick." Impressed, he made a mental note of it.

The public show was held the next evening at London's Victoria Palace Theatre. Three thousand spectators had crowded in to witness the results, but Arnold was too busy in the confusion backstage, pumping himself up for his public unveiling, to take much notice of what was happening on the other side of the curtain. Mostly he tried to listen to the snatches of conversation that he could understand with his limited English. As he listened to the conversations of the other bodybuilders, waiting his turn, he heard endless theories. Some contestants were talking about the idea of taking a sauna just before a competition to wring every last bit of fluid out of their system. Others were talking about the benefits of tensing and flexing to promote something called "vascularity." When another German competitor began translating for Arnold, and he could finally understand exactly what was being said, he also understood something else for the first time. Bodybuilding was "not a sport but a very complex science."

When it was his turn to pose, the announcer furnished an enthusiastic introduction: "And now, ladies and gentlemen, allow me to introduce the new sensation from Germany, Mr. Europe, Arnold Schwarzenegger. He is nineteen, already a fantastic top bodybuilder, and this is his first time in an international competition. Let's give him a great welcome."

As he took the stage, the applause was deafening, unlike anything he had experienced at the smaller contests he had competed in to this point. As he caught his first glimpse of the jammed auditorium, he was suddenly afraid that he would freeze up, unable to pose at all. To avoid what would have been a disastrous beginning to his international career, he fixed his gaze on a spotlight high up in the ceiling and struck his first pose. As the applause increased, the warm rush of adrenaline and adulation that he would crave for the rest of his life washed over him. As he concluded his routine, the applause for the unknown young newcomer was deafening, and he didn't want to leave the stage.

Albert Busek, who had flown in that day and was in the audience, later described the scene. "Nobody knew who he was, but he was a sensation," the German editor told *Flex* magazine. "From the moment the fans saw this new giant onstage, it was like a thunderstorm had struck. They began cheering 'Arnold! Arnold! Arnold!' like crazy. With his charisma, Arnold, who was always comfortable onstage, connected with the fans and they couldn't get enough of him."

When Arnold finally left the stage, somebody pushed him back out for an encore as the audience clamored for more. "I told myself that it made the entire four years of training worthwhile," he told himself at that moment. It was the first encore of the evening. Was it possible that he had defied the odds and triumphed at his first appearance?

But if he entertained that possibility even for a split second, reality sank in the moment Chet Yorton emerged into the spotlight. Arnold watched from the wings as the American ripped off his poses one after another "like a machine," keeping each muscle tensed as he hammered his poses. *Bang! Bang!* his calves popped out like diamonds. Arnold had never before seen a bodybuilder flex his leg muscles. This went against the European idea of concentrating only on the size of the chest and arms. In awe, he watched Yorton's facial expression, "proud and relaxed," expressing only one attitude—*I am the winner.*

Indeed, when the judges presented the trophies, Yorton had easily won the tall class as well as first over-all. But to the surprise of nearly everybody, Arnold came in second. It was a remarkable achievement for a rookie, and there wasn't a person in attendance that evening who didn't think Arnold would be clutching the winner's trophy before long.

8.

The Age of Schwarzenegger

On the Monday following the contest in London, Schwarzenegger returned to Munich in triumph. None of his financial benefactors had expected him to place higher than fifth or sixth. "Second place was almost a miracle," recalled Albert Busek. "We all knew that he was now on his way to the top. Nothing would stop him."

When he had finally reached the top—in body-building, in Hollywood, in business, and in politics—pundits regularly made a sport of analyzing how he did it. His reaction to losing Mr. Universe provides a fairly good glimpse. Once he got over the disappointment of coming home without the top trophy, he immediately set out to understand exactly where he had faltered so it would never happen again. Because of his already massive ego, it was all the more remarkable to those around him to watch Arnold honestly assess his weaknesses, dissecting every area of his development and routine for answers. It was an approach that he would bring with him to each subsequent phase of his life and career and that would serve him remarkably well as he climbed the ladder to the pinnacle of every profession he chose.

Whereas most bodybuilders focused all their energy building up their strongest assets—arms, chest, or biceps—Arnold was determined to focus on his shortcomings until he could genuinely be called the best-built man in the world. Assessing what he called his "glaring weak points," he knew from watching Chet Yorton that his legs, and especially his calves, were embarrassingly underdeveloped. He immediately set to work training his calves twice as hard as any other muscle, reportedly wearing shorts in the gym and inviting the other bodybuilders to mock his "girlie legs" as a motivational exercise.

He compiled lists and charts and pored over every element until training literally became a twenty-four-hour-a-day job: he dreamed of new poses in his sleep. He was remarkably self-aware, and his checklist concentrated on not only physical weaknesses but also psychological weaknesses, even delving into his family upbringing.

"Because of my strict parents," he wrote, "I was very disciplined. However, I didn't get certain things I needed as a child, and that, I think, finally made me hungry for achievement, for winning in other ways, for being the best, being recognized. If I'd gotten everything and been well-balanced, I wouldn't have had my drive. So, as a result of this negative element in my upbringing, I had a positive drive toward success and recognition."

Haunted by the remarkably precise, machinelike posing routine that Yorton had used to secure the title, Arnold was determined to work on his poses until he could hammer them out the way his rival did, only better. He would pore over muscle magazines, circling and cutting out the photos of the poses he liked, sometimes saving only the hands or the twist of the torso. He even studied photos of models and dancers in poses he believed would suit bodybuilding, searching especially for "symmetry and elegance." Aiming for a distinctive routine—something "strong and powerful and beautiful"—he collected twenty poses until he had a routine that said *Arnold*.

Trying his new routine out at an exhibition, he invited friends to criticize anything they didn't like— the more ruthless the critique, the better. The way a sports team watches game films to scout its opponent,

Arnold would spend hours watching films of his rivals posing, to determine their weak points and posing strategy. With mathematical precision, he timed their posing transitions, calculating where he could insert three poses to their one, at the same time displaying more body parts to the judges. He spent as much time, he later explained, concentrating on mental attitude as on his physical training, a strategy he learned from his old friend in Graz, Karl Gerstl, who had used the same training methods to become an international karate champion.

Meanwhile, Rolf Putziger announced that he was getting out of the gym business in order to concentrate on publishing his magazine and selling protein supplements. He offered to sell the gym to Arnold, who still had barely a pfennig to his name. It was a remarkable opportunity to both train and gain independence from a boss, and Arnold knew that he would find the money. Applying the same relentless drive that he put into his training—managing other gyms, giving private lessons, and selling food supplements on the side—he managed to scrape together the down payment and the money for the gym equipment. His fame from placing second at Mr. Universe had attracted a steady membership to the gym, and plenty of acolytes wanted to train with the pride of Munich, bringing in more revenue every week. But there were loans to be repaid, and improvements were needed to the facilities. "It was a struggle, a hell of a struggle," he later recalled.

A few months earlier, on the night he placed second in the Mr. Universe contest, Arnold was approached by one of the judges, Wag Bennett, who said through an interpreter that he preferred Schwarzenegger's body to Yorton's and had in fact voted for Arnold to win. Bennett, who—with his wife, Dianne—was among the most influential people in British bodybuilding, owned a gym located in an old Victorian house on Bromford Road in London. That evening, he invited the young Austrian runner-up to his house for dinner along with Albert Busek, who translated.

"Arnold really couldn't speak English and he just stood there—this big, gauche Austrian hick who was literally bursting out of his clothes. He told me then he wanted to be the biggest bodybuilder in the world," Bennett later recalled of the dinner conversation that evening. "And the richest. And the greatest. He wanted to live in California and own an apartment block and be a film star."

Impressed by the scope of his ambition, Bennett and his wife never forgot their dinner guest and were determined to cross his path again. Later that fall, Arnold received a letter from the Bennetts inviting him back to England for a series of bodybuilding exhibitions they were promoting all over the country.

Arnold flew back to London a little skeptical about posing for the public with no title at stake but eager for the fat paycheck that Bennett had promised him. The British couple, whom he would one day refer to as his "British parents," invited him to stay at their house in Forest Gate. "This was a boy of nineteen who didn't have a pot to piss in," Bennett recalled of Arnold's arrival. "Even his trousers only came halfway down his leg. Dianne had to take him round the corner to buy him a pair of booties."

It turned out that Bennett had an ulterior motive for inviting Arnold to England. He had been judging contests for many years and knew what it took to win. He believed that with a little polish, Arnold Schwarzenegger could become the world's greatest bodybuilder. Bennett could see how much Arnold had improved in the brief time since the contest in September. He knew he could offer no constructive advice about physique or form. But he was convinced he had the secret weapon that would enable Arnold to best all comers—posing to music. When he made the suggestion, Arnold's first reaction was indignation. "I had won second place in the Mr. Universe contest. What makes him think he can show me how to pose?" he thought.

Arnold was confused by the suggestion that he pose to music, all the more so when Bennett explained what music he had in mind, a semiclassical sound track. It reminded Arnold of the "boring" music he had to endure at Alfred Gerstl's salons years earlier. He liked modern, jazzy music, anything with a beat, something that "moved." But Bennett patiently explained that for the purpose of the exhibition, he had to use something more complex, something with "depth and texture."

The sound track was from the movie *Exodus*—an epic film about the founding of the state of Israel. As Bennett played the record on the hi-fi in his living room, Arnold's first reaction was embarrassment, then laughter. "I can't pose to that," he protested. Bennett urged him to at least try. With nothing at stake, and Bennett paying him the grand sum of ten pounds per exhibition, Arnold reluctantly agreed. Soon Bennett showed him how to hit the most dramatic poses in time to the high points of the music. He taught his new protégé to move and turn to the rhythm and the flow; he also showed films of other bodybuilders posing, explaining what he thought worked and didn't work. It was a marked contrast to the *Bang! Bang!* posing routine used by Chet Yorton months earlier, but something gradually dawned on Arnold that he would never forget. Bodybuilding was as much show business as sport. If he was to rise to the top, he would need to become a showman. Still, he imagined that the new routine made him look slow and clumsy. He would never use it in a serious competition. He would be laughed off the stage.

His attitude changed on the night of his first exhibition, at London's Crystal Palace. The moment he stepped onstage, "everything fell into place." It was just as Wag Bennett had predicted. The 2,000 spectators roared with approval when the music came up and quieted when it went down. Before, he explained, his posing had been "like a silent film." Now it was like a talkie. It gave his routine a whole new dimension, with Bennett manipulating the lighting to throw shadows on his body and the music stopping and starting dramatically. "The results amazed me," he recalled. After the show, for the first time in his career, the audience crowded around him, clamoring for autographs. "What a feeling that was to write *Arnold Schwarzenegger* across the program. All of a sudden I was a star," he recalled. The reaction was the same in Newcastle, Belfast, and Portsmouth. He now had a completely new posing routine and was ready to show it off in competition.

Returning to Munich, he brought along the *Exodus* music and took it with him to every competition. Before he went on, he would instruct the stage manager how to light him and when to open and close the curtains. Soon the buzz about his new routine had spread across Europe and he was invited to exhibitions in Holland and Belgium. His fame was spreading fast.

He was now a genuine professional, commanding as much as 100 marks for one exhibition, a princely sum that helped him quickly pay off his gym debts and gave him a little extra money in his pocket for the first time in his life. "If Hercules were to be born today his name would be Arnold Schwarzenegger," wrote one German newspaper. Fame and fortune, however, were hard to handle, especially for a young man whose ego was already boundless. "I was becoming a star, being interviewed and photographed, and I let that go to my head," he later admitted.

Indeed, Schwarzenegger and others were quickly earning a reputation as troublemakers, starting bar-room brawls, driving recklessly through the streets, and playing increasingly cruel jokes on helpless victims. As he confessed years later, his public notoriety simply raised his ego to new heights.

"I already felt I was better than anyone else. I felt as if I were a Superman or something," he explained.

"That was my attitude: macho. I was strong and I walked the streets feeling and acting tough. If someone made the slightest remark or gave me trouble I would hit them over the head."

At the time, this obnoxious streak appeared to be confined to Munich. Every few weeks, he would fly to London and stay with the Bennetts, who observed a very different side of him—another paradox that would frequently show itself over the years. In London, he would help out around the house, displaying his Austrian sense of order. Dianne Bennett was especially grateful for his help with her two young children; he would take them swimming on weekends and pick them up after school. "He was very gentle with them; they loved him," she observed, speculating that her motherly affection toward Arnold might have helped him develop "more mundane characteristics such as liking family life."

Dianne had taken it upon herself to teach Arnold English, working with him for hours at a time. But as he began to pick up the language and she observed his bombastic side, she occasionally regretted it. "At first, when Arnold would talk about what he intended to do with his life, I tended to take it with a pinch of salt," she later recalled. "He'd sit there and explain—albeit in rudimentary English—how he was going to be the greatest bodybuilder of all time, and that he wanted to own real estate and be a movie star. We'd all be going, 'Yeah, yeah, yeah. . . . He's all mouth and no trousers.' "

Before he met the Bennetts, Dianne recalled, Arnold had "never actually read a book." She took it upon herself to send him titles that she thought he would find interesting. Prophetically, one of the first books she sent him was a biography of his future grandfather-in-law, Joseph Kennedy.

But if the Bennetts' language lessons and advice about posing had a lasting effect on Arnold, these paled in comparison with the service they did him by introducing him to one of their close friends in late 1966. Ever since the afternoon at the Graz Cinema when Arnold first laid eyes on Reg Park in *Hercules and the Vampires*, the South African bodybuilder turned film star had been his idol. Even after he began to accumulate titles of his own, his hero worship never waned. If anything, it intensified as he read everything he could about Park's training regimen, studied every move and every gesture Park made, and envied Park's "perfect calves." To Arnold, Park was the epitome of the perfect bodybuilder. Once a month for years, he had written Park a fan letter asking for advice. He would occasionally receive a form letter and an autographed picture, but never a personalized reply. Then one day, a few months after Mr. Universe, he received a letter from Park. This time, to his excitement, Park replied that he had heard of Arnold and was looking forward to meeting him sometime. Park would be doing an exhibition in London the following January. Maybe they could meet up there. Arnold immediately wrote to Wag Bennett and asked if he could do the same exhibition as his hero. Bennett immediately gave the go-ahead.

The day came in mid-January 1967. Arnold was training at Bennett's gym when he heard that Park would be arriving within the hour. "I was like a child," he recalled. "I was going to meet my idol for the first time." He later compared the moment to the feeling a girl gets when she has a crush on a boy. Finally, he rushed forward to say how excited he was to meet Park. His English was still limited and Park spoke no German, but there was an instantaneous bond between them. Park later recalled that at this first meeting, Schwarzenegger said his mother thought for a long time that he was gay because he had pinups of Park, shirtless, all over his bedroom wall.

"There was something about his look, his drive. He was hungry to get to the top and I thought this kid is going to be better than me one day." Still, Park was

gracious, and even though he may have been further-
ing the career of a future rival, he immediately invited Arnold to join him on his upcoming tour of the
United Kingdom and Ireland. At the first stop on the
tour, in fact, Park introduced Arnold as "the next
Mr. Universe." In a few years, he told his young fans,
Arnold Schwarzenegger would be the "greatest thing
bodybuilding has ever seen."

In the ten days they toured together, Arnold learned
more about his craft than he had in the last year in the
gym. Park taught him the finer points of bone structure
and that a bodybuilding exercise routine had to be tai-
lored to the shape of an individual body. Most important, the South African cleared up much of the mystery
and confusion Arnold had confronted about the "principles" of other champions. As Park dispensed advice,
Arnold wrote it all down to take it back to Munich,
anxious to put it into practice. "I knew from the first
time I met him that one day the pupil would become
the master," Park later recalled.

At the end of the tour, Arnold asked whether he
could come to South Africa to train with Park and possibly do an exhibition. Park extended the invitation but
made it contingent upon one thing. "First you must
win Mr. Universe," he said, adding that he was confident this would happen in 1967.

When Arnold returned to Munich eager to work even harder toward that goal, he trained almost exclusively according to the principles Park had taught him. He also knew that he would have to take his self-criticism to a new level, working harder than ever before on his remaining faults. Each month he hired a photographer to shoot his routine so he could study it in minute detail, with a magnifying glass, for flaws. The other bodybuilders commented on his remarkable improvement, and Arnold's confidence soared. But Park's influence, he later claimed, went beyond the gym. It also "made me want to become a better person," he explained.

As he became more and more satisfied with his physical progress, "then gradually I could allow myself to admit how bad I was in other areas." Realizing that he had become nothing more than a "punk" and a "bully," he now vowed to become a better human being, "just a normal guy." The macho persona, he claimed, was now "gone." Others who knew him would later dispute this, but there is no question that his scrapes with the law, his brazen cruelty, and his drunken barroom brawls were now less prevalent. That may have been due more than anything to his increased focus on the upcoming Mr. Universe contest, which gave him little time to do anything but train

and run the gym when he wasn't on the road performing exhibitions.

Arnold began to hear rumors of a new potential rival,
Dennis Tinerino, who had just won Mr. America and
was being touted by muscle magazines as the next Mr.
Universe. Nervously, Arnold collected all the photos
he could of the twenty-one-year-old New Yorker with
the perfect physique, who he had to admit had better
legs. In the days before rules about conflicts of interest
would have made it impossible, Wag Bennett was once
again serving as one of the judges and he had already
seen Tinerino in action. Eating breakfast with Arnold
at the Royal Hotel on the morning when the contest
began, Bennett informed his Austrian "son" that it
would certainly be close. Arnold had been accompanied
to London by his editor friend Albert Busek, whom he
dispatched to locate and check up on the American favorite. Busek dutifully found Tinerino and persuaded
him to be photographed for *Sportkraft Revue.* When
Busek returned to report on his findings, Arnold could
immediately tell that he was impressed. "Arnold,"
Busek declared, "Tinerino *is* incredible."

At the prejudging that afternoon, Arnold finally got
a chance to observe his rival up close. They even had a
chance to talk briefly, but both men used the opportunity to play psychological head games—a strategy they

had learned from boxers like Muhammad Ali, who had famously been using it to great effect at prefight weigh-ins.

When Tinerino asked how he was, Arnold, whose English was steadily improving, replied, "Fantastic! It's the kind of day when you know you're going to win." As the prejudging began, an increasingly confident Arnold made sure to stand right next to Tinerino, wanting to give the judges a side-by-side comparison. He had learned a lesson from Chet Yorton the year before, and this time he had registered last so that he would be judged last, becoming what he described as the "final attraction."

As he hit his catlike poses, one after another—chest, back, double biceps—the room erupted with applause, though such displays were usually frowned upon during the sedate prejudging phase. The positive reaction from the officials, fellow bodybuilders, and some of the press sent a rush of adrenaline through Arnold's body, even as he continued flexing. Yet Tinerino had also performed well. It was clear to Arnold that, up close, the American had better abdominals and calves.

The winner would not be announced until the next evening, at the public show. That meant waiting an entire day until he would know whether he was about to be crowned the youngest Mr. Universe in the history of the contest. It was the longest day of his life. "All I could do was wait and not let on that not a single cell in my body would accept second place," he recalled. The next night, at the Victoria Palace Theatre, 3,000 spectators broke into thunderous applause the moment Arnold walked onstage and began his routine. He knew that the judging had already taken place and that the contest was already won or lost, so he decided to treat the occasion as an exhibition. "My routine became ballet," he recalled. As he finished, striking the last pose, the crowd broke into a spontaneous chant of "Arnold! Arnold! Arnold!" He came back for the only encore of the evening, as the crowd went crazy. Finally the announcer quieted down the auditorium and announced the third-place and second-place winners.

Then, "Ladies and gentlemen, the winner, Mr. Universe 1967 . . . Arnold Schwarzenegger!"

The Age of Schwarzenegger had begun.

9.

Business Learning Curve

When he woke up on Sunday morning after his victory the night before, Arnold was on top of the world. After five years of training for this moment, he was finally Mr. Universe. Or was he?

As he entered the dining room for breakfast—a scene he would later describe as "something out of a Marx Brothers film"—there were bodybuilders everywhere, some piling ten eggs onto their plates, some with two steaks, each replacing the calories they had sacrificed in the days before the contest in an attempt to emphasize muscle over fat. In other words, this was standard post-competition fare. But as Arnold walked in, they interrupted their gorging long enough to gather around and congratulate the new champion. Most of them were genuinely happy for his success.

"Next up is Sergio Oliva," said one competitor, hugging Arnold affectionately. "No," said another, "the next one is Bill Pearl." As they swarmed around him, he heard many of the great names of the bodybuilding world, people whom he had read about in American muscle magazines but who were nowhere to be seen in London that year. The words served to jolt him back to reality as he realized that there were in fact three Mr. Universe pageants and he had won only one of them. The NABBA also held a professional Mr. Universe pageant, crowning Bill Pearl that year; and its rival federation, the IFBB, also held a contest, where Sergio Oliva had recently triumphed. And there was the Mr. World contest, held in New York, where Rick Wayne had emerged triumphant. The ultimate contest was Mr. Olympia, which Sergio Oliva had also won. If Arnold wanted to call himself the best bodybuilder in the world, he would also have to win those contests.

"That was my next challenge," he later recalled, "to be the best, the ultimate winner. I vowed to keep going on and on and on until everybody in the world said, 'Yes, it's him. It's Arnold, he's the best.'"

When he called his parents to tell them the news, the response was not what he expected. Though they were happy to hear about his victory, he felt they would have been happier to hear that he had just finished college. Their unenthusiastic reaction was heartbreaking to him. Reflecting on it, he acknowledged to himself that much of what he did was designed to obtain the approval of his parents. He felt that he understood them and their shortcomings better than they understood him.

The fact is that Gustav and Aurelia still didn't see where bodybuilding was going to take him. But Arnold already knew exactly where it would take him, and he told anybody who would listen. First, he would get to America, then he would become a millionaire, then he would head to Hollywood and become a movie star. That was how his idol, Reg Park, had done it, as had Steve Reeves and countless other champions. He would follow in their footsteps but be even greater. He was as sure of this as he had been about becoming the youngest Mr. Universe in history. He had achieved that feat three years earlier than even the most optimistic of his friends had predicted. There was no stopping him now.

A few weeks after his triumph at Mr. Universe, his father went to watch him perform at an exhibition in Stuttgart and, to Arnold's excitement and relief, was impressed by the amount of applause his son received. It was not until she saw him win Mr. Olympia five years later, however, that Aurelia would fully accept her son's chosen career and understand how successful he had become.

As Reg Park had promised when they met in London months earlier, he flew Arnold to South Africa in December 1967 to stay with him and his wife and participate in ten exhibitions across the country. When the telegram came from Park, Arnold recalled, he was in his "glory." He trained as hard for the South African exhibitions as he had before Mr. Universe, wanting to impress his boyhood idol. "I don't know how many years I'd dreamed about being like Reg Park; then, all of a sudden, I was really almost like him. People remarked on it," he wrote. "They said we shared the same rugged quality." Arnold had never before seen anything like Park's Johannesburg estate, featuring an Olympic-size swimming pool in the front garden, surrounded by acres of flowers and trees. As he traipsed through the antique-filled house, he couldn't help thinking that this was the house of a star. Park and his wife, Marion, were wonderful hosts, treating Arnold like a member of the family. Indeed, he later told Laurence Leamer that they were a model of what he wanted his own life and family to be. "We would sit down to dinner in a very civilized way, and we would discuss the day," he recalled of that visit, adding, "I'll always remember him making me do calf-raises with 1,000 lbs. at 5 o'clock in the morning." Park would later claim that Arnold "fell in love with my wife. She was what he wanted." He apparently meant it in an innocent way, suggesting that Schwarzenegger admired her homemaking skills. But the fact is that more than one of Arnold's closest colleagues, and even his friends, would later accuse him of hitting on their wives. The British bodybuilding official Lud Shusterich told Wendy Leigh that he personally witnessed Arnold that same year waiting for a fellow bodybuilder to go to the bathroom before turning to his young wife and saying, "Listen, I only live down the block. Why don't you come up to my apartment with me?" Shusterich claims he later lectured Arnold about his boorish behavior, chastising him and saying that he was not a gentleman.

The Parks took Arnold to parties, dinners, and films, introducing him to all their friends. He felt like a member of their family, at least until Park got him in the weight room and put him through the wringer. Arnold was anxious for a brutally honest assessment of his physique. He was counting on his mentor to tell him what he had to do if he truly wanted to be the world's greatest bodybuilder, besting the American monsters whom he would soon face in elite competition.

Park immediately singled out Arnold's calves, which were still puny compared with the rest of his body. When Park mocked him for the 150-pound weights he was putting on the calves machine—replacing them with 800 grueling pounds—he knew that he had not been working hard enough to reach the ultimate plateau.

Whatever Park asked of him, he would gladly do, comparing himself to a "panting puppy dog at his master's feet," lapping up the tidbits that Park threw at him. The workouts were torturous, but Arnold never complained. He had no time for his fellow bodybuilders who whined and complained incessantly through every workout. He relished the pain, and in the end that's what set him apart from virtually every rival. He would do whatever it took to be the best and was happy to do it. His secret? The idea of pain, he later explained, became a "pleasure trip." He simply converted pain into pleasure—not for its own sake but because every agonizing moment meant he was growing, getting better, moving one step closer to becoming the best. He never shared this thought with anybody at the time, fearing that people would think him a "masochist" or a "weirdo."

By the time he returned to Munich, bodybuilders from all over Europe were clamoring to train with the new Mr. Universe. Gym membership doubled practically overnight from 200 to 400 members. Business was booming and Arnold was in his element. At the end of each week, he would host a huge barbecue, keeping the beer and wine flowing, as he and his friends pretended to be gladiators, "male animals," but acting more like cavemen, collecting women and trading them like cattle.

Again, he was gaining as much of a reputation for bad behavior outside the gym as he was for his international achievements in his chosen sport. The locals knew more about his scrapes with the law, his increasingly frequent drunken brawls, and his run-ins with American tourists than they did about his bodybuilding titles. "I was living in Munich at the time, hanging out with night people—entertainers, hookers, and bar owners—and I had a girlfriend who was a stripper. I was an innocent boy from a farm town, but I grew up fast in Munich," he later recalled. It was only the realization that such behavior was affecting his training, his focus, that made him vow to curb his antics. As his gym became a going concern, Arnold knew he needed more business savvy in order to realize its full potential and become a millionaire by his twenty-fifth birthday— one of his newly formed goals as he discovered he had a knack for business and he enjoyed thinking of new ways to succeed. He enrolled in a Munich business school, thus adding one more burden to his already full schedule. If he wasn't training or partying, he was studying, and his friends didn't know how he managed to keep up the almost inhuman pace. "Arnold, you're crazy, you're going to burn yourself out. Slow down," he recalled them warning him. But those closest to him already knew that when Arnold focused on something, he never gave anything less than a Herculean effort, befitting every bodybuilder's dream film role.

One of the great sporting traditions in Munich is the annual stone-lifting competition held during Lent to mark the start of the "strong beer" season. Competitors stand on two footrests resembling chairs and, with no warm-up, pull a giant stone weighing more than 500 pounds from between their legs over the head with a metal handle. An electronic monitor measures how high the stone is lifted. In the spring of 1968, Arnold entered the contest and set a new record. The media heralded the achievement, which went a long way toward shattering the stereotypes of bodybuilders as lummoxes with lots of useless muscles but no actual power. Franco Columbu, who was a champion power-lifter, had long since discovered that Arnold possessed both, as they regularly competed to outdo each other in the weight room.

The NABBA Mr. Universe (professional) contest was scheduled for September 21, 1968, in London. Arnold knew he would have no trouble at all taking the title. He knew that his workouts with Park and his vastly improved calves put him in a different league than any of his immediate rivals. But he was also acutely aware that the world's elite bodybuilders would not be competing in London. Instead, they opted for the Mr. Universe competition put on by NABBA's rival federation, IFBB, and held a week later in Miami. This is where the top Americans competed, and it made the NABBA contest seem like a mere pretender by comparison. Arnold desperately wanted to go to America and match up with the men he had read about for years in the U.S. muscle magazines. Yet no invitation was forthcoming—at least not yet. He knew that winning the contest in London would at least put him on the radar in America, and as he prepared to compete, he was already dreaming of the next competition and a trip to the promised land of bodybuilding.

As expected, he made short work of the competition in London. By the time the thunderous applause had died down and Arnold had accepted his trophy and the accompanying accolades, Albert Busek had slipped out of the auditorium and sent a telegram to his chief contact in America about his protégé's latest victory.

The next morning, Arnold was awoken by a knock on his door. It was a bellhop bringing him a telegram—an invitation to come to Miami immediately, all expenses paid, and compete at the IFBB Mr. Universe contest. Even more significant than the long-awaited invitation was the man who sent it—a man whose life and career would soon become inextricably linked with Arnold Schwarzenegger, and who would indirectly draw me into writing a book about the present-day governor of California. The man's name was Joe Weider.

10.

A Modern-Day Moses

When Joe Weider was growing up in Montreal in the 1930s, he was frequently beaten up by bullies, targeted because he was Jewish and small. He tried Charles Atlas's method, but it didn't do a lot to build his physique. He opted instead for the more traditional method of weight training, but equipment was expensive and his family was very poor. The sons of penniless Jewish immigrants, Joe and his younger brother Ben grew up in a cold-water flat, fending off hunger during the lean years of the Depression. What happened next is a rags-to-riches story that has become part of the lore of bodybuilding and would eventually forever change the sport.

The story goes that, unable to buy weight-training equipment, a young Joe found a scrapped axle and two flywheels in a junkyard and fashioned them into a barbell, which he lifted over his head repeatedly. He dropped out of school at the age of twelve to support his family, but spent more time working out than working.

"I was very weak and confronted by a lot of people who made my life difficult, so I figured the best way to overcome that was to strengthen my body," he recalled years later. By the time he was sixteen, he could bench-press 330 pounds. Needless to say, bullies were no longer a problem.

That same year, 1939, Weider purchased a second-hand mimeograph machine and, in his parents' back parlor, put together his first publication: a four-page newsletter called *Your Physique*. He mailed it to 600 weightlifters whose names and addresses he had collected from the letters-to-the-editor page of the top bodybuilding magazine of the day. Soon he had a regular subscriber base at 15 cents an issue and the money was pouring in. While most of the money being made in bodybuilding during that era came from selling training equipment, Weider saw that the future was in advice and eventually supplements. By 1940, a year and a half after he started publication, he had already accumulated a fortune of $10,000, a staggering sum for an upstart publisher. By 1942, when Weider persuaded the largest magazine distributor in the world to sell

Your Physique on newsstands, circulation had reached 50,000 copies a month. When he couldn't find a Canadian printer to handle the huge press run, he relocated from Montreal to Jersey City, New Jersey, where he added another company, selling bodybuilding instructional booklets through the mail.

His success began to worry the man who was then the reigning fitness king, Bob Hoffman, publisher of the magazine *Strength and Health*. Hoffman was an admirer of the German philosopher Friedrich Nietzsche, and his magazine idealized the Nietzschean superman. Nietzsche had also inspired one of Hoffman's contemporaries, Adolf Hitler, and the bodybuilding impresario was reported to be an avid admirer of Hitler.

This began to show in the anti-Semitic broadsides he published in his magazine attacking Joe Weider, his up-and-coming rival.

"Hoffman couldn't stand any competitor," Weider later explained. "He had his magazine, *Strength and Health*, and he was writing mostly about strength training because he was interested in winning weight lifting at the Olympics. He figured I was taking good potential athletes and encouraging them to do bodybuilding. He was losing his grip. Plus Hoffman was very prejudiced. He loved the Nazis. He didn't like minorities. He thought Hitler was making the German people strong, teaching them strength through joy and all that kind of stuff."

Hoffman was also a successful promoter, controlling many of the top bodybuilding contests of the day, and using them to promote his magazines and a number of fitness-related products. Hoffman believed in weight lifting to develop strength, and he frequently maligned bodybuilders in his magazines, mocking them as "boodybuilders," odd-shaped and effeminate. Weider in turn maligned Hoffman's ideal strongman, and the rivalry intensified as the young Jewish kid became more and more successful. In 1946, Joe's younger brother, Ben, joined the business and immediately suggested that they form their own association to compete with the various weight-lifting federations controlled by Hoffman and others, notably the Amateur Athletics Union, which concentrated mostly on the Olympic sport of weight lifting. The result was the creation of the International Federation of Body-Builders (IFBB), founded the same year, with Ben as its president.

"Remember, if you go back to the 1940s and 1950s, bodybuilding was laughed at," Joe later recalled. "Doctors thought you'd get an enlarged heart. They thought an athlete's heart was bad for you. Coaches thought if you exercised you'd become muscle-bound and wouldn't be able to play sports. That's what we fought against all those years. When we founded the IFBB, everyone thought we were nuts."

By the 1950s, the Weiders had succeeded in loosening Hoffman's stranglehold and were well on their way to their goal of making bodybuilding a respectable sport. As the brothers' empire expanded, Joe's ego appeared to expand just as rapidly. He had already made countless enemies for his allegedly ruthless approach to business. "He loved getting an edge on you any way he could," the former editor of one of his magazines told the *New York Times*. "It was his whole philosophy of being superior to the ordinary guy." One of his former associates, Dan Lurie, who was his partner in a dumbbell business in the 1940s, also believes Weider was ruthless. "Every person who goes into business with him has scars where they got hurt. He left me penniless. . . . Joe is a brilliant man, there's no question about it. But he's invented everything. Listening to him, he invented fresh air, the sunshine, the moon, the stars," Lurie told *Newsday* in 1988.

But Joe Weider was just as famous for his lofty opinions on how bodybuilding can change the world, which would frequently appear in his publications as if he fancied himself a modern prophet. In the July 1950 issue of *Your Physique*, for example, he issued ten predictions about how bodybuilding would change the world. Among these:

I PREDICT that bodybuilding will become the chief form of systematic exercise and physical activity, and that it will come to be looked upon as one of the greatest forces in the field of preventive medicine.

I PREDICT that the principles of good bodybuilding—which include a balanced diet, adequate sleep, plenty of fresh air, ample sunshine and regular workouts—will become basic principles of living.

I PREDICT that bodybuilding will become the steppingstone to every other sport and physical activity.

I PREDICT that bodybuilding will spread to every corner of the world and that it will one day be recognized as the king of all sports and physical activities.

I PREDICT that bodybuilding will one day become one of the greatest forces in existence, and that it may be hailed as the activity that actually saved civilization from itself.

The predictions would later spark mocking comparisons, and his critics would charge that Joe thought of himself as a modern-day Moses. But despite his religion, Weider appeared to prefer a slightly different biblical comparison, when he gave an interview years later about the influence of his flagship publication.

"They always refer to *Muscle and Fitness* as the bible of bodybuilding," he told *Newsday* in 1988. "I wondered why they would say that and it dawned on me—I don't want to be arrogant—take Christianity; it has Jesus as the central point, so I figured maybe I'm the central point. Then the Church had its commandments—we had our Weider Principles. Then they have their archbishops and cardinals and we have our champions. They have their missionaries—our champions go all over the world teaching how to train. Maybe all this put together unconsciously struck people as *Muscle and Fitness* being the Bible."

Responding to a question about how he had accumulated so many enemies, he once told the *Los Angeles Times*, "You think anybody says negative things about Jesus? About Moses? You get a lot of atheists and devil worshipers that hate God. Why should I be loved by everybody?"

Early on, Weider realized that magazine sales alone would not sustain a successful business. The real money was in supplements that could be sold as fast as they could be produced to bodybuilders and weightlifters constantly searching for an extra edge. The magazines provided the perfect editorial and advertising platform for the wide range of supplements that the Weiders' companies produced and distributed. These ranged from vitamin powders to amino acids and proteins that—despite what the ads claimed—many experts believed were worthless in developing a stronger physique. The government as well occasionally challenged some of Weider's sensational claims. He has been hit by the Federal Trade Commission with claims of misleading advertising and unfair and deceptive acts, claims which he settled without admitting guilt. A superior court judge once ruled that his company was guilty of false advertising for promoting a weight-loss shaper that could take off a pound a day.

Despite his flaws, however, many credited Weider with revolutionizing modern bodybuilding, and he has countless acolytes willing to sing his praises. There is no doubt that, compared with his bigoted rival Hoffman, who died in 1985, Weider was positively farsighted. In 1953, before the dawn of the civil rights movement, when blacks never appeared on the cover of white magazines, he featured a twenty-year-old black man, Leroy Colbert, as the model on the cover of his magazine *Muscle Power.* The edition lost money, as predicted, because it could not be sold in the South, but Weider stuck to his guns and his liberal principles, gleaned from his Jewish parents.

Along the way, there were many business setbacks and a run of bad luck, including the dismantling of his distributor, the American News Company, which he claimed failed to pay him $7 million in back debts.

By 1968, when a young Austrian bodybuilder named Arnold Schwarzenegger first appeared on his radar screen, Weider was undeniably one of the world's major players in bodybuilding, controlling a significant chunk of the market. But the competition was fierce, rival federations were eating into the IFBB's hegemony, and Weider was scrambling for a savior. The fact was that bodybuilding had still not gained mainstream respectability and its practitioners were still considered skeptically by much of the population. Joe Weider was well aware why the sport he loved had never caught on in the public's imagination, why his "Ten Predictions" had not yet been realized. There was one very good reason and, as it turned out, one perfect solution.

I'm probably as far removed from the world of bodybuilding as is humanly possible. I've barely set foot in a gym. But as it turned out, the Weiders and I have something important in common. We are both from Montreal. And while Joe moved to the United States more than sixty years ago, his brother Ben remained behind, running a portion of the fitness empire from

Canada as well as the IFBB, where he spent decades pressing to have bodybuilding recognized as an Olympic sport. Ben was a major figure in my hometown, very well respected in two areas—fitness and Napoleonic history. For much of his life, he was a very dedicated Napoléon scholar whose passion was to find out everything he could about the life of the French emperor—and his death. It was long assumed that Napoléon Bonaparte had died of cancer in exile. But in the course of his research, Weider became convinced that the emperor had actually been assassinated by a French general who had been deported with him to Saint Helena and had ended up working as a wine steward there. For forty years, Weider worked to prove his theory, which was at first mocked by other Napoleonic scholars who derided him as a charlatan and an amateur. A Parisian professor reportedly once told him, "Ben, French Napoleonic historians think guys like you are great. But watch out—if you make too much fuss and rock the boat, we'll squash you like a bug."

In 1982, Weider published a book, *The Murder of Napoleon*, which was translated into more than forty languages and sold more than 1 million copies. The book, however, was virtually ignored in France. But persistence and the Weider fortune paid off. He spent

huge sums of money trying to prove his theory sci-
entifically and eventually it bore results when he sent
preserved strands of Napoléon's hair to various international laboratories, which found unnaturally high
traces of arsenic. Still, historians scoffed. It was at this
point that Weider thought to send the strands to the
FBI, which ran one of the most sophisticated toxico-
logical crime labs in the world. According to Roger M.
Martz, head of the Toxicology Division of the FBI, the
concentration of arsenic present in the hairs sent by
Weider was sufficient to be considered by the bureau
as positive proof of poisoning. That was enough to
convince many previous skeptics, who conceded that
Weider's theory might be plausible after all.

In Montreal, Weider was a very prominent member
of the Jewish community and was a longtime financial
supporter of the YMHA, which was eventually named
for him. Besides being a writer, I am also a longtime
musician, and a few years ago I was hired to play a
benefit at the Y. Afterward, I was introduced to Ben
Weider and we hit it off immediately, mostly talking
about sports. Soon after that, we had lunch at Montreal's Snowdon Deli, ostensibly to discuss a future film
project, possibly a miniseries, involving his Napoleonic
research. On that occasion and at many subsequent
lunches—always at the Snowdon Deli—we ended up

talking about almost everything except Napoléon. Ben was an absolutely fascinating man, very gentle and soft-spoken. He was nothing at all like his bombastic brother, whom I never met, though he did tell me that Joe was his hero. The film project never really got off the ground. Sadly, Ben died in 2008 before anything could come of it, but we did spend considerable time discussing Arnold Schwarzenegger, about whom Ben never said a harsh word. On the contrary, it was clear that he admired the Governator immensely. It was my acquaintance with Ben Weider that first got me thinking of doing a documentary and eventually a book about the man who said at his funeral, "Ben Weider was like a father to me."

To hear Schwarzenegger tell the story, Joe Weider's invitation to come to Miami took him completely by surprise, so much so that he had only a gym bag when he arrived at the airport for his journey to America. That isn't entirely true. In fact, Weider had been keeping his eye on the Austrian Oak for quite some time and was receiving regular reports from the U.K. editor of his magazine *Muscle Builder/Power*, Ludwig Shusterich, who had already featured Arnold on the cover of the July 1968 issue. Lud, as he was known, had told Arnold that an invitation to Miami was certain if he won the contest and that he should be ready. In fact, Arnold appears to have had at least one transatlantic telephone conversation with Weider at Lud's office—at which the American promised a plane ticket—prior to the Mr. Universe contest. It was Shusterich who brought Arnold to the American embassy to secure a visa so that he could travel to Miami and compete. That visa would later become a source of considerable controversy.

Arnold had not, in fact, left all his worldly possessions behind in Munich. And he was already in talks to have somebody manage his gym while he was absent, implying that he planned more than just a short trip to Miami. His biographer Wendy Leigh has suggested that his eagerness to travel to America, and even stay there, may have been prompted not "by rashness but by calculation." She refers to his admitted "scrapes" with the Munich police, though neither she nor I could find any evidence of a criminal record.

Whether or not Weider's invitation took Arnold by surprise, however, there is no doubt that everything appeared to be going according to plan. For the first time in his life, he would truly be competing against the world's best. If he won here, he could finally call himself Mr. Universe and mean it. And, despite the fact that he knew the Americans were in a different league, he was completely confident that he would walk away with the trophy, because "victory was in my blood." His confidence was immediately boosted when he arrived at the auditorium and people crowded around to have a look at the Austrian Oak, whose reputation had built up quite a buzz from the other side of the ocean.

When he began to pose, there was at first an uncomfortable silence from the crowd. This puzzled Arnold, who was used to a different reaction when he flexed for the first time. Is it that much different in America? he asked himself. But then he realized that the spectators were, in fact, "studying" him, sizing him up. As he rose up and expanded every muscle fiber in his body, there was an audible gasp. Suddenly, the crowd started chanting, "Arnold! Arnold!" At that moment, he knew he was in America to stay. He also thought the crowd's reaction meant he had the contest locked up. So it was all the more devastating when the emcee made the announcement: "In second place, Arnold Schwarzenegger." The trophy that year went to Frank Zane, whose elegant posing routine and chiseled features were undeniably better than those of his Austrian competitor. Still, the loss was devastating for Arnold, who later confided that he was "overhelmed, crushed" by the defeat.

Years later, when I asked Zane about this contest, he told me that going in, Arnold clearly believed that he was better than anybody else and that he was going to sweep in and win his first American contest. "Arnold was a raging egomaniac and he absolutely hated, *hated* to lose," Zane recalled. "But you have to understand, we all were to some degree—all day long we are looking at our bodies, we pose onstage all oiled up and glistening about 98 percent naked so everyone can examine us. We are referred to as Greek gods. . . . I am fairly sure you could not do this stuff if you didn't have a healthy ego."

A few minutes after the trophies were handed out, still reeling, Arnold came face-to-face for the first time with Joe Weider, who later described the moment. "After the contest, I found Arnold backstage sitting next to the winner's trophy. He was petting it," Weider recalled. "He told me he wanted to win that title more than anything."

Despite the second-place showing, Weider had instantly recognized the potential of the twenty-one-year-old visitor, who was still not fluent in English. On the spot, he asked the sobbing youngster if he would like to come to California and "train with the champions."

Arnold didn't hesitate in his response: "That's my dream."

They quickly worked out an arrangement for Arnold to spend a year in America and provide regular reports about his training methods to various Weider magazines, for which he would also pose. In exchange, Weider would provide a car, an apartment, and a small weekly salary.

A few days later, Arnold Schwarzenegger arrived at the mecca of bodybuilding: the neighborhood of Venice, in Los Angeles, California, home of two shrines that had long been associated with the sport—Muscle Beach and Gold's Gym. Muscle Beach actually had its origins during the Depression in Santa Monica, a couple of miles south of its current location. Bodybuilders from all over America descended to a small stretch of beachfront near the Santa Monica pier where they could train in the sunshine and sea breeze and show off their muscles to passersby. Among the famous names who trained there were the future fitness guru, Jack LaLanne; and Steve Reeves, who would later inspire a young Arnold Schwarzenegger. For years, until it was closed by the city of Santa Monica in 1959 after a sex scandal involving bodybuilders and underage girls, thousands of spectators would regularly gather to watch the musclemen working out and giving exhibitions. It was the prime reason, in fact, that

Southern California became the world's capital of bodybuilding.

In the 1960s, the location moved to neighboring Venice, which was also home to a gym that would forever be associated with Arnold Schwarzenegger and other bodybuilding champions. Three years before Arnold arrived in California, Joe Gold had built a state-of-the-art gymnasium for bodybuilders who were tired of training on the primitive equipment at the nearby Muscle Beach Gym, affectionately known as "the Dungeon," with its splintery two-by-four benches and pulleys taken from a nearby boatyard. The new gym saw an immediate influx of top bodybuilders, weightlifters, and wrestlers. Even celebrities such as Jim Morrison worked out there. Gold himself was quite a character, the son of Russian Jewish immigrants who became interested in bodybuilding at the age of twelve when his sister-in-law designed a device for strengthening her arms; it was crafted from buckets and broom handles she found in their father's junkyard. After World War II, during which he served as a machinist in the merchant marine, Joe became a professional bodybuilder and toured the country as part of Mae West's traveling revue. Finally, in 1965, Gold decided he wanted to settle down and build a place of his own where bodybuilders could find a home. It was an instant success.

In 1968, however, Gold's Gym was not yet the only gym in Los Angeles where bodybuilders would congregate. In North Hollywood twenty years earlier, Vince Gironda had established a no-nonsense training facility, nicknamed the "muscle factory." Vince was known for his military-style training methods and for demanding complete obedience. His customers crossed him at their peril. Still, his methods were known to be effective, and his regulars included many of the early bodybuilding greats as well as countless Hollywood celebrities. Among those who trained there regularly were Robert Blake, Cher, Clint Eastwood, Denzel Washington, James Garner, Brian Keith, Tommy Chong, and Erik Estrada.

Joe Weider was still living in New Jersey, but he had paid Vince Gironda to take care of Arnold, find him an apartment, and get him into shape; and it is here that Arnold first trained, despite his later claim that it was actually at Gold's. When Schwarzenegger walked into Vince's Gym for the first time, Gironda wasn't at all impressed.

"The guy was a sissy," he told Nigel Andrews. "I'd demonstrate exercises to him he couldn't do. He didn't have the balls. The first day he came to see me, he walked up to my desk. He'd put on a pair of trunks and he came up from the back room. He told me who he was and he wanted me to assess his body. I looked him over and I said, 'You look like a fat fuck to me.'"

Arnold was taken aback by his first encounter with the legendary gym owner. "He took off mad. He came in wanting me to adore him and I told him he was a big fat German sausage," Gironda added. Undoubtedly, he was testing the newcomer's mettle. In fact, he was immediately impressed by the young immigrant's physique, though he forever lamented Arnold's inability to follow instructions. Schwarzenegger's success, Gironda reflected, was due to tenacity alone rather than to any ability as a student.

Gironda's harsh methods eventually drove Arnold to Gold's Gym, where the atmosphere was decidedly different. It was a place where bodybuilders trained together, told jokes, and reportedly obtained steroids, which were banned at Vince's Gym. Gold's was much more like Arnold's own gym in Munich, which was a place for hard work but also had a jovial atmosphere.

"Arnold was a great guy, always kidding around," Gold recalled years later of his initial impressions of Schwarzenegger. "I had my own nickname for him. I nicknamed everyone in the gym. It was easier than remembering their names. I couldn't pronounce Arnold Schwarzenegger, so I called him Balloon Belly. I used to have a lot of fun at Gold's. That's the object of going to a gym, having fun."

More than four decades after Arnold Schwarzenegger first trained there, I arrived in Muscle Beach without the slightest clue about how I was going to cultivate sources and contacts who could enlighten me about those early golden years. There were bodybuilders everywhere, men and women, their bodies glistening with oil and sweat as they grunted and lifted weights, occasionally stopping to flex for the onlookers or practice their posing technique. None of them looked like candidates for Mr. or Ms. Olympia and none appeared old enough to have been here during Arnold's era. I assumed, however, that many of them could point me in the right direction and provide me with the names and numbers I needed to get started.

And then I had an idea. I decided to pose as a bodybuilding promoter from the United Kingdom, who wanted to recruit talent for a "World Bodybuilding Championship" to be held at London's 02 Arena in mid-November 2010. This proved surprisingly easy. I was immediately introduced to an African-American bodybuilder, Joe Wheatley, who is a local promoter, staging bodybuilding productions in conjunction with the City of Los Angeles Parks Department. When I told him my cover story, Wheatley proved incredibly helpful, facilitating numerous introductions and conveying instant credibility when I wandered the area "auditioning" contestants. Although virtually all the musclebound men and women I talked to told me they had been inspired by Schwarzenegger's success, few were particularly helpful when it came to providing insights about the Governator, and none except Wheatley had actually met him. Some had been present a few years ago when Joe Weider was inducted into the Muscle Beach Hall of Fame, a ceremony at which Schwarzenegger spoke and introduced his friend and mentor. In fact, although the beach is lined with bronze plaques of various bodybuilding greats—such as Frank Zane and Arnold's best friend, Franco Columbu—Schwarzenegger himself is conspicuously and curiously absent from the Hall of Fame.

To my surprise, many of the bodybuilders were actually critical of Schwarzenegger. One complained, "He's not the same person he used to be by any stretch. The last time I saw him here he was biking with one of his kids. He drove right by without stopping. He really has no interest in us anymore." Another builder, Keith, deplored Arnold's admission that he used performance-enhancing drugs. "He brings us much more negative publicity than positive," Keith told me. "He should have kept his mouth shut about using so much steroids. He sold us out so he could run for office. Now everybody thinks we got these bodies by using drugs."

Later, I discovered why Schwarzenegger and the bodybuilders in Venice haven't exactly formed a mutual admiration society. A few years ago, in a broadside against what Muscle Beach has become, he called the bodybuilders who hang out there "bums and parasites."

"Just take a walk along Venice Beach on any sunny day," he said, "and you'll see the numbers of muscle guys who are unemployed. They have to live. But instead of going out and getting some kind of job, they lie on the hot sand and dream up ways of making easy money."

Despite their lack of acquaintanceship with Schwarzenegger himself, and his apparent lack of respect for their ways, many of them provided a wealth of contacts—names and numbers—of bodybuilders who did know Arnold and who had worked out with him back in the day. Many of them still work out at Gold's Gym and occasionally at Muscle Beach.

Through a fortuitous connection with Gold's Gym, I also established a number of key contacts. The gym that Joe Gold established forty-five years ago as one location had long since expanded to become one of the world's largest fitness chains, operating in more than thirty countries. A few years ago, I was commissioned to do a series of corporate videos for the Gold's Gym Wall Street franchise by Blake Thompson, a marketing rep for Gold's Gym New York. The connections I made then would prove very valuable while I was researching this book.

It didn't take long after Arnold arrived in Los Angeles for him to resume his womanizing ways, taking up where he left off in Munich. But now it was easier than ever. Southern California had become known as a flesh factory, especially at Venice Beach, where hot, tanned women strutted around throughout the day in bikinis. Some, known as "muscle honeys," hung out at the beach admiring the bodybuilders' physiques, or outside Gold's Gym, where the groupies congregated waiting for the men to finish their workouts.

According to Carl Jenkins, who frequently worked out at Gold's and Muscle Beach during that period, Schwarzenegger was incredibly bold in his approach to women. "A lot of the guys were tomcats—that's why many of them became bodybuilders in the first place— and there was a lot of sex going on. Remember, it was the whole free love era; none of the guys were shy around women. But Arnold was just unbelievable. He'd see a beautiful woman on the street or wherever he was and he'd go right up to her and say, 'Do you wanna fuck me?' His English wasn't all that great but he had that phrase down pat. It wouldn't always work. . . . I never witnessed him get the proverbial slap in the face, but often the women would walk away disgusted. He'd usually succeed after a while. That probably happened a few times a day. I wasn't usually present, but everybody would tell stories about witnessing it. We'd watch this in awe and think it was some kind of European thing, but nobody else had the balls to hit on women so blatantly."

A Muscle Beach regular, Armand Tanny, told Wendy Leigh a similar story, recalling a time he saw Arnold approach a bikini-clad girl on the beach and announce, "I want to fuck you." One of his friends intervened, explaining that he was a foreigner and didn't "understand our ways." But the girl wasn't interested in excuses. She wanted to take Arnold up on his offer, and did.

Joe Weider would fly to L.A. frequently for magazine photo shoots and to check up on his stable of bodybuilders, which included a number of top names besides Arnold. Joe was always one to keep up with gossip, and it didn't take him long to hear about some of Arnold's exploits. The womanizing didn't bother Joe a bit—on the contrary—although he was sometimes a little shocked at some of the excesses.

As Arnold himself confessed in a 1977 interview with Peter Manso of *Oui* magazine, he and his fellow bodybuilders didn't always have to leave the gym to find a woman to sleep with.

"Bodybuilders party a lot," he explained, "and once, in Gold's—the gym in Venice, California, where all the top guys train—there was a black girl who came out naked. Everybody jumped on her and took her upstairs, where we all got together." Asked if he was referring to a gang bang, Arnold replied, "Yes, but not everybody, just the guys who can fuck in front of other guys. Not everybody can do that. Some think that they don't have a big-enough cock, so they can't get a hard-on. Having chicks around is the kind of thing that breaks up the intense training. It gives you relief, and then afterward you go back to the serious stuff."

11.

Dumbbell Queers

When Joe Weider first hooked up with Arnold Schwarzenegger, his company was taking in around $1 million a year. Not bad, but not the stuff of empires. A few years later, after an extraordinary partnership that inextricably linked the names Weider and Schwarzenegger in the public mind, that total had soared to $28 million annually, and eventually the empire was worth hundreds of millions of dollars. Each man has frequently and publicly given credit to the other for their shared success. Most industry analysts, in fact, have credited Schwarzenegger with the meteoric rise of bodybuilding to mainstream respectability and the growth of Weider's company as the world's largest fitness empire. Ben Weider was very open about what he and many in the industry felt was the reason.

"It was Arnold who finally helped us overcome the gay thing," he said. "That's how my brother used him and it worked beautifully. Straight guys started buying our products and we never looked back."

To explore the history of homosexuality and bodybuilding, one needs to go back to the beginning, to the father of modern bodybuilding, Eugene Sandow. Sandow abandoned his wife and took up with the male piano player who provided the musical accompaniment on his tours. When he retired, he and his boyfriend bought a house together in New York City. One of the items most prized by turn-of-the-century homosexuals, in fact, was a postcard featuring Sandow completely nude except for a fig leaf. Ironically, the trophy given to today's winner of Mr. Olympia is a statue of Sandow. It is not difficult to figure out why some gay men would be drawn to the spectacular bodybuilders. The renowned artist Michelangelo allegedly used his gay lover as the model for the famous statue *David*—showing the rippling physique of a naked man—which has stood in the center of Florence for centuries, representing the idealized example of male beauty.

The nude postcard of Sandow was also probably the genesis of the bodybuilder as a gay pinup—a role that continues to this day but reached its peak in the 1950s with the advent of "physique" magazines. Soon after the end of World War II, a Los Angeles photographer, Bob Mizer, founded the Athletic Model Guild as a modeling agency for male bodybuilders. He then sold the photos he took by mail, attracting a mostly gay clientele, though women were known to order them as well. In 1951, he began to publish his photos in a magazine he founded, *Physique Pictorial*. Many of the top bodybuilders of the day, including Steve Reeves and Jack LaLanne, appeared in the pages of Mizer's magazine, which became a lucrative concern. A few years later, he began to shoot cheesy low-budget eight-millimeter films featuring the same models—either posing as bodybuilders or wrestling in pairs—with campy titles such as *Aztec Sacrifice* and *Days of Greek Gods*.

Mizer's successful magazine spawned a slew of imitators with titles such as *Adonis, Tomorrow's Man, Young Adonis,* and *Body Beautiful.* Although these publications pretended to showcase the human body and promote physical fitness in a nonsexual manner, their intention and target audience were obvious and they frequently ran afoul of government censors. They never featured full frontal nudity, but they occasionally pushed the boundaries with a glimpse of bare buttock. The bodybuilders always sported a "posing pouch," which covered the genitals but blatantly showed off their package.

American obscenity laws allowed women to be photographed tastefully in states of undress as long as the photos were billed as "art." But no such license was permitted for men, and Mizer was charged with obscenity on numerous occasions and even served six months in prison for distributing male nudity. Eventually, as obscenity laws were relaxed in the 1960s, the photos became bolder and many bodybuilders, including Arnold Schwarzenegger, ended up supplementing their income by posing nude for Mizer and other publishers.

According to *The Gay and Lesbian Encyclopedia*, "Physique magazines were arguably the most openly—and self-affirmingly—gay male publications available to a wide American audience." Many gay Americans, in fact, first discovered their sexuality by looking at these magazines.

It is difficult to determine how many of the bodybuilder models were gay themselves and how many were heterosexuals simply seeking to supplement their income. But there is no doubt that gay men, starting with Eugene Sandow himself, had long ago embraced and taken up bodybuilding in large numbers, even though homosexuality was still taboo and they had to be careful who knew their secret. Was Wardell B. Pomeroy of the Kinsey Institute correct when he warned that bodybuilding might "lead to an unhealthy interest in other boys' bodies"? Or is this a chicken-and-egg question?

In his book *Little Big Men*, the sports sociologist Alan M. Klein of Northeastern University notes that he spent six years studying the subculture of bodybuilding at an unnamed California gym, thought to be Gold's. He concluded from his research that homosexuality is very common among bodybuilders and that many of them finance their pursuit by "hustling."

"As hustlers," writes Klein, "bodybuilders are generally paid to engage gay men in a range of behaviors that, at one end, includes simple escort services, becomes more sexually explicit, as in appearing at gay parties (for example, popping out of a cake nude) and, at the other end, includes the only authorized sex act: allowing a gay male to perform oral sex on the hustler."

The bodybuilders he interviewed estimated that anywhere from 30 percent to 80 percent of the men used to hustle or currently hustled. He determined that hustling has a number of benefits, both financial and social, for the bodybuilders, making them "part of the sport's influential network." Most important, the underground economy enables the bodybuilder to finance his training and lifestyle.

"This is a constant conflict in myself because I don't have to be [a hustler]," one world-class bodybuilder told Klein. "But I trained for the Mr. America contest eight hours a day—eight hours of some sort of training. I couldn't do that working 12 hours a day in some shipyard. I simply couldn't do it."

In addition to gay bodybuilders, the culture has always attracted gay men who attach themselves to the fringes of the sport, hoping to pick up muscular boys. It is these men who become the clientele for the hustlers, and the phenomenon is by no means limited to American bodybuilding culture, as Schwarzenegger discovered when he first arrived in Munich in the mid-1960s.

In fact, one of those homosexuals was his benefactor, the late Rolf Putziger, who hit on the nineteen-year-old Arnold on his very first day in the Bavarian capital. After giving the new arrival a tour of the city and his gym, Putziger brought him back to his house, where Arnold was scheduled to stay until he got settled. But when he got there, he discovered there was no extra bed—there was only a couch, which was too small and uncomfortable for somebody his size. After a few days of these awkward sleeping arrangements, the gym owner suggested that Arnold sleep in his bedroom. Arnold immediately packed his bags and left the house.

Nevertheless, Arnold worked for Putziger for more than a year before buying the gym away from him. He was, apparently, very practical when it came to business, even then. Years later, I asked Arnold's old friend and competitor Rick Wayne, a three-time Mr. Universe, about how Arnold handled the gay culture surrounding his sport.

"I remember a couple of times he would tell stories about being in London early in his career," Wayne told me in 2010, "and he would be partying with rich, British gay men that loved musclemen—Arnold never, at least in front of me, ever said that he actually went with them, but he often said he indulged these guys for all it was worth. He was always looking for investors and business opportunities, so if some of these dandies wanted to take him out to dinner or partying because they were turned on by him, Arnold would let them think that maybe, just maybe, there might be a chance." Years earlier, Wayne told Wendy Leigh about a gay Spanish millionaire, Oscar Heidenstam, who used to hang around after the Mr. Universe contests in London. Wayne revealed that Heidenstam had pulled out a stack of photos of Arnold posing in his underwear at Heidenstam's house after Heidenstam said he paid

Arnold $1,000 to spend the weekend there. He did not, however, claim that the two ever slept together.

By the time Arnold arrived in America a year later, there was already a well-known group of similar gay "sugar daddies" in Southern California who would finance the lifestyles of gay and, occasionally, straight bodybuilders in exchange for certain favors. They would often put the bodybuilders up at their houses. My contacts at Muscle Beach eventually led me to a former bodybuilder, Calvin, now living outside San Diego, who claims he took advantage of one such sugar daddy for almost three years in the mid- to late 1960s.

"That the only way I could afford to train," Calvin tells me when we meet at Seal Beach in La Jolla, California. "I wasn't the only one."

Asked if he was actually gay, he says, "I guess at that time I would describe myself as bi. I had women too. Not anymore. I'm full-fledged queer now." He quickly dismisses, or clarifies, Klein's statistics on the prevalence of gay bodybuilders. "Look, at that time, it was hard to know for sure. You didn't advertise it, though with some it was obvious and it definitely wasn't a big deal unless you were really good. There's no way that more than half of the guys were gay, maybe 25 or 30 percent would be a good guess. It was a lot but not the majority. Venice wasn't an uptight place; you could be gay and you wouldn't be hassled, although you were still supposed to be discreet. In the gyms, there was a lot of talk about fags and queers but that was just the way guys talked. They'd call somebody a fag if he wasn't lifting enough weight. It wasn't because they were homophobic. I think there were enough of us around that everybody was comfortable with it."

I asked him if he knew Schwarzenegger. "Yeah, I knew him, but I wasn't in his league, know what I mean? He was really big and really good. There were a bunch of those guys who hung around each other, a little clique. They didn't spend a lot of time with us unless we were world class like them. We'd watch them train, occasionally go for beers, but we didn't hang out.

"Arnold had a sponsor, Joe Weider, who I think was paying him, so that gave him some money in his pocket—I don't know how much. I think he did pose for photos, probably gay stuff, but I don't think he had to hustle. I remember when he brought Franco Columbu over, they were always together and people at first thought they had something going, but I don't think so. I guess today I know he's straight so that might cloud my perception. I don't know what I thought back then. He was always going after girls, talking about fucking them, very crude. Sometimes we'd think that guys like that were covering, pretending to be straight. There was a lot of that with the closeted bodybuilders. I was like that at first, a little bit. But I don't think that was the case with him. He never gave off a really gay vibe, although the gays loved him. They loved all the top guys. I'm sure he had lots of offers."

Arnold was regularly featured in Weider's publications, dispensing training techniques and posing for regular photo shoots in the magazines that were quickly making him a superstar in bodybuilding circles around the world. At the time, those same magazines were beginning to step up the message that bodybuilding wasn't for sissies.

Weider himself regularly gave interviews in which he worked to debunk the "myths" about homosexuality and bodybuilding. "As far as lack of interest in women among bodybuilders is concerned," he told one interviewer, "I have personally never seen a group of heterosexuals more interested in women, nor a group more successful with women." An ad for one bodybuilding supplement in one of his magazines declared, "A woman wants a man who's strong and solid—this is what turns them on—not a car or money or pretentious crap like that. So let that jerk with the car eat his heart out. While he goes home alone with $250,000 worth of Lamborghini wrapped around him—man, I got what I want wrapped around me."

As Ben explained to me, the success of the Weider companies depended on insecure heterosexual guys joining gyms to acquire the body that would attract girls. To this end, they would buy supplements, powders, proteins—whatever it took—all supplied by the Weiders and advertised in their publications, often featuring an endorsement by none other than Arnold Schwarzenegger.

In his deconstruction of the industry, *Little Big Men*, Alan Klein studied Weider's publications very closely and discovered that they had a very obvious mission. "Heterosexuality is enshrined in the pages of *Muscle and Fitness*," he wrote. "Each issue abounds with full-color ads of men and women together, enjoying each other in some wholesome way. Forty years ago Charles Atlas ads ran in comic books and also reinforced heterosexuality. In both Weider's and Atlas's ads, the message is that if one looks like a man some woman will drape herself over him."

Now, with Schwarzenegger, as Ben had explained to me, Joe had the embodiment of the heterosexual superman he had long been craving to take his sport to the next level and shatter its effeminate image. Arnold was all too willing to go along with him. Like Weider, and probably at Weider's behest, he never missed an opportunity to evangelize about how bodybuilding was the domain of straight macho men like him.

"I know more plumbers who are fags than I do bodybuilders," he told one magazine.

At the peak of his career, perhaps with the same goal in mind, he told what seems almost certainly to be a fib to Jim Stingley of the *Los Angeles Times* when he claimed, "I personally don't know of any competitive bodybuilders who are homosexuals. But there is a lot of homosexual following around bodybuilding. Like when you go to a competition, you will see them. And in gyms, like here, you will find homosexuals signing up to become members of the group so they can just watch you working out. Because we are to them what maybe some female sex symbol is to me. I mean, I would love to watch Brigitte Bardot going to a gym and doing some bend-over lateral raises. A lot of people think we are homosexual because we attract them. Because to them, you know, we are heaven."

A couple of years later, perhaps tired of lying and gay-bashing—which didn't represent his true views—he finally came clean and admitted that many bodybuilding champions had, in fact, been gay, telling the magazine *New Times*, "When it comes to sex,

I don't give a shit what anyone's trip is. Two of the last five Mr. Americas were gay."

In 1977, he told *Oui* magazine that gay bodybuilders don't bother him a bit. "Gay people are fighting the same kind of stereotyping that bodybuilders are: People have certain misconceptions about them just as they do about us. Well, I have absolutely no hangups about the fag business; though it may bother some bodybuilders, it doesn't affect me at all." In the years since then, his public statements about gay rights have become increasingly more enlightened; this is one of the many social issues that have alienated Schwarzenegger from his Republican base.

In fact, so far only one top bodybuilder has publicly come out as gay: Bob Paris, who won Mr. Universe in 1983 and came out of the closet six years later in an interview he gave to *Ironman* magazine. When I caught up to him in Vancouver, where he had long ago retired from the sport, Paris explained that he finally came out in 1989 because "I wanted to stop living a lie publicly, I wanted to be proud of myself, every aspect of myself, not just my accomplishments. I wanted to marry my partner and I wanted it known that I was gay before that became a public matter."

I asked him why, given the sport's huge gay fan base, more bodybuilders haven't followed his example in the years since. "No, no, no, it is a sport but it is still big business," he replied. "How many Hollywood executives and directors and producers are gay men? Now how many of them are openly gay men? A much smaller number. There is prejudice and bigotry out there and homophobia is still pretty rampant."

Before he came out, Paris had been under contract with Joe Weider; he was one of Joe's stable of elite bodybuilders, appearing regularly in the magazines, endorsing products, and allowing his image to be used as Weider saw fit—much as Schwarzenegger himself had done a decade earlier. According to Paris, though, when he came out, Weider cut him loose and failed to renew his contract. Paris's recollection of what transpired serves as a cautionary tale for other gay bodybuilders.

"It's all about selling their products," Paris explains bitterly, "and Joe knows that gay bodybuilders aren't good for business."

12.

Just Like Ali

S chwarzenegger was hungry. He knew he was on the cusp. But he could not call himself the best bodybuilder in the world until he had acquired the titles that still eluded him. The next important rung on the ladder was the 1969 IFBB Mr. Universe. Previously, he had lost this contest to Frank Zane a day after arriving in America in September 1968. In preparation for the fall of 1969, Arnold spent a full year sculpting exactly the body he knew he needed to finally claim his rightful place. He was already the biggest bodybuilder in America, but perhaps somewhat too big. For five hours a day, every day, at Gold's and Vince's, he concentrated on chiseling his body into a "masterpiece," and in the process took off the twenty excess pounds that he had concluded were unnecessary to achieve his desired look. His sheer determination left the other bodybuilders in awe. They had never before seen the level of self-discipline that Arnold applied to his career.

"Arnold is the most goal-oriented person I have ever met," Frank Zane told *Sports Illustrated* in 1975. "It takes so much knowledge to do what he has done, an understanding of anatomy, nutrition, your own body. And discipline and self-control. He is very practical. Whatever he does must be useful to him in some way, in the direction of whatever goal he has set."

By the fall of 1969, Arnold was convinced he had finally achieved the "look"—the look he had envied in other greats—rippled, cut, veins bulging. He was ready. This was evident the moment he took the stage on September 13 at Mr. Universe, which was held at the Brooklyn Academy of Music. This time there was no mistaking who was the best. All seven judges awarded Arnold first place. But it was a hollow victory. Looking at the opponents he had just beaten, he knew that one was missing—Sergio Oliva, who had chosen to compete instead at the Mr. Olympia contest, the premiere event in the bodybuilding world and a title he had won the previous two years. Joe Weider had deliberately scheduled both contests on the same weekend, for reasons that are still a mystery. Arnold would have preferred to compete against Oliva, but he was under contract to Weider, who demanded that he enter Mr. Universe, perhaps fearful that he wasn't ready to compete against Sergio. Now, with his trophy in hand, Arnold finally convinced his benefactor, later that evening, that it would bring great credit to Weider's magazines and products if he could claim the Mr. Olympia crown and finally erase any doubt about who was the world's greatest bodybuilder. Weider finally agreed, confident that his boy would blow Oliva off the stage. When Arnold arrived at New York's Town Hall auditorium, however, and got his first glimpse of the massive black Cuban bodybuilder up close, he saw for himself why Oliva was known as "the Myth."

"It was as jarring as if I'd walked into a wall," he later recalled. "He destroyed me. He was so huge, he was so fantastic, there was no way I could even think of beating him. I admitted my defeat and felt some of my pump go away. I tried. But I'd been so taken back by my first sight of Sergio Oliva that I think I settled for second place before we even walked out on stage."

Albert Busek concurred, describing Oliva as a "freak of nature with his twenty-seven-inch waist, massive thighs, and twenty-one-inch arms—he was unbelievable."

Indeed, when the judge's verdict was announced, Oliva had won his third consecutive Mr. Olympia.

Arnold was gracious in defeat—the last he would ever suffer in a bodybuilding competition—and reached over to hug his opponent, even kissing Oliva on the cheek.

A few days later, he unexpectedly flew to London and easily won the NABBA Mr. Universe title—the fourth Mr. Universe he had now won—but there was no longer any glory in second-rate titles. He later said he did it to spite all the American bodybuilders who were competing in other contests just to get away from him. But he knew there was now only one competitor who mattered. His one-year agreement with Weider had expired, but he pleaded for an extension so that he could train hard to beat Oliva next time around. Weider agreed. At the same time, Arnold begged Weider to bring over his old friend Franco Columbu from Munich as a training partner.

It had been months since Arnold and his Sardinian friend had trained together, competing with each other to see who could bench-press the most weight or complete the most reps. It had also been a long time since Arnold had a partner to chase women and tear up the town, which is what the two had become most known for in the taverns and streets of Munich, where their antics had become legendary. But a lot had changed for Arnold since he had seen Franco last. He had been forced to shelve his formerly wild ways, owing to a change in his domestic situation. Arnold finally had his first serious girlfriend.

On a July 4 weekend in 1969, Arnold was having lunch at his favorite deli, Zucky's, at Fifth Avenue and Wilshire in Santa Monica, with a friend, Robert Kennedy, who was involved in publishing muscle magazines, when a young waitress named Barbara Outland—sitting at the counter on a break—caught his eye. His usual response when that happened was the direct approach, a technique he hadn't refined much since his days in Germany: "Do you want to fuck?" But there was something about this woman that was different, something in her smile that made him deviate from his standard question. As a regular at Zucky's, he had seen her a number of times before, but he wasn't used to these feelings. Women, he frequently explained, were meant to be sexual playthings. Anything more was a distraction from the serious business of training. Yet now he decided to do something uncharacteristic. "You are so sexy," he declared, sitting down beside the nineteen-year-old. "I must ask you out on a date." When her manager had warned her a day earlier that Arnold had been talking about asking her for a date, her first reaction was "revulsion" that this "hideous man" would dare to ask her out. But when he finally made his move, she couldn't help being curious. By 1969, she later recalled, musclemen had become a metaphor for "insecure self-centeredness, foppish vanity, and assumption of certain homosexuality." But there was something about his manner that intrigued her. She smiled and reluctantly accepted his invitation.

Kennedy later confided that Arnold had told him, "I really like this girl. I really like her." According to Kennedy, this was something Arnold had never before said about any other woman. Their first date took place two weeks later on the night of the Apollo moon landing, and they watched the historic event on television in Barbara's living room. All the while, she couldn't help noticing Arnold's tacky taste in clothes and was glad that their first date wasn't taking place in public.

"That was the thing about Arnold," she later recalled, describing the "pitiful little European clothing" he wore. "Polyester pants and pointy shirts and those awful 'under' T-shirts. It was an embarrassment to me at the time." She nearly laughed out loud when she noticed his pointed black leather shoes, which accentuated his "athletic pigeon-toed swagger." Communication was difficult because, according to Outland, Arnold could speak barely 200 words of English. But he listened, intrigued, as she talked about John F. Kennedy's vision and the impressive scientific achievement that had led to Neil Armstrong's walk that night.

When they started dating, her friends—"with their lawyer and doctor husbands"—frowned on the musclebound Neanderthal. But Outland claims to have discovered a sweet, sensitive side that belied their stereotypes. Still a virgin, Barbara resisted Arnold's advances for months. In between workouts, Outland—who would later become a college professor—worked with him on his English, which was improving rapidly. At the end of their summer romance, however, Outland resumed her university courses, moving back to San Diego for her senior year and living at her sorority house. She assumed that her relationship with Arnold had been merely a summer fling until he started calling the sorority house and telling her he missed her. Soon he was flying her back to L.A. on weekends, and the two resumed their relationship. In the fall, she finally gave in to him. She was hooked.

For his part, Arnold genuinely seemed to enjoy his new domestic arrangement. "I was impressed immediately by something I felt about her," he recalled, "something that was different. . . . I could describe it as an inner warmth, the wholesomeness one associates with a hometown girl. Our dating was different, too, from any I'd ever done. She took me to meet her parents. This also impressed me. There was a healthy atmosphere in their home. They seemed to have communication. They felt love and respect for each other and expressed it."

Franco Columbu had arrived in America soon after Arnold and Barbara began seeing each other, and at first he and Arnold shared an apartment in Santa Monica, working out together at Gold's Gym. Eventually, Arnold and Barbara got their own place on Sixth Street in Santa Monica, later moving into an apartment building Arnold had purchased. In the four years they lived together, Barbara thought she had "tamed the beast," domesticating the Austrian wild man. It was only a matter of time, she believed, before Arnold would retire from bodybuilding and propose. But she was living a fairy tale in more ways than one. Unbeknownst to her, the beast was untamable.

Almost from the moment Columbu arrived, he and Arnold took up where they left off in Munich, chasing women and carousing on the beaches of Venice and Santa Monica. The bodybuilder Dick Tyler, a friend of both, revealed to Wendy Leigh that the pair had confided in him that "they had so many women that they couldn't keep track of who was who. They would just wake up in the middle of the night and they would each have a girl with them. Women were for their own pleasure."

In the course of my own research, three women told me they had slept with Arnold during this period, but none had any photos or witnesses to prove the claim. Then I discovered a woman who claims to have slept not only with Arnold but with Franco Columbu as well. And she has a trove of photos to back up her statements.

Kellie Everts was an aspiring female bodybuilder when she first met Schwarzenegger in the early 1970s.

"When I met him I had been trying to get some attention as a female bodybuilder, but no one was taking that seriously," Everts told me in 2010. "It was divided between people thinking I was some kind of flake to people deciding that I was some new sort of lesbian who wanted to have big muscles like a man and have soft, petite girlfriends caressing my huge muscles. . . . Neither was true—I saw bodybuilding as a way of making the already beautiful female form even more beautiful."

She says that it was Joe Weider who made the initial introduction after she had appeared in the pages of one of Weider's magazines, *Muscle Training*. She claims that at the time they met, both she and Arnold were "walking around in a constant state of arousal," always looking for sex. They got together a few times, she recalls, whenever "the opportunity presented itself," but that a meeting wasn't something they would plan in advance.

"We were not like committed partners or anything like that," she says. One of the women I met who claims to have slept with Arnold told me that he wasn't particularly good in bed, that he was like a "jackhammer." I asked Everts whether she shared that view.

"He was massively muscular," she replies, "and when we were having sex the power and energy of his body was awesome. Feeling the energy and the blood pumping and surging through his muscles was very erotic, and the fact that I was muscular too meant he was feeding off my energy as well, feeding off my strength and power—while men have the thrusting power during sex, women have the gripping, clenching, drawing-in kind of power—so when both bodies are very strong and powerful, naturally sex becomes very strong and powerful too. Having sex with Arnold was like working out in a lot of ways, but in a powerful, spiritual, sensual sense—it was a workout of the senses that our muscular bodies sent to a heightened place of sensuality that those not so in touch with their bodies can never get to.

"If you're asking whether he was good in bed," she continues, "the answer is yes and no. Like a lot of guys, once he starts he goes until he gets off, and if his woman gets off in the process, great, but that is not the priority. But he enjoyed it so much that it ended up being very enjoyable for me too. One time we were both in town, he called me and asked if I wanted to get together and work out together and catch up—so we worked out in his hotel gym. After we went to his suite and showered, then just naturally we started doing it in the shower, then on the bathroom floor, then moved to the bed, then moved to the chair in front of the picture window . . . just having a great time."

For about a year, she claims, she was involved in a "love triangle" with both Columbu and Schwarzenegger, until the IFBB Mr. America and Ms. Americana show in 1972, when Arnold caught her having sex with Franco. From then on, she says she incurred the "wrath of Arnold." Everts, who would go on to become Miss Nude Universe and later a preacher, produces a slew of photos of herself with both bodybuilders, including a classic shot of Arnold riding on her shoulders while she flexes her muscles.

It was only after they broke up in 1973, revealed Barbara Outland years later, that Arnold confessed he had been cheating on her during their relationship. She was stoic about the discovery and not particularly surprised, given what she had witnessed among the bodybuilding groupies who hung around the gym. "Women threw themselves at Arnold, men threw themselves at him, but in a way he did pretty well," she continued.

"How would any of the rest of us have done if we were being told, 'You can have anything you want with anybody's body'? You'd really have to have your moral code nailed down."

Of the many contradictions in the astonishing rise of Arnold Schwarzenegger, few are as glaring as a snapshot from his earliest days in America. When he was governor of California years later, one of the most pressing issues he faced was the growing problem of illegal immigration. Given the political climate and his Republican affiliations, he probably had little choice but to promise a crackdown and employ harsh rhetoric denouncing illegal immigrants. But in the late 1960s, when he first arrived in America, Arnold Schwarzenegger was almost certainly an illegal immigrant himself.

When Arnold arrived in America during the fall of 1968, he was traveling on a B-1 visa, which is issued to foreign athletes wishing to train and compete in America as well as to practitioners of other professions seeking to visit temporarily. The visa, for example, might be issued to a rock band touring the United States and then recording an album, or to an engineer traveling from abroad to install a computer system. However, the terms of the visa explicitly bar the holder from drawing a salary in America.

Yet in his 1977 autobiography, Arnold makes it clear that he did draw a salary. "My part of the agreement was to make available to Weider information about how I trained," he wrote of his first 1968 contract. "He agreed to provide an apartment, a car, and to pay me a weekly salary in exchange for my information and being able to use photographs of me in his magazine."

In a 2003 interview with the *San Jose Mercury News*, Joe Weider revealed that he paid Schwarzenegger a salary of $200 a week. "I paid him right away," Weider said. "How do you think he was going to live?" This contradicted a statement by a spokesman for Schwarzenegger that he had been paid a salary of only $65 a week. Whatever the figure, however, any salary would have violated the terms of his visa and would have been illegal.

When the newspaper interviewed immigration attorneys about the potential violation and presented the known facts, six lawyers asserted that if the account was true, he broke the law. "It allows you to come in to conduct business, but to be gainfully employed, you need a visa that allows you to be gainfully employed in the United States," said the New York-based immigration attorney Steven S. Mukamal. "It would seem that Mr. Schwarzenegger violated his own status."

But when the newspaper presented its findings, Weider suddenly changed his story and said he couldn't recall if he had paid Schwarzenegger $200 per week after all. "I thought I paid him around that, but I'm not sure," Weider said. "I don't think I paid him exactly weekly. He was paid when he needed some money."

According to Crystal Williams of the American Immigration Lawyers Association, Schwarzenegger might have faced deportation for violating the terms of his B-1 visa had his arrangement with Weider been known at the time.

"Things were a lot looser in 1968 than they are today," she explained. "Generally, they were not paying as much attention back then as they do today. If you change from a B-1 to working status without disclosing that you were working beforehand, that could be considered fraud—and that's very serious."

In 1969, more than a year after he arrived in America, Arnold received an H-2 visa, which now allowed him to work in the country, under some restrictions. It was around that time that he and Franco Columbu started a bricklaying company, called Pumping Bricks. Their exploits are now legendary, thanks to stories the two frequently told—after Arnold began to gain fame—about taking advantage of rich Americans. On ABC's *20/20*, Franco related one such anecdote. "One of our workers nearly ruined a patio job by laying the bricks crookedly," he said, chuckling. "Then Arnold said, 'Don't worry. We will talk to the lady.' I said, 'Talking to the lady won't move these bricks.' Arnold said, 'No matter what happens in a construction site, you have to be able to sell what you have created.' Arnold convinced the lady that the bricks, by being off, were a new European style."

About their venture, Arnold later explained that Franco "was the technical expert; I cut the deals." According to Columbu, his Austrian partner was particularly adept at finessing deals with clients, using European terms such as centimeters instead of inches and making a "complex" job sound like a bargain. Franco once bragged to *California Business* magazine about a job they did following an earthquake, when they were called by a woman whose house had been partially damaged. A previous contractor had estimated the job at $5,000, including $4,000 for simply knocking down the chimney.

"Arnold looked at it," recalled Franco, "and said, 'What if we got a big rope and swung like Tarzan onto the roof and lay on our backs and pushed the chimney over with our feet?' So it took us about ten minutes to knock down the chimney once we got the rope on it, and we made $1,000. The lady was so happy she gave us the bricks." Arnold proceeded to sell those bricks to another client, calling them "antique bricks."

But it was another story, which Arnold told on *The Tonight Show* in 1981, that is perhaps the most famous legacy of Pumping Bricks. Talking to Johnny Carson, he said that he and a friend (Columbu) had placed an ad in the *Los Angeles Times* after the 1971 Sylmar earthquake, offering their services as "European special bricklayers." Arnold explained that his job was to give an estimate and negotiate a price with the customer. "Meanwhile, Columbu climbed up on the roof to check the chimney. . . . He pushed all the chimneys over so they fell down." Hearing the story, Carson raised his eyebrows and replied, "What a racket! You go and push chimneys down and then rebuild them." To that, Arnold responded, "Exactly. . . . So we had a business going very successfully for a year." A spokesman for Schwarzenegger later chalked up the story to "shtick." Nevertheless, operating the company itself may once again have violated the terms of Arnold's H-2 visa.

Meanwhile, Arnold had kept his eye on the prize— the bronze statue of Eugene Sandow presented to the winner of Mr. Olympia. He now worked out longer and harder than ever, always with one image fixed in his mind—Sergio Oliva, the only man who stood between him and that trophy. He vowed to "destroy the myth." But first there was a stop in London for the NABBA Mr. Universe contest, which would be a good tune-up for Mr. Olympia in New York two weeks later. When he arrived in London, however, he was in for a shock. Reg Park had decided to make a comeback twenty years after first competing and had chosen Mr. Universe as the breakout competition.

"I couldn't believe it," Arnold recalled. "Here I was competing against my idol, whose pictures I'd hung up all over my bedroom, whose words I'd lived and trained by." Competing against Park posed a genuine dilemma. Should Arnold drop out of the competition, which was essentially meaningless by this point in his career? He knew Park didn't have a chance to beat him, and he was severely conflicted about showing up his father figure and mentor. But in the end, he decided that leaving would be "stupid." Beating the forty-two-year-old South African, he reasoned, would be good for his ego and "good for publicity." Beside, he didn't think of this as beating his idol. He thought of it more as being able to "step up beside him, to finally share an equal place with him." As it turned out, the competition wasn't even close. The disciple had finally surpassed the master. Wendy Leigh quotes Rick Wayne as a witness to the interaction between the two men backstage before the contest. Park was pumping up furiously while Arnold stood gossiping and laughing with the other competitors. Finally, in a moment of frustration at his old friend's apparent indifference, Park is said to have exploded, "Dammit, Arnold. Will you can the bullshit until after the contest!" To which Arnold replied, "Contest, what contest?" The episode, and especially the humiliation factor, later prompted countless oedipal comparisons by various biographers and Schwarzenegger-watchers who can never resist summoning Freud to explain his fellow Austrian's complex personality. But, as Frank Zane noted, it was simply a reflection of Arnold's need to win, no matter what the cost—physical or human.

An hour after beating Park, Arnold flew to Columbus, Ohio, to compete in the Pro Mr. World contest, run by his future business partner, Jim Lorimer, who whisked Arnold across the Atlantic in a private jet so he could get to the Ohio contest on time. What Lorimer had failed to tell him was that the headlined bodybuilder at Mr. America that weekend was Sergio Oliva, whom Arnold thought he wouldn't have to meet until October 3 in New York at Mr. Olympia. Arnold wasn't yet ready mentally, but he knew he was in the best physical shape of his life. The reaction in London had showed him that he had now achieved "perfection," the body he had been envisioning, willing, in his mind since he had placed second to Oliva in New York a year earlier.

At the prejudging, comparing himself with Oliva, he felt confident but nervous. It was going to be close this time. As the announcer took the microphone, the crowd was hushed; the spectators knew they might be witnessing a historic turning point in the sport.

"In third place . . . Dave Draper. In second place . . . Sergio Oliva." As the announcer called out his rival's name, Arnold could hear his opponent beside him mutter, "Oh shit!" The crowd went wild, chanting, "Arnold! Arnold!"—a chant that by now he was very familiar with.

Despite defeating his only real rival, however, Arnold knew that Mr. World was hardly a meaningful title. If he was to take his rightful place atop the sport, he would have to repeat the feat at Mr. Olympia two weeks later, in front of a much more experienced judging panel and a New York crowd that would probably be much more in favor of Oliva, who was both Latino and black, two of New York's most populous demographics. In addition, Arnold knew well that Oliva hadn't been at his best in Columbus, assuming he would have no serious competition with Arnold 3,000 miles away at Mr. Universe. The surprise entrant threw him off his game. Yet the judging was very close. Anything could happen in New York, and most watchers still assumed that Oliva was better than the Austrian upstart.

It was billed as the "Bodybuilding Battle of the Century." In the audience at New York's Town Hall auditorium, the fans were in a frenzy. Each camp had its fanatical following, and the fans were desperate to get a piece of their guy. Backstage, word reached Arnold that people were offering $100 for a lock of his hair, $500 for his trunks. The police had to hold back the hordes from rushing onstage. Cries of "Sergio" drowned out the smaller contingent of Arnold's fans, and it was clear who the crowd's favorite was. Arnold merely stared at his rival as they warmed up, watching his every move, sizing up his opponent.

Finally, it was time for the showdown. Both men received a rapturous welcome from their legions of followers. Then they started posing. Arnold had studied films of his opponent's techniques for hours on end, and by now he probably knew Oliva's routine better than Oliva knew it himself. He knew exactly how to time his own routine to full advantage, whipping off two or three lightning-quick poses for every one of Sergio's. Finally, the two were clearly exhausted and Arnold whispered in Oliva's ear that they should leave the stage. "After you," Arnold politely suggested. But as the Cuban departed, the cheers of the crowd turned to boos. Unaware that it was Arnold's idea, they believed Oliva had retreated from the showdown. And as their boos mingled with cries of "Coward," Arnold did something that Oliva has never forgiven him for to this day. He remained onstage to thunderous applause, knowing that Sergio had been vilified moments before for following his suggestion. It was one of the most significant turning points in the history of bodybuilding—the moment when Arnold Schwarzenegger became the undisputed hero of the sport.

It was a mere formality by the time the results were announced and Arnold was presented with the Eugene Sandow trophy that finally acknowledged him as the best in the world. "I was King Kong!" he later recalled of that moment. But, although he had been gracious in defeat a year earlier, he now reverted to the bully that the people of Thal and Munich had come to loathe.

He boasted to anybody who would listen about how he had "tricked" Oliva and described the boos that greeted Oliva as "music to my ears," knowing there could be no return for his greatest rival.

"I improvised those things," he bragged in the pages of *Muscle Builder/Power.* "It was my doing and it was kind of unique in the sport. I've seen it with Ali, I've seen it with other sports, but in bodybuilding it was unique."

The comparison to Muhammad Ali was especially telling. In the bodybuilding world at least, the rivalry between Schwarzenegger and Oliva is easily as compelling as that of Frazier and Ali—fittingly because Schwarzenegger had watched Ali from afar for many years. What he admired most about the outspoken heavyweight champion was not his boxing ability but his sense of showmanship. Wag Bennett had told Arnold years earlier that bodybuilding was not a sport but show business. In order to succeed, one had to be an entertainer. And while this skill plays only a small role in boxing, Arnold had sensed that it was hugely important in his own sport. Knowing that Ali was famous for composing improvised doggerel—"Floats like a butterfly, stings like a bee"—Arnold tried his own hand at poetry, writing a verse to his defeated opponent that he published as an open letter to Oliva in *Muscle Builder:*

> *Sergio, I'm so sorry you had to lose*
> *'Cause now you might turn to*
> *Sin and booze*
> *If you do, watch out for your wife—*
> *I hear she packs a knife*

Fifteen years later, in fact, Oliva's wife, Arlene, would shoot her husband in the abdomen with a gun.

13.

Hercules in New York

Joe Weider likes to tell the story of what happened afterward on the night Arnold Schwarzenegger won the 1970 Mr. Olympia contest. Weider had booked a hotel suite for himself, Arnold, and Franco Columbu, along with assorted members of their entourage. As they were preparing to retire for the evening, a knock came on the door of the suite. It was Sergio Oliva. He had nowhere to sleep that night and was wondering if he could have a bed. Arnold was reluctant to let his defeated opponent share their quarters, but Weider finally acquiesced, saying, "There's enough rooms; let him stay." At seven o'clock the following morning, they were awoken by the sound of bedsprings going up and down in Sergio's room.

"I peek into Sergio's room and there he is," recalled Weider, "leaning on the edge of the bed, doing triceps dips with his feet upon a chair. I went back to Arnold and said, "Sergio Oliva's training in there." And he said, 'Why? The contest's over.' I went to Sergio's room again and asked, 'OK, Sergio, why are you training after the contest?' He looked at me like I was nuts! Of course, he was preparing for next year's contest."

The story is meant to illustrate how competitive Oliva was, how eager for a rematch. But in fact it also tells a completely different and very revealing story. It demonstrates that, although Oliva had been the undisputed world's greatest bodybuilder for three years, until that very weekend, he couldn't even afford a hotel room.

"People say that we [the Weider brothers] chew up bodybuilders and spit them out," Ben Weider told me, "but that's not true. We take very good care of our people." Technically, he's correct. Once you were on Weider's roster, you were well taken care of, although the financial rewards were still scanty. But it was obvious that Joe Weider had no use for those he couldn't profit from. And Sergio Oliva was one of those people. Although Weider had embraced a number of black bodybuilders, such as Ricky Wayne and later Robby Robinson, they tended to be charismatic and prompt to bend to Weider's strong will, at least in the beginning. But Oliva was testy, he was considered more Latino than black, and Weider had concluded that he wasn't particularly marketable. Weider acknowledged this when he told a reporter, "I put Sergio on the cover and I sell x magazines, I put Arnold on the cover and I sell 3x magazines."

What few people realized is that the most prize money Schwarzenegger or Oliva had ever earned in a competition was $1,000. Weider and other promoters were making millions from the sweat and hard work of these musclemen, many of whom were forced to hustle just to pay the rent. Arnold was luckier than most because Joe Weider had recognized his potential early on. Yet the contract he had signed for $200 a week had also put him in a form of what he would later call "indentured servitude." As he rose to the top and watched Weider profiting from his fame, he began to resent it. He wanted more.

"I'd begun to look at bodybuilding as a kind of vehicle," he explained. "It feels good being the best-built man in the world, of course, but the question always comes up: Okay, how can you use that to make money? I had been increasingly more involved in business since the year I bought the gym. I no longer had to prove I was the greatest bodybuilder of all time."

Despite the stereotypes, Arnold Schwarzenegger was anything but stupid, even then. He was acutely aware that Joe Weider was using him and the other bodybuilders.

First, he demanded and received a raise, but that barely covered his rent and his dates with Barbara. His business with Franco was sporadic. He wanted more. About Weider, he later wrote that the man had "two personalities. The warm, beautiful private man and the shrewd businessman at the office." Business had fascinated Arnold ever since he ran a successful gym in Munich. With the same sense of purpose he applied to his training in the gym, he made a decision about his future. "I wanted to build an empire," he recalled. He asked Weider how he could get a piece of the action. Sensing rebellion in the ranks, Joe finally suggested to his protégé that he start his own mail-order company.

With Barbara's help writing and editing in English, he marketed a series of training courses and sold photo albums, T-shirts, posing trunks, personalized programs, and other items through the mail. Capitalizing on his newfound fame, he also established bodybuilding training seminars throughout the world—as far away as Japan, Australia, South Africa, Canada, France, and Mexico, where the name Schwarzenegger now had considerable cachet.

As his enterprises expanded, he also continued to defend his titles, knowing that those bodybuilding championships were good for business. "Eventually, I wanted every single person who touched a weight to equate the feeling of the barbell with my name," he explained. "The moment he got ahold of it, I wanted him to think, 'Arnold.'"

Arnold became so fixated on business deals that they even began to affect his sex life. "Many times, while I was getting laid, in my head I was focusing on a business deal," he confided to Laurence Leamer.

Because of the complicated contract that bound him to Joe Weider, the two had to work out numerous details to allow Arnold to expand his business in such a way as not to threaten the Weiders' own empire. This necessity led to much tension over the years, mostly involving business disputes. Arnold later hinted at those troubles, describing business dealings with Weider that were "not so pleasant." He was realistic enough to understand that he couldn't expect Weider to put Arnold's welfare above his own, and he didn't blame Weider for that. Arnold had been burned more than once back in Munich and was very cautious.

By 1975, he had become so frustrated with Weider and other bodybuilding tycoons that he gave a blistering interview to *Sports Illustrated* about the money side of the business, uncharacteristically naming his mentor as one of the culprits.

All of these magazines—Weider's, Hoffman's, Lurie's—I call them comic books, circus books! Those headlines! HOW ARNOLD TERROR-IZED HIS THIGHS! Hah! THIS is JOE'S BICEPS SPEAKING! Why are Joe's biceps talking to anybody? It is not that much of a biceps. Joe exposes Lurie and Lurie exposes Joe and Hoffman is against everybody and can't tell Ben from Joe, or says he can't. Why won't these guys get together? I will tell you why. It is because none of these silly people are really interested in bodybuilding anymore. They are interested only in the money that can be made from it. Each of them says he is for bodybuilding, but these men are not. They are knocking the sport down. I ask Joe why he prints such junk—why is everybody bombing and blasting and terrorizing, all those silly words? Joe says it sells the magazine. Period.

Eventually, all was forgiven. "Me and Arnold never had a falling-out," Ben Weider told me. "We always got along great, but I didn't work as closely with him as Joe did. They fought constantly—they would be standing there screaming into each other's face; sometimes they wouldn't speak to each other for weeks at a time. But they loved each other too. And I think they both knew that they needed the other. We did very well being associated with Arnold, but he also did very well from us. He'll be the first to admit that."

Indeed, Weider also gave his young protégé some sound business advice that would serve Arnold very well in years to come. When Arnold started to make his first real money, he asked Joe where he should invest it.

Weider later recalled his response. "I said, 'Don't go into any business. It's best to take it and invest in real estate. It always goes up. And you don't have to do much, so you can work on being famous.'" By the end of his second year in America, Arnold had already saved $28,000, a not inconsequential sum in 1970.

To hone his entrepreneurial skills, Arnold enrolled in business courses at Santa Monica college and at the same time struggled to understand the American economic system.

Since the days when, as a teenager, he had sat in the darkened Gaidorf Kino cinema in Graz watching his hero, Reg Park, on the screen, Arnold Schwarzenegger had three unshakable goals. The first was to become the world's greatest bodybuilder. That would somehow lead directly to his second goal—to make a lot of money and have the lavish lifestyle that Park enjoyed. But his ultimate ambition was to become a movie star so that someday teenagers could worship him on the big screen the way he idolized Park. It was a dream he shared with everybody who would listen: his father, Kurt Marnul, Alfred Gerstl. None of them, however, took him very seriously; they dismissed the dream as the folly of youth.

Imagine the excitement, then, when in 1969, Joe Weider told him Arnold was up for a part in a Hollywood movie. Even better, he would be playing Hercules, the role that launched the careers of Reg Park, Steve Reeves, and other famous bodybuilders turned movie stars. The producers hadn't been able to find an actor who had the right physique to play Hercules, so they contacted Weider, asking if he knew anybody who might fit the bill. Weider informed them that he had the perfect candidate. "I told them he had acting experience and that you could run a projector on his chest, it was so big," Weider recalled. The next day, he brought Arnold, still completely unknown, to a Hollywood office to meet the filmmakers.

"Weider is such a hype artist," Arnold told *Sports Illustrated* in 1987, recalling his audition. "He did all the talking, I was just standing there like an idiot. He tells them, 'This guy's a Shakespearean actor in Europe!' And they believed him."

Before long, they flew him to New York, where he spent twelve weeks filming for the enormous sum of $1,000 per week. "You know, little did they know. Literally, I couldn't even speak the English language well enough to say my lines," he says, laughing. "I had to study day and night to just say the lines so someone can loop over the lines. But that really was the moment when I saw it really could happen, that I could be a movie star. So I went after it even more strongly."

To this day, it's unclear whether the producers meant the film to be a comedy or a slightly campy drama in the tradition of the "sword and sandal" epics on which Reg Park had cut his teeth in the 1950s. The plot is somewhat ludicrous and involves Zeus casting his son, Hercules, out of Mount Olympus to find adventure on earth. In the fish-out-of-water antics that follow, Arnold meets a number of eccentric characters who introduce him to the ways of New Yorkers. Eventually, Hercules becomes a professional wrestler, much to the dismay of Zeus, who is watching all this warily from his perch on Mount Olympus. Believing his son is making a mockery of the gods, Zeus dispatches a number of his minions, including Mercury, to wrangle the young god back where he belongs, but Hercules defies their efforts. The highlight of the film involves Arnold riding a chariot through Times Square.

When the film was released in February 1970, it was widely derided, and it has since become somewhat of a cult classic, on many critics' lists as the worst movie of all time. "Arnold Schwarzenegger's film debut was a Herculean effort . . . to sit through," mocked the *Newark Star Ledger*.

In the credits, Arnold is billed as "Arnold Strong," and his English was so poor at the time of filming that the producers dubbed in an American voice, adding to the camp element. Today, the movie is available on DVD, with the original version featuring Arnold's voice, although he has long since disowned the project and claims it was the one movie he regrets doing. Nevertheless, the experience gave him a taste of the actor's life, and he knew he wanted more.

At the 1971 Mr. Olympia in Paris, Arnold defended his title with ease, but it was a hollow victory because Sergio Oliva had not been permitted to compete. Oliva had participated in a match that wasn't sanctioned by the IFBB, and the Weiders used it as an excuse to suspend him from that year's Mr. Olympia. Many insiders felt that this was done to prevent Arnold from being dethroned. The epic rematch that the bodybuilding world had been lusting for would have to wait.

Oliva's chance would come a year later, in Essen, Germany. It was his opportunity to finally avenge his 1970 defeat and reclaim the throne that his supporters believed was rightfully his. But in a match that was later compared to the "Thrilla in Manila" rubber match between Frazier and Ali, when Ali finally settled the question of who was "the Greatest," Arnold took home the Sandow trophy once again. When the judges announced their decision, many onlookers were surprised. Even Joe Weider's magazine *Muscle and Fitness* later acknowledged that Oliva may have been better. "Sergio had improved significantly," it wrote, "and came in as big and sculpted as ever, so much so that many bodybuilding insiders felt he had the decidedly superior physique."

Arnold's longtime friend Albert Busek later appeared to acknowledge that Oliva had the better body going in, but rationalized Arnold's victory by claiming that Oliva had used the wrong tactics.

"In Essen, Sergio—as he had become famous for—pumped up backstage for an hour," Busek recalled. "He just grew before your eyes. I saw him and thought he was unbeatable."

While Arnold attributed his victory to psychological warfare, Oliva had a different explanation. He believed that the Weiders, by virtue of their control of the

IFBB, made sure their man, Schwarzenegger, emerged victorious. By 1972, Arnold had become a veritable marketing machine for the Weider empire, appearing regularly on the cover of the Weiders' magazines, endorsing their products and supplements, and bringing in a huge new fan base. Joe Weider himself had said that Arnold's photo on the cover sold more than three times as many magazines as Sergio's and that Arnold was a marketing bonanza.

Was Oliva simply being a sore loser or could the Weiders indeed have influenced the outcome? Undue influence is a charge echoed by many other bodybuilders over the years, but it is difficult to prove. There is no doubt that Ben and Joe Weider exercised enormous control over the IFBB, selecting and hiring the judges and setting the rules. Their decision to bar Oliva from the 1971 contest underscored the ability they had to micromanage their competitions to their advantage.

The controversy demonstrates one significant flaw of bodybuilding, and one major reason why, unlike weight lifting, it has never been made an Olympic sport, despite four decades of effort by Ben Weider to persuade the IOC of its merits. As with figure skating and gymnastics, which have also aroused their share of controversy over the years, the results of bodybuilding are decided by a judging panel. But, unlike those sports, bodybuilding has no genuinely objective criteria such as "landing" or "dismount" on which the judges can base their decision. It has only a number of vague, subjective factors like "muscularity," "proportion," and "symmetry." This opens up the possibility of undue influence. I never discussed this controversy with Ben Weider, but he had given a number of interviews over the years denying charges that he and his brother have exerted influence on the results.

14.

Admiring Hitler

It was hard to believe that anybody would offer Arnold another movie role after the fiasco of *Hercules in New York*, but Robert Altman was looking for a tough guy to play a hit man in his new film *The Long Goodbye*, based on the classic Raymond Chandler novel. Elliott Gould would be playing Chandler's detective Philip Marlowe, transported to the 1970s from the typical 1950s film noir in which he usually appeared. David Arkin, an actor who played in most of Altman's films, happened to be a buddy of Arnold's and recommended him for the small part. This time, however, despite his thick Austrian accent, Arnold needed no dubbing; the hit man was a deaf-mute. The lasting image of this character today is the cheesy mustache he sported in his only scene. The movie, which was released in 1973 to an underwhelming response from the public and the critics, died a quick death, and Arnold's career as an actor had once again failed to ignite.

Around the time Altman's film was in production, Arnold encountered the two men who would change all that. Charles Gaines was a thirty-year-old associate professor of creative writing at a small New Hampshire college when *Sports Illustrated* assigned him to report on a bodybuilding competition to be held in Holyoke, Massachusetts. Gaines brought along his friend George Butler to take photos. Neither of them knew much about bodybuilding other than the clichés.

"What you've got to understand is that back in the early 70s bodybuilding was the least glamorous sport in the world," Butler later told *Flex* magazine. "The prevailing view was that it was purely homosexual, that bodybuilders were totally uncoordinated, and that when they grew older their muscles would turn to fat and that they had no intelligence whatsoever." Gaines himself thought the sport compared to "midget wrestling."

The scene the two witnessed that night was strangely compelling. The event was minor, with the title "Mr. East Coast" on the line. But when Gaines and Butler saw hundreds of screaming bodybuilding fans filling the makeshift hall, they thought it was like something out of a Fellini film, a unique microcosm of American culture. They resolved to open the eyes of the American public to the heretofore obscure sport. Little did they know that they would soon accomplish this more successfully than Joe Weider and Charles Atlas combined and become what *Flex* magazine would later describe as the "Lewis and Clark of American bodybuilding."

The magazine article that Gaines wrote about the event was so well received that he and Butler decided to write a book about the bodybuilding world. They received a sizable advance from Doubleday.

"I saw this as a great story and I saw the whole scene as something that was just waiting to be examined and given some . . . some credence if you will," Butler told me in 2009. In September 1972 they headed to the Mr. America contest, where they encountered the reigning champion, Arnold Schwarzenegger, for the first time. The morning after the contest, they had breakfast at a Howard Johnson's at Forty-ninth and Broadway and discovered a raw but fascinating character they knew they had to tap. Butler would later describe his first impression of Arnold as "naive and ingenuous" but "crafty as all get-out" and "the quickest read I've ever met." They decided on the spot to feature him as a central character in the book.

But when they turned the manuscript in to Sandy Richardson, who was editor in chief at Doubleday, he wrote them a disheartening letter: "I want my money back. No one will ever read this book and no one will ever be interested in Arnold Schwarzenegger."

Although the book featured a number of other top bodybuilders of the day and had Ed Corney, rather than Arnold, on the cover, Arnold was far and away the most compelling character and the authors exalted him as a kind of bodybuilding god. In retrospect, the most telling and prophetic passage in the book, published in 1974, was a quote from Arnold predicting his future course: "I will go into movies as an actor, producer and eventually director. By the time I am 30, I will have starred in my first movie and I will be a millionaire. . . . I will marry a glamorous and intelligent wife." The book became a *New York Times* best seller, and Arnold's name and sphere of influence expanded even farther.

Meanwhile, Gaines had Arnold in mind for another project he had in the works. In 1972, he had published *Stay Hungry*, a well-received Hemingwayesque novel about a sensitive bodybuilder named Santo who is training hard to become Mr. Universe and a southern gentleman named Craig Blake who is seeking to buy the gym where Santo trains. The novel was optioned as a Hollywood film, to be directed by the well-regarded Bob Rafelson, who asked Gaines to do the screenplay. When Gaines suggested Arnold for the part of Santo, it took only one meeting for Rafelson to agree. For the film, Santo was quickly turned into an Austrian emigré to fit Arnold's thick accent. When Arnold heard that Rafelson would be the director, he was thrilled—this was the guy who had made Jack Nicholson cry in *Five Easy Pieces*. Nor did he object to Rafelson's demands on the set, but he was a little taken aback by the director's critique of his physique.

Two months before production started, he recalled, the director contacted him and told him, "I'm afraid of hiring you for this film, Arnold. You're just too goddamn big. You weigh two forty, and if you're in a scene with Sally Field you'll dwarf her. I'd like you to be much leaner and more normal-looking in street clothes."

"You worry about your film and I'll worry about my body," Arnold replied, asking the director what would be the ideal weight. The reply was 210 pounds. When Arnold stripped down and stepped on the scale on the first day of filming, he weighed 209. The acting itself wasn't as easy, and so Rafelson arranged five weeks of acting lessons. They appeared to pay off, and Arnold put as much effort into his performance as he usually did in the gym.

"I was ripped out of the mentality of being an athlete, where you have to keep the blinders on all the time," he recalled. "I tapped a well that I'd never tapped before."

Jeff Bridges had been hired to play Blake, and Sally Field appeared in a role that was a far cry from her innocent persona in *Gidget* and *The Flying Nun*, appearing in a nude scene that shocked many of her fans. Arnold turned in a surprisingly strong performance as Santo, though many critics later noted that he was merely playing himself. Writing in the *New York Times*, Vincent Canby was distinctly unimpressed: "The movie apparently means to respect these body builders, and as long as Mr. Schwarzenegger keeps his clothes on, it does. However, when the camera, at the end of the film, roams over physiques so carefully and lovingly exaggerated they seem about to burst, you suspect the movie of being a freak show that couldn't care less about its freaks." But *Newsweek* singled out Arnold's performance: "Arnold Schwarzenegger, a former Mr. Universe, is surprisingly good as the muscle man with heart—and pectorals—of gold."

The film was something of a box office flop when it was released in 1976; but Arnold's film career took a huge leap forward the following January, when he was named the surprise winner of a Golden Globe Award for Best Acting Debut in a Motion Picture. Backstage on the evening of the awards, he would meet another winner— Sylvester Stallone, clutching the trophy he had been given for *Rocky*. Their paths would soon cross again.

Ever since their book, *Pumping Iron*, was released to great acclaim, Gaines and Butler had harbored an ambition to turn it into a documentary. Only a film camera could capture the sweat, the raw energy, the ambition, the pathos of the bodybuilders and their lives. But when they sought funding for such a venture, they were turned down repeatedly. Butler approached 3,000 people, one at a time, to finance the project, but with little luck. He then thought to shoot some test footage at a tournament, mostly featuring Arnold, and screen it for potential investors. But when he gathered 100 people in a New York apartment and showed them the footage, the playwright Romulus Linney (father of the actress Laura Linney) stood up and said, "George, I'm going to speak for all your friends in the room. If you ever make a movie about Arnold Schwarzenegger, you'll be laughed off Forty-second Street."

Yet the two plodded on, gaining some funding, though far from enough to realize their vision. They decided to start filming with what they had and raise the rest as they went along. But it didn't take long for the production to encounter an ironic ghost from Arnold's past.

"I was very short on money," Butler recalled years later, "so I went to this lab in New York and I had just come back from shooting the initial part of the film and I asked them if they'd give me some credit, which is the kind of thing they normally do when you get going in the movie. This was a place called DuArt Lab and the owner of it is someone named Irwin Young. So I went in with my hat in my hand and asked him if he would give me $15,000 worth of credit. He said, 'Tell me what you're doing,' and I said, 'Well, I'm making a movie about bodybuilding.' Then he said, 'Does it have anything to do with Arnold Schwarzenegger?' and I said, 'Yes.' So he said, 'Forget it. I won't give you any credit. I had a movie in here called *Hercules in New York* and they never paid a bill and they owe me thirty grand.' "

Eventually, Butler raised $400,000, enough to produce one of the most successful documentaries in the history of the genre to that point. Arnold had been contemplating retiring from bodybuilding in 1974 to pursue his other dreams and at one point even announced that he was through with the sport. He had won every title that mattered. Sergio Oliva had quit the sport not long after the 1972 Mr. Olympia, and Arnold was now undisputedly the world's greatest bodybuilder. His businesses had succeeded beyond his wildest dreams and he had already earned his first million, comfortably invested in real estate at Joe Weider's suggestion. But Gaines and Butler persuaded him that the film could make him a star. They intended to follow a number of bodybuilders training for the 1975 Mr. Olympia contest in Pretoria, South Africa. To stand any chance of actually winning, Arnold would have to regain the thirty pounds he had lost for *Stay Hungry*, but he quickly agreed to do it, recognizing the potential. With Arnold on board, production began.

Butler recalled how the film came together and how Arnold eventually came to dominate the story, although that was never the filmmakers' original intention. "Once we started it took on a life of its own and the force of Arnold's personality and the dominance he had over his sport at the time made his contribution very meaningful," he told me years later. "And remember, I had never made a film before, never went to film school. I had never even read a book on filmmaking—it was the story that fascinated me and I knew this story had to be told very visually, so I thought documenting the event from as many angles and perspectives would make for a wonderful movie, and it did. Arnold of course wanted to be the center of attention and he did everything he could to make sure he had the camera on him as often as he could."

Arnold had been taking ballet lessons for some time to perfect his posing routines, an idea he borrowed from boxers who took ballet to refine their footwork. Still, the film's opening sequence is quite incongruous, featuring Arnold and his friend Franco Columbu in a New York ballet studio being guided by a female instructor in a leotard as they gracefully flex their massive muscles to classical music.

Some of the most memorable scenes in the film involve Arnold's graphic comparisons between bodybuilding and sex. "It's as satisfying to me as coming is," he says, chuckling, "you know, as having sex with a woman and coming. Can you believe how much I am in heaven? I am like getting the feeling of coming in the gym, I'm getting the feeling of coming at home, I'm getting the feeling of coming backstage when I pump up, when I pose in front of 5,000 viewers. I get the same feeling, so I'm coming day and night."

In this scene and many others throughout the film, Arnold's humor, charisma, and geniality jump off the screen. Each time he appears, his screen presence positively radiates. It is no wonder that many viewers believe the film is exclusively about him rather than about the other bodybuilders who also appear. The cameras follow him to Gold's Gym, to Muscle Beach, to a federal prison where he puts on an exhibition for male and female inmates. It's not even particularly jarring to hear a black prisoner commenting afterward, "He's got a beautiful body, man." So thoroughly had Arnold heterosexualized the sport by 1975 that a line like this doesn't even raise an eyebrow. A few years earlier, it would have taken on a very different meaning in a film about bodybuilding.

The film actually chronicled the quest of four bodybuilders: two amateurs vying for Mr. Universe and two professionals competing at Mr. Olympia. The competitors at Mr. Olympia were Arnold and Lou Ferrigno, a still unknown giant from Brooklyn who was far and away the biggest bodybuilder on the circuit, at six feet five and 285 pounds. Ferrigno clearly posed a genuine threat to Schwarzenegger's dominance. In contrast to the brash chutzpah the viewers see in Arnold throughout the film, Ferrigno's story is largely told through the prism of his relationship with his dad, Matty, an overbearing Italian stage father living his dreams vicariously through his reticent son.

Even though it is clear that Ferrigno was in much better form than Arnold, he ended up in third place in his weight class, behind a French competitor, while Arnold won both the class and the overall title, taking his sixth straight Mr. Olympia. Ferrigno never did win Mr. Olympia, but he had some consolation two years later when he beat out Arnold for an iconic television role as the Incredible Hulk.

The last scene shows Arnold smoking a celebratory joint while sporting a T-shirt that reads, "Arnold is numero uno."

When the film was released in 1977, to great acclaim, it was an immediate sensation and Arnold became a star almost overnight. But there was also a great deal of controversy, and the filmmakers soon found themselves on the defensive about charges that they had scripted and staged certain portions of the film for dramatic effect. Arnold himself admitted that he had made up some of the stories he told. "There were certain things that were not true and that's why we never call it a documentary, we call it a docudrama," he explains. "Because certain things were created in order to make it more interesting. It was very clear that the only way we could raise the money to make the movie was to make it more dramatic. They said let's create a hero, let's create a villain, let's create a guy who psychs out his opponents, let's create a guy who falls for that." He claims that the filmmakers' original intention was to make Lou Ferrigno the villain, the 285-pound monster who would vanquish little Arnie Schwarzenegger. "But then they discovered he was actually quite vulnerable, that he had a hearing problem, that he relied on his father for a lot of stuff, that he was a huge guy but didn't necessarily have the presence to win, so they switched it around. They made me the villain who plays tricks on people, who psychs out his opponents and that wipes out the competition year after year." He decided, he says, to make himself out to be like a machine, calculating, a guy who doesn't care about his own friend; he says that he was willing to do a whole psych-out on Lou Ferrigno. "I loved Lou," he says, "there was no reason to psych him out, I knew I was going to win, that he just wasn't there yet." One of the most memorable passages in the film had Arnold telling a story to the camera about the coldness necessary to be a champion. His father, Gustav, had died in 1972 and he used the family tragedy as a backdrop to illustrate his point.

"I have to cut my emotions off before a competition," he says in the film. "I trained myself for that to be totally cold and not have things go into my mind. It was the same story when my father died. My mother called me on the phone and she said your dad died and this was exactly two months before a contest. She says, 'Are you coming home for the funeral?' I said, 'No. It's too late. He's dead, there's nothing to be done and I'm sorry, I can't come.' It actually caused the greatest conflict with my girlfriend. She said, 'It doesn't bother you?' and I said, 'No.'"

But Arnold later claimed that this never happened; it was an anecdote he borrowed from a French bodybuilder four years earlier when he heard the man say he couldn't go home for his father's funeral because he had to stay focused. "I stole that story. I said, 'I have to say that story. People will be shocked. People will be writing about that story, that's how you sell the tickets.'" Most of the later revisions, Arnold claimed, are things that made him look bad, that critics singled out, unflattering aspects of his personality that he was anxious to sanitize.

But a subsequent investigation by the *New York Times* discovered that Arnold had in fact skipped his father's funeral, despite his claim that the incident was made up. Subsequently, he furnished a number of conflicting explanations over the years about why he didn't attend. He had a leg injury; he didn't hear about it in time. The truth will probably never be known, though it may be as simple as the fact that he hated the man who had abused him and was not particularly sentimental about his death.

I asked George Butler about Arnold's claims regarding the manipulation of the plot. Was much of the film scripted for dramatic effect, as he claims?

"We did do that at a few points, but that was for cohesion," Butler explained; "and I would tell Arnold that we needed something here or there and could he think of something from his youth or from previous competitions that would bridge the gaps or would enhance the understanding of his world. That he just thought up things as he was going along I didn't know about until later."

The controversy over how much of *Pumping Iron* was true, however, paled in comparison with what followed. In 1997, Butler circulated a proposal for a book he intended to call *The Master Plan*, about what went on behind the scenes while he was making *Pumping Iron*. It purported to contain verbatim transcripts of material that was not used in the film. The most explosive alleged that Arnold had expressed admiration for Adolf Hitler. In one interview that ended up on the cutting-room floor, for example, Arnold is asked, "Who do you admire most?"

The response: "It depends for what. I admired Hitler, for instance, because he came from being a little man with almost no formal education up to power. And I admire him for being such a good public speaker and for what he did with it."

In his proposal, Butler claims that at the time of filming, he considered Schwarzenegger a "flagrant, outspoken admirer of Hitler." In addition, he claims to have seen Arnold playing "Nazi marching songs from long-playing records in his collection at home." More alarmingly, he "frequently clicked his heels and pretended to be an SS officer."

When the *New York Times* got hold of Butler's proposal, it asked Arnold for an explanation, but he claimed not to recall making those statements. "Let me tell you something," he replied. "It's one of those things that if you come from that background, you get accused a lot of times of being that, of being a Nazi. So you know I despise anything that Hitler stands for, anything he has done, hated the Nazism, hated what was done during the Second World War." He added that he did consider the Führer to be a "great public speaker" but that Hitler had used his talent for "something negative."

When the controversy exploded, Butler claims he went back to his house in New Hampshire and found a different transcript of the interview in question. This one differed from the wording he had mentioned in the book proposal:

"I admire him for being such a good public speaker and for his way of getting to the people and so on," Arnold says in the second transcript. "But I didn't admire him for what he did with it. It's very hard to say who I admire, who are my heroes." Butler said his transcribers may have had trouble getting down the correct wording because of Arnold's thick Austrian accent.

When the *Times* contacted Peter Davis, who had actually conducted the interviews, he stuck by the original transcript, saying that's the way he remembered it. But Davis pointed out that Arnold's words had been taken out of context and that Schwarzenegger went on to say he had changed his views about Hitler while growing up in Austria. "He went right on to say, basically, as soon as he woke up, his hero became John F. Kennedy, and he was shaking his head at himself," Davis recalled. He did not explain the SS marching songs or the Nazi-style clicking of heels that Butler had witnessed. The matter could have been cleared up simply by viewing the outtakes, but Arnold had in fact purchased all the footage from Butler in 1991 for a sum of $1.2 million. When the *Times* asked to view the footage, he was somewhat cagey.

"I don't know where they are now but I'm sure we have them," he said. "I've never held them in my hand."

Among the other claims Butler made in the book proposal was that Arnold had said he wished he could experience the rush and adulation of speaking to a huge crowd of people. "The feeling like Kennedy had, you know, to speak to maybe 50,000 people at one time and having them cheer, or like Hitler in the Nuremberg stadium and have all those people scream at you and just being in total agreement with whatever you say."

At another point in the transcript, Arnold appears to have an authoritarian streak.

"We can't live without authority," he tells the filmmakers. "Because I feel that a certain amount of people who were meant to do this and control, and a large amount, like 95 percent, of the people who we have to tell what to do and how to keep order. That is why I am all for it. . . . I feel if you want to create a strong nation and a strong country you cannot let everybody be an individual, because everybody has his own opinions and you can't just stick together as a strong nation. Then you have to tell people what to do and you can't just let them float away. In Germany there was a lot of unity. The German soldiers were the best, and with the police force and everything."

But he takes pain to stress that he doesn't approve of what Hitler did with his army. "It was misused on the power. First, it started having, I mean, getting Germany out of the great recession and having everybody jobs and so on and then it was just misused. And they said, let's take this country, and let's wipe out this country, and let's wipe out whole Europe, and let's get America, and so on. That's bad."

The ghostwriter of Arnold's 1977 autobiography, Arnold Kent Hall, claims that he too saw Arnold twice imitate Hitler "for laughs," and even produced two photos of Arnold pulling his hair down over his fore-head, using his comb as a Hitler mustache and raising his arm in a mock Nazi salute. "To some people that is funny and to some people it is not funny," Hall said, explaining that it was in the beginning phase of Arnold's acting career.

These were not the only potentially embarrassing photos taken of Arnold during this period. Butler had taken thousands of photos, including numerous nude shots and other possibly compromising shots that Arnold was anxious to keep away from the public eye. As part of his 1991 deal to sell the rights to the *Pumping Iron* footage and outtakes, Butler also agreed to let Arnold's associate Neal Nordlinger comb through his extensive collection with an eye to exorcising unfavorable images. According to the memo I obtained:

The sellers agree that Nordlinger has the right to examine in the presence of Butler all of the still photographs of Schwarzenegger owned and/or controlled by Butler or any affiliate thereof and Nordlinger may destroy any of such photographs and negatives of such photographs, as well as copies thereof, which in Nordlinger's opinion are either embarrassing to Schwarzenegger or in any way reflect negatively on Schwarzenegger's professional or private life.

Nordlinger destroyed forty-three photos, and Butler has never revealed their contents or explained just how embarrassing they might have been.

Butler has reconciled with Arnold after an initial falling-out about the book proposal. Today he downplays the accusations in the proposal and says he doesn't believe Arnold admires Nazis. Nevertheless, I was anxious to discover for myself whether there was anything to his original allegations. As the son of a Holocaust survivor, I was particularly anxious to know whether Arnold's vast fortune and long tentacles have been used to cover up the truth and to sanitize his real views about race. Is he an anti-Semite? A racist? Can the apple really have fallen that far from the tree?

This was one of the very first questions I asked Ben Weider when I first met him several years ago. The question was a natural one, since at the time I knew very little about Schwarzenegger's past except for a vague memory about the controversy over the allegations of Nazism.

"I can tell you that Arnold is not a Nazi sympathizer. I have known him for a long, long time. As you know, I am a very proud Jew. If I thought he was a Nazi or a Jew-basher, I wouldn't have anything to do with the guy and neither would my brother. Take it from me. Did he say some stupid things at the beginning of his career? The guy had literally got off the boat from Austria, the place where Hitler was from. His father was a dyed-in-the-wool Nazi. He grew up just after the war. I'm sure he grew up hearing a lot of not so nice things about Jewish people. But he had a lot of Jewish friends later on. My brother has been like a dad to him. He hated his own dad, you know. He told me the guy beat the shit out of him, so it's not like he's likely to cling to his father's beliefs."

It was a convincing defense, and I knew Ben well enough to know that he wouldn't have anything to do with a Nazi sympathizer. Still, the Weiders have never been particularly objective about their longtime cash cow.

To make sense of the past, I needed to tap the contacts I had acquired during my undercover foray on Muscle Beach. By now, Schwarzenegger was so powerful and his mentor Joe Weider's influence so far-reaching that their tentacles extended everywhere I searched. One person I contacted, a onetime bodybuilding power player and potential key source, told me outright he is terrified to go public. He wrote me, explaining why he was reluctant to cooperate. "They basically ruined and bankrupted me."

One person who had no such compunctions, one of the few elite bodybuilders who have been willing to publicly criticize both Weider and Schwarzenegger, is the former Mr. Universe, Robby Robinson, a formidable figure in the history of bodybuilding known as the "Black Prince." Robinson was a former friend and colleague of Arnold's and was under contract to Joe Weider for years. In fact, Weider created a statue of himself, prominently displayed in his office, featuring a bodybuilder's perfectly sculptured physique that he admits was based on the body of Robinson. I concluded that the Black Prince could be the perfect person to serve as a consultant for my own planned documentary and open doors in the bodybuilding world that might otherwise be closed to me and my cameras.

I met with Robinson for the first time one day at Venice Beach's French Market café. As he took me on a tour of the landmarks, including the original Gold's Gym, where he and Schwarzenegger had trained together more than thirty years ago, he painted a picture of Arnold Schwarzenegger very different from the devious but good-natured rascal portrayed in *Pumping Iron*, a film in which Robinson also appeared.

He describes the so-called golden age of bodybuilding—the early to mid-1970s when Arnold was in his prime—as the "feudal kingdom of Joe and Arnold." Conditions for most bodybuilders, he recalls, were brutal. The most prize money a champion could hope to win, he says, was $1,000. As Robinson saw it, Weider was accumulating a vast fortune from the sweat of his minions while giving them virtually nothing in return.

"If you complained about the bad conditions back then," Robinson continues, "(Joe) Weider would blacklist you. The money we made was impossible to survive on. We all needed to do other things on the side. Not Arnie. Weider took care of him." It got so bad, Robinson reveals, that at one point he and his fellow athletes attempted to form a union.

"Arnold pretended he was interested, even attended some meetings, but then he backstabbed everyone by telling Joe Weider what we were up to," he recalls.

Robinson also claims that Arnold told him he had started taking steroids in Austria at the age of fourteen and that he still took a massive amount when they were training together. "It was still legal. I did it too," he says.

Although there is really no way for him to prove it, Robinson believes the judging at competitions was corrupt, deliberately slanted to favor Schwarzenegger. "They all saw Arnie as the great white hope," he says, complaining that black bodybuilders were at an immediate disadvantage because they didn't fit into Weider's marketing plans. "I lived in a warehouse, making less than $200 per week," he recalls. "I had to leave America and go to Europe because Weider kept it as a cult. He made it slavery. Racism to the fullest. He gave Arnie seminars, showcases, and put it all into him. He put nothing into the black bodybuilders."

Arnold, he claims, was well aware of the situation, took advantage of it, and even taunted the black bodybuilders with racist insults. "Arnie certainly harbored racist views because he was brought up in that environment. He tried to hide from everyone that his father was a Nazi, but there were times in the locker room when he seemed to brag about it. It was frightening."

Robinson's most startling claim was that Arnold regularly called him a "nigger." The most blatant example—which he says was witnessed by seven or eight other bodybuilders—took place at a banquet after San Diego's Russ Warner Classic when Arnold started shouting, "Down with blacks, nigger this, and blacks that for several minutes while everybody just sat there in shock."

I tell him I need confirmation or some other proof. "Call Ricky Wayne," he tells me. Rick Wayne is one of the all-time greats, the first black superstar of the sport, a three-time Mr. Universe and two-time Mr. World who knew Schwarzenegger well and trained with him for years, although Wayne's own peak years came before Arnold's reign. Wayne definitely had the credibility and the firsthand knowledge to confirm or deny Robinson's explosive claims. And if anything, what Wayne told me was even more shocking. Now the editor of a newspaper in Saint Lucia, Wayne was all too glad to fill me in on the bodybuilding scene of the 1970s. Was Arnold really a racist, as Robinson claims?

"That's a tough one," he tells me. "I mean, I'm a black man who has known and been friends with Arnold for almost forty years. There were other black guys that he trained with and competed with and did business with, so it would be hard to see him as a flat-out racist, but he did have an insensitivity streak a mile wide."

Wayne describes the period during the filming of *Pumping Iron* when he and the other bodybuilders had been recruited by Arnold to participate in the movie and sign releases. Arnold, he said, had some kind of arrangement with the producers and was getting a considerable sum of money for his participation.

"We were at Arnold's house and he had gathered us and I staged a walkout and said I wanted nothing to do with it if the only one getting paid for it was Arnold. It was then agreed that we would all get something—I think it was a hundred bucks a day. But Arnold hated that—he hated that I stood up to him and—that was when I would hear him say, 'Nigger this, and nigger that.' That's the first time I saw the racist slurs directed at me personally, but he would talk that shit all the time. We were all very close to Joe Weider at the time. I wrote for his publications often, and it was even assumed that Arnold was going to one day take over the Weider empire, but (Arnold) wanted to go in a different direction. I remember watching Arnold following Joe around one day making one anti-Semitic remark after another—telling awful Jewish jokes, pretending he was Hitler, doing the salute—poor Joe was so upset that he was almost crying over it."

He recalls another troubling racial slur. "I remember him talking to me once about apartheid in South Africa and listening to him saying that it was a good thing and that if the black people were ever allowed to have any power, it would be a mess and this beautiful modern country would sink into the mud, things like that—remember, he was saying this stuff about South Africa knowing that the competition (in *Pumping Iron*) was actually happening in Pretoria."

Like Robinson, Wayne says Arnold was a heavy user of steroids. "In fact, I remember it was Arnold that gave me my first bottle of Dianabol," he recalls. "We all did whatever we could to get the edge. Arnold would do virtually anything to win—he would hit on a guy's girlfriend to knock him mentally off his game. He was a winner in competition because he was a great competitor—he didn't care what he would have to do to win; winning was, and is, everything to him."

Wayne's account seems to confirm a story told by yet another black bodybuilder to Wendy Leigh twenty years ago. Dave DuPre, who also appeared in *Pumping Iron,* told her that one day while they were working out at Gold's Gym, Arnold told him, "Black people are inferior. You are not capable of achieving the success of white people. Black people are stupid." DuPre also claimed that he heard Arnold make a number of anti-Semitic remarks. "He would make fun of the Jews. If anybody looked Jewish, he would point it out and tell them that they were inferior. I would remind him that it was a Jew who had brought him to America. Then he would shut up."

The stories that Wayne and Robinson told me were eye-opening, but I wasn't interested in performing a hatchet job. That accomplishes nothing except to present a one-dimensional, inaccurate portrait of your subject. I needed a bodybuilder who could give me another side of the story, but I already knew that few of Arnold's friends were willing to talk to me without getting a formal go-ahead from Arnold himself. This made a documentary almost impossible, even undercover, because in California—unlike other locales where I had produced exposés in the past—it was illegal to film with a hidden camera, and most of the bodybuilders still live in California. But I needed to get the inside scoop from somebody who still admires the subject of my book. I already knew who was on top of my wish list—Lou Ferrigno, the Incredible Hulk himself, who is said to be still close to the governor, despite having been bested in the most famous bodybuilding tournament in history, his ignominious defeat preserved on celluloid and watched by tens of millions of people over the years.

I had already been warned by another former bodybuilder that Lou wouldn't say a negative word about Arnold, "because he got the same preferential treatment from Weider as Arnold did. He and Arnold were spoon-fed by Weider because they were white, good looking, and marketable all over the world."

Another of my contacts tipped me off that, despite his lucrative acting gigs—most recently, he had played himself for years on *King of Queens*—Ferrigno still supplemented his income by taking on private fitness clients. This was the perfect entrée for me, but there was just one problem. One of the recent private clients happened to be Michael Jackson, who had hired Ferrigno to get him into shape prior to *This Is It*, the tour that the singer never lived to perform. Only a few months earlier, I had written a book about Jackson's final days, *Unmasked*, that ended up number one on the *New York Times* best-seller list. As a result, my face was everywhere, appearing on virtually every major television talk show nonstop for weeks. Ferrigno had to have seen me and was sure to be suspicious the moment I walked through his door. The book itself had been very controversial and, as a friend of Michael's, Ferrigno would want no part of helping its author— unless he actually read it.

The truth was that *Unmasked* was an extremely sympathetic portrait of the singer and ultimately proved that he was innocent of the charges of child sexual abuse that had dogged the final years of his life and destroyed his career. When his own family members read my book and realized that it cleared his name and reputation of the heinous charges, many of them, including his father, Joe, embraced me and offered their encouragement. However, it was another of the book's revelations that ended up getting even more attention. I had exposed the fact that the singer was gay and had interviewed two of his former lovers, both adult men. When that fact came to light, the homophobia of a large segment of Jackson's fan base reared its ugly head, sparking calls from all over the world to boycott the book.

Given his prominence in both Hollywood and the world of bodybuilding, where gays are everywhere, I didn't expect Ferrigno to mind the revelation all that much. I suspect that like most of Jackson's entourage, he already knew. But I wasn't about to take any chances. After I used the private number I had been given and talked to him personally, introducing myself as Alfred Newman and agreeing to pay $400 for a one-hour workout, I chose the most outlandish sunglasses I could find, a pair that would surely disguise my now well-known features.

When I arrive at his palatial house in Santa Monica, not far from the original Muscle Beach, Ferrigno greets me warmly and introduces me to his wife, Shanna. He then takes me to an extension in the back where he has built a huge private gym. I ask Lou if he could put me through the same workout he did for Michael for *This Is It*. "No problem," he says. "It's tough, but I think you can do it."

He starts me on the hang bars doing sets of ten lifts pulling myself up to the bar. It's grueling and I cannot believe Michael had been able to pull it off, given what I know about his health—especially during his final months, when he was skeletal. But I hold my tongue. Then Ferrigno gets me on the treadmill for fifteen minutes. This exercise is followed by repetitions, lifting small weights. He then takes out a large ball, the same blue ball that Michael had worked on. He has me do the same repetition: lifting my stomach up while I'm lying on the big plastic ball. "If you do this, in a short time you will lose your pot and won't look like you're expecting twins," he tells me.

Although I am anxious to talk about Arnold, we spend most of the first half of the workout discussing Jackson. He says he had trained Jackson for two decades, including two to three times a week in the months leading up to the tragically aborted *This Is It* tour.

When he discovers I'm from the Laurentian Mountains near Montreal, he tells me he knows the area well and travels to Montreal frequently for comic book conventions and trade shows where he signs autographs and Hulk memorabilia. He had been there just three months earlier, in fact. I steer the subject to Jackson. What was he like?

"Michael loved to play pranks," he reveals. "He was very funny and very cooperative. The only time I ever got mad at him is when he showed up at my gym at ten o'clock at night wearing a mask. I had to tell him: Michael, don't worry; there's no paparazzi around. Then he'd take off his mask."

I ask him about his own background. "I grew up in Brooklyn and had a dad who I had mixed feelings about. Many times we didn't see eye to eye. My dream was to live in California. I moved there in 1976 and lived on the beach for the first two weeks. I didn't have a dime. Fortunately, Joe Weider discovered me and lent me a couple hundred bucks and got my career started. I'm still good friends with Joe. I had dinner with him a few weeks ago. His brother Ben passed on last year. Joe couldn't attend the funeral, because he has health problems. I don't think he wanted to go back there. Joe was a good businessman. Lots of people might have had issues with him, but I didn't. We're still close to this day."

It was just the opening that I needed to bring up Arnold Schwarzenegger. "We've been good friends for thirty years," he tells me. "He was a great athlete. He always worked hard. I still see him often. In fact, in three weeks I'm going to his Arnold Classic in Ohio. He brings me in every year."

Was Arnold the greatest of all time? I ask. "No, that would definitely be Sergio Oliva," Ferrigno says, pointing to a photo of the black Cuban great on the wall alongside a gallery of other top bodybuilders. I notice there is no photo of Arnold among them.

"Nobody could top Sergio," he continues. "But Arnold was great. He probably worked the hardest of anybody. He and Robby Robinson were probably tied for second place as the best I ever saw," he says, refer-ring to my most recent interview subject.

I tell him I once heard that Arnold had directed racial slurs at Robinson. Did he ever any hear any of that stuff?

"Sure," he replies without hesitation. "But that wasn't Arnold being a racist, that was him trying to get a rise out of somebody. He didn't mean that stuff. He'd always be saying stuff like that, mostly in fun. He wasn't the only one—that's the way the guys talked in the gym. I think he used to call me a wop or a dago or something because I was Italian, but I didn't take it se-riously. It was just part of the whole scene. Don't read too much into it."

I tell him I'm Jewish. Did Arnold ever badmouth the Jews?

"Probably, the same way he did everybody else, but he wasn't an anti-Semite, believe me. No way. Joe and Ben Weider are Jewish; they were very close. He had lots of Jewish friends—they'll all tell you he likes Jews. Hey, come on, look where he worked before he was governor. Hollywood. Let me tell you, I work there too. You're not going to get far in Hollywood if you're an anti-Semite. The Jews don't control the business, that's a myth, but they're everywhere and a lot of them are pricks like lots of others in the town, but a lot of them are wonderful people, most of them are. If you're an anti-Semite going in, you'll change your mind in a big hurry. They should make every Jew-hater work in Hollywood for a year."

He tells me that a lot of the other bodybuilders were resentful of Arnold because of his popularity. "I don't know exactly what it was, but people on the scene were jealous," he says. "I think it was because he made so much money and got the royal treatment from Joe Weider. I can understand their concerns, but Arnold always worked hard."

The entire time I worked out with him, I kept my zebra sunglasses on, telling him that I had a condition that made me sensitive to light. Nevertheless, he told me twice during our session that I seemed "familiar." The entire time I was with him, I was terrified that my identity would be discovered and I would get my butt kicked by the Incredible Hulk. But the session ended uneventfully. He told me that I had done well and that if I came back regularly, my pot would disappear in no time.

My hour with Ferrigno had given me a more objective perspective on Arnold's personality and attitudes in the 1970s. But there was still one person I needed to talk to in order to get an idea of what he's like today— his longtime best friend, Franco Columbu, who spent more time with Arnold during that golden era than anybody else alive and has kept up the close friendship for more than forty years. Arnold's Sardinian body-building colleague was, even then, studying to be a chiropractor, and he now practices chiropractic medicine in Los Angeles. I knew he would never grant me an official interview, but there was one surefire way to talk to him. I decided to make a chiropractic appointment, complaining that I had recently taken up weight lifting and was now suffering from a number of related back ailments. The only problem was that Columbu was one of the most highly regarded chiropractors in Southern California, with a roster of celebrity clients a mile long. There was a waiting list of more than six months, I was informed when I called to make an appointment. That's when I decided to drop a name I knew might open the door. "Tell him I'm an old friend of Ben Weider from Montreal," I told the receptionist. "He always told me Dr. Columbu was the best." Sure enough, I was given an appointment almost immediately. When I arrived at the nondescript Santa Monica office, Columbu's receptionist gave me some forms to fill out detailing my medical background. I answered no to everything on the form, even though I had undergone a surgical procedure just two weeks earlier. I wanted to see if he would notice my condition without my disclosing it. He didn't.

In the waiting room, there were a number of blown-up photos of Dr. Columbu during his heyday as a world-class bodybuilder and powerlifter. On the table in the waiting room, there was a book called *Arnold Schwarzenegger's Encyclopedia of Modern Bodybuilding.*

After I finished filling out the forms, Columbu appeared and introduced himself. I couldn't help but notice that he had dyed his hair the same brown-gold color as that of his friend Arnold. He was still broad-shouldered, but he had long ago lost his once formidable physique. I was a little shocked at how short he was, no more than five feet six. He looked to me like a large fire hydrant.

His accent was still thick. "I'm from Sardinia," he announced. He asked me how I had found out about his practice, and I told him I was an old friend of Ben Weider, who said he was the best in the business. "Any friend of Ben is a friend of mine," he told me. "I love Canadians. By the time I'm through with you, you'll feel like a new man."

Ushering me into a small room, he asked me to lie down on a massage-type table and started to feel the pressure points in my back, which he told me is too straight. "I need to bend it into proper shape," he informed me. He put me through some rigorous exercises and then had me lift weights. Then came the sales pitch. He recommended a special Swiss shoe called MBT. He happened to be wearing it and would be glad to sell me a pair then and there. "I sell them at least 20 percent cheaper than if you order them online." He also told me I would have to see him once a week for "the next few months," and then every two weeks after that. At $220 a session, this plan could run into some serious cash. I told him I'd be traveling a lot and would have to check my schedule. The whole time I couldn't help thinking he sounded more like a businessman than a medical professional; and I remembered his notorious first enterprise, Pumping Bricks, which he and Arnold ran together in the early 1970s. As I was getting dressed, I took the opportunity to bring up the subject of Arnold for the first time. I asked how Arnold was doing. "He comes in here all the time and I work on his back," Columbu told me. "He takes very good care of himself. He's one of the fittest people I've ever met."

I said Ben Weider had told me that Columbu and Arnold used to be pretty "wild." He laughed.

"That's when we were young," he told me. "We've grown up since then. Now we're boring. All we do is play chess." I told him that as a son of a Holocaust survivor, I was a little shocked when I heard that Arnold had once said he admired Hitler. Columbu immediately reassured me. "I've known him for over forty years and if there's one thing I can tell you, it's that Arnold never had an anti-Semitic bone in his body. I didn't know him in Austria, but I knew him practically since he was a boy and he always hated Hitler. Always. When he was young, he used to say crazy things to shock people—that's the way he was, you know—but he didn't mean it; it was always to get a rise. I remember long before he went into politics, before he met Maria even, that he was a big supporter of Israel; he always rooted for Israel. Ben could tell you that. He loved Arnold. People say, 'Some of my best friends are Jews,' and you right away get suspicious, but in Arnold's case, everybody close to him was Jewish."

He laughs. "Well, maybe not everybody," he adds. "I'm not a Jew."

I couldn't directly ask Columbu about his friend's alleged Nazi sympathies, for fear of arousing his suspicion. But I still didn't quite know what to make of Butler's assertion that, during the 1970s, Arnold was a "flagrant, outspoken admirer of Hitler." In the years since he became an international celebrity, the publicity machine surrounding Schwarzenegger has become a master of damage control, responding to any negative publicity with a tightly controlled spin. One of the most effective techniques has been to rally the vast array of Arnold's fiercely loyal friends and colleagues, in both Austria and America—what one biographer terms the "Arnia"—who can be summoned to defend their famous friend at a moment's notice. Almost as soon as Butler's allegation initially surfaced, reporters were quietly directed to contact Arnold's old instructor, Kurt Marnul, in Graz. When they did so, he told them a story that he had apparently never told before to the numerous biographers and media figures who had interviewed him about Arnold over the years. Nor did Arnold himself ever tell the story in the hundreds of interviews he has granted about his youth.

Now, Marnul claimed that in the early 1960s Alfred Gerstl had regularly summoned him to send his weight-lifters to break up neo-Nazi rallies in Graz and that Arnold frequently participated in those rallies. Marnul claimed that he once saw Nazi soldiers kill three people at a concentration camp—two Jews and one child—and that this motivated him to break up neo-Nazi rallies later in life. "It's absurd. It's 100 percent wrong that [Arnold] could have ever liked Hitler," he declared. And while it's possible that the gym owner himself might have broken up neo-Nazi rallies, when Gerstl was contacted, he didn't quite back up Marnul's story about Arnold's participation. However, he was no less adamant in rejecting Butler's allegations.

"[Arnold's] father was an old Nazi—there were many of them around then—but Arnold was completely the opposite," says Gerstl. "He's a committed antifascist. Arnold isn't a Nazi and he never was one."

The idea of a youthful Arnold battling neo-Nazis in the streets—widely reported after Marnul told the story—makes for a compelling and heroic image, but it has about as much basis in reality as the *Terminator* movies. The truth, it seems, is somewhat milder. In the early 1960s, a bold Graz schoolmaster organized a field trip to Mauthausen, Austria's notorious Nazi concentration camp, which has been preserved as a museum. Right-wing (but not neo-Nazi) groups, which for decades discouraged any reminder of Austria's Nazi past, staged a rally denouncing the teacher. Arnold, it appears, may have participated in a counterdemonstration organized in part by Alfred Gerstl and his People's Party to denounce the protesters. This appears to be the extent of Arnold's antifascist activities, and even it is sketchy because Arnold himself has, curiously, never mentioned it. Indeed, he appears to have acknowledged that, as a young man, he once admired Hitler until he "woke up" and his hero became John F. Kennedy.

Nevertheless, by the time I completed my own investigation, I had become convinced to my satisfaction—and relief—that Arnold Schwarzenegger is no Nazi sympathizer, or even an anti-Semite, and that if he ever held those abhorrent views, he abandoned them a long time ago. In fact, in the years since his reign as a bodybuilder, Arnold appears to have shed most of the anachronistic attitudes of his Austrian youth and become quite enlightened on many social issues. Indeed, by the time *Pumping Iron* introduced him to the world in 1977, he was well on his way to a more enlightened worldview. And yet, despite his serious long-time relationship with Barbara Outland, he still appeared to cling to at least one neanderthal attitude— his stated belief that women were simply "sexual playthings."

He was about to meet the woman who may or may not have changed that.

15.

Meeting Maria

Long before he became a member of the Kennedy family, it seems, Arnold was almost obsessed with the Kennedys, and with John F. Kennedy in particular. When he paid more than $750,000 for a set of the former president's golf clubs a few years ago, people simply assumed that the purchase was a tribute to his in-laws.

But to gain some insight into Arnold's fascination with the clan that has been described as America's equivalent of royalty, one has only to travel back to the week when *Pumping Iron* premiered in September 1976.

George Butler had given a lot of thought to how he wanted his new film promoted. Instead of launching it in Los Angeles, the center of the bodybuilding world, he decided to hold the premiere in New York, center of hip celebrity culture. It was exactly the cachet he wanted associated with the film. Butler had no desire to reach the people who traditionally attended body-building events. He was seeking to introduce Arnold Schwarzenegger, and the still obscure sport, to a whole new audience. And he knew just the man for the job.

Bobby Zarem was considered an up-and-coming public relations genius, a superflack. Among his clients at the time were Dustin Hoffman, Cher, Cybill Shepherd, and James Caan. A couple of years earlier, Zarem had famously rented the Fifty-seventh Street subway station and invited 700 guests to a black-tie dinner to promote the Who's rock musical *Tommy*. He was still a year away from developing the iconic "I ♥ New York" ad campaign, but he was already being referred to as the "prince of pitch."

Zarem's task as press agent was to round up as many celebrities as possible from his vast network of contacts to attract attention in the gossip columns that Butler knew would make or break the film. The director was particularly anxious to attract Andy Warhol, whose nightly presence at Studio 54 had garnered nonstop buzz for the famous disco in New York and around the world. But when Zarem met with Arnold Schwarzenegger, there was only one celebrity on Arnold's wish list—Jacqueline Kennedy Onassis. She was the one person he most wanted to meet, he confided—the woman who had been married to his hero, JFK. Zarem told Arnold he'd see what he could do. Fortunately, he happened to have a friend who worked for America's most famous widow, and it took only a phone call and a hastily improvised luncheon to achieve Arnold's wish.

Zarem arranged a get-together at Elaine's, one of Manhattan's most fashionable hot spots, a few days before the actual launch. Among the invited guests were Warhol, Paulette Goddard, and George Plimpton, along with assorted other glitterati assembled from Zarem's Rolodex. And an hour after the luncheon began, who should walk in the door but none other than Jacqueline Kennedy Onassis herself. Arnold was starstruck at first when he was introduced to the glamorous former first lady, and the two didn't have a lot to talk about. "She likes very much where I came from," Schwarzenegger later recalled of their conversation. But the brief chit-chat was all Zarem needed to put his plan into action. He had a photographer waiting, ready to snap a photo of Arnold speaking to Jackie. That was all it took. The next day, the photo appeared in newspapers all over the country, conferring not only instant credibility on the upcoming film but overnight celebrity by association on Arnold.

The premiere itself was no less celebrity-packed, probably as a result of Jackie O's imprimatur. Paul Simon, Mikhail Baryshnikov, James Taylor, Carly Simon, Tom Wolfe, and countless others jammed into the Plaza Theater to see what all the fuss was about. Laraine Newman, one of the hot new Ready for Prime Time Players on *Saturday Night Live*, showed up only because the show's producer, Lorne Michaels, gave her his ticket. When a journalist asked her why throngs of celebs would come out for a film about bodybuilding, she replied, "Oh, they're probably bored."

One of the moviegoers was even less enthusiastic. "Ugh! All these ghastly people showing up for muscles!" complained the daughter of the acclaimed Broadway composer Richard Rodgers. Indeed, at the front of the theater prior to the screening, Arnold had assembled five bodybuilders, including Lou Ferrigno, to pose and flex for the assembled crowd. Meanwhile, he mingled, wearing a tuxedo that had to be custom made when no rental could be found to accommodate his massive frame.

Butler's effort proved successful beyond his wildest imaginings as news of the film and countless interviews with Arnold began to appear in the nation's media, including countless references in the gossip and society pages. All of a sudden, it seemed everybody wanted a piece of him, and the film hadn't even been officially released yet. Arnold was reveling in the adulation and took full advantage of it, sensing that he had only a short time to get noticed and capitalize on all the attention.

His ex-girlfriend Barbara Outland recalled that Arnold's ego had made him "insufferable" even before *Pumping Iron* made him a star, noting that after his role in *Stay Hungry* he was "classically conceited—the world revolved around him." By the time *Pumping Iron* brought an even brighter spotlight, George Butler recalled the way Arnold was beginning to talk about his future. "He was enormously intelligent and enormously crude, and he said then that he had a recurring dream that he would be king of the earth. He had a master plan. He wanted to be a movie star, a millionaire, and have enormous power."

He was already talking to his friends and mentors about acquiring enormous power, and he had frequently confided in his friends and colleagues his eventual plan to enter politics one day. But as the media called him for profiles—looking for the same kind of entertaining and outrageous quotes that he had supplied in the film—he appears to have let his guard down, giving the kind of candid interviews that no savvy politician would ever allow in the public arena. Indeed, many of his quotes from this period would be used against him when he did decide to run for political office more than a quarter century later. The most notorious interview he gave at the time was for a Q and A with the now-defunct *Oui* magazine, the same interview in which he bragged that he and his friends had participated in an orgy with a black groupie at the back of Gold's Gym. Having elicited this sordid gem, the interviewer decided to pursue the sex theme and see just how much further Arnold was willing to open up:

OUI: Do you think that your familiarity with your body gives you a sounder mind sexually?

SCHWARZENEGGER: I don't have any sexual hang-ups, but I'm sure there are bodybuilders who have trouble with sex, and obviously the body building hasn't helped. Still, if you're in touch with your body, you certainly have an enormous sexual advantage. The mind-body connection is the same in sex as it is in training. If I tell myself to train the thighs, then the calves, it's boom, boom, mind-thighs, mind-calves, mind-this, mind-that. And it's the same with fucking— mind-cock. You're in touch. You realize you have a body. Ninety percent of the people, though, don't realize that there is anything below the head. They think that the head is carried around by something very mysterious, and they're not aware that it's the body, something they should be in tune with.

OUI: Stirling Moss, the British racing-car champion, claimed that he'd never fuck the night before a race because it would sap his competitive drive. Does anything like that apply to bodybuilders, say, on the eve of the Mr. Olympia contest?

SCHWARZENEGGER: I get laid on purpose. I can't sleep before competition and I'm up all night, anyway, so instead of staring at the ceiling I figure I might as well find somebody and fuck.

OUI: Doesn't it take the edge off your performance?

SCHWARZENEGGER: No, why should it? For ten years, I've been building a physique. It's not going to run away after one night. What Moss and others are talking about is a totally mental thing: If you feel that something's going to affect your body, then it definitely will. I've always found that sex gives me a kind of calm, and I'm much more in control because of it. It's the same for friends of mine who are also top bodybuilders. The guys who are working their way up often say they have to sleep ten hours a day and they try not to get laid more than three times a week, but, sooner or later, most of them find out that all this means shit. Whether you sleep two hours or ten, get laid a dozen times a week or not at all, eat three meals or five, at the end of the week you look absolutely the same; there's no difference.

OUI: So you believe in writing your own rules?

SCHWARZENEGGER: Exactly. There are bodybuilders who are afraid of indulging in sex or even of playing other sports for fear of harming their bodies. I think that's silly. What's the use of building your body if you don't use it? At the Mr. Olympia contest in 1972, we had girls backstage giving head, then all of us went out and I won. It didn't bother me at all; in fact, I went out there feeling like King Kong.

But if his comments about sex later offended the morals crowd, his candid admission about his illegal drug use may have been even more damaging among his future law-and-order Republican base.

OUI: Do you use dope?

SCHWARZENEGGER: Yes, grass and hash—no hard drugs. But the point is that I do what I feel like doing. I'm not on a health kick. I know I should take vitamins, for example, but I forget half the time. I just can't be bothered carrying around a lot of little bottles. Once I get outside the gym, I forget all about body building. I can look at a chick who's a little out of shape and if she turns me on, I won't hesitate to date her. If she's a good fuck, she can weigh 150 pounds, I don't care.

When he was in London promoting the film the same year, he gave an equally revealing, wide-ranging interview to *Time Out* magazine. The reporter is evidently eager to discover how Arnold's adopted country reacts to his candid and outrageous views about sex.

"What I want to do is make Americans aware that they're fucked-up when they equate everything a person does with some sexual trip," Arnold explains. "You know, if you hold a pencil in your hand, it's a phallic symbol and you really want to hold a cock in your hand. And a football coach doesn't really want to be a coach, he likes to slap football players' asses . . . he's a latent homosexual. And it goes on and on and on, all the fucking time. . . . America is so money-oriented. Thank God! It's always helped me! But it has its disadvantages because the psychiatrists know their business doesn't mean a thing if there are no sick people around, and so they make everybody feel guilty. You know, all New York City is running to a psychiatrist. All America thinks it has sexual hang-ups. Everybody's running to shrinks."

It was entertaining stuff, and the reporter lapped it up, begging for more. "Nixon was always being attacked sexually," Arnold continues. "It was always said that he was a fag and that he had no sexual relations with his wife for 15 years and that was why he liked power. And Hitler had only one ball, and that was why he wanted to conquer the world."

In an age when celebrities carefully chose their words to conform to a tightly controlled image, molded by publicists, it appeared that the public on both sides of the Atlantic couldn't get enough of Arnold's candid and refreshing outlook.

During one of my conversations with Ben Weider a few years ago, I asked, "Do you think Arnold set out to bag a Kennedy?" It was a flippant, offhand remark and I wasn't really expecting a serious answer. But Ben gave it a moment's thought before answering.

"It's not like he sat down and plotted how to marry a member of the Kennedy family," he said. "I don't think it was premeditated, but he did always say he was going to marry somebody prominent or famous. It was part of what he called his 'plan.' I know he was enamored of President Kennedy, so maybe when he met Maria, the thought was in his mind that he might get to sleep with a Kennedy. But there was nothing calculated about it; he found the right woman for him and he went for it. And she happened to be a Kennedy."

The bodybuilder Rick Wayne, who was a friend of Arnold's when he met Maria, told me he was convinced that the Kennedy name is what attracted Arnold.

"Oh, yeah, he was really quite open about that," recalls Wayne. "That he was that close to power really excited him. When he met her, he couldn't stop bragging about it; he was spouting some bullshit about how she reminded him of Bobby Kennedy, whatever the hell that meant."

There are conflicting accounts of how that meeting came about in the first place, how a musclebound, semi-articulate immigrant found himself hobnobbing with American royalty. According to one version, Maria's brother, Bobby Shriver, had seen *Pumping Iron* and became an instant fan of Arnold. So when his extended family was compiling the guest list for its annual Robert F. Kennedy pro/celebrity tennis tournament, he suggested the suddenly famous Austrian bodybuilder. The rest of the clan had never heard of him, but had no objections. The second, and more likely, version involved Bobby Zarem making a few phone calls and getting Arnold invited to the event, which was organized every year by RFK's widow, Ethel Kennedy, to benefit her slain husband's memorial foundation. Arnold would be replacing another invitee, the actor James Caan, who had another commitment. That, at least, is the story Zarem told in later years.

The gathering took place on August 28, 1977, at the Forest Hills Tennis Stadium in Queens, the day before the U.S. Open was scheduled to begin. Arnold had arranged some tennis lessons in Malibu so he wouldn't embarrass himself, but as a natural athlete he had little trouble with most sports. Somebody on the organizing committee must have had a sense of humor, pairing Arnold with another massively built sportsman, the great Rosie Grier of the NFL. The former New York Giants defensive tackle had an emotional connection to the Kennedy family, having served as a bodyguard for Robert Kennedy on the night RFK was assassinated in the kitchen of L.A.'s Ambassador hotel nine years earlier. Grier was, in fact, the man who had grabbed the gun out of Sirhan Sirhan's hand a moment too late to save Kennedy's life; but Arnold had arrived in America only two months after the assassination and probably had no idea about his teammate's historic role. The *New York Times* later described their doubles match as the "highlight of the day" after Arnold and Grier removed their shirts to display their gargantuan torsos before dispatching their opponents in three sets.

The night before the tournament, Ethel Kennedy had hosted a banquet for the participants. After dinner, Arnold was chatting with Tom Brokaw when the future NBC news anchor saw twenty-one-year-old Maria Shriver nearby and introduced her to his new friend. Maria claimed that after a brief chat and a dance with the burly bodybuilder, she was instantly "smitten." For his part, Arnold claims he had no idea he was chatting with a member of the American aristocracy until he met her again following the tournament while she was chatting with her cousin Caroline and Maria impetuously mentioned that her family would be heading to their compound in Massachusetts after the match on their private jet. Would he like to tag along? It took him a little while to register the fact that the compound in question was in Hyannis Port and that the family she was referring to was the most famous in America.

When Maria Shriver was a little girl, she would frequently come downstairs in her pajamas to find her uncles Jack and Bobby huddled with her father planning a political campaign. She has never publicly discussed her uncles' tragic deaths when she was eight and twelve years old, respectively. Her mother, Eunice, grew up playing touch football with those same uncles—her elder brothers—under the watchful eye of Maria's grandparents, Joe and Rose. But Eunice was even closer to her older sister, Rosemary. When Rosie, three years older than Eunice, was in her teens, she began to experience violent mood swings. Her volatility concerned her parents, who took her to a series of specialists, one of whom diagnosed mild mental retardation, though her recently discovered early letters and diaries show her to have been an intelligent and articulate young woman. When she was twenty-three years old, a doctor told her father about a new procedure that could calm Rosemary's mood swings. It was called a lobotomy. One didn't argue with Joe Kennedy, and Rosemary reluctantly agreed to undergo the treatment. The procedure went drastically wrong, however, leaving Rosemary in an infantile state for the rest of her life. Her parents institutionalized her and rarely visited her. The tragedy proved particularly devastating for Eunice, then twenty, who became a regular visitor at St. Coletta's Institute for Backward Children, where Rosemary was sent.

As the result of her sister's experience, Eunice became a lifelong advocate for children with disabilities and eventually founded the Special Olympics, which became her passion. Joe was particularly impressed with his daughter's abilities, once reportedly lamenting, "If that girl had been born with balls, she would have been a hell of a politician."

Because of her mother's devout Catholicism, Eunice was educated in a convent school and grew up very religious. At one point, she had even planned to become a nun before concluding that she liked boys too much. Her dates were strictly chaperoned, and she was expected to find a good Catholic husband. Among her suitors was the red-baiting Senator Joseph McCarthy, whom she was dating until she met a young man her father had hired to run the family's Merchandise Mart in Chicago, Illinois. His name was Robert Sargent Shriver and Eunice immediately knew he was the one. Sargent Shriver would later become one of the most prominent and respected American personalities, but as a young college student, he played a prominent—and rarely discussed—role in one of America's darkest chapters.

In 1940, a year after the war in Europe had begun, Shriver was an undergraduate at Yale University. He got together with a small group of fellow students—a group that included future president Gerald Ford and future Supreme Court justice Potter Stewart—to form an organization called the America First Committee. Across the Atlantic, most of Western Europe had already fallen to Hitler, and England was under siege. In the White House, President Roosevelt was doing what he could to help England ward off a Nazi invasion, but his hands were tied. A powerful isolationist movement was sweeping the nation, led by a onetime aviation hero, Charles Lindbergh—the man who had captivated the world with his solo flight across the Atlantic a decade earlier. Lindbergh's increasing sympathy for Nazi Germany, however, would permanently tarnish his reputation, despite later efforts of biographers attempting to dismiss his isolationism, as well as his anti-Semitism, as youthful naiveté.

When Shriver and his fellow students got together to formulate their founding principles, their aim was merely to keep America out of the war in Europe, which they believed was none of America's concern.

There is no evidence that the original founders had any Nazi sympathies. Yet before long, the group had been hijacked by an assortment of rabid anti-Semites, American fascists, and other elements of the extreme right. At its peak, the America First Committee had nearly 800,000 members and could fill huge arenas with its fervent antiwar rhetoric. President Roosevelt, who appeared desperate to commit American troops to stopping Hitler, came to regard the committee as one of the greatest threats to democracy, and captured German cables revealed that the Nazis viewed the organization as its strongest propaganda asset. The Nazis secretly channeled funds to the committee through the German embassy in Washington, along with tens of thousands of dollars that they arranged to be donated to another important asset, the Republican Party, which was also fiercely isolationist at the time.

The organization eventually imploded after an address by its most prominent spokesman, Lindbergh, in Des Moines, Iowa, in September 1941. Before a crowd of America First loyalists, Lindbergh blamed the British, the Roosevelt administration, and "the Jews" for attempting to push America into the war. The resulting outcry, and revulsion from all walks of American life, spelled doom for the movement, and in any case its aims became obsolete less than three months later when the Japanese invaded Pearl Harbor.

Although Lindbergh never admitted that his isolationist views were misguided—and even appeared to downplay the Holocaust after the war when he wrote that the American troops had also committed atrocities—Shriver would later acknowledge that the America First Committee and his own youthful isolationism had been a mistake. He also volunteered for the U.S. Navy, becoming a skilled aviator. When he entered the Kennedy family in 1953, however—marrying Eunice in a lavish Catholic ceremony—Sarge's prewar isolationism was probably not an issue. The Kennedy family patriarch, Joseph, had played a far more important role in the isolationist movement as America's ambassador to England during the Munich crisis of 1938. Joseph, who had accumulated a vast fortune as a bootlegger during Prohibition, helped persuade the British prime minister, Neville Chamberlain, not to stand up to Hitler—and Joseph himself was known to harbor considerable sympathy for the Nazis, at least before Pearl Harbor.

And Joe wasn't the only Kennedy with baggage unbecoming a future liberal dynasty. I had a conversation with JFK's former adviser Arthur Schlesinger Jr. at a reception in New York during the late 1990s when he told me something I will never forgot. "Remember," he said, "even the Kennedys weren't always Kennedyesque." He told me that both John and Robert Kennedy had flirted with McCarthyism during their early political career. It's no wonder, then, that Joe McCarthy himself was invited to Eunice's wedding in 1953. He even presented the couple with a silver cigarette case inscribed: "To Eunice and Bob from one who lost." Maria was born two years later.

Sargent Shriver would eventually go on to become an integral player in the Kennedy political machine, though the family was said to have kept him on a very tight leash, lest he become too politically ambitious himself. After campaigning hard for JFK in 1960, coordinating the crucial West Virginia primary that clinched the nomination, Shriver was rewarded for his efforts when President Kennedy appointed him the first head of the Peace Corps.

In 1964, when Lyndon Johnson was considering whom he was going to choose for his ticket as the vice presidential candidate, he was anxious to have somebody connected to the Kennedys, to capitalize on the leftover goodwill toward the family following JFK's recent assassination. He toyed briefly with naming Shriver until he heard from the Kennedys, through an envoy, that "if you're going to name a Kennedy to the ticket, it had better be a real Kennedy, which Shriver is not." Johnson eventually appointed Shriver ambassador to France, where the young Maria had a splendid view of the Eiffel Tower from her bedroom. When his appointment was over, the family—which by then included Maria and her four brothers—returned to the Shriver estate in Maryland where Maria had grown up. In 1972, Shriver finally got his chance at high office when the Democratic presidential nominee, George McGovern, chose him as the vice presidential candidate for the doomed campaign. In later years, Shriver's family name came to be associated with political dignity. "The Shrivers are Kennedys without the tawdriness: all that great taste and less scandal," one political adviser told *Vanity Fair*.

Growing up in such an intensely political household, Maria—the future first lady of California—would later complain that she was desperate to go into anything but politics. And despite her maternal family ties, she has always claimed that she was anxious to distance herself from her image as a Kennedy.

"All these commas—the daughter of, the girlfriend of, the granddaughter of, the niece of—I hate them! What absolutely drives me is to be considered as somebody outside the commas, somebody considered for her work alone," she would later declare.

Maria is fond of telling a story about how one of her brothers fell down one day at the family compound in Hyannis Port, and immediately burst into tears. Bobby Kennedy chastised the child, saying, "Kennedys don't cry," at which point Sargent Shriver lifted the sobbing boy in his arms and said, "That's OK, you can cry. You're a Shriver." Whether the story is apocryphal, as seems likely, or not, it is supposed to underscore her independence from her famous clan.

She likes to claim she has never even read a book about the Kennedy family. Everything she knows she learned from the family members themselves. But, according to a former colleague at CBS News, that doesn't ring true.

"That's nonsense," the former broadcast producer told me in 2009. "First of all, she's a Kennedy from head to toe. She's very talented in her own right, but most of what she has she owes to her lineage. And she's never been afraid to use her family when it suits her purposes. In the early days, a lot of people didn't even know she was a Kennedy. Her last name was Shriver and she wasn't particularly well known. But she let people know in a hurry who her uncle was. She'd always find a way to work it into the conversation. As for never reading a book about the family, that's ludicrous. Just look at the topic of her senior thesis at the university. She did it on the role of religion in John Kennedy's presidential campaign. Do you really believe she wrote that without ever reading a book about him?"

One of her other claims is far more believable. Maria has frequently said that she was bored by the stifling society crowd she grew up with. Because she was a Kennedy, her romantic options were thought to be limited to the East Coast liberal intelligentsia with whom her family hobnobbed.

"Everyone assumed that I was supposed to marry someone like a John Kerry, some preppy that had gone to Harvard or Yale," she later recalled. "I didn't want to marry those boys—I did not like them. I had been around them my whole life. I interrupted the story line. I wanted out of that suffocation. I wanted someone different."

So when the twenty-one-year-old Maria met Arnold Schwarzenegger on that sweltering August day in New York, he certainly fit the bill. Arnold was definitely different from anyone she had met before. That was apparent when he arrived at the fabled Kennedy compound for the weekend, although the family was so used to the assorted cousins bringing guests—boyfriends and girlfriends—that his appearance was not as odd as one might think. Nor was he quite as much a fish out of water as he would later describe himself.

The way Arnold described the weekend, he was distinctly uncomfortable in the midst of the famous clan until he hit it off with matriarch, Rose Kennedy. Because she happened to speak German, this bond was formed immediately.

He later described the encounter to *Penthouse* magazine. "Rose Kennedy was great. She speaks perfect German; so we spent the whole weekend talking to each other in my native tongue. We went for several long walks together and talked about Austria at length. The odd thing was that she knew everything about my country. Music, art, opera, books, even history. I was on my toes every second with her."

I recently spoke to a friend of Timothy Shriver, Maria's brother, who was often present at family occasions when Arnold was there, though it's unclear whether he witnessed the weekend in question. He told me that many of the stories that later circulated about Arnold and the Kennedys were "fiction," apparently scripted to cast both parties in a positive light and capitalize on the humor of the unlikely pairing. But the friend tells me that Arnold did indeed hit it off with Rose.

"I think Maria had told him that he would have to get the old lady's seal of approval, so she made sure they got to spend some together and told him to turn on the charm," he said. "She also told him that Rose was very religious, so she encouraged him to play up his own Catholicism, talk about going to church, that sort of thing. I don't speak a word of German, so I don't know what they ever talked about, but she seemed to like him."

Maria and Rose weren't the only ones taken with Arnold. Most of the Kennedys liked the big genial guy with the funny accent, who was all too willing to joke around, and to try his hand at sailing, water skiing, or the traditional Kennedy pastime, touch football. He even agreed to play a set of tennis with Sarge, losing rather badly, though, contrary to subsequent reports, Arnold didn't let his future father-in-law win. That was preordained, since Sargent Shriver had been playing all his life and Arnold had taken up the game only three weeks earlier. Nor did Arnold ruffle many feathers when he told Eunice, "I just want to tell you. Your daughter has a great ass." Uncle Teddy, among others, was famous for saying much worse.

Neither the Kennedys nor the Shrivers were particularly snobs. Unlike most of their eastern establishment friends, they didn't place a high value on culture and breeding; that is perhaps why they were Democrats. There was something they valued much more than blue blood. "The big thing we learned from Daddy,"

Eunice Kennedy once said, "was win. Don't come in second or third—that doesn't count—but win, win, win." And Arnold was a winner—the best in the world at his chosen sport.

One of John F. Kennedy's friends once observed something about the aura of the family. "These people just had a feeling that they existed outside the laws of nature," he said. "There was no other group so handsome, so engaged. There was endless action, endless talk, endless competition. It was as simple as this: the Kennedys had a feeling of being heightened, and it rubbed off on people who came into contact with them."

Whether it was youthful rebellion, a desire to shock her family and friends, or a genuine connection that drew Maria to Arnold right from the start is anybody's guess. Not surprisingly, like the women who regularly threw themselves at him on Venice Beach, she admits that his looks played no small part in the attraction, but there was more.

"It was instant and physical," she told Marie Brenner of *Vanity Fair.* "I found him attractive, funny, and original. He was independent. He was alone. I traveled everywhere in a pack. I thought in a pack. I acted in a pack. I was part of an umbrella name. I was not original. I was part of 'Which Kennedy are you?' "

Indeed, Arnold has claimed that he believes Maria was attracted to him because he was so different from her family, which he calls "the clones," and that she was yearning to break free from the Kennedy-Shriver mold. He fit the bill perfectly.

"Everyone in the family thinks exactly the same," he told Brenner. "If her mother says it is green, it is green. If her father says it is black, it is black. When you are in the family, you think this is normal, and then you meet someone from the outside and the lights go on. Here was a guy who was free."

But Maria has also hinted that, in fact, Arnold's boundless ambition—a trait he shared with both sides of her family—was the real attraction. Like all the Kennedy progeny, she too was ambitious, and she had been contemplating a career in broadcast journalism. Her photogenic features and famous bloodline guaranteed that there would be plenty of offers. And, despite his inherent sexism, Arnold wasn't the least bit threatened by successful women. Or perhaps they drowned each other out when they discussed their respective ambitions.

"When I first met him, he talked a lot about visualizations," Maria told Brenner. "He talked to me about where you wanted to be, where you wanted to go. . . . Arnold wanted to be a star. He wanted to be famous! I thought it was great. Everyone I knew was so serious. It was 'You can't do that! You have to be successful.' Arnold was like an explosion of fresh air. 'You want to go and do TV? Great! Do it! You have a dream? Go for it. Let's get a convertible and ride around in it!'"

For his part, Arnold had described his ideal woman to the *New York Times* a year earlier. "The lady with me has to look good, too," he explained. "And I definitely want to have one that's brighter than I. Then I can learn. I like an aggressive woman who can talk and is not always in the background." Maria appeared to qualify on all counts.

The gathering in Hyannis Port proved to be no weekend fling.

"I'm very heavy in love," Arnold told the *Washington Post* not long after he began dating Maria. "On the 1-to-10 scale of love, I'm 10 in love."

There was only one problem with the burgeoning fairy-tale romance. Her name was Sue Moray.

In July 1977, a month before he met Maria Shriver for the first time, Arnold was walking along the Venice Beach boardwalk indulging in his favorite pastime, girl watching, when he spotted one he liked, a beautiful blonde on roller skates. But as with Barbara Outland before her, he sensed that this was not a woman who would respond to one of his crude come-ons. Sue Moray was a twenty-five-year-old Beverly Hills hairdresser when she ran into Arnold that day. It was "lust at first sight," she later told Wendy Leigh, admitting that she recognized Arnold from *Pumping Iron*. She was flattered when he stopped to chat, thinking in the back of her mind that she was about to be picked up by a celebrity. But then she caught his eye wandering, checking out the other girls as they went past. "You're really a whore, Arnold, a beach whore," she said flirtatiously. Arnold insisted that he was no such thing, but he was instantly intrigued by this ballsy young woman. He asked for her phone number and as he wrote it down, Leigh reveals, he made a note: "Roller skates." Moray noticed that there were a number of other phone numbers in the book, with notations like "Big breasts" and "Black hair."

They started dating a few days later, beginning a relationship that Moray would later describe as a "lusty encounter." It didn't take her long to move into his Santa Monica apartment, where they satisfied their mutual physical needs with great regularity. She revealed to Leigh that, from the start, they had an open relationship. "When he was in town, he would be committed to me and I would live with him and go to work from his house. We would be faithful when we were both in L.A., see each other exclusively, and not go out with anyone else. But when he was out of town, we were free to do whatever we wanted and to date anyone else we wanted."

He did insist on one caveat. When he was out of town she was free to date anybody she wanted—except bodybuilders. It seemed like a reasonable request. They even liked to compare notes on whom they had been with, which Moray described as a "turn-on" for both of them, though she claims Arnold got mad when she described her own intimate encounters. Thus, neither of them was under any illusions about monogamy. So, a month later when Arnold returned from his vacation with the Kennedys in Hyannis Port, he had no compunction about bragging to Sue that he had spent time with John Kennedy's niece.

Maria has always claimed that it was "love at first sight" when she met Arnold. She knew instantly that he was the man she wanted to spend her life with. Today Arnold tells much the same story. In reality, however, it took him many years to come to that decision.

It would be a long time before Maria Shriver learned of Sue Moray's existence.

16.

Hollywood Calls

Movie offers weren't exactly pouring in, despite Schwarzenegger's Golden Globe and the critical acclaim for his role in *Stay Hungry*. Arnold had a theory about what the problem was. It was his accent that was holding him back, he believed. He had desperately wanted to land the Superman role that made Christopher Reeve a star, but who ever heard of a Superman with an Austrian accent?

The box office success enjoyed by the man of steel in 1978 had, however, ignited an interest in bringing comic book characters to the big screen, and that opened up another door. The great Italian filmmaker Dino De Laurentiis had seen *Pumping Iron* when it came out and had immediately thought of the charismatic bodybuilder who stole the show in that documentary to play the lead in a film he was creating at the time, *Flash Gordon*.

Arnold had secured an agent, Craig Runar, but, as noted above, he wasn't getting a lot of offers, a situation that Runar also later ascribed to the fact that Arnold had a thick German accent, which did not ingratiate him with an industry that is largely Jewish. Still, Runar had arranged for a sit-down meeting between Arnold and De Laurentiis, who had taken Hollywood by storm since arriving from Italy, where he had cut his teeth producing Fellini's films and had gained an international reputation. Runar had informed Arnold that this producer could be his ticket to stardom. But the meeting between the Austrian and the Italian wasn't an immediate success.

"I walked in, and I just kept staring at this desk," Arnold later recalled. "It was enormous. Antique. Probably from Italy somewhere. And he was standing behind the desk. And only his shoulders and his head stuck out above it. I just couldn't figure it. So I asked him, 'Why does a little man like you need such a big desk?' And he went crazy." But for De Laurentiis, Arnold's less-than-refined manners weren't the deal breaker. He just kept focusing on that accent—a cross between a Nazi storm trooper and a caveman, he thought. Of course, his own accent sounded a little like Chico Marx and was frequently imitated in Hollywood by friends and foes alike. So when De Laurentiis said that he couldn't use Arnold because the Austrian accent might be unintelligible to moviegoers, Arnold was taken aback. He later described the scene to *Sports Illustrated*, imitating the Italian producer by flourishing a cigar and waving it aggressively as he recalled the day he was rejected for the film.

"You have an accent! I cannot use you for Flasha Gordon! Nah! Flasha Gordon has no accent! I cannot use you! Nah!"

Arnold acted offended. "I said, 'What do you mean, *I* have an accent? I barely can understand *you*.' And that was the end of the meeting. Exactly one minute and 40 seconds on the clock. My agent said it was the fastest meeting he ever saw."

De Laurentiis, however, didn't hold a grudge. The man who had made *Serpico* and *Barbarella*, among other highly regarded films, was already looking ahead to another project, in which the dialogue was not nearly as important as the look. The producer he had partnered with, Ed Pressman, thought the man De Laurentiis had recently rejected for *Flash Gordon* just might fit the bill. They had received the green light to produce a big-budget studio adaptation of *Conan the Barbarian*, the fantasy character popular in sword and sorcery tales dating back to the 1930s. They had already signed a hot new director, Ridley Scott, to helm the project, but when De Laurentiis told his director who he had in mind for the role of Conan, Scott was dead set against it, fearing Arnold's poor English would ruin the film. Arnold was always acutely aware that his poor English would limit him to certain types of roles. "Of course I knew that my accent was something that was going to work against me," he told the journalist Chris Heard. "I knew that I would only be seriously considered for a certain kind of movie, but that was fine with me, that was the kind of movies that I wanted to make—I loved watching the old Steve Reeves historical action movies—so if I was able to do movies like that I would be doing what I wanted to be doing." He clearly saw *Conan* as exactly that kind of film, and who ever heard of a barbarian who spoke perfect English?

Normally at such an impasse, the producer would simply keep searching for his lead actor. But De Laurentiis had sensed some quality in Arnold; something told him that Arnold was perfect to play his hero—though Wendy Leigh claims that De Laurentiis initially rejected Arnold for the role, describing the Austrian muscleman as a "Nazi." Whatever the truth, rather than ditching Arnold, he instead found himself another director, and this proved fortunate for Scott, who went on to direct *Alien* instead. With a new director, John Milius, on board, Arnold signed on for $250,000 and even negotiated a part for his best friend, Franco Columbu. But the movie wasn't scheduled to begin filming until the fall of 1980.

Meanwhile, he had landed some less auspicious acting jobs, including playing a psychopathic womanizing bodybuilder named Josef Schmidt on an episode of the TV show *Streets of San Francisco*, starring Karl Malden and Michael Douglas. At about the same time, coincidentally or not, he signed on for another film, *The Villain*, starring Michael Douglas's father, Kirk, as a bungling bandit and Ann-Margret as the love interest. The film, directed by Hal Needham, who made *Smokey and the Bandit*, was a western farce, featuring Arnold as a shy cowboy. It had a dreadful script. When *The Villain* was released in 1979, it was savaged by critics, who singled out Arnold in particular for his lack of acting chops. The *New York Times*, which called the movie "as dopey as it is interminable," described Arnold as "more of a weight on the movie than even he might be able to lift." A number of critics suggested he stick to bodybuilding because it was clear he would never be an actor.

But, as it turned out, the critics' lambasting of *The Villain* was just what Arnold needed. Years later, after becoming a star, he posted the film's harshest reviews on his wall to remind him of their redeeming effect. He would later recall the moment his life and career turned around. "I asked myself what did I do to become the world champion in bodybuilding," he reflected. "It was five or six hours of training a day. And then I had to ask myself am I doing that right now and the answer was no."

As he had always done while training for a tournament, he created a strict regimen for himself: voice lessons, acting lessons, even accent removal lessons. As he had once done in the gym, he spent hours on end studying the ways of Hollywood, watching classic films, paying attention to the technique of the greats. Upon reading the script of *The Villain*, he knew it was subpar. Yet the $275,000 pay had been hard to resist. He vowed to let his instincts, rather than monetary considerations, guide his future career decisions.

Maria's own career was starting to take off. Ever since she was ordered to ride in the press plane as a seventeen-year-old while volunteering for her father's ill-fated vice presidential campaign in 1972, she knew she wanted to be a journalist. "It was the best thing that ever happened to me," she would later declare. With her family's connections, it didn't take long for the offers to pour in, and she started her first broadcast job at Philadelphia's station KYW-TV soon after graduating from Georgetown University. Kennedy or no Kennedy, however, she didn't take long to earn the respect of her colleagues, who were impressed by her work ethic, her creative ideas, and her willingness to learn from more experienced veterans. Maria Shriver was no dilettante, and she moved quickly up the ladder, receiving an offer to associate-produce a news magazine show for a Baltimore station.

Around the time he met Maria, Arnold had published his autobiography, *Arnold: The Education of a Bodybuilder*, and he was about to embark on a nationwide promotional tour for the book, which would go on to become a hugely popular best seller. In October, as part of the tour, he was scheduled to sign books in Washington, D.C., and he invited Maria, who lived nearby, to meet up with him while he was in town. She took him to a Halloween party in Georgetown and the two spent most of the weekend together seeing the sights and getting better acquainted. This is the trip that Arnold would later claim marked the beginning of his serious interest in Maria, when he realized for the first time that he was "in love."

It was also the beginning of a long-distance relationship that would last for the next nine years. On weekends, Maria often flew to L.A. to be with

Arnold, and he frequently made the trip east to be with her, staying at the nearby Maryland estate of her parents, who were beginning to realize that the relationship was serious. The Shrivers had come to enjoy Arnold's genial company and appeared to have no problem with the relationship, although many of Maria's friends—typical East Coast snobs—were not as accepting and wondered why she would be involved with a vulgar bodybuilder. But her parents had come to see beneath the surface and concluded that there was more to their daughter's new boyfriend than met the eye. Around that time, a friend of the family told *People* magazine, "It's nonsense to think that the Kennedys don't like him. Everybody enjoys Arnold; he's so much more than you might expect." Eunice was especially thrilled that Arnold appeared eager to embrace her pet cause, the Special Olympics, and made himself available to help promote the event or to give whatever other help she might need. It is a cause that eventually became almost as dear to his heart as it was to Eunice's. Anticipating that there might be wedding bells in the future, Sargent gave Arnold a Labrador puppy as a birthday present. "Dad said to pay attention to how Arnold treats the dog," Maria later recalled, "because that way I'll know how he'll treat children."

Perhaps she should have paid less attention to how he treated the dog and more to how he was treating her. For she still had no idea that Arnold was deeply involved with Sue Moray and almost certainly with many other women. To illustrate how closely his two serious girlfriends overlapped, Barbara Outland recalls in her biography that Arnold brought Sue as his date to her parents' house on Christmas Eve 1977, more than two years after she and Arnold had broken up. A few days later, Maria flew to L.A. to spend the New Year's Eve weekend with him. Moray claims she was told, "She's coming. You're out of here," forcing Sue to temporarily move out of the house she still shared with Arnold.

For months, they continued their passionate relationship, even after Arnold returned from a trip and gave Sue gonorrhea, which almost certainly was not acquired from Maria. "I was outraged," she later revealed to Wendy Leigh. "Arnold just said, 'Look, what if I came and gave you a cold—would you be outraged? You know I sleep with other people.'" As late as August 1978, a year after he first began dating Maria, he and Sue were still involved, though it wasn't easy for her to read the countless media stories about his public relationship with Maria, which had become a staple in the society and gossip columns whenever they appeared at a public event together. Finally, Moray told Leigh, she announced she was no longer willing to share Arnold with the Kennedy princess. She packed her belongings and drove away. But after a few blocks, she had a change of heart and turned around. Returning to the house, she claims she found Arnold crying like a baby. "I've never seen a man cry so hard," she recalled. She finally moved out for good at the end of the summer, convinced that Arnold was destined to choose Maria, but they continued to sleep together well into the fall.

Arnold had long since retired from competitive bodybuilding to devote himself to his film career. He had bowed out of bodybuilding on top and had nothing left to prove. He had repeatedly insisted that he would never return to his old sport, even if his movie career failed to take hold.

"The idea was to cut the competition off cold. Boom!" he told *Sports Illustrated* about his decision to quit while he was on top. "To have this energy that wants to reach out and hold on to the attention, the victory, all the things that bodybuilding brought me, but suddenly there is nothing to hold on to and that energy must now be channeled into acting, full-heartedly. Rather than wimp out and say, 'Well, if this doesn't work, I can always go back to bodybuilding.'"

But in 1979, he was hired by CBS to do network commentary for that year's Mr. Olympia contest in

Columbus, Ohio. Frank Zane, who had bested Arnold at the 1968 Mr. Universe, was the winner that year, receiving the Eugene Sandow trophy for the third time in his career. When Arnold, TV microphone in hand, asked Zane how it felt, the reigning champion did not hesitate. "Arnold, it feels even better than it did the last time I beat you," he said, according to the story Zane told Wendy Leigh.

It was at this moment that Arnold apparently decided to make him eat his words. The next day, Arnold hit the gym and resumed his old daily six-hour training regimen. It wasn't until the day before the 1980 Mr. Olympia, however, that he officially announced he was coming out of retirement, surprising the entire bodybuilding establishment, which was convinced he was long past his prime and didn't stand a chance. For his part, Arnold denied that his decision to compete had anything to do with revenge against Frank Zane. He simply wanted to be in peak shape, he claimed, for his upcoming film, *Conan*, due to begin shooting soon after the contest took place. But, as it turned out, he had actually secured funding for a documentary film called *The Comeback*, which would chronicle his attempt to win his seventh Mr. Olympia title.

When Arnold showed up at the tournament, held that year in Sydney, Australia, he was convinced he still had enough of his old magic to win one more title. But upon his arrival, the night before the prejudging, he discovered that the format of Mr. Olympia was not the way he remembered it. Before the officials knew Arnold would be competing, the Weiders' IFBB federation had changed the rules and eliminated the traditional two weight classes that had always characterized the competitions. The new change would seriously affect Arnold's chances because it meant he would have to compete against everybody at the same time.

To the shock of virtually everybody connected to the contest, Arnold claimed his seventh title the next day, despite a near-consensus that he was out of shape and far from worthy of the trophy. Many in the crowd appeared to agree, as a loud chorus of boos immediately rang out through the auditorium; this was the first time in his career that Arnold had been booed. To this day, it is the most controversial result in the history of Mr. Olympia.

The Australian competitor Roger Walker, who finished sixth that year, echoed the belief of many others that a fix was in. "I'll tell you something," he recalled years later. "Arnold flew over in his own plane, with his own film crew. They followed him to the toilets, showers, everywhere. They were here to promote and publicize his new movie. There was *no way* he was going to lose, and everyone knew it."

Arnold didn't give much thought to the controversy about his 1980 victory, although it dogs his legacy to this day. He had already turned his attention to his upcoming role in *Conan*, which he was convinced would make him a star. This time his instincts were sound. *Conan*, he would later observe, "was God's gift to my career."

17.

Box Office Gold

When Robert E. Howard arrived home one afternoon in 1936, he found a doctor waiting with some grim news. His beloved mother had only a few months to live. He proceeded to walk quietly to his car in the driveway, take a Colt .38 out of the glove compartment, and shoot himself in the head. The suicide of the thirty-year-old Texan also marked the demise of the character he had created a few years earlier for an obscure pulp magazine, *Weird Tales*, in which he chronicled the quest of a hero named Conan.

During the Hyborian Age, following the destruction of Atlantis, a barbarian was born on a battlefield, the son of a blacksmith. By the time he was a teenager, young Conan was already a fierce warrior revered throughout the land. In his stories, Howard described

Conan as "a tall man, mightily shouldered and deep of chest, with a massive corded neck and heavily muscled limbs . . . His brow was low and broad, his eyes a volcanic blue that smoldered as if with some inner fire." After he helped destroy the outpost of his people's enemy tribe, Conan began to wander, beginning the adventures chronicled by Howard in a series of twenty-one stories that would eventually see the light of day in magazines, serials, and comic books, acquiring a legion of loyal followers over the next forty years. In his travels, Conan was variously a mercenary, a pirate, and an outlaw, encountering evil wizards, giant snakes, tavern wenches, monsters, and princesses. Eventually he became king of Aquilonia, where, despite the often savage violence of his previous encounters, he reigned with gentle nobility, though his enemies were constantly plotting to oust him and he lamented that "these matters of statecraft weary me as all the fighting I have done never did." Eventually, Conan is deposed and must battle to regain his throne.

Howard's stories were clearly aimed at teenage boys lusting for adventure and daring during the bleak days of the Great Depression, but he always made clear that his antihero was the embodiment of his own personal philosophy, which rejected the idea of an ordered society. "To hell with the psychologists and city-bred psychoanalysts and all the other freaks spawned by our rotting civilization," he once said. "Barbarism is the natural state of mankind. Civilization is unnatural. It is a whim of circumstance. And barbarism must always ultimately triumph."

One thing that immediately jumps off the page is how, despite his savage appearance, brutal tactics, and sheer brawn, the title character is very clever, displaying an incongruous intelligence that allows him to think his way out of countless situations where violence alone won't help him.

Ben Weider once told me what he believed was the secret to Arnold Schwarzenegger's success. "The thing about Arnold," he said, "is that people constantly underestimate him. I'm not sure if it's the funny accent or his bodybuilder look, but he's actually very, very intelligent. Once you get to know him, that's immediately obvious, but people are always underestimating him and I think that's the way he likes it. He uses that to his advantage over and over."

Indeed, the brains behind the brawn may have convinced *Conan*'s producers that Arnold was the perfect choice to play the lead in the film they had been trying to get off the ground for years before receiving the green light from a nervous studio.

Almost a year before production commenced, Arnold was already preparing for the role, with the same attention to detail and hard work that he had applied as he tackled every other endeavor. Immersing himself in the character of Conan, he taught himself to wield a sword and an ax. He spent hours in front of a mirror practicing how to smile naturally with paint on his face and how to push his hair out of his eyes the way a barbarian would. He also had to slim down so that his muscles looked less imposing because, as he would later explain, "in the barbarian age, you don't have food every day."

While he was waiting for principal photography to begin, he costarred in a network movie, *The Jayne Mansfield Story*, with Loni Anderson playing the blond bombshell, the star of countless schlocky B movies before her death at thirty-six. Arnold portrayed Mansfield's husband, the 1950s bodybuilder Mickey Hargitay, who stands by helplessly as his wife descends into a maelstrom of addiction and despair. The lackluster script and Anderson's unconvincing portrayal resulted in a critical dud; but, as with *Stay Hungry*, in which he also played a bodybuilder, most critics believed Arnold was convincing as Mansfield's hapless foil. The *Washington Post*, in fact, noted that he gave the movie "a certain lunkheaded charm with his fractured phonetic line readings."

In January 1981, three months after *The Jayne Mansfield Story* was broadcast, *Conan* finally began shooting in Spain. A few days later, Dino De Laurentiis approached Arnold on the set—an encounter that Arnold later recalled fondly. "He said to me, 'Hey, Schwarzenegger, *you're* Conan.' He was so proud that he had picked the right guy."

The public seemed to agree. When *Conan the Barbarian* premiered in May 1982, it far exceeded the studio's expectations, grossing $9.6 million on the opening weekend and eventually more than $100 million. The executives were thrilled, but the critics were far from impressed. The film, wrote the *New York Times*, "is an extremely long, frequently incoherent, ineptly staged adventure-fantasy set in a prehistoric past." Arnold's performance, however, was frequently singled out as the one bright spot. According to the *Washington Post*'s reviewer, Arnold was "one of the few actors who can and does look convincing biting off a vulture's neck while pinned to a cross. Schwarzenegger is ideal as a hero who has to do battle with both stupendous snakes and seductive sorceresses."

Despite the overall critical drubbing, the industry agreed on one thing. A star had been born. Arnold sounded not at all surprised by the sudden burst of media attention, hailing him as Hollywood's new action hero. All was going according to the carefully crafted plan. "I see Conan as a step closer to getting me where I want to go—the top, the same category as Clint Eastwood, Charles Bronson, Dustin Hoffman," he told *People* magazine during the week of *Conan*'s release. "I'm planning to throw myself into acting. I will not give up until I am there—where I ought to be," he revealed to another publication.

Five years of hard work, patience, and humiliating reviews had finally paid off. It was what he always told the throngs of aspiring bodybuilders who arrived at Gold's Gym believing they would be Mr. Olympia. Endurance, hard work, and patience were the secrets, he counseled. But most weren't willing to put in the work necessary to achieve the desired results. Now he found telling comparisons between his old profession and his new one.

"I'll tell you why there are so few bodybuilders in acting," he told a UPI reporter. "It's the same reason why so few top professional athletes in any sport make good in show business. They all want to start at the top. But they can't.

"Acting has to be studied and learned like any other profession. If an athlete reaches the top in his field and enters acting, he has to start at the bottom all over again. You can't allow your ego to get in the way. You have to listen to other people, ask for help and, what's hardest for athletes, having other people tell you what to do and what not to do."

But Arnold knew that if he wanted to reach the top, it would require more than just a weekend of good box office returns. In fact, he believed it wasn't enough to simply sell the movie, as the studio publicists demanded. He would have to sell himself. It was a lesson he had learned as far back as *Stay Hungry*, and it may be the reason why he walked off with an unlikely Golden Globe for that film. The director of Arnold's first successful Hollywood venture later recalled his impressive salesmanship.

"When we had screenings of *Stay Hungry*, Arnold would literally wait by the door and introduce himself to people walking out," said Bob Rafelson. "He would say, 'Hi, I'm Arnold Schwarzenegger, do you want to talk to me?'"

By the second week that *Conan the Barbarian* was in theaters, Arnold was already being described by awed veterans in the industry as a master of salesmanship. It is a talent that persists to this day and that many feel is the secret to his ultimate success. "Self-promotion comes as naturally to Schwarzenegger as flexing his triceps," *Newsweek* once declared.

For Arnold, it was a no-brainer. "You have to let the world know what you have out there. It doesn't make

any sense to just work on the product but not on getting it out there," he explained.

In later years, describing his knack for self-
promotion, writers would usually summon the adjec-
tive "shameless." Arnold would not have argued with
that characterization. As far back as his 1977 autobiography, he wrote, "I knew I was a winner. I knew I was
destined for great things. People will say that kind of
thinking is immodest. I agree. Modesty is not a word
that applies to me in any way."

To the surprise of the producers, who usually had
to drag their reluctant stars on grueling promotional
tours, Arnold insisted on being involved with every
facet of the marketing for *Conan* as well as for each of
his subsequent films.

Reporters assigned to profile him noted how Arnold
stage-managed every aspect of their interview sessions, controlled who could take photos, and answered
only the questions he approved of. Usually this was the
domain of interfering publicists, but it was soon apparent that Arnold was his own publicist. He didn't need
anybody else to manage his image or even devise the
marketing.

After he was successful, he would tell a reporter,
"When people come to me with a script or concept,
I tell them, 'Before we shoot the first frame, we have

to shoot the poster. What is the image? What are we trying to sell here? Say in one sentence what the movie is about. You can't? Then how are you going to sell the movie? So forget that. Next project.'"

He was also well aware of his popular appeal long before the studios discovered it. One of the producers of *Conan*, Edward Pressman, recalls seeing Arnold in New York at about the time *Pumping Iron* was released and was impressed at how many people recognized him during that period when he was still a relative unknown. "Even then Arnold drew crowds," Pressman told Nigel Andrews. "People treated him as a movie star long before he was one."

The week *Conan* was released, the studio polled moviegoers to determine what drew them to the film. "According to Universal's research," reported the *New York Times*, "the movie is drawing a fanatic crowd of followers of 'Conan.' The studio also discovered that Mr. Schwarzenegger, five times Mr. Universe, has a surprisingly large following. The lure of body building is apparently summed up in Mr. Schwarzenegger's torso."

The industry realized it had a phenomenon on its hands, and suddenly Arnold was in high demand. Offers began to pour in, but his contract with De Laurentiis had already committed him to film a sequel,

Conan the Destroyer, which was scheduled to begin shooting in October 1983, this time in Mexico. Now— unlike the last time he flew out from LAX—he would now be traveling with an American, not an Austrian, passport.

On September 17, 1983, he stood with 2,000 others in a naturalization ceremony at L.A.'s Shrine Auditorium, raised his right hand, and swore allegiance to his adopted country, which was now his own. With Maria by his side, and waving a tiny American flag, he sang the national anthem and then told reporters, "This is the realization of the dream I have had ever since my childhood, to come to America and become an American. I really am convinced, after traveling all over the world and having seen all the places there are to see, that this country is the No. 1 in the world. It's like joining a winning team."

Most of the assembled media people paid more attention to his red-white-and-blue suit than to his heartfelt display of patriotism. It wasn't the first time he had sounded like a cheerleader for the American dream. He had been singing the virtues of the United States almost from the moment he arrived in 1968, frequently contrasting it to the country he had left behind, which usually came up short in such comparisons.

Arnold pumping iron in his Muscle Beach days. *(Keystone Press Agency)*

Nobody trained harder than Arnold.
(Keystone Press Agency)

Master of the Universe doing his *Baywatch* pose.
(Keystone Press Agency)

Arnold with two of his favorite pursuits: beautiful women and weight-lifting.
(Keystone Press Agency)

Arnold really is the Last Action Hero. *(Fame Pictures)*

Even the Governator can't
beat back Father Time.
(Fame Pictures)

Undeterred by their many difficulties, Arnold (who now seems to let Maria wear pants in public) and Maria remain a couple. *(Fame Pictures)*

Arnold loves a good stogie. *(Fame Pictures)*

Arnold has always put his family before anything else. *(Fame Pictures)*

The Governator, confident, handling intense pressure. *(Fame Pictures)*

Muscle Beach was the best place to hang out to get stories about Arnold. *(Ian Halperin)*

Despite their reported disagreements through the years, Arnold remains close with Stallone. *(Fame Pictures)*

Lou Ferrigno shed light on Arnold's early days. *(Ian Halperin)*

Racism is rampant in Muscle Beach, according to Robby Robinson. *(Ian Halperin)*

Arnold trained at Gold's Gym with some of the world's top bodybuilders. *(Ian Halperin)*

Undercover with one of Arnold's oldest friends, Dr. Frank Columbu. *(Ian Halperin)*

Infiltrating the Republican Party to get the goods on the Governator. *(Ian Halperin)*

"My dream was to end up in America," he had declared. "When I was ten years old, I dreamed of being an American. At the time I didn't know much about America, just that it was a wonderful country. I felt it was where I belonged. I didn't like being in a little country like Austria. I did everything possible to get out."

Ignoring the frequent public denigration of his homeland, Arnold's old mentor, Alfred Gerstl, pulled political strings to allow him to keep his Austrian citizenship, despite regulations that prohibited dual nationalities.

A month earlier, Maria's own dream came true when she was offered a long-sought network job, as West Coast correspondent for CBS News, working out of the Los Angeles bureau. Best of all, it allowed her and Arnold to be close instead of commuting from coast to coast as they had been doing for the previous six years. The media were constantly abuzz with speculation about whether she and Arnold would ever tie the knot. But, asked by the *Miami Herald* whether wedding bells were imminent, Maria, now twenty-seven, immediately quelled expectations and denied plans to set up housekeeping. She did admit, however, that her friends and family were surprised that she and Arnold had stayed together for as long as they had.

"It's like when a man shows up with a model who's on the cover of all the magazines, and everyone says, 'Oh, God, it will never work.' You never know what goes on with two people," she told the paper. Maria's cousin Christopher Kennedy Lawford told me that the Kennedys and the Shrivers had reservations at first about the prospective new addition to the family. "There was some skepticism, sure, but there was also skepticism about Maria becoming a high-profile TV reporter," he said. "I don't think Arnold's movie star status really bothered anyone too much. His life story, the immigrant guy with a big dream who made spectacularly good—that was admired. His vocal Republican status—now, that was another thing; that was something a lot of the family found they had to . . . tolerate."

Although most of the media coverage of the couple was positive, focusing on social events they jointly attended, one item was not as welcome. In late December 1983, Arnold returned from shooting the *Conan* sequel to spend New Year's weekend with Maria. But in the early hours of December 29, the pair got into a car accident that, to this day, has never been satisfactorily explained.

Shortly after midnight, on the Interstate 10 freeway, ninety miles east of L.A., the jeep Arnold was driving careened into a fence and rolled down a forty-foot embankment. The accident resulted in a minor leg injury to Maria, who was in the passenger seat. A California highway patrolman, Greg Transue (whose name was misspelled as Transu in subsequent accounts), arrived at the scene, where Arnold told him he had pulled over to allow Maria to drive but had misjudged the width of the road's shoulder. At the time, Arnold didn't have a driver's license. When the UPI news service got wind of the accident, it contacted Transue, who gave the details. The first story to hit the UPI wires in the P.M. news cycle of December 29 reported, "Transu said Schwarzenegger, 36, would be cited for driving without a license. He said the body builder might have been drinking at the time of the accident."

But by the A.M. cycle on December 30, the story had been altered. Now the newswires reported, "Transu said Schwarzenegger, 36, would be cited for driving without a license. He said there were no indications the body builder had been drinking."

Rumors have circulated for years that Shriver's well-connected family made a phone call, resulting in the excision of any reference to alcohol, but no evidence has ever surfaced to link the Shrivers to the change. If the initial reference had been a mistake, standard UPI procedure was to publish a correction and send it on the wires, but no such correction was ever issued, suggesting that something else was at play.

I contacted the highway patrol, requesting the original incident report, but the patrol informed me that it no longer has those records. I also tracked down Transue himself, who now lives in Susanville, California, and still works as a trooper for the state highway patrol, but he refused to comment.

The first time he met Arnold Schwarzenegger in 1982, James Cameron was an unknown twenty-eight-year-old Canadian filmmaker who had only one film under his belt: *Piranha 2*, an awful sequel to a modestly successful horror film called *Piranha*, about beachgoers attacked by mutant flying fish. He had originally been hired as the special effects coordinator, his specialty, but was asked to take over the project when the original director was fired after a dispute with the producers. The sequel was filmed in Italy, with a predominantly Italian crew, and Cameron couldn't even communicate with most of the personnel on the set. The result was, predictably, a mess. In his 1986 book *The World's Worst Movies*, Tim Healey dubs Cameron's debut "a strong contender for anyone's list of all-time horror turkeys." The director himself, who now acknowledges the sheer awfulness of the film, jokingly refers to it as "the finest flying killer fish horror/comedy ever made."

Given the results of his first film, it's a miracle that anybody let him make another one, but, having cut his teeth working for the legendary B movie king Roger Corman, he had enough contacts and goodwill in the industry to land a modest $6.5 million budget for a new science fiction adventure project, *The Terminator*, which he had written and pitched with a friend, the producer Gale Anne Hurd.

The movie, set in modern-day Los Angeles, involved a cyborg assassin sent from the postapocalyptic future and programmed to murder a waitress named Sarah Connor—the mother of a yet unborn rebel leader—while a guerrilla fighter named Kyle Reese is dispatched from the future to protect her. Cameron had already received the green light from an independent studio, Orion, but had not yet assembled his cast when he saw *Conan* and immediately envisioned Arnold for the role of the hero, Kyle Reese. He called Arnold's agent and set up a meeting.

Arnold was immediately intrigued. This was the kind of action movie that he believed perfectly suited his image. And Reese was certainly a more sympathetic character than his last role, a bloodthirsty barbarian. But as many directors had already discovered and many more soon would discover, Arnold was not content to simply show up and read the lines in the script. He was intent on having as much input as possible. And once the directors put aside their first impressions, drawn from the funny accent and the Neanderthal physique, they were always impressed. Here was an actor who knew what he wanted and instinctively understood what the public wanted as well. Arnold was convinced that if the character of Reese was to work, he needed the right cyborg opponent, someone who was "cold, lethal, and machinelike." It would be the Terminator role that would make or break Cameron's film, he argued. Arnold later recalled what happened as his meeting progressed.

"After I was through with this whole spiel, and this took half an hour, of hyping Jim Cameron about how this person has to appear in order to be really true to the character the way he wrote it, he said, 'You are the Terminator. You should play the Terminator.' I said, 'No no no no no, wait a minute. The guy only has 24 lines. Don't do this to me.' I said, 'I want to play the hero.'"

But after some thought, he realized Cameron was right. "Deep down inside," he recalled, "I knew that I could do more with the Terminator character than I could with the Reese character because it just somehow clicked. I just fell in love with that character, I visualized how he should act and walk and talk and do all those things."

Once again, his instincts were impeccable. The release of *The Terminator* in October 1984 conferred overnight superstar status on both Schwarzenegger and James Cameron.

To most of Hollywood, the advance premise had all the makings of another *Piranha 2*. But as the critics gathered for press screenings, watching Arnold as a programmed killer, they quickly changed their tune. *Daily Variety* described the film as a "blazing, cinematic comic book, full of virtuoso moviemaking." *Newsweek* reported that the film's many climaxes "will melt the hinges of your jaws." Arnold's performance received mixed reviews. "The title character of this film speaks English with a terrible accent, never says more than one sentence at a time, is as expressive as a rhino and moves as gracefully as an anvil with legs," declared *People*. "In other words, he was born to be played by Arnold Schwarzenegger." Janet Maslin, an influential film critic for the *New York Times*, provided a backhanded compliment: "Arnold Schwarzenegger is about as well suited to movie acting as he would be to ballet, but his presence in *The Terminator* is not a deterrent. This is a monster movie, and the monster's role fits Mr. Schwarzenegger just fine. Schwarzenegger is marvelous as the villainous title character in what for him is a bold change."

In the end, however, it wasn't the critics but the public who would make or break the film, and moviegoers voted with their wallets, making Cameron's film the top-grossing movie in America the week it premiered. For the second time in a row, Arnold had proved he was box office gold. And Hollywood wasn't the only place where he was a hot commodity.

In a number of interviews, Arnold had let slip that he was a dyed-in-the-wool Republican. The admission was unusual enough for someone in an industry dominated by ardent Democrats, where prominent Republicans could be counted on the fingers of two hands. What made his Republicanism all the more noteworthy was the fact that he was dating a Kennedy princess, a member of America's most famous Democratic dynasty. The way Arnold always told it, he had arrived in America in the midst of the 1968 presidential campaign between Richard Nixon and Hubert Humphrey. When he heard Humphrey's promises, they sounded a little too much like the socialism he had left behind in Austria. He liked Nixon's free enterprise approach and asked a friend what party

Nixon belonged to. When the response came back—Republican—Arnold decided on the spot that he was a Republican too.

Now, with an actor in the White House, also a Republican, the time was auspicious for Arnold to come out of the closet with his Republicanism. His friends, who had heard him muse about his own political ambitions for years, couldn't help letting slip their hope that Arnold would follow Reagan into the political arena.

"When you think of things that Reagan is putting his finger on—the new patriotism, the cheerfulness, the optimism, the voracious work ethic—I can't think of a person better placed than Arnold to capitalize on that," the author of *Pumping Iron*, Charles Gaines, told *Esquire*.

Sensing a great story, reporters seemed to seize any opportunity to ask Maria how she could date a Republican. "Our relationship isn't built on political philosophy," she told one newspaper, annoyed and perhaps a little embarrassed.

In August, Arnold was invited to give a breakfast speech at the Republican national convention in Dallas, where Ronald Reagan, whom he called his hero, was being renominated to run against the Democratic nominee, Walter Mondale. Arnold met Reagan for the first time shortly after midnight on the evening Reagan accepted the nomination. He was in awe, taking special note of how young the septuagenarian president seemed. "God, when I'm his age, I hope I'm still alive. He's remarkable," Arnold said afterward.

According to his biographer Laurence Leamer, one reason Arnold identified with the president was that the two had something important in common. Reagan also had an abusive, drunken father who shamed him and his family. "The President's buoyant optimism was in part his thrusting upwards out of the darkness," Leamer wrote. For the first time, Arnold began musing aloud to friends that he might like to be president one day. Nobody paid much attention to such ridiculous talk. Not yet.

As 1985 dawned, Arnold was still reveling in the success of *The Terminator*, and he had signed up with the producer Joel Silver for another action adventure, *Commando*. Arnold would play a retired special operations officer, John Matrix, who returns to action when his daughter is kidnapped by a deposed dictator holed up on a South American island. The film had a hot new director, Mark Lester, whose previous film, the Stephen King thriller *Firestarter*, starring Drew Barrymore, had created much buzz the year before. Playing opposite Rae Dawn Chong, Arnold's character, a single father motivated by love of a child, was sympathetic and was made more so by the incongruous humor of the dialogue. Lester claimed he wanted to create a James Bond–style film, and the script was full of witty one-liners, reminiscent of Sean Connery. To the surprise of everybody, Arnold delivered these quite effectively, helping to soften the often sadistic nature of the character he played. Many viewers were beginning to take note of Arnold's infectious sense of humor, familiar to anybody who watched him in *Pumping Iron.*

"When you meet [Arnold]," Joel Silver told *People* magazine, "you imagine he's going to be a quiet, stoic, big construction of a guy, and he's like one of the Three Stooges."

But the film was also replete with gratuitous violence and brutality, a fact that could not be obscured by the witty dialogue.

Once again, Arnold managed to deliver a box office hit: *Commando* was the top-grossing film for two weeks after its release in October 1985. Critics didn't know quite what to make of the film. Most appreciated the humor but were unimpressed by the interminable mayhem. And it seemed to more than one that they had seen it all before. Many reviewers couldn't resist comparing *Commando* with another recently released

Hollywood action thriller, *Rambo*, also packed with blood, violence, and a revenge motif. "In the 1985 body-count sweepstakes, *Commando*, the new Arnold Schwarzenegger vehicle, makes *Rambo* look like a Shriners' convention by comparison," declared the *Arkansas Gazette*. "Arnold Schwarzenegger is back, making *Rambo* look like a refugee from the Folies Bergère," noted the *Washington Post*. More than one review suggested that *Commando* was simply copying *Rambo*. One newspaper described the film as "*Rambo*, but with more yuks."

But while Arnold's latest film was unanimously declared the winner on the scale of violence and mayhem, it still ranked far behind *Rambo* at the 1985 box office and in the public consciousness. More important, the actor who played Rambo was still the number one star in the world, the undisputed king of the action genre. Arnold Schwarzenegger had never settled for number two and he wasn't about to start now. As in the days when Sergio Oliva and Frank Zane stood in his way, he knew exactly what he had to do.

18.
Cutting Stallone
Down to Size

Sometime in the 1960s, about the time Arnold Schwarzenegger arrived in America, a new breed of filmmakers came of age. They regarded films as art, not money machines. They sometimes called themselves auteurs. People like Polanski, Scorsese, Schlesinger, and Hopper ushered in a new era that also signaled the end of an old one. This was good news for moviegoers, but not so much for the studios, which had come to rely on some tried and true staples that had nothing to do with art and everything to do with putting asses in the seats. Among these were a couple of genres personified by the iconic John Wayne: war movies and westerns. The Duke and his imitators could for decades count on drawing a demographic crucial for the studios' bottom line—men.

As a talented and cerebral breed of new filmmakers plied their trade and made some of the greatest films of all time, however, the demographics became sharply skewed toward women. Men, it seems, were simply not interested in sensitive portrayals of the human condition. They were more interested in football, which saw a huge spike of popular support as American males turned away from watching movies and preferred to stay home watching sports on TV. The success of *The Godfather* in 1972 offered new hope and a revival of a genre—the gangster movie—but it wasn't enough to sustain a trend. The men were still staying away in droves. It took an unlikely figure to change all that, and the outcome might never have happened if Sylvester Stallone hadn't dropped out of beauty school.

Michael Sylvester Gardenzio Stallone was born in New York during the first wave of the postwar baby boom. His parental lineage is a tad unusual—he is the son of a hairdresser and a wrestling promoter. This would not be so strange, except that his father, Frank Sr., was the former and his mother, Jackie, the latter. As a child, Frank had come to the United States from Sicily and learned the hairdressing trade after he gave up his original show business aspirations because of stage fright. Jackie was the daughter of a French socialite of

Russian Jewish descent. When Sylvester and Frank Jr. came along after the war, Frank Sr. stayed at home with the kids in their seedy Hell's Kitchen apartment while Jackie worked as a chorus girl in Billy Rose's revue at the Diamond Horseshoe nightclub. After they were estranged, Jackie would appear on the *Howard Stern Show* to make the dubious and unlikely claim that, when she got pregnant with Sylvester, Frank insisted she have an abortion. Instead, she faked the procedure and Frank didn't know until after she had given birth.

When Sylvester was five, the family moved to a suburb of Washington, where Frank opened up his first beauty shop. It eventually expanded into a chain, making Frank a wealthy man and allowing him to indulge in a new hobby, polo. The marriage broke up when Sylvester was eleven, and for years he lived alternately with each parent.

Despite his privileged upbringing, Sylvester was a troubled kid, and he was expelled from a series of exclusive Catholic schools for unruly behavior. Around this time, his father gave him a piece of advice: "You weren't born with much of a brain, so you'd better develop your body." It's a line he would eventually recycle for *Rocky*, but heeding the advice, he took up weight lifting and built up a powerful physique. Fortunately, his mother at the time owned a gym called Barbarella's, so he had easy access to the equipment.

Around the same time, he decided he might like to follow in his father's footsteps and become a hairdresser, so he dropped out of high school and enrolled in a cosmetology school to learn the trade. Quickly realizing it wasn't what he wanted to do, he hadn't the heart to break this to his father.

"Some woman would walk in with eight hairs on her head and say, 'Make me beautiful,' he later recalled. "I'd say, 'Lady, give me a break.' One day I cropped the heads of most models they used at the beauty school. I just went snip, snip, snip. I thought OK, that should be enough to get me thrown out." It did.

Shortly afterward, Sylvester was sent to an exclusive private school for troubled boys outside Philadelphia so that he could obtain his high school degree and eventually go to college. There, he played football, excelled in fencing, and eventually straightened himself out, thanks to weekly psychotherapy sessions. When he couldn't get into any U.S. universities, because of his poor marks, his father paid for him to attend the American College, located in the Swiss Alps, where he developed a love for drama after winning the role of Biff in a school production of *Death of a Salesman*. His nickname in Switzerland was "Studly" and he became best-known for charging students five francs to sneak their girlfriends into the boys' dorm. Eventually deciding to pursue acting seriously, he enrolled as a drama major in his junior year, transferring to the University of Miami. But in 1969, three credits short of graduation, he inexplicably caught a plane to New York, where he was convinced a Broadway career awaited him.

Like many a starving young actor, however, he quickly discovered that the competition was fierce and stardom wasn't as easy to acquire as he had assumed. His father had cut off his allowance when he dropped out of school and he was forced for the first time to make it on his own, which proved no easy task. His first part was in an off-off-Broadway production of *Desire Caught by the Tail,* the only play ever written by Pablo Picasso. His salary: $10 a week. "For a year or so, I really perfected the part of being rejected," he later recalled.

In 1970, after being evicted from an apartment because he couldn't come up with the rent, Stallone had been homeless for a short period when he was offered $200 to appear in a soft-core porn film, *The Party at Kitty and Stud's.* "It was either do that movie or rob someone, because I was at the end—the very end—of my rope," he later recalled. The next couple of years were tough. He drove to Hollywood in a $40 jalopy he had purchased from a friend and managed to land a few small roles, including a tiny part as a strangler in Woody Allen's film *Bananas* and as a thug in Jane Fonda's thriller *Klute*.

In 1973, he seemed to have his first big break when he auditioned for and won a role in *The Lords of Flatbush*, a movie about a Brooklyn street gang. The movie introduced both Stallone and another unknown, Henry Winkler. The reviews of Stallone's performance were universally positive and it looked as though he was on his way, but instead it was Winkler who became a star, landing the role of "the Fonz" in *Happy Days*, while Stallone continued to languish waiting for his big break. In 1974, he married a young woman, Sasha Czack, whom he had met while she was employed as an usher in the same movie theater where his younger brother, Frank, worked.

Between auditions, he wrote. And as more than one director had already discovered when he offered to write his own dialogue for various projects—and when he received a credit for script doctoring for *The Lords of Flatbush*—he appeared to have considerable talent. He had come up with a gritty, promising screenplay called *Hell's Kitchen* about three struggling fictional brothers from his old neighborhood. Paramount optioned it for a film, but Stallone objected when he learned that it was going to be turned into a TV movie instead of a feature. He pulled the plug, although the executives told him this would be career suicide.

He attempted to sell the script elsewhere, but when he had meetings with producers, he suffered the same fate Arnold Schwarzenegger had repeatedly encountered in his early days. "They only looked at my muscles instead of my brains," he recalled.

On March 24, 1975, Stallone was watching Muhammad Ali fight an obscure white boxer, Chuck Wepner, on a closed-circuit broadcast in New York City. Stallone, a fan of Ali's, was surprised as the fight progressed to see everybody around him cheering for Wepner, who surmounted huge odds and repeated pounding and somehow managed to go the distance, even knocking the champion down once. As he watched the crowd's reaction to the scrappy underdog, Stallone immediately had an idea for another film, but, contrary to Hollywood legend, he didn't go home that night and proceed to write the script over the next three days. He was already working on a screenplay about a Philadelphia taxi driver who runs for mayor. Only after he pitched that idea unsuccessfully did his agent suggest he try his hand at the boxing idea, which he had casually mentioned over lunch in March.

That's when he went home and started dictating a script to Sasha, who pounded away on a small portable typewriter, offering invaluable suggestions and ideas along the way. For three days they wrote, barely eating or sleeping, and popping caffeine pills to stay awake.

When they were finished, Stallone knew he had something special—the tear-jerking story of a working-class Philadelphia underdog, Rocky Balboa, who almost becomes heavyweight champion of the world. He wasted no time setting out to sell the script. It didn't take long, though first he had to polish the draft into a much tighter, more inspirational story. His original script, for example, had Rocky throwing the fight, and the protagonist was a much rougher, less sympathetic character who spent much of the movie swearing. Less than three months after the Wepner-Ali fight, Stallone's agent had brought the script to two independent producers—Irwin Winkler and Robert Chartoff—who in turn pitched it to United Artists (UA). A month later, UA got back to them, very interested.

The studio knew it had a potential hit, and it made an appealing offer: depending on the versions told in later years, this was anywhere from $18,000 to $315,000. There was only one catch. Stallone insisted on playing the title character himself. The studio, however, wanted an established star such as James Caan or Paul

Newman. Casting an unknown was just too risky. But Stallone wouldn't budge.

"I kept saying no until finally they gave in and said, 'Oh Jesus, let's forget all this and let him have a shot at it,'" Stallone recalled years later. In the end, the studio agreed to his demand only on the condition that the budget would be reduced from $1.75 million to $1 million and that Stallone would agree to accept $20,000 for the script plus union scale for his acting. Fortunately, his agent also negotiated 10 percent of the profit as a condition for reducing the price of the script.

A few months later, shooting began. Stallone later recalled what was going through his head on that day, in 1975. "When we started shooting," he told *Playboy*, "we were on Broad Street in Philadelphia at 4:30 in the morning and it was 19 degrees outside. I got dressed in a trailer and as I was about to walk out, I looked at myself in a mirror that was hanging next to the door. And I thought, 'Oh, God, this is it. Sylvester, you've bluffed your way, you've bullied your way, you've badgered your way and you've begged your way into this position. If you don't pull it off, your name is gonna be synonymous with failure. Pretty soon, people aren't going to say, "Hey, you made a bomb." They'll be saying, "Hey, you made a Stallone." It's all up to you. Can you do it?'"

A few months later, audiences delivered their verdict on his performance and his film, which was pronounced a masterpiece by countless reviewers and a box office smash by the public. Roger Ebert of the *Chicago Sun-Times* speculated that Stallone could become his generation's Marlon Brando. The film was nominated for ten Academy Awards, including two nominations for Stallone himself: for Best Actor and Best Original Screenplay. The film ended up winning the Best Picture award that year and was the highest-grossing film of 1976, earning more than $220 million worldwide, a staggering figure for that era. Stallone failed to win an Oscar, but he did walk away with a Golden Globe, and it was at the Golden Globe ceremony where he first met Arnold Schwarzenegger after the unknown Austrian had wowed critics with his performance in *Stay Hungry.*

While Arnold's career continued to languish for years, Stallone's took off immediately. A hugely successful sequel to *Rocky* followed, along with numerous critically acclaimed films, including *F.I.S.T.* and *Escape to Victory.* His star was continually rising, and it reached another height in 1982 with the release of *First Blood,* in which he played a Vietnam veteran named John Rambo—a performance that garnered critical praise along with enormous box office receipts.

Meanwhile, he continued to churn out more successful additions to the *Rocky* franchise, but it was the sequel to *First Blood*, not *Rocky*, that made Sylvester Stallone a cultural icon.

In 1985, a few months before Arnold starred in *Commando*, Stallone appeared in *Rambo: First Blood Part 2*, which basically rewrote the history of the Vietnam War to declare America the winner. In the age of Reagan, it was just the kind of movie that would resonate in a country tired of the perpetual soul-searching and guilt America had experienced since Vietnam and Watergate. Americans had found two new heroes, both larger than life, to lift them out of their malaise. One occupied the White House, the other the big screen. Ronald Reagan sensed the same thing and seemed to regard Stallone's film as a personal call to arms.

In June 1985, Lebanese extremists hijacked a TWA flight and flew it to Algiers, where they held a number of passengers as hostages. After a tense standoff, thirty-nine passengers were released. When President Reagan stepped before reporters at the White House to express his reaction to the release, he declared, "After seeing *Rambo* last night, I know what to do next time this happens." A few months later, when he was battling for a tax reform package before Congress, Reagan said, "Let me tell you, in the spirit of Rambo, we're going to win this thing." These extraordinary references by the commander in chief, coupled with regular invitations to visit the White House, bestowed an almost mythic image on Stallone, who was almost as popular as the perpetually optimistic president.

While most Americans watched approvingly as Stallone's status rose—viewing it as a real-life *Rocky*, a story of an underdog making good—there was at least one bystander who wasn't impressed.

Arnold Schwarzenegger must have fumed as he saw somebody else occupying the exalted status that he felt was rightfully his, as he saw his hero, Reagan, embrace what he considered a less worthy rival while he himself watched from the sidelines. It was time, he concluded, to cut Stallone down to size. At the same time as Arnold was making a respectable $3 million per picture, Stallone was getting $15 million and was now the number one box office star in the world. Arnold vowed to reverse that situation, and as always, there were no half measures.

The first salvo came in a 1985 interview he gave to Britain's *News of the World* while promoting the London premiere of *Commando*. "I'd be angry at hearing my name mentioned in the same breath as Stallone's," he said dismissively. "Stallone uses body doubles for some of the close-ups in his movies. I don't.

We probably kill more people in *Commando* than Stallone did in *Rambo*, but the difference is that we don't pretend the violence is justified by patriotic pride, All that flag-waving is a lot of bullshit. And if killing is done with good taste, it can be very entertaining indeed. I've made a better film than Stallone's and I'm happy to wait for time to prove me right."

Neither the critics nor the public seemed to agree, and this only further fueled his resentment. A few months later, *GQ* magazine heralded an interview it had conducted with him by announcing that Arnold was "spoiling for a feud." Indeed, it was hard not to come to that conclusion in reading what he had to tell the magazine about Stallone when the interviewer asked him whether there was a rivalry between the two.

"As intense as I am about my training or acting when I do it, at the same time I have fun with it," he responded. "I don't take it all that seriously. I mean, I had the best-built body in the world. You have to keep a sense of humor. I think Sylvester Stallone, as far as I knew him, is extremely intense all the time, even when it comes to the gym. It's continuous competition. If you're doing 120-pound curls, he will say, 'I can do 130.' He's obsessed, and that carries through in the way he dresses, how hard he tries to belong to charity organizations. It's all *Rocky*. It doesn't come from, you know (he points to his heart). There's no love there. And people see that. . . . I think that's the difference between him and me."

Stallone, who was born into privilege and was far more sophisticated than his image would suggest, was already known around Hollywood as a discerning art connoisseur and collector. Arnold had been schooled in art by Joe Weider, but his knowledge lagged far behind that of his rival, so this was yet another area where Stallone had bested him. It clearly rankled, if we can judge by an interview he gave to James Cameron's biographer Christopher Heard. When Heard asked about Stallone, Arnold replied testily, "His *Rocky* is one of the great movies of all time—but he turned into a different kind of actor when he got really successful—a different kind of person. Just because a guy can afford to put a Rodin statue in his fucking living room does not mean he is an art historian. Sly is not half as smart as he thinks he is."

But it wasn't until Arnold's *Playboy* interview that the public really caught wind of just how much animosity existed. After Arnold tells the interviewer, Joan Goodman, how much he admires Clint Eastwood, the "king of the box office," she points out that there is currently a Hollywood actor even bigger than Eastwood.

PLAYBOY: Are you forgetting your friend and fellow action-movie mogul Sylvester Stallone? Isn't he the highest-paid actor?

SCHWARZENEGGER: First of all, I don't know about that. Second, he is not my friend.

PLAYBOY: Why not?

A.S.: He just hits me the wrong way. I make every effort that is humanly possible to be friendly to the guy, but he just gives off the wrong vibrations. Whatever he does, it always comes out wrong. I'll give you an example. We had breakfast together not long ago, because we are making films for the same company. We discussed not getting in each other's way and when the films should be released. It was a very agreeable conversation on every subject, and then he said, "You've got to become a member of my new club." I said, "What club?" He said, "It's going to be an all-male club with no women allowed. Just like in the old days. Only men. And we sit around and smoke stogies and pipes and have a good time." I told him it was the worst thing he could do. That we're living in a very sensitive time period when women are struggling for equality. I said that I didn't agree with half the stuff they were talking about, but a club like that would offend every smart woman in the country. I said to stay away from it. "If you want just guys, invite them up to your house. That's what I do."

PLAYBOY: He's had some trouble with his image lately, hasn't he?

A.S.: Just because you're a big star doesn't mean you have common sense about these things. Listen, he hired the best publicity agents in the world and they couldn't straighten out his act. There's nothing that anyone can do out there to save his ass and his image. Just the way he dresses. Seeing him dressed in his white suit, trying to look slick and hip—that already annoys people. And the gold ring and the gold chains that say, "Look how rich I am"—all that annoys people. It's a shame no one taught him to be cool. He should have L.L.Bean shoes and corduroy pants with a plaid shirt. That's cool; that's how a director should look, rather than have that fucking fur coat when he directs.

The media feasted on the feud, which made colorful copy. "There's a new sheriff in town," one paper announced, prematurely declaring that Arnold was nipping at Stallone's heels in the quest to be number one. And as critics seized on the similarities between *Rambo* and *Commando*, speculating on whether Arnold was trying to copy Stallone, what few realized is that the two men had something in common besides their films.

Shortly after Arnold wrapped up shooting *Conan the Destroyer* in 1983, Dino De Laurentiis had asked for a favor. He was having trouble securing funding for another comic book–inspired film, this one featuring a strong female character, effectively a female version of *Conan*. He wondered if Arnold wouldn't mind attaching himself to the picture and taking a small supporting role. By then, the producer had become what Arnold later described as a "father figure like Joe Weider" and he couldn't say no, even though he was queasy about a project in which he couldn't be the star. The film was *Red Sonja*, based on a fictional bikini-clad barbarian who had first appeared in a *Conan* Marvel comic book. Having secured Arnold's participation, the producer embarked on a quest to find his star. She had to be formidable—strong enough to serve as a role model for the young female moviegoers he was trying to attract but also beautiful enough to persuade men to buy tickets.

He finally found his Sonja on the cover of a European fashion magazine. She was Brigitte Nielsen, a striking Danish model whose six-foot frame and stunning features were just what De Laurentiis had in mind for his title character. Nielsen would later describe herself as "Amazonian," but the media preferred to refer to her as a Valkyrie or a Viking because of her Scandinavian roots.

Twenty-one years old at the time De Laurentiis discovered her, Brigitte had been brought up in Copenhagen, the daughter of a librarian and an engineer. Still a teenager, she had been sitting in a café one day when she was discovered by a fashion photographer, Marianne Diers, who wondered if the stunning blonde had done any modeling. After taking a few test shots, Diers hooked Brigitte up with a modeling agency, and it didn't take long for her unique look to grace the covers of some of Europe's top magazines. She moved to Milan, fashion capital of the world, where she walked the runway and attracted a great deal of attention, though she had not yet received much in America.

When she was nineteen, she met a Danish musician, Kasper Winding, and moved in with him. The two were married less than a year later and had a baby boy together. When the call came from Hollywood, however, she hopped onto the next plane, leaving her husband and infant son, Julian, behind. By the time she signed her contract to star in *Red Sonja*, she had forgotten all about her husband, and she didn't bother to inform him of her plans until her film was already in theaters.

By then, she had met two other men who could serve her boundless ambition the way a struggling musician never could. It took only a few days after filming began in Rome for Nielsen to catch the eye of her costar, who by that point had already been dating Maria Shriver for more than seven years. As usual, Arnold wasted no time getting what he wanted, and Brigitte was all too eager to hook up with a movie star. Their first sexual encounter took place in his trailer. Not long afterward, on October 11, the newspaper *Vienna Kurier* was the first to report their fling. It may have been this story that filtered through to Maria. Arnold's old girlfriend Sue Moray, still in regular touch with her former lover, revealed to Wendy Leigh that Arnold told her Maria had assigned spies to report to her from the set. But, according to Moray, that wasn't enough to get Arnold to back off. He was so "sexually intoxicated" by the free-spirited Nielsen that he couldn't resist, Moray claimed.

On a break from filming in December, Arnold flew with Brigitte to Austria, where they stayed with his mother, Aurelia, who had met Brigitte on a visit to the set a month earlier. Once again, the *Vienna Kurier*, eager to report every move of Austria's famous native son, reported on the ongoing affair. The paper also reported that Arnold had recently hooked his costar up with his agency, ICM. "She is heavenly," he declared to the reporter. "If I could, I would have her in Hollywood tomorrow."

He was already having her all over Europe, and Maria was said to be furious, especially because of the public manner in which he chose to conduct the liaison with his costar. But when filming wrapped up, so, apparently, did the affair. Moray told Leigh that Arnold confided he was dismayed by how Brigitte had callously dumped her infant son. "And she was too reckless for me," he told her.

Years later, Arnold would reveal to Laurence Leamer more details of his time with Nielsen. "She said, 'I want to move to America and be your wife or woman,'" Arnold recalled. "I said, 'I have a girlfriend I'm very serious about. I am committed to Maria.' She said, 'I am unbeatable.'" But he had made his choice.

When *Red Sonja* was eventually released, it proved to be an embarrassing setback for Arnold's film career, which had enjoyed considerable momentum up until that point. He was said to be furious at De Laurentiis, who had promised that his role would be minimal. Instead, the producer had kept in virtually everything Arnold shot, attempting to capitalize on his box office appeal. It wasn't enough, however, to save the film from a critical and box office disaster. "*Red Sonja* is not the least bit exciting, or sexy, or even funny," declared the *Chicago Tribune*. "Instead, it's lumbering, oddly prim and laughable."

During the promotional tour, there was no mention of the off-set high jinks enjoyed by the two stars a few months earlier. Instead, the media had another romance to write about. In the same week that the film hit the theaters in July 1985, Nielsen inexplicably announced that she had become engaged to Sylvester Stallone, who had recently left his wife and longtime collaborator, Sasha, after ten years of marriage.

What happened between the time Nielsen broke off her affair with Arnold a few months earlier and the surprise engagement is still up for debate, and it would play a crucial role in the course of Arnold Schwarzenegger's life and career.

A few years ago, I went undercover in Hollywood for a book and documentary exposé about the entertainment industry. Along the way, I infiltrated the shadowy Church of Scientology as a gay actor seeking to be turned straight; tagged along with a drug dealer who supplied celebrities; got offered a job by a Hollywood madam as a gay escort servicing famous actors and other high-powered figures; and landed a part in Martin Scorsese's film *The Aviator*, acting opposite Leonardo DiCaprio and Jude Law, although my scenes ended up on the cutting-room floor.

The contacts and sources I cultivated while working on that project eventually proved invaluable while I was working on this one. One of those contacts happened to have been a member of Sylvester Stallone's entourage when Stallone was still the biggest draw in Hollywood during the 1980s. This contact was still peripherally connected to the entertainment industry, and I looked him up and asked him what he recalled about the legendary feud. His response surprised me.

"That was all bullshit," he proclaimed. "Arnie and Sly were good pals; they were both in on the gag. I'm not sure who started it, but I remember whenever they got together they'd be ragging on each other, insulting one another, even at public events, and then they'd laugh about it. They'd be comparing their bodies and putting down the other one. Sly would say, 'You've gotten fat, Schwarzenegger,' and Arnie would act like the Terminator. When he started saying those things about Sly in the magazines, I think he gave him a

heads-up or it was thought up by a publicist or something. I don't remember—it was a long time ago—but
I do remember Arnie gave this *Playboy* interview and
he was saying all these things about Sly and acting like
a feminist or something about Sly starting a men's club
that was offensive to women. We all cracked up about
that because everybody knew Schwarzenegger was the
biggest hound in Hollywood; his whole life was a men's
club. He'd get together with his friends and smoke
hundred-dollar cigars and talk about chicks they were
going to bone. I mean, Sly was a member of that club at
one point. Naw, they always were buddies. That didn't
mean anything."

This could explain why they went in together on a
partnership in a restaurant chain, Planet Hollywood,
and why they have teamed up on countless projects in
the years since. In fact, just recently, Schwarzenegger
announced that he planned to shoot a cameo in an upcoming Stallone movie, *The Expendables*, which may
be released before he leaves the governor's mansion in
early 2010. Could the two of them really have buried
the hatchet so easily after the bitter animosity and the
nastiness that rose to the surface between them during
the mid- to late 1980s? Or was it indeed all an act?

Wendy Leigh clearly didn't think there was anything phony about the feud on the day when she was

invited to visit Stallone in Arizona on the set of *Rambo III* in February 1988. At the time, she was a well-regarded Hollywood correspondent for Britain's *News of the World,* a newspaper owned by Rupert Murdoch. Publicly, Stallone had almost always remained above the fray, refusing to comment about Schwarzenegger's continuous sniping except for a brief interview he gave to *Hollywood Magazine* revealing that he had called Arnold personally after the *GQ* article to inform him that his comments were silly. "I told him there was room for both of us, so why backstab," he told the magazine. Other than that, he had never let on that Arnold's criticism bothered him in any way. But within half an hour of meeting Stallone, Leigh later wrote, she had no doubt that he was out for Schwarzenegger's blood.

"I never did anything to the fucker," Stallone told her. "But he's always been out to get me. Now he's gone too far."

He proceeded to share some scuttlebutt that had until then only been rumored. "He had an affair with Brigitte," Stallone confided, referring to his ex-wife, whom he had divorced a year earlier after two years of marriage, when he caught her cheating with another man. "She was in Austria with him, met his mother, found out a lot about him. I could give you a great story."

Over the next month, Leigh claims, Stallone plied her with stories about his archrival, one juicier than another but many "impossible to substantiate." Assuming that Stallone might one day deny his involvement, the British reporter began to secretly tape their conversations. Meanwhile, she began musing aloud that she was considering writing a biography of Schwarzenegger. Stallone was immediately enthusiastic about the prospect.

"I'll get you an agent, an accountant, a publicist, 24-hour-a-day bodyguards. Anything you want," he told her. Leigh claims there was never any suggestion that Stallone would actually finance the book or exercise any editorial control. However, he did arrange an agent and put Leigh in touch with his publicist, Paul Bloch. He also provided her with a number of sources attesting to Schwarzenegger's affair with Brigitte Nielsen, along with countless other revelations and juicy tidbits. One of those revelations would eventually cause a worldwide firestorm.

"I think of Schwarzenegger every night before I go to sleep," Stallone confessed to Leigh.

In the spring of 1989, she showed him the first draft of the book she planned to call *Arnold: An Unauthorized Biography*. In her presence, he read it from cover to cover. As he sat devouring the book, she received considerable insight into the behind-the-scenes world of a Hollywood sex symbol. In the adjoining room, she recalls, Stallone's assistant fielded phone calls virtually nonstop. Almost all of them were from women offering their sexual services. Occasionally, he would put a call through to Stallone, who would pause long enough from his reading to talk to the women and turn down their propositions. After rejecting one caller, he turned to Leigh and said: "Honey, reading this is better than getting four fucks."

While she was working on her manuscript, Arnold gave an interview to ABC's *Good Morning America* expressing regret for some of the things he had said about his fellow action star in the *Playboy* interview, and he suggested that he had been quoted out of context. But by this time, Stallone was not in a forgiving mood.

"What he had to say was uncalled for, and was not something that's easily forgotten," he told Leigh. "An apology to me doesn't remedy the situation. I consider this a real betrayal and something that is not got over easily. Eventually, the matter will have to be settled in another fashion."

Shortly before she turned in her completed manuscript, Leigh claims, her publishers, Contemporary Books, received at least two calls from Schwarzenegger's people demanding that they scuttle the book. One caller implied that if they shelved it, he would write a book for them instead. But the publishers stood firm and issued the book as scheduled in early 1990.

The finished product was an impressive biography—thoroughly researched, well documented, and, above all, fair. It was so fair, in fact, that Leigh apparently received an angry phone call from Stallone claiming that the book was "too nice"—nicer, apparently, than the first draft he had read months earlier. She told him she had never promised him a hatchet job. Yet she was about to receive what she described as an "object lesson in Hollywood power politics." The planned publicity campaign, she revealed, ran into repeated obstacles as numerous television shows suddenly scrapped her appearances because, she believes, they feared the wrath of both Arnold and his studio benefactors. As a result, few people ended up reading the first important chronicle of Arnold's early life and career.

Leigh claims that not long after the book was released, Arnold—suspecting his rival's hand in helping her—began to tell friends that Stallone was upset at him for more than simply his disparaging magazine interviews. Arnold allegedly claimed that he had deliberately dumped Brigitte Nielsen on Stallone, knowing how volatile she was. He had allegedly arranged for them to meet through his attorney, Jake Bloom, whom

Brigitte knew from the filming of *Red Sonja*. Their subsequent marriage and bitter divorce had given Arnold the last laugh.

But, as it turned out, that's not how Stallone and Nielsen met at all. The way they both later told the story, he met his future wife after she sent him a nude photo of herself and he called her to ask her for a date.

Were all these stories simply cleverly conceived by both rivals to provide the illusion that there was an ongoing and dramatic feud, which would further their careers by giving moviegoers a chance to take sides? It certainly seemed that way around the time Leigh's book was released, when the two action stars found themselves together at poolside during the Cannes Film Festival. With paparazzi snapping away, the two musclemen began to do a tango together, laughing and appearing as if they were the best of friends. Less than a year later, they suddenly announced their partnership in Planet Hollywood. For years afterward—to the present day, in fact—they appeared together in public, joking and ribbing each other, with no sign of animosity on public view.

Leigh remains convinced that this friendship is phony, not the feud itself.

"That is how Hollywood works," she wrote in the *London Daily Mail*, revealing Stallone's role for the first time in 2005. "If it suits Schwarzenegger and Stallone for the world to think of them as good buddies, that is how millions of people will think of them. And since 1991 it has suited them for us to do just that. . . . Looking back on the whole curious saga, the main emotion I feel for Stallone is pity. He may still be fabulously wealthy, but he is forever locked into playing best friends with a man he secretly despises."

And how does Leigh feel, having been used as a pawn by Stallone?

"I truly do not regret my pact with the Hollywood devil," she declares unapologetically, "because, for better or worse, it brought me unprecedented insight into the lives and secret machinations of the celluloid gods we choose to worship."

19.

Tying the Kennedy Knot

Arnold and Maria's relationship had been going on for eight years, and questions were coming more frequently, especially from their families. What were their plans? Were there wedding bells in their future? Neither had even hinted publicly that they planned to make a life together, and it was clear to those who knew him that Arnold had been seeing other women on and off for years. Many assumed that Maria was merely what one friend of Arnold's called "Kennedy arm candy"—somebody he could bring to public functions to enhance his social status while continuing his usual womanizing.

This theory was given further credence by the fact that the two had never even lived together. Instead, Maria lived with her brother Bobby in Santa Monica, about ten minutes away from where Arnold resided.

In 2009, I had lunch in New York with a former colleague of Maria's from CBS News who had her own theory about why they kept separate residences.

"I obviously can't prove it," she told me, "but a bunch of us were convinced that Maria was a thirty-year-old virgin. She was literally saving herself for marriage."

I found that hard to believe, especially given her longtime relationship with Arnold Schwarzenegger, who made no secret of his unquenchable sexual desires, but she did key me into something that lends credence to the idea: "Maria is no garden-variety Catholic. She's the real thing, maybe the only one I ever met unless you count the time I interviewed a priest."

Indeed, unlike most of her Kennedy cousins, who are hardly poster children for their religion, I have learned that Maria Shriver is a true believer—much like her mother and grandmother. So devout was her mother, Eunice, in fact, that she was a rare Democrat who was staunchly pro-life and frequently took the party to task for its pro-choice platform. Before her death in 2009, both Eunice and Sargent were daily communicants; that is, they received communion from a priest every day, not just on Sundays. However, Maria seems even more devout than her parents, if that is possible—closer in this respect to her grandmother Rose, who claimed that her deep religious beliefs helped sustain her through countless family tragedies. So strong was Rose's Catholicism that Pope Pius XII named her a papal countess of the church. Maria has claimed that her grandmother was her spiritual guide and is responsible for her devotion to the church. "I'm a practicing Catholic and devout Catholic, who goes to Mass every single day," she regularly tells audiences.

It is hardly difficult to imagine someone as devout as Maria Shriver refusing to engage in premarital sex, which is a mortal sin in her religion. But it is also hard to imagine Arnold Schwarzenegger involved in an eight-year platonic relationship.

Perhaps a clue can be found in something Arnold's ex-girlfriend Sue Moray—who was dating him before and after he met Maria—told Wendy Leigh. Despite the fact that she and Arnold had an open relationship and would often confide in each other about their sexual escapades, Arnold told Sue, "She's young. I don't sleep with her; she's just a friend." He continued to deny that he and Maria were sleeping together, and Leigh naturally concludes that this was a subterfuge. But why would he lie to Sue about sleeping with Maria when he was completely up-front with her about his other sexual partners?

As their relationship progressed, Arnold would tell friends who asked that they had to keep up appearances because Maria was a Catholic.

Whatever the truth, Arnold was clearly not suffering from enforced celibacy. His old bodybuilding friend Rick Wayne told me that after Arnold started dating Maria, "he was getting a blow job backstage a couple of minutes before he went out to compete. . . . he was really enjoying himself—and remember, when he bedded a woman, whether it was a one-off thing or someone he was seeing casually, he was so into himself that he actually believed he was doing the woman a favor, that she was going to have the time of her life with him just because it was him."

His affairs were legion. But what about Maria, who, when she was young, had contemplated becoming a nun? Her former colleague believes that she finally got married not because she wanted to settle down with Arnold, but because she wanted to have children. Maria would, in fact, later confide to Laurence Leamer that she turned down marriage proposals from Arnold twice before she finally said yes.

On my trip to Arnold Schwarzenegger's birthplace in 2009, his childhood friend Karl Kling—owner of the Thalersee inn—directed my attention to the edge of the lake close to the inn where Arnold used to do pull-ups from the branch of an oak tree. At the end of a path, there is a rowboat propped up vertically, its oars sticking down as if holding the boat upright. Facing out from inside the boat was a giant photo of Maria Shriver and Arnold Schwarzenegger, smiling, with an inscription in German identifying it as the Boot des Versprechens (the boat of the proposal). It was in this boat, I was told, that Arnold finally popped the question to Maria Shriver in the middle of the lake in August 1985 (though I later learned that the boat is actually a replica of the original).

The way Arnold's longtime friend and business partner Jim Lorimer tells it, he was the one who finally persuaded Arnold to tie the knot. Lorimer was visiting Arnold in Santa Monica in the late spring of 1985 and the two were lounging in the Jacuzzi just after midnight. According to the story Lorimer told Laurence Leamer, he advised his friend, "Arnold, you've been going with this girl now for eight years. The relationship has stood the test of time. She has a career, you have a career; you're very successful, and nobody could accuse you of marrying the girl for her money. You don't need anybody's money. You don't have to work for the rest of your life. But you've got to experience all of life's processes. And that means marriage, stable home, children and grandchildren. You've got to make the move and ask her to marry you."

Lorimer, who claims that Arnold thanked him for the advice but was generally dismissive, believes it was his impassioned plea that finally persuaded his friend to pop the question. The implication is that Maria was just waiting to be asked and Arnold was procrastinating. Yet Maria herself claims that she turned Arnold down twice before finally accepting his proposal.

For his part, Arnold says that he was already planning to ask her long before his late-night session in the Jacuzzi with Lorimer. He finally decided to do so in August, on a trip to Thal to visit his mother.

"I carried the engagement ring around with me for half a year," he told the *Los Angeles Times* in 1989. "I could never find the place I thought was right. I went to Hawaii and thought maybe this is it. What a stupid thing, everybody goes to Hawaii to get engaged. Then another trip and another. Finally, we went to Austria. I was showing Maria the place where I grew up. We were driving by this lake and I said, 'Would you like to go rowing?' She said, 'I would love to.' There we were in the middle of this lake that I learned to swim in, in my home village. I thought, 'This is great, this is it,' and I pulled the ring out and proposed right then. It became a very romantic day. Later, I told her I did this on water so in case she said no I could throw her in."

The question of why Arnold finally decided to tie the knot is easily answered. It was all part of "the plan"— the carefully orchestrated timeline, which he had charted for his life at an early age and which appeared to guide many of his decisions. According to his first serious girlfriend, Barbara Outland, Arnold was very organized when it came to planning such decisions. "He was a prolific goal setter," she told the *Daily Telegraph*. "He would write the most extraordinary targets on little index cards on January 1. Ridiculous things, like starting a mail-order business or buying a BMW. And, by the end of the year, they'd all be done."

She didn't know that Arnold had already vowed to one day marry into a prominent family, but when it came to settling down, Barbara soon discovered, to her dismay, that in more ways than one, she didn't fit into his plans. It was, in fact, his refusal to marry her that had prompted Outland to break up with him a decade earlier: she wanted marriage and kids and he said "he couldn't go there" because he wasn't ready. "He said he didn't want to marry until he turned forty," she recalled. When Arnold rowed out to the middle of the lake and proposed to Maria that August afternoon in 1985, he was less than two years short of his fortieth birthday.

Clearly, Arnold was now ready. Less clear is why Maria waited so long. Perhaps her career was more important to her at that stage. "My mother got married at 30," she had recently told a reporter. "She was working before she got married. My mother has always worked and raised a family. She had a husband who respected her and encouraged her. I think I should work. But I think people should go through cycles in their lives. Right now, work is the most important thing to me."

Was it his recent high-profile affair with Brigitte Nielsen that finally persuaded the thirty-year-old Maria to settle down with Arnold, despite his tendency to stray? Or was it indeed her longing to start a family? Whatever it was, her reaction to Arnold's proposal was decidedly less romantic than he remembered it. She later told *Us* magazine that when Arnold popped the question for the third time, she replied, "Hey, Arnold, what's so special about today? Have I been especially *good* lately? Have I gotten really *beautiful*?"

She said yes, but they still had not set a date. That became even more complicated upon her return to the states, when her agent called with some career-changing news.

In 1980, a reporter had asked Maria—still a relatively neophyte broadcaster—where she wanted to be five years from now. She answered, "I'd really like to be on one of the morning news shows." The morning shows tend to have only one female anchor, and at the time, the prospect seemed unlikely. Diane Sawyer was firmly entrenched at CBS, Jane Pauley on the *Today* show, and Joan Lunden at *Good Morning America*. In the interval, however, Sawyer soon jumped to *60 Minutes* and was replaced on the *CBS Morning News* by the former Miss America turned broadcaster, Phyllis George. Then five years after Maria had first been asked the question, George suddenly announced her resignation—she had drawn severe criticism for asking an accused rapist and his victim to hug on live television—and there was an opening. Everybody in the business coveted the job, but it was now being offered to Maria, who had impressed many in the industry with her professionalism, poise, and on-camera presence while working as the CBS Los Angeles correspondent for the last several years.

"Her Kennedy family connections certainly didn't hurt, but those kinds of business decisions aren't based on who you're related to," recalls a former colleague. "CBS was a billion-dollar business and they wouldn't have hired her if they didn't think it was good for business. She was the perfect choice."

Maria was nothing if not ambitious and did not hesitate to accept the job even though it would take her across the continent from her new fiancé. In the end, she explained to the *New York Times*, practical considerations won out.

"I had to make a wrenching decision," she said. "It was the job I'd always wanted. But I had worked a long time at that relationship, and I had just finally gotten it where I wanted it, and all of a sudden, I was faced with moving 3,000 miles away and pursuing a very demanding job. But I knew that if I didn't take it, there were other people who would."

She and Arnold talked it over, he urged her to take the job, and they decided they would somehow make it work, despite the distance.

Again, it appears to be religion that Maria turned to for guidance. "I'm a firm believer, a religious person. I was born and brought up Catholic, and I believe that God is watching over this and that I will be able to do both," she told the *Times* about her conflicting loyalties to both Arnold and her career.

They decided on a spring wedding, and she flew to New York to start her new job.

Six weeks before the Shriver-Schwarzenegger wedding, scheduled for April 26, 1986, the *New York*

Times revealed some shocking news about one of the leading candidates in the election campaign then under way in Arnold's homeland.

On March 5, the newspaper published a report alleging that Kurt Waldheim—a former secretary-general of the United Nations and the leading candidate in the Austrian presidential election scheduled for May—had served under a German army command that fought brutal campaigns against Yugoslav partisans and engaged in mass deportations of Greek Jews during World War II. The *Times* also revealed the existence of documents suggesting that Waldheim had voluntarily enrolled in a Nazi student union—the National Socialist German Students' League—as well as a branch of the notorious Brown Shirts, the SA, after Austria was annexed to Nazi Germany in 1938. When he was eventually drafted into the German army, the Wehrmacht, he served on the staff of a war criminal, General Alexander Löhr, the "butcher of the Balkans," who was eventually executed in 1945.

The news of Waldheim's Nazi ties was especially surprising because he had always publicly claimed to be a devout anti-Nazi. In 1981, in fact, Waldheim had given an interview to the *Times* claiming that he had joined the anti-Nazi Austrian youth movement and that his father was an outspoken anti-Nazi who was jailed by the Gestapo for his opposition. "We lived in constant fear.," he told the paper. "My father had to present himself to the authorities regularly. We were always shadowed by the police."

But the World Jewish Congress uncovered documents in the Austrian archives proving that Waldheim had in fact concealed his Nazi past in what the organization called "one of the most elaborate deceptions of our time." Waldheim immediately denied the charges and claimed they were the result of a "conspiracy." The documents presented by the *Times*, however, left little doubt that he had voluntarily joined two separate Nazi organizations before the war.

He was cornered and had to admit that he had indeed belonged to the two groups, but insisted he had joined only to shield his family from persecution.

In his 1986 autobiography, *In the Eye of the Storm*, Waldheim wrote that his military career had ended in December 1941, when he suffered a leg wound on the eastern front. He was discharged and permitted to finish law school at Vienna University, where he graduated in 1944.

However, military records captured by the Allies after the war proved that Waldheim was actually assigned to a German unit in Salonika, Greece, and later to Yugoslavia, where he served as an interpreter.

Once again, Waldheim was forced to acknowledge his membership in these units but claimed that he had a minor role.

In Salonika, Waldheim's commanding officer was General Löhr, who, according to the Holocaust historian Gerald Reitlinger, was "perhaps more implicated in Jewish deportations than any other Wehrmacht commander." Reitlinger reveals that under Löhr's command, 42,380 Jews were deported from Salonika to death camps at Treblinka, Auschwitz, and Lubin.

Informed of these statistics, Waldheim insisted he knew nothing about them and that his activity consisted merely of analyzing reports on enemy troop movements.

"I regret these things most deeply, but I have to repeat that it is really the first time that I hear that such things happened," he said. "I never heard or learned anything of this while I was there. I hear for the first time that there were deportations of Jews from there." More documents would eventually emerge—including a 1945 CIA report—proving that Waldheim was actually a German intelligence officer and not simply an interpreter.

Commissioned by the World Jewish Congress to comb through archives in Germany and the United States, Dr. Robert E. Herzstein, an expert in European history, discovered more incriminating papers in Washington's National Archives, captured from Waldheim's former military unit after the war. One set of documents discovered by Herzstein contained daily intelligence reports on "mopping-up" operations as well as interrogations of prisoners in Croatia and Greece. These reports bore the signature of a Lieutenant Kurt Waldheim and were very damning.

According to Herzstein, these operations consisted of "extermination campaigns directed against hostages, civilians, alleged harborers of partisans and entire villages." In 1944, Waldheim put his initials on a packet of anti-Semitic propaganda leaflets to be dropped behind Russian lines. One of them declared, "Enough of the Jewish war, kill the Jews, come over."

Curiously, as the evidence accumulated that Waldheim had been involved, directly or indirectly, in Nazi atrocities and that he had lied about his wartime role, his popularity in Austria soared. His small lead in the polls before the revelations had now doubled, in part because of a backlash led by Waldheim's People's Party, which suggested that his opponents were behind the "smears." The allegations also set off a disturbing wave of anti-Semitism as Waldheim's supporters accused the Jews of trying to bring him down. This was not especially surprising, as Austria had persistently refused to come to terms with its role in the Holocaust. The country had resolutely refused to pay compensation to the Nazis' victims and, after 1970, had refused to investigate Austrian citizens who were senior Nazis, many of whom went on to lead prosperous lives after the war with virtually no repercussions for their involvement in Nazi crimes against humanity.

Inexplicably, Waldheim ended up with a landslide victory in the presidential election in May, setting off worldwide revulsion. The U.S. Justice Department had already put him on a "watch list," declaring him persona non grata, forbidden to travel to the United States. Many Western countries followed suit, making Waldheim an international pariah for his entire term of office. This posed considerable problems, since the post is largely ceremonial and usually requires the officeholder to travel abroad for state visits, funerals, and other such occasions.

Reeling from the international condemnation, the Austrian government eventually decided to appoint an international committee of historians to probe their new president's activities between 1938 and 1945. Their report, issued in 1988, found no direct evidence that Waldheim personally participated in a war crime, although they did conclude that he "must have known of the war crimes committed by the unit in which he served from 1942 to the end of the war, German Army Group E. It was responsible for sending thousands of Jews, civilians, partisans, and Allied commandos to concentration camps, forced labor and death." This contradicts Waldheim's repeated assertion that he had no knowledge of such atrocities. In contrast, the report found that "he repeatedly went along with unlawful acts and thereby made it easier for them to be carried out." Nobody had ever suggested that he directly participated in war crimes; it was claimed only that he knew about them, so his subsequent assertion that the report vindicated him is disingenuous at best.

The famous Nazi hunter Simon Wiesenthal studied the commission's findings and was especially alarmed by the account of Waldheim's time in Salonika, Greece. Over the course of several weeks, the Jewish community—which, before the war, formed one-third of the population in Salonika—was sent to Auschwitz. Taking note of Waldheim's denial that he knew anything about those deportations, Wiesenthal stated, "I could only reply what the committee of historians likewise made clear in its report: I cannot believe you." Wiesenthal reiterated that there was no evidence found by the committee that Waldheim took part in any direct war crimes, but that he was definitely guilty of lying about his military record.

However, Neil Sher, head of the U.S. Justice Department's Office of Special Investigations, took issue with the conclusion that Waldheim had participated in no direct war crimes. "Under the Nuremberg standard, one who is involved in the implementation and facilitation of deportations of civilians is culpable of war crimes," Sher declared, adding that the United States found that Waldheim "personally participated in persecution" of civilians while serving as a lieutenant in the German army during World War II, "and the evidence against him is overwhelming."

Around the time the first charges were leveled against Waldheim in the spring of 1985—when new revelations about his Nazi affiliations were emerging every day—he received an invitation to the wedding of Arnold Schwarzenegger and Maria Shriver. It was only fitting. Months earlier—during the trip to Austria when Arnold proposed to Maria—he had been introduced to Waldheim through the connections of his old mentor, Alfred Gerstl.

Gerstl's own political mentor was Josef Krainer, the powerful governor of Styria, who was part of a family political dynasty dating back to 1945 when his father was elected governor. (The elder Krainer would serve for twenty-three years.) Gerstl had turned to Krainer when he needed a favor two years earlier, and Krainer had pulled strings to allow Arnold to keep his Austrian citizenship after becoming an American. By 1985, however, Schwarzenegger was close enough to Krainer that he no longer needed Gerstl as a go-between. Each time he returned home to visit his mother, he would pay a visit to Krainer at the Burg, a stately fifteenth-century castle, built by Emperor Frederick III in Graz, which now houses offices of the Styrian provincial government.

Arnold was impressed by the worldliness of Krainer, and was said to be thrilled that he had the ear of someone so powerful. For his part, Krainer knew that Arnold was Austria's most famous export and was eager to use Arnold's fame for his own political ends. Krainer also took any opportunity to extol the virtues of his party's conservative free-market ideology to his famous visitor, who was tremendously receptive.

Through Krainer, Arnold also got to know Werner Kopacka, the correspondent in Graz for Austria's largest newspaper, *Kronen Zeitung*. According to Kopacka, Arnold had by that time become fascinated with Austrian politics and would call him regularly about developments in his homeland. "He wanted to know everything, all the scandals, all the political news, and why this politician or that one lost the elections," Kopacka told Joe Mathews, author of *The People's Machine*.

Josef Krainer was a longtime political ally of Waldheim, who was running under the banner of the Austrian People's Party in the coming election. When Arnold showed up in Graz in August 1985, Krainer arranged a get-together to introduce Arnold and Maria to Waldheim. The trio immediately hit it off, and Arnold offered his full support. A month later, in September 1985, Krainer arranged for Arnold to sign a letter to his fellow Austrians endorsing Waldheim, who eventually featured the endorsement on his campaign posters. At that time, the charges about his Nazism had not yet surfaced. When they did arise the following March, it did not stop Arnold from adding Waldheim's name to the guest list—which included a number of other dignitaries, such as Pope John Paul II and Ronald Reagan—although some claim the invitations were sent out before the political storm broke on March 5.

Two days before the scheduled April 26 wedding, the U.S. government placed Waldheim on its official watch list. This would have prevented him from attending the wedding even if he wanted to, but he was too busy campaigning for the May election and had already sent his regrets.

On the day of the ceremony, most people were not even aware of Arnold's links to Waldheim, so it would not be accurate to claim that the controversy cast a pall over the proceedings as the wedding got under way.

The ceremony took place on a Saturday morning in the historic St. Francis Xavier Roman Catholic Church in Hyannis Port, where generations of Kennedys had been baptized, married, and buried. The scene outside the church was like a royal wedding, which is indeed what this was, as thousands of spectators thronged the streets hoping for a glimpse of the celebrity attendees. Locals claimed that they had not seen as much commotion in the town since John F. Kennedy was president.

About forty-five minutes before the scheduled 11 A.M. wedding, limos began pulling up outside the church, depositing the 450 attendees. Despite the run-up, the guest list wasn't particularly star-studded. Considering Arnold's exalted status in Hollywood at the time, there were surprisingly few big names. Most of the notables were, in fact, friends of Maria or the Kennedy family, people like Tom Brokaw, Forrest Sawyer, Quincy Jones, Oprah Winfrey, and Abigail Van Buren, otherwise known as "Dear Abby." Andy Warhol, who brought Arnold's *Conan* costar Grace Jones as his escort, had been invited because Arnold had commissioned him to paint a portrait of Maria as a wedding gift. The pair showed up twenty minutes late in an orange Volvo, befitting their eccentric reputations. Among the rumored attendees who were no-shows were Clint Eastwood, Dan Rather, Barbara Walters, and Princess Caroline of Monaco. Their names had repeatedly surfaced in the weeks leading up to the wedding but they themselves were nowhere in sight.

Franco Columbu served as Arnold's best man, and the guest list included many of Arnold's longtime friends, including bodybuilders; friends from Austria, Germany, and England such as Albert Busek and Wag Bennett; and numerous business associates.

"Arnold has always surrounded himself with his old friends, most of them unknowns, as opposed to other movie stars who hobnob only with other celebrities," a former bodybuilder and onetime friend of Arnold told me. "People think it proves he's a genuine person, and maybe he is, but that's not the reason. These are the only people he can trust to keep his secrets—and, believe me, he's got a lot of secrets. These are the Arnie loyalists; their devotion to him is absolute and he knows they will never betray him, never sell their story to a tabloid."

As the guests disembarked at the steps of the church for the ceremony, Arnold drove by in his limo. Passing the cheering throngs, he rolled down the window and waved to the crowd, holding a cigar in one hand, before driving to the back of the church and preparing for his entrance.

The bride wore a stunning $10,000 Dior wedding dress, complete with a ten-foot silk train, but the crowd paid more attention to Maria's aunt, Jackie Onassis, as she emerged from her limo. "Oh, she's so gorgeous," one woman gushed to reporters before nearly fainting from excitement.

Sargent Shriver escorted his daughter down the aisle to the strains of the Wagner bridal march from *Lohengrin*. Caroline Kennedy served as Maria's maid of honor and Maria's longtime friend Oprah Winfrey recited Elizabeth Barrett Browning's poem "How Do I Love Thee (Let Me Count the Ways)." As the couple left the church, the organist played "Maria" from *The Sound of Music* and the crowd roared its approval.

The newlyweds and the other guests were whisked back to the nearby Kennedy compound for the reception. There, under two huge tents set up for the occasion, a seven-foot, eight-tier, 425-pound carrot cake awaited them. The only sour note concerned Arnold's elderly mother, Aurelia, who had flown in from Austria for the occasion. According to Schwarzenegger biographer Laurence Leamer, several of the wedding guests took note of how badly Aurelia was treated by the Kennedy family, telling Leamer that the Kennedys didn't even bother to greet the mother of the groom. Maria, however, later adamantly denied that Aurelia had been treated shabbily. "I've never seen in my lifetime a woman treated as a queen as that woman was," she told Leamer.

However, it wasn't Aurelia's treatment that grabbed the attention of most wedding guests that afternoon. Instead, it was life-size papier-mâché statues of Arnold and Maria with her wearing a traditional Austrian dirndl and him wearing lederhosen. The guests couldn't take their eyes off this kitschy display, which they soon learned was a gift from Kurt Waldheim. The pope merely sent a blessing, President Reagan a telegram.

If the guests were wondering why the disgraced Austrian politician would be sending a gift to Arnold and Maria, it didn't take them long to discover the reason. Reporters had been kept strictly away from both the wedding and the reception. The Shrivers had even used their powerful political connections to have the airspace over Cape Cod closed to traffic for the afternoon to prevent a news helicopter from taking photos, as had happened at other recent high-profile celebrity weddings.

Maria's friends in the media would not, of course, blab. But in the end Andy Warhol's diary, published after his 1987 death, provided a glimpse of something that happened during the afternoon which Arnold and Maria would probably have preferred to remain a secret.

At one point during the reception, Arnold tapped a spoon on his champagne glass to get the attention of the guests, then directed people's attention to the papier-mâché statues, which he informed them were a present from his friend Kurt Waldheim, and proposed a toast:

"My friends don't want me to mention Kurt's name, because of all the recent Nazi stuff and the U.N. controversy, but I love him and Maria does too, and so thank you, Kurt."

The surprising gesture to the Austrian politician—whose name had been plastered all over the newspapers just a day earlier in connection with the ban on his travel to the United States—was later confirmed by another guest, Terry Smith, a correspondent for CBS News. The toast was said to have caused Jackie Onassis to pale visibly. In addition, Arnold's longtime friend Richard Burkholder told Wendy Leigh that Arnold "wished Kurt Waldheim was at the wedding. He also assured everyone that Waldheim hadn't done what he had been accused of."

Whether or not Arnold had heard the most serious allegations against Waldheim before he sent the candidate an invitation to his wedding, there was no doubt that he had been fully briefed by the time he visited Austria again in August 1986, three months after Waldheim had won his nation's election with 54 percent of the vote. On that visit, Arnold made it a special point to visit the new president at his summer home, outside Salzburg. During this visit, the two men spent almost three hours together and were photographed extensively by the Austrian media.

Those close to Arnold, including members of the Kennedy family and reportedly Maria herself, wondered why he chose to stand by an accused Nazi rather than distance himself from someone so controversial.

20.

Hardly a Honeymoon

Their honeymoon was a quick jaunt to Antigua, with both newlyweds having to go back to work almost immediately—Arnold to wrap up his latest film, *Raw Deal,* and Maria back to the set of the CBS *Morning News,* which she couldn't afford to leave for long, as she feared that her bosses might be tempted to make her replacement permanent.

"The ratings were lousy," confides a former CBS colleague. "They thought bringing in Maria would make the show more competitive, but it didn't happen. The show was stuck in third place and we weren't anywhere near second. She had to have known she was in trouble because there was open speculation in the papers that they might be looking for a replacement."

Asked by Boston's WBZ-TV how he and Maria would manage to start a family, being on different coasts, Arnold deflected the question with one of his trademark off-the-cuff replies. "We have over-the-phone sex," he quipped.

Acknowledging that this method might not work biologically, however, he turned serious. "We fly back and forth as much as possible and we run up thousands of dollars in phone bills, but there's no way we can have children with her on the East Coast and me on the West Coast." Still, he said he was very supportive of her career. "It's only a temporary thing. But she should do it because she'll be happy the rest of her life because she's done it."

To another reporter, he said, "I don't need to have Maria around me all day long. I'm independent enough also to understand that Maria needs her own life and career and I'm happy that she's goal oriented and wants to accomplish a lot of things and be competitive out there." He admitted that it was hard for him at first to get used to the idea of strong career women. He was raised to believe, he confessed, that the ideal woman stayed at home. But that was before he was "reeducated" in America and understood the value of women's "doing their thing."

"It's an asset for a woman to have these qualities. You can have more interesting discussions, talk more intelligently with such a woman," he told the Brisbane (Australia) *Courier Mail.*

After Arnold wrapped up shooting *Raw Deal,* there wasn't time for him to spend more than a couple of days with his new wife before he had to fly to Mexico to begin shooting his next film, *Predator.* By this point, Arnold had carved out a niche for himself as an action star, guaranteed to draw young men as well as international audiences with his macho image. In at least one way, he was like his rival Stallone, who was still number one at the box office: critics didn't know what to make of him. Tempted though they may have been after a golden era that produced some of Hollywood's most riveting and acclaimed dramas, reviewers couldn't simply dismiss his films as trash, though at the same time these films were hardly cinematic masterpieces. There was something about Arnold's on-screen presence—an almost indefinable quality—that kept even the most discerning critics in their seats, despite their better instincts. The *New Yorker*'s Pauline Kael articulated that sentiment in her review of *Raw Deal,* in which Arnold played a former FBI agent enlisted to destroy a mob organization from the inside.

"It's reprehensible and enjoyable, the kind of movie that makes you feel brain dead in two minutes—after which point you're ready to laugh at its mixture of trashiness, violence, and startlingly silly crude humor. As a lawman who infiltrates the biggest mob in Chicago, Arnold Schwarzenegger is a puzzling, cartoon phenomenon, like a walking brick wall."

In *Predator* Arnold played the leader of an elite team assigned to rescue hostages from a communist guerrilla force in the jungles of Central America. Meanwhile, the team is hunted by an extraterrestrial creature, who has arrived on a spaceship. Playing Major Dutch Schaefer, Arnold brings a moral bearing to his character, which one reviewer described as a "killing machine with a heart."

Again, there is a lot of violence and not a lot of artistic merit, but somehow Arnold's performance is compelling and the reviews were generally good. The *Syracuse Post-Standard* noted particularly how much his performance had improved from his earlier films. "He has obviously been taking acting lessons, for his intonation and his timing are near perfect. If he'll never be the next Laurence Olivier, he may well be the new John Wayne."

And, despite the almost nonstop violence, more than one reviewer incongruously made note of Arnold's comic timing. When *Predator* was released, his films were perhaps as well known for their memorable one-liners as for anything in the plot. Some critics believed, in fact, that Arnold's comedic talent and ability to put across catchphrases helped overshadow his often wooden acting.

In *Conan the Barbarian*, for example, the most memorable line was delivered by Conan after he was asked by a Mongol general what was the best thing in life.

"To crush your enemies, see them driven before you, and to hear the lamentation of the women!" he replies—a line that many young men would repeat in the halls of their high schools for years to come, often with a thick Ah-nuld accent.

In its 1984 follow-up, *Conan the Destroyer*, a girl remarks to Conan, "I suppose nothing hurts you."

"Only pain," he replies.

In *The Terminator*, as Arnold loads a shotgun in a shop, the clerk tells him, "You can't do that."

"Wrong," he replies, shooting the clerk dead.

In *Commando*, the film with perhaps more memorable one-liners than any of his others, an army general asks his character, Matrix, whether he's "left anything for us."

"Just bodies," he replies.

When he commandeers a seaplane, the heroine, Cindy, tells him, "This isn't a plane, this is a canoe with wings!"

"Then get in and start paddling," Matrix retorts.

In *Raw Deal*, his wife throws a cake at him in a drunken fit, and he simply replies, "You should not drink . . . and bake."

These witty one-liners often served to humanize an otherwise brutal character and have redeemed the somewhat formulaic action movies. But there definitely were Americans who didn't find anything funny about the orgies of gratuitous violence between the bon mots that characterized most of Arnold's films during this era.

The spectacular rise in popularity of the action film during the 1980s had prompted soul-searching and a backlash among American conservatives, who often looked for any excuse to bash Hollywood and excoriate the industry for corrupting young minds.

In 1992, the film critic and prominent social conservative Michael Medved would publish a book called *Hollywood vs. America: Popular Culture and the War on Traditional Values*. In it, he declared that America's long-running romance with Hollywood was "over," articulating what many of his fellow conservatives had been saying for years about the influence of Hollywood films. In language that had once been used exclusively to attack pornography, Medved fired a shot across the industry's bow, purporting to speak for "tens of millions" of disenchanted Americans who he claimed now saw the entertainment industry as an "alien force that assaults our most cherished values and corrupts our children." The "dream factory," he concluded, had become the "poison factory."

He named Schwarzenegger, among others, as having a role in spreading the poison. This was nothing new to Arnold, who had been watching the rising storm for years. In 1988, for example, he received a dubious honor from the National Coalition on Television Violence, which named him the most violent actor of the year, with a score of 146 atrocities per hour in his latest film, *The Running Man*.

But Arnold had no time for such criticism, as he made clear when *Playboy* asked him whether he thought too much violence was bad for people.

"If I thought it was, then I wouldn't do those films," he responded. "As far as I'm concerned, it doesn't influence people. I watched violent movies all my life and it had no influence on me. Something on the screen doesn't turn a person into a killer unless there's something already wrong with him. And I don't think when you make a movie you can say, 'There's some crazy person out there who may take this the wrong way, who may do something crazy.' If you did that, you would never make a movie."

Asked what he thought about studies showing that screen violence negatively affects young people in particular, and about efforts by parent groups to stop it, he was equally dismissive.

"Yeah, yeah, I know about the P.T.A.," he said. "But this is just parents who don't want to take responsibility for controlling their kids. They work or are divorced or something. They think they don't have the time. Besides that, the press and the TV news focus on violence—real violence—all the time. Every local news show starts with how many killings happened that day."

The drumbeat of criticism, and his hostile response, indicated the first visible schism between Arnold and a sizable segment of his fellow Republicans and would later help account for his antipathy to the far right wing of his chosen political party.

There was one thing he didn't say when responding to such criticism, but he and the studio execs who hired him were well aware of it. Violent action films were good for business and were rapidly helping Arnold narrow the gap between him and Sylvester Stallone, his longtime rival for box office supremacy. Stallone was still ahead, but not by much, and Arnold could sense the tide beginning to shift.

For his semi-authorized 2005 biography, *Fantastic*, Laurence Leamer interviewed Arnold's longtime friend Sven-Ole Thorsen, the bodybuilder turned actor who appeared in many of his films. Thorsen told Leamer that in 1988, following the release of Arnold's latest film, *Red Heat*, he walked in on his friend reading an issue of *Variety*, a tear running down his cheek. Thorsen asked what was wrong, Arnold replied, "Fucking *Red Heat*." Thorsen was confused by his distress. "Come on," he said. "It's number two. Come on."

"You don't understand," Arnold replied. "I want to be number one."

Ironically, the genre that he had made his own would not finally vault him into the top spot. Instead, a rather unlikely film was about to cement his reputation as one of the most powerful and profitable actors Hollywood has ever seen.

A few years earlier, Arnold was on a ski trip in Colorado with Maria when he happened to bump into the hot young director Ivan Reitman, who had directed the huge 1984 comedy hit *Ghostbusters*. Reitman would later recall his first encounter with Arnold.

"He comes up to me in the lobby of some club and says, 'You're that *Ghostbusters* guy, right.' And I said, 'Yeah, hi, I'm Ivan Reitman,' and he said, 'You know, I can be a Ghostbuster.' I just sort of looked at him and wondered what he actually meant by that. What he was trying to tell me is 'Look, I'm actually a pretty funny guy and I think I can do comedy.' " The director was highly skeptical.

But after seeing Arnold flawlessly deliver many of his memorable one-liners in film after film with a straight face, Reitman no longer thought the idea of Arnold as a comedian was so far-fetched. Those who knew Arnold outside his tough guy film persona already knew his comedic side.

At his 1988 Friars' Club roast, he delivered some of the funniest lines that club members had heard from a roastee in many years. After George Carlin described his first impressions upon meeting Arnold, "He's so lifelike," Arnold retorted, "You thought you'd embarrass me with that filth. Well, I heard worse language in Hyannis Port when they found out I was a Republican . . . I'm such an easy target. It's one of the rare nights when people can insult me and know that I won't kick their butts."

Riffs on the Kennedy-Republican connection were already a standard feature of Arnold's repertoire, and he trotted out amusing variations on the theme whenever he could.

The Kennedys were equally adept at joking about their unlikely in-law. "Who wants to argue with Arnold when he can hold you upside-down by your ankles?" quipped Uncle Teddy to one reporter.

In 1988, Reitman was developing a new project about a perfect physical specimen who goes in search of his fraternal twin brother, only to discover that his twin is a short, stocky small-time crook. He had already cast Danny DeVito, the always hilarious star of *Taxi,* as the diminutive brother. Now he thought of Arnold as the perfect foil. However, the studio, Universal, was extremely nervous about the idea of starring somebody like Arnold Schwarzenegger in a high-budget comedy, especially given its recent track record. Also, Reitman's 1986 film, *Legal Eagles*—filled with expensive big-name stars—had sunk at the box office. According to estimates by *Daily Variety,* the studio's summer film a year earlier cost $65 million to make, yet brought the studio less than $50 million in box office revenue. Universal couldn't afford another flop, and no one besides Reitman had much hope for the new project. The risks were just too high. But the director was not willing to let the idea go, convinced it would be a hit. Coming up with a new idea, he approached the studio with an offer it couldn't refuse.

Reitman, Schwarzenegger, and DeVito would work on the picture for no money up front (other than the compulsory union scale). But in lieu of a salary, the trio would split a percentage of the box office receipts from the first dollar—an unheard-of arrangement that would allow the picture to be made for the measly sum of $15.5 million. If the film was a dud, Universal would be protected. If it was a hit, the director and his two stars would clean up.

DeVito and Reitman would each receive a two-sevenths share of the predetermined percentage, while Arnold would receive three-sevenths, since he was by then commanding almost $10 million a picture.

The arrangement paid off better than even Reitman could have imagined. Moviegoers loved the film, and so did many of the critics, who singled out Arnold's comedic talents in particular.

"*Twins* keeps up some very high spirits, and proves that muscleman Schwarzenegger can handle comedy as adeptly as he has his strong man roles," raved UPI. "He plays the gags for all they're worth, and gives the role of Julius some very hilarious moments, both visually and with very bright comedic timing."

Even papers that weren't particularly enthralled with the film acknowledged Arnold's performance. "For years interviewers have been laughing at Arnold Schwarzenegger when he said he'd like to try a comedy," wrote the *Boston Globe.* "Well, Cary Grant he isn't, but he's the main reason that *Twins*, an otherwise pretty synthetic one-joke entertainment, works."

The figures were staggering. Thanks to the unusual profit-sharing arrangement, Arnold ended up with 17.5 percent of the film's $110 million domestic gross, plus a lesser share of its $100 million international take, netting him between $20 million and $25 million, thought to be the most anybody had ever made on a single film until that point. When his fellow stars heard how he had fared, many of them insisted on a similar arrangement for their next film, initiating a complex financing system that has permanently changed the way the film industry operates.

In his next film, *The Running Man*, Arnold returned to the familiar action genre. This science fiction thriller is about a mild-mannered construction worker, Douglas Quaid, played by Arnold, who buys a virtual holiday to Mars from a company that implants memories. He discovers that he is actually a Martian freedom fighter and must revisit a nightmarish world, struggling to determine what is real and what is fantasy while battling a corrupt Martian dictator intent on killing him.

The film, released in 1990, cost almost $75 million to make, this time with no complex profit-sharing to cushion the risk; but it too was wildly successful, bringing in more than $120 million domestically and securing Arnold's reputation as the biggest box office star in the world, finally leaving Stallone in the dust for good.

With this kind of box office clout also came tremendous power, which would soon prove extremely useful when he faced the first serious threat of his Hollywood career.

As he was filming *Twins* two years earlier, Arnold had gotten wind of a British reporter, Wendy Leigh, nosing around, asking questions of his friends, colleagues, and Hollywood associates. It was clear she was writing a very unauthorized biography. Arnold was nervous. The secrets she might uncover could do incalculable damage to his reputation and standing in Hollywood and beyond. At the time, the worst that was ever said about him was that he was a Republican—a subject that prompted gentle ribbing in the media, given his Kennedy connections. Little was known about his past, and few people seemed to care. He had come from the same quaint European country where *The Sound of Music* was set, but little else was written about his early years, and even when something else was written, the media usually relied on his 1977 autobiography for the details.

Only Arnold himself knew just how much Leigh might come up with, and he definitely didn't want that information disseminated. He must have been especially wary because of her involvement in a 1988 piece in Britain's newspaper *News of the World*, which hinted that Arnold may have held anti-Semitic, perhaps even pro-Nazi views, and that he was a "secret admirer of Hitler." He had filed a libel suit both against the newspaper and against Leigh herself, even though she had not written the article. She later claimed that he had named her to intimidate her into backing down on the biography she was writing. And although the newspaper apologized and settled out of court for a small sum, Leigh refused to settle. She may, however, have toned down her own book, which was finally released in the spring of 1990.

Two years later, *Spy* magazine got hold of the settlement papers that Leigh had been offered by Arnold's lawyers. *Spy* claimed that the settlement offer demanded "a promise from Leigh not to address in her book allegations [allegations—other than the use of steroids, which Schwarzenegger denies] of Arnold's homosexual experiences, his use of steroids, his sale of steroids, his theft of automobiles or his involvement in passport forgery."

She categorically refused the settlement, and the suit was still pending when she published *Arnold* in 1990. But the book itself makes no mention of any of those subjects other than Arnold's use of steroids, which he has himself admitted. In the years between the piece in *News of the World* and the publication of the book, however, Leigh received an eye-opening education on how far the Governator was willing to go to suppress the book.

When Leigh began contacting friends of Arnold for her book, she immediately discovered that many of them either had been advised not to talk to her or had been coached on what to say. The friends who agreed to be interviewed, in fact, immediately began pumping her for information about her project, leaving her with the impression that their questions had been "dictated by Arnold."

One bodybuilder confided to her that Arnold had asked him to get Leigh over to his house and tape-record her without her knowledge so that the tape could be played back for Arnold.

After his former girlfriend Sue Moray had granted Leigh an interview, she claimed that Arnold chastised her for speaking to the biographer without his permission. Another former girlfriend, Barbara Outland, suddenly received a registered letter from Arnold after years of virtually no contact. It was sent from the location of his latest film, shot in Mexico, and Arnold wrote that he wished she were there. "Arnold, what in hell is going on?" she thought to herself. She discovered exactly what was going on when she received a call from his assistant a few weeks later asking if she had been contacted by an author writing an unauthorized biography. Outland had indeed been contacted but told Leigh she didn't want to participate, as she informed the assistant.

Now she understood the registered letter, as she recalled in her 2006 memoir. "Plain and simple," she wrote. "He was kissing my ass by telling me he wished I were in Mexico with him, buttering me up for the inevitable Wendy Leigh phone call he knew would be made. It annoyed me that he chose to use such a ploy with me."

Before Leigh's book was published, Franco Columbu and one of the Weider brothers contacted her publishers, Contemporary Books, offering them the choice of either a large amount of money or a biography cowritten with Arnold if they would agree to shelve Leigh's book.

In the period leading up to the publication of *Arnold*, Leigh's publishers suffered four separate break-ins in one month, though no connection to Arnold or his people was ever proved. Contemporary Books claimed that because of these incidents, it was necessary to hire security guards, move the production schedule up three weeks, accelerate the printing of the book, and move the printing to a hidden location. The publishers also began using secret passwords and a phony title to throw snoopers off the trail. "I was also told Arnold Schwarzenegger had deep pockets and could put me out of business," recalled the head of the publishing company, Harvey Plotnick. Leigh herself claimed that she received "strange" late-night phone calls, "whispering that I'd better be careful."

Rick Wayne told me that he had once planned to write a biography of Arnold, but that members of Arnold's publicity machine had threatened to tie the book up in the courts for the rest of his life, costing him every penny he had in legal fees. He knew they weren't bluffing.

It wasn't the first time Arnold or his people had employed similar tactics to control his public image. "Arnold has achieved his position in the world largely because he wields ruthless control over his press," wrote Charles Fleming in *Spy*. "As one Paramount executive says, 'Arnold exercises power the way the old-fashioned moguls did—they could cover up anything, make any problem go away.'" It was these kinds of stories that convinced me of the need for subterfuge when I embarked on my own unauthorized project two decades later.

Much of Arnold's success in suppressing negative stories about him had been orchestrated by his longtime publicist and fellow Austrian, Charlotte Parker, who at one point was known as the "most loathed woman in Hollywood."

For years, Parker had ensured that media coverage of Arnold was tightly controlled. But as he became the world's number one box office star, this task became considerably easier. Fleming observed, "The reason Arnold gets his way with journalists is not a mystery: They need him more than he needs them. Arnold sells magazines; Arnold attracts viewers. If you don't play by Arnold's rules, then you don't get access to Arnold, and that's a difficult proposition for any magazine or television show that focuses on entertainment. In the case of a media conglomerate, the movie division may be upset if the company's newspapers or magazines offend Arnold."

The publicist for Leigh's book, Bruce Lynn, claimed that he believes Charlotte Parker threatened producers of TV shows by saying they would never interview Schwarzenegger again if they put Leigh on the air. "People told me that," Lynn revealed to the *Columbia Journalism Review*. He claims that the booker for a national TV show told him, "No way. We're doing Arnold for the movie [*Total Recall*], and we don't want to upset him."

"All publicists make deals," explained Lynn, "but this is the first time I've ever been censored." When

Kitty Kelly released her biography of Oprah Winfrey in 2010, she would experience much the same fate, as producers confided that they couldn't risk incurring the wrath of the powerful talk show host by booking Kelly. Parker has always denied such stories, but there is no question that she made a habit of controlling her client's media access with a strict set of guidelines, to which interviewers had to agree in order to secure an interview with Arnold. Such interviews, she dictated, could be only for a cover story. They had to focus on whatever movie Arnold happened to be promoting at the time, and reporters were forbidden to touch on certain topics. Parker would end an interview instantly if her rules were breached.

In June 1990 alone, Arnold's face was on the cover of five separate magazines, and, as the *Guardian* noted, "Arnie did not have these covers thrust upon him: he chose them." This respected British newspaper credited the unprecedented feat to Parker's ability to leverage Arnold's power. "If there is ever such a thing as the Second Coming, the Almighty would be well advised to use Arnie's press agent," the paper declared.

When he didn't have Parker running interference for him, Arnold had no compunction about taking matters into his own hands. In May 1987, as Arnold and Maria were entering Manhattan's Regency Hotel, a photographer attempted to take pictures of the couple. He told the *New York Post* what happened next: "Schwarzenegger came up to me and twisted my arm behind my back, grabbed me by the back of my hair and pulled my head back, arching my whole body."

At New York's Liberty Café the same year, the photographer Michael Schwartz almost suffered the same fate. He claims that after he began to take photos of Arnold seated at a table, the actor got up, walked over menacingly, and threatened him: "If you take my picture again I'm going to break your face."

When Leigh's book was finally released, it was largely either ignored or disparaged. A whispering campaign suggested to journalists that it was nothing more than a tabloid hatchet job. But James Willwerth, a veteran correspondent for *Time* magazine, thoroughly investigated her thirty-four pages of notes for a profile he was writing on Schwarzenegger at the time and claimed to have been very impressed. "It was very well reported," he told the *Columbia Journalism Review*. "My nose told me that the book was on target."

Although the book itself was actually quite balanced and generally fair, it was soon obvious that one revelation above all others threatened to do considerable damage. This was a disclosure that, once public, could not be easily contained. And to hear Arnold tell it, the shocking information that Leigh uncovered was as much a surprise to him as anybody else.

But it had taken only a visit to Berlin's national archives for Leigh to uncover the document she had been searching for. On July 4, 1938—when membership in the Austrian Nazi Party was still illegal—Gustav Schwarzenegger applied for membership and was accepted. On the fading document still held within the archives, Leigh could still make out most of his membership number, 8439?80, one digit being obscured.

Upon the book's publication, Elan Steinberg, executive director of the World Jewish Congress, immediately looked into Gustav's past and confirmed for reporters that he was indeed a Nazi, saying, "We have copies of his Nazi membership cards." But the story still didn't get a lot of play in the media and it was soon obvious why not. This is a story that Charlotte Parker had in the past denied, and now she sprang into action. Reporters who wished to ever get another interview with Arnold Schwarzenegger were warned not to ask or report about Gustav's Nazi ties. At Cannes that year, reporters seeking to interview Arnold were handed an agreement to sign. "I didn't read it very closely," revealed Garth Pearce of London's Word Star Media Service. "But it said that I would not mention the book by Wendy Leigh. . . . I didn't know the book, I didn't know the references, so I just signed so I could go along with seeing him. No one ever asked me to sign anything like it before."

Leigh was understandably upset. "[Parker] said that there's going to be major trouble if they publicize this and print that it's true," she told *Newsday*. "This is no reflection on Arnold, so why lie? I can understand the publicist of a major star denying that that person is gay. But this has been documented. Arnold could just say it's true and denounce it." For her part, Parker refused to even discuss why she had attempted to suppress the story that Arnold's father was a card-carrying member of the Nazi Party. "Ridiculous. I have no further comment," she told a reporter.

One of the shows that had contacted Leigh about a potential appearance was CNN's *Larry King Live*. She was never officially booked, but soon after the initial contact, in May 1990, Schwarzenegger himself appeared on the popular talk show. King took the opportunity to ask him about the book.

KING: You know, it got almost no attention, so I guess that asking is almost weird, but a biography came out about you, and it was labeled "the truth about Arnold Schwarzenegger," and "Nazi" and all this kind—and nobody read it, to

my knowledge. I've asked people "Did you read
the book" "No." I guess it didn't sell.
SCHWARZENEGGER: Trash doesn't sell.
People are smart enough.
KING: Did you read it?
SCHWARZENEGGER: No, I never read it, no.

Although he and his publicist had succeeded in
containing much of the damage, especially the fallout
about his father's dark past, Arnold knew that there
was more to the story than a membership card tucked
away in a dusty archive. He also knew that, although
people couldn't hold him accountable for the sins of
his father, he had rather publicly embraced another
high-profile Nazi, Kurt Waldheim. Sooner or later, his
association with two Nazis might come back to haunt
him. In a peremptory attempt at damage control, he
turned to a longtime friend for advice—and, like many
of those who had guided him in the past, this one was,
appropriately, Jewish.

Arnold Schwarzenegger's association with Marvin
Hier dates back to at least 1984, when Arnold attended
a fund-raising dinner for L.A.'s Wiesenthal Center,
named for the famous Nazi hunter. Charlotte Parker
had persuaded him to attend the dinner, a benefit for
the new Museum of Tolerance, a combination Holo-

caust museum and memorial to victims of racism and genocide worldwide. The director and founder of the center was a charismatic rabbi, under whose leadership it had become one of the most respected human rights agencies in the world. Marvin Hier had been particularly adept at enlisting Hollywood figures, executives and actors alike, in his fund-raising efforts. Parker had known him for years and had promised to send her high-profile client to this dinner. It was the beginning of Arnold's long association with Hier and the Wiesenthal Center. Just as important, it was the beginning of a financial commitment: Arnold would soon be donating at least $50,000 to the center every time he appeared in a film, and sometimes considerably more.

Hier wasn't quite sure why Arnold had embraced his cause so enthusiastically. "How many Austrians do we have that are interested in wanting to come forward?" he told Laurence Leamer. "So, I knew there was something that was driving him to be involved with this, but for a number of years I didn't know what it was."

Whatever Arnold's motivation for contributing millions of dollars to the Wiesenthal Center over the last quarter century, Hier is convinced that he is sincere in his commitment, just as I am after conducting my own investigation into Arnold's attitude toward Jews and Nazis.

It wasn't until 1990, however, that Hier learned Gustav Schwarzenegger was a Nazi. Following the publication of Wendy Leigh's biography, Arnold quietly requested that Hier look into his father's past, suggesting that he himself knew nothing about Gustav's Nazi affiliations.

But what Arnold didn't know at the time is that Wendy Leigh hadn't learned about his father's sinister activities simply by coming across a faded membership card. It was, in fact, Brigitte Nielsen who stumbled upon the secret when she visited Aurelia Schwarzenegger with Arnold during their clandestine affair in 1984. After she married Sylvester Stallone a year later, she confided the secret to her new husband, who in turn shared it with Leigh while helping her research the biography a few years later. What Nielsen discovered on that trip astonished her, as Leigh finally revealed in 2003 when she disclosed Stallone's role.

"Arnold's mother had pictures all over the house of his father dressed in his Brown Shirt uniform, Stallone told me. Arnold made no bones about the fact that his father had been a member of the Nazi Party," Nielsen told Leigh. Is this why Arnold had quietly been donating money to the Wiesenthal Center for years?

But neither the photos on Aurelia's mantel nor Gustav's long-dormant membership card told the whole story. Arnold's Nazi demons were destined to haunt him at least one more time.

Years later, in the middle of Arnold's 2003 gubernatorial campaign, the *Los Angeles Times* discovered more skeletons in Gustav's closet. He hadn't merely joined the Nazi Party in 1938, as the Wiesenthal Center claimed in its own 1990 investigation. The *Los Angeles Times* discovered that Gustav had voluntarily enlisted in the Nazi SA, or "Brown Shirts," Hitler's most ardent loyalists. During the war, he was in fact a storm trooper, a member of one of the vicious paramilitary units that committed some of the war's worst atrocities—not simply a member of the German army as he had always claimed. Still, there was no evidence linking Gustav himself to any war crimes, and the political damage was minimal.

21.
An Arnold Classic

In the beginning of June 1989, Maria took some time off from her busy schedule and flew to Mexico, where Arnold was wrapping up *Total Recall.* As usual whenever she had some time with her husband, she took a few moments to discuss their social calendar. It wasn't easy juggling their schedules, especially given the fact that they still lived on opposite coasts. After finalizing a number of dates, Maria had one more item to bring up.

"Oh, and it would be good if you have some time on December first," she said.

"What's that?" asked Arnold.

"That's when you will become a father."

There had been rumors for some time that the couple had been having problems reproducing. It had been three whole years since the wedding, and still no heir. There was even a widely reported rumor that they had consulted a sex therapist. But on December 13, 1989, their press agent announced that Maria had given birth to a little "Schwarzenshriver" following a nearly sixteen-hour labor. Arnold was with her every moment and had cut the cord moments after little Katherine Eunice was born.

"It's great to be part of the delivery," he told reporters as he emerged from the hospital. "You really respect the woman more. The pain and the hours and hours of pure torture brought us even closer together."

Arnold had made it clear that he had a very definite philosophy about raising children. His views, in fact, didn't sound much different from those of his strict Austrian parents. "I believe kids have to be treated with an iron fist," he told *USA Today*. "They should know that they are not able to make their own decisions. They have to respect their parents completely. They have to learn—to polish their own shoes, iron their own shirt, arrange their things. Every day. They have to respect their parents completely."

As she had feared, Maria had been fired from her morning anchor job at CBS not long after her 1986 wedding, because of poor ratings. NBC offered her a job as a correspondent in Los Angeles, but, according to the *New York Times*, she was "said to be reluctant," probably because the job would be considered a demotion; there was also a significant pay cut, from $500,000 a year to about $150,000. Still, as Nigel Andrews noted, it was decidedly "odd" that she would hesitate to take a job that would allow her to work in the same city as her husband.

In the spring of 1987, she finally jumped to NBC as cohost of the *Sunday Today* show, along with Garrick Utley. It meant moving back to New York and eventually to Washington, D.C., when the show switched locations a year later—but again, the couple had vowed to make this work. Maria was even busier after she was offered the prestigious anchor position on Saturday's NBC *Nightly News* broadcast.

With the birth of her baby, however, Maria shifted her priorities. She announced that she would be discontinuing her two jobs and would instead work part-time, hosting a series of news specials, *First Person with Maria Shriver*, which appeared a few times a year on NBC in prime time and could accommodate her new schedule as a mother.

Publicly, Arnold portrayed himself as a doting father who was happy to help his wife with the domestic duties of parenthood. "He's changing diapers, warming bottles, doing the whole trek," Maria told Larry King eight months after the baby was born. By most accounts, Arnold was indeed enjoying fatherhood and was certainly a more hands-on father than Gustav had ever been. "I have my soft side and I help with Katherine in any way I can," he told the *Independent*. "I feed her and hold the bottle and have her lie on my chest in the morning and I burp her." He claimed that he even enjoyed changing her diapers and "getting up in the middle of the night to rock her to sleep," though a reporter for the *Miami Herald* witnessed his diapering efforts and labeled them "clumsy," noting that it took him more than an hour to learn the technique. This suggests that such stories were merely for media consumption.

Arnold was clearly intent on having his fans believe that he and Maria were just like any typical middle-class American parents. "I couldn't do what I hear your English aristocrats do," he told Nigel Andrews. "Which is to leave the kids to nannies, see them for half an hour a day, and then send them away to school."

But the idyllic domestic picture didn't tell the whole story. He and Maria employed a team of nannies and a variety of other domestic help in their $2.8 million Pacific Palisades mansion and were anything but a typical family. Most tellingly, Arnold went back to work soon after the baby was born, spending long hours on the set of his new film, *Kindergarten Cop*.

With the success of *Twins,* both he and Ivan Reitman were anxious to put his comedic talents to the test one more time, and the director had the perfect vehicle—about a tough detective, played by Arnold, who is forced to go undercover as a kindergarten teacher to catch a drug dealer. By this point in his Hollywood career, his former bodybuilder physique had been scaled down deliberately and dramatically, in part because it wouldn't suit some of his movie roles, in part because there was little time to train.

When the film was released, it was another huge hit, though it was beaten out for top Christmas honors by Macaulay Culkin's surprise hit, *Home Alone,* and the reviews were far less favorable than those for *Twins.* Still, it grossed almost $100 million domestically and another $110 million overseas, underscoring Arnold's continuing box office clout.

Most important, Arnold was set to begin filming the sequel to *The Terminator,* which was virtually guaranteed to be a huge hit.

Like Arnold, Maria was not particularly keen on staying at home being a full-time parent. She returned to work very quickly after the birth of Katherine, flying with the baby and two nannies around the country as she worked on show segments in Seattle, Washington, and New York. In one of the more ironic segments she filmed for *First Person,* about privacy and the press, she tackled the issue of her own lack of privacy and how she was pained by the unwanted attention she constantly received as "a member of the Kennedy family and as the wife of a famous movie star."

Few sympathized with her plight, and this was one of the few times that Maria wasn't treated with kid gloves by her media colleagues. "You can send your tax-free contributions to Saving the Celebrities," wrote Walter Goodman in the *New York Times.*

Arnold would frequently echo his wife's complaints publicly, but, according to his former girlfriend Sue Moray, he actually craved the attention that came with the life of a celebrity. Moray told Wendy Leigh a story about how, before he was a superstar, she and Arnold were stranded in Denver because of a snowstorm. Needing to get to Aspen, they decided to rent a car, and when they met a man from Little Rock in the same situation, they invited him to share the car rental.

"Arnold was always complaining because people came up and bugged him for autographs," she told Leigh. "But when he realized that this man from Arkansas had never heard of him, he spent the entire trip explaining who he was and who he knew."

Years later, as his film career began to decline and requests for autographs became less frequent, Arnold dropped the pretense altogether and admitted that for him there is no such thing as unwanted attention.

"That is movie star bullshit, loss of privacy," he told James Cameron's biographer Christopher Heard in 2000. "We all want people to come see our movies, we make good livings off of people knowing who we are, loving to come watch our movies, every actor that dreams of being successful dreams of being famous— one goes with the other in this business—so to say once you get what you dreamed of that you wish people would leave you alone is fucking bullshit—if no one wanted to see you or nobody was suddenly curious about you then you would no longer have a fucking career and you would be back to saying, 'I wish people would ask for me again.' Any actor that wants his privacy back should stop making movies and move to a cabin in the fucking mountains."

There wouldn't be much privacy for Arnold in 1991 as he filmed the much-anticipated *Terminator 2: Judgment Day*, otherwise known as *T2*. Upon its release, it became his most successful film to date and also produced the line for which he would forever be associated: "*Hasta la vista*, baby." With a budget of $102 million, it was the most expensive film ever made, but it more than doubled that figure in domestic box office receipts alone, bringing in $205 million. The original

Terminator had grossed only $38 million domestically, so *T2* represented a 434 percent improvement over the original, a record that stands to this day.

In December 1990, a cover story in *Time* magazine crowned Arnold "the movies' top star." By then, his films had already taken in well over $1 billion at the box office, and that was before *Kindergarten Cop* and *T2* added almost another billion to the total. With this kind of box office clout, he was commanding as much as $15 million per picture, as well as unprecedented percentages of merchandising, profits, and other perks. Like most film stars, he was now a very rich man. But unlike most of his peers, he had wealth extending far beyond his earnings as a movie star.

Since long before he had ever appeared in a movie, Arnold had acquired a reputation as a very shrewd investor—a reputation he cultivated whenever he could.

He often told the story that when he was eleven years old, he embarked on his first business venture, buying ice cream pops for 1 Austrian schilling and selling them for 3 schillings to the tourists who came to visit the lake near his boyhood home in Thal. "I had two choices," he later recalled of his motivation. "Do I want to make some money to afford the things I want to buy, or don't I want them? I wanted them badly. I wanted a bicycle,

I wanted to buy myself some gym clothes, so I had to come up with ideas to make money. My father was not going to give it to me."

When he arrived in the United States in 1968, he couldn't help noticing Joe Weider's keen instinct for business. He vowed to learn all he could from the successful fitness mogul, who immediately advised him that the only surefire investment was real estate. It was a piece of advice that he never forgot.

"The first money he got from shows he invested," recalled his best friend, Franco Columbu. "Once he did about five shows in South Africa and then I joined him and we did another five. He said, 'I'm not going to touch any of this money; I'll put it all away.' We came back and he put every penny of it in an apartment building. Two years later, he bought a bigger one."

The same went for the money he made in his bricklaying business with Columbu and the proceeds from his early mail-order business. It was the primary reason he could claim to be a millionaire before his twenty-third birthday, despite the fact that the most he made from winning a bodybuilding tournament in those days was $1,000. While his colleagues were hustling gay sugar daddies or selling steroids to survive, Arnold was planning, saving, and thinking about life on a larger stage.

Through his early years, Arnold always strove to understand how business works and how he could work the angles to his advantage. Throughout his bodybuilding career, he was taking evening business courses at Santa Monica City College and later at UCLA. In 1977, he enrolled in correspondence courses at the University of Wisconsin and somehow managed to persuade the university to grant him a B.A. with a major in business administration and the marketing of fitness, although he had completed far fewer than the required credits. There is some suspicion that his future in-laws may have had an influence in the decision: the school later admitted that the degree was specially created for him and that he had received credits for his work promoting the Special Olympics—Eunice Shriver's pet project.

"You don't only have to make the money," he later explained, "you have to know how to spend it wisely and not buy stupid toys and all those things people do." Instead of buying fast cars and throwing money around, he continued to invest shrewdly, driven by a credo that he outlined in his 1977 autobiography, in which he described how the lessons he learned building his physique could be applied to business.

"Body building changed me entirely," he wrote. "I think I would be a different person now if I'd never trained, if I just worked somewhere. It gave me confidence and pride and an unlimited positive attitude. I can apply my success to everything. The same with business. I'm so determined to make millions of dollars that I cannot fail. In my mind I've already made the millions; now it's just a matter of going through the motions."

Investing in real estate near his Venice Beach base when the area was still a sleepy suburb of Los Angeles, he wisely anticipated the Santa Monica boom of the 1970s and 1980s, accumulating a significant amount of real estate on the town's lucrative main street, which would eventually have high-end boutiques, restaurants, and luxury developments. As his movie career flourished, and he started to receive regular multimillion-dollar paychecks, he was able to expand his holdings significantly, into the riskier area of commercial real estate.

"Arnold is one of the brightest guys I know," declared Al Ehringer, one of Arnold's partners in a $10 million commercial and residential complex they purchased near the Santa Monica–Venice line. "He's a very shrewd businessman." The pair named their venture LBMG, for "Local Boys Make Good."

Not all his investments, however, proved particularly shrewd. In the early 1990s, he started an Austrian-style delicatessen called Schatzi on Main in the Santa Monica strip. It was a place where he could hang out with his friends, negotiate film deals, and smoke his trademark $25 cigars—first introduced to him by Eunice Shriver in 1977—while eating the dishes he loved from his youth, schnitzel, noodles, and strudel. But the restaurant was a perpetual money loser, and restaurant critics seemed to take particular delight in excoriating the mediocre food, which they would often compare to Arnold's acting. Eventually, he sold the business.

"Ninety percent of my investments have been very, very profitable," he told *Business Wire* in 1986. But this may have been something of an exaggeration. Arnold seemed to get into trouble whenever he invested in a project outside Santa Monica. Among his investments that went sour were commercial projects in Denver; Columbus, Ohio; and San Francisco.

In some of these ventures, he was not afraid to use his celebrity to further his business interests, as the owners of a mall in Denver learned when Arnold invested in a rival mall there. He immediately started to aggressively court commercial tenants who had already signed letters of intent with another complex, raising some ethical questions.

He also may not have been entirely forthcoming about whom he was taking advice from. "I invest my money myself. I don't have a business manager and

I have been doing it ever since my first hour in this country," he told the *Times* of London in 1991. "I'm not keen on stocks because I don't want to lose a million dollars because someone somewhere has had a vision we should let the hostages go or the cannons or guns are pointing in the wrong direction. I would rather do more concrete investment like real estate, and like everything else you just have to have a lot of knowledge and go about investing it in the proper way."

But when Arnold eventually entered politics and was forced to partially disclose his business holdings, it emerged that he had in fact invested millions of dollars in the stock market, and that he had a wide range of financial advisers handling his investments, though it is certainly possible these relationships began after 1991.

And occasionally there was more to some of Arnold's supposedly shrewd investments than meets the eye. When he teamed up with Sylvester Stallone and Bruce Willis in 1991 to launch Planet Hollywood, the trio left the impression that they had put their own money into the theme chain, once again perpetuating the idea that Arnold was Hollywood's shrewdest entrepreneur. In fact, the three stars were just the front men for a consortium that paid them in stock to use their names. At first, the company was wildly successful, and the media had countless features on Arnold's wily business practices. Years later, however, after the company filed for Chapter 11 bankruptcy, the truth came out when Arnold cashed in his stock, once worth $15 million, for less than $200,000.

Other investments were decidedly more successful, and none more so than a venture in which Arnold could put his vast knowledge of bodybuilding to good use. In 1970, a young Arnold Schwarzenegger was flown on a private jet from London to Columbus, Ohio, to compete in a fledgling tournament, Pro Mr. World, run by a former FBI agent and insurance executive named Jim Lorimer. After winning the contest and collecting the $500 prize, Arnold told Lorimer it was the best-run event he had ever participated in. "Then he said to me when I retire in five years, I want to go into promotion and really raise the stakes for this sport," Lorimer later recalled in the *San Jose Mercury News*. "I'm going to come back to Columbus, Ohio, and ask you to be my partner."

Lorimer was skeptical and didn't think much about the promise until, sure enough, Arnold telephoned in 1975 and announced that they were going to go into the bodybuilding promotion business together. Within four years, he told Lorimer, they would raise the top prize from $1,000 to $100,000. He had always been critical of the low prize money available in his sport and, despite their friendship, had publicly claimed that the Weiders were exploiting bodybuilders. He vowed to change this, and, with Lorimer's help, that's exactly what he did.

First, the two persuaded Joe Weider to let them bring the Mr. Olympia contest to Columbus from New York. They were willing to take all the financial risks. It was a headache that Joe was happy to give up; also, Joe trusted Arnold enough to let him take the reins, as long as he continued to allow his name to be associated with the Weider brand, endorsing products and appearing in the magazines.

That first year, they raised the prize money to $10,000 and still managed to bring in a $10,000 profit for themselves, attracting 4,000 paying spectators to Columbus's Veterans Memorial Auditorium.

Eventually, the Weiders snatched back Mr. Olympia, fearing that Arnold would use it as a way to horn in on their empire. But in 1989, Arnold and Lorimer started the Arnold Classic: an annual bodybuilding competition and sports showcase in Columbus that immediately became the most lucrative strongman competition in the world. It also brought the two partners countless millions in profits as they expanded the event into a "fitness weekend," featuring gymnastics, martial arts, and cheerleading competitions. Eventually, it grew to include 10,000 athletes and a top prize of $130,000, realizing Arnold's early vision.

Although the Arnold Classic clearly capitalized on his name and reputation to bring in huge profits, Arnold regularly refused to lend his name to most outside ventures, giving up, over the years, tens of millions of dollars in potential endorsements—what most celebrities regard as easy money.

Something just didn't sit right with Arnold about these kinds of commercial opportunities. "Although there was a lot of money there, I just tried to stay out of it," he told *California Business* magazine about his reasons for forgoing such endorsements. "Like pressing a tire together and popping it, looking like a gorilla in a zoo somewhere and saying, 'I've trained for 20 years, but I was not able to rip this tire apart.' I just never felt comfortable with that kind of stuff."

Nevertheless, he had run his own mail-order business for a long time and continued to do so, hawking books, seminars, and videos with titles such as "How Arnold Builds His Chest Like a Fortress," as well as T-shirts, souvenir photos, calendars, and other profitable merchandise. At the Arnold Classic every year, hundreds of attendees would line up and pay $250 to be photographed with Arnold as part of a special VIP package.

Still, he wisely resisted the kind of high-profile shilling that would have brought in untold millions but would have ultimately undermined the Arnold brand. It helped that he no longer needed the money.

It's almost impossible to determine just how much Arnold Schwarzenegger is worth, given his complex web of investments, real estate holdings, and multifaceted ventures. Estimates have ranged from $250 million on the conservative side, to $1.2 billion before the real estate bubble burst in 2008.

Whatever the figure, there is no question that he is an extraordinarily wealthy man. And yet, as his friends and associates long ago discovered, the almighty dollar has never been what motivates Arnold. There is something that he has always valued far more, though he also knows that money can go a long way in helping to obtain it.

From the moment when he was fourteen years old and watched John F. Kennedy thrill the crowds in Vienna, Arnold Schwarzenegger has lusted after one thing above all else—power.

22.

Reagan's Resonance

We always knew Arnold would go into politics," Ben Weider once told me. "It was only a question of when. And we knew he wasn't going to run for dogcatcher or whatever small-time office Clint Eastwood ran for. It was always going to be something big. That's the only way Arnold does things."

He was referring to Eastwood's 1986 election as mayor of Carmel-by-the-Sea, significant perhaps because the actor was one of the few other high-profile Republicans in Hollywood. The Republicans had, in fact, long courted Eastwood for higher office, but he always made it clear that he had no political ambitions beyond running the sleepy hamlet of Carmel.

Arnold, in contrast, had never really bothered to disguise his political ambitions, at least not with his friends and colleagues. Years later, in 2004, he would appear at the Republican convention and give a stirring speech about how he first got interested in politics and, more important, how he became a Republican, invoking his inspirational immigrant's journey from Austria to the promised land of the United States:

> When I was a boy, the Soviets occupied part of Austria. I saw their tanks in the streets. I saw communism with my own eyes. I remember the fear we had when we had to cross into the Soviet sector. Growing up, we were told, "Don't look the soldiers in the eye. Just look straight ahead." It was common belief that the Soviet soldiers could take a man out of his own car and ship him back to the Soviet Union as slave labor.
>
> Now my family didn't have a car—but one day we were in my uncle's car. It was near dark as we came to the Soviet checkpoint. I was a little boy. I was not an action hero back then. But I remember—I remember how scared I was that the soldiers would pull my father or my uncle out of the car and I would never see them again. My family and so many others lived in fear of the Soviet boot. Today, the world no longer fears the Soviet Union and it is because of the United States of America!

*As a kid—as a kid I saw socialist—the socialist
country that Austria became after the Soviets left.
Now don't misunderstand me: I love Austria and
I love the Austrian people. But I always knew that
America was the place for me. In school, when the
teacher would talk about America, I would
daydream about coming here. I would daydream
about living here. I would sit there and watch for
hours American movies, transfixed by my heroes,
like John Wayne. Everything about America—
everything about America seemed so big to me, so
open, so possible.*

*I finally arrived here in 1968. What a special
day it was. I remember I arrived here with empty
pockets, but full of dreams, full of determination,
full of desire. The presidential campaign was in
full swing. I remember watching the Nixon and
Humphrey presidential race on TV. A friend of
mine who spoke German and English translated for
me. I heard Humphrey saying things that sounded
like socialism, which I had just left. But then I
heard Nixon speak. He was talking about free
enterprise, getting the government off your back,
lowering the taxes and strengthening the military.*

*Listening to Nixon speak sounded more like a
breath of fresh air. I said to my friend, I said,*

"What party is he?" My friend said, "He's a
Republican." I said, "Then I am a Republican."
And I have been a Republican ever since!

By the time of his speech at the 2004 convention, he had fine-tuned the tale somewhat from the version he had offered at various points over the years, no longer telling his audience that Humphrey and Nixon's TV debate was his political epiphany. After the first few times he told the story, he must have heard that there was no presidential debate in 1968. Arnold's best friend, Franco Columbu, also frequently tells the story, suggesting that he was watching the debates with Arnold. However, Columbu emigrated to America only in 1969, when Nixon was already in the White House. One wonders if Arnold had one of his scriptwriters produce a good explanation when he decided to venture into politics. Still, it is entirely plausible that Arnold would have embraced Nixon's free market, fiercely anticommunist philosophy, since he had grown up in Graz listening to the political views of his mentor, Alfred Gerstl, a prominent member of the conservative Austrian People's Party whose own views weren't so different from those of the Republican leader.

Reagan's 1980 election undoubtedly had a special resonance for Arnold, and he could often be heard referring to the actor turned politician as his hero. "President Reagan symbolized to me what America represented—hope, opportunity, freedom," he would explain. However, Reagan already had his own Hollywood action figure, Sylvester Stallone, and never seemed to pay much attention to Arnold. But in 1988, with Reagan's second term coming to an end, Arnold sensed an opportunity to court his successor.

The Republican nominee was Reagan's vice president, George Herbert Walker Bush, a comparatively bland figure who was locked in a tight electoral battle with the governor of Massachusetts, Michael Dukakis. Arnold let it be known to party leaders early on that he was willing to help. They were lukewarm at first, aware that many Republicans held Hollywood in contempt and that Arnold didn't necessarily represent the family values that Bush had made a cornerstone of his campaign. It was the time of the backlash against violence in film, and Arnold Schwarzenegger had been made a symbol for the "poison factory." He was given a relatively minor role at the Republican convention that summer and mostly kept out of the spotlight.

However, in the waning days of the campaign, when Bush's strategists looked at the electoral map, they were very worried. No Republican has ever won the White House without winning Ohio, and Dukakis was extremely strong in the industrial Midwest. The Arnold Classic hadn't yet been launched, but Arnold's longtime friend and business partner Jim Lorimer suggested to his Republican contacts that Arnold was extremely popular in Columbus, where the two had staged numerous contests over the years, as well as in large swaths of Ohio. Bush would practically be living in Ohio during the end of the campaign, so important was the state to his chances. His people put out a feeler for Arnold to accompany him on this swing and warm up the crowd before the candidate gave stump speeches.

Arnold was all too happy to oblige. Four days before the election he accompanied Bush to Columbus and provided one of the most memorable lines of the campaign. At a rally of 50,000 boisterous spectators in front of the Nationwide Insurance headquarters, where Lorimer worked, Arnold introduced Bush as a "real live action hero," adding his standard joke about being a Republican married to a Kennedy. "It is true that I have different political views from my wife," he said, but he assured his audience that this was not a problem: "Everything is just fine, especially since I got used to sleeping in the garage," he joked.

He then talked about his role as a bad guy in *The Terminator* before delivering the zinger that would appear on most national newscasts that evening:

"I only play the Terminator in my movies. But when it comes to America's future, Michael Dukakis will be the real terminator."

The speech was so successful that Arnold was invited to accompany Bush to Illinois and New Jersey, where he often received louder cheers than Bush. Lorimer would later claim that the two struck up a genuine friendship chatting on the campaign plane, and that the unlikely pair seemed to have formed a lifelong mutual admiration society. At the end of each rally, Bush would raise arms with Arnold, who he said embodied the immigrant spirit.

In the end, Bush won the election and some political analysts credited Arnold with carrying Ohio, the state that had put the new president over the top. It was generally assumed that Arnold would receive some reward for his role, and Bush hadn't even been inaugurated yet when the *Washington Post* reported what the reward might be.

The day after Bush attended the premiere of *Twins*, at the Kennedy Center, the *Post* wrote that Arnold had met with the president-elect's transition team about heading up the White House Council on Physical Fitness and Sports, a long-ignored section of the Public Health Service. The council had been created by Dwight D. Eisenhower four decades earlier, after a study found that American children had fallen far behind their European counterparts with regard to fitness. It reached its zenith during the Kennedy administration but had been largely neglected ever since, with a paltry budget of only $1.4 million. Arnold now let it be known that he would like to revitalize the position. Indeed, he seemed an ideal candidate and the appointment appeared to be in the bag.

However, the inauguration came and went; most White House posts were long since filled: and still no announcement had been made, though there had been at least one inquiry from the transition team about Arnold's citizenship status and it had appeared that the vetting process was well under way. Arnold was puzzled, but no explanation was forthcoming. Finally, in June, he received the first hint about what may have been the holdup when a White House aide called him on location in Mexico City to ask whether he had ever used steroids. A few weeks later, the personnel office alerted him that his publicly stated love of cigars might also be a sticking point. He knew that neither of those issues was a deal breaker, though soon afterward he suddenly embarked on a public crusade to ban steroids in bodybuilding. But unbeknownst to Arnold, since the *Post* reported on the prospect in December there had in fact been a quiet but concerted lobbying campaign to keep him from the position. The National Coalition on Television Violence, for example, had sent a letter pointing out that Arnold's films averaged more than 100 violent acts per hour. A Texas delegation of the United Methodist Church complained that the post would largely involve talking to kids about physical fitness and that Arnold was a very "poor role model for children." Letters from individual Americans had also poured in opposing the appointment by a ratio of more than five to one, undoubtedly engineered by conservative groups urging their members to write.

At the same time, his biggest Hollywood rival, Sylvester Stallone, was clandestinely seeking to top Arnold once again, lobbying for the position himself and mining his old contacts in the Reagan administration. Stallone even sent the White House a pointed reminder that Arnold had smoked a joint at the end of *Pumping Iron.*

Eventually, a rather unlikely figure would secure the coveted appointment for Arnold—his mother-in-law, Eunice Shriver. Joe Mathews, a political correspondent for the *Los Angeles Times*, discovered that Eunice had written a series of letters to the White House extolling Arnold's virtues, noting that he was the "number one star" in the United States and pointing out how much dedication he had shown to her cherished Special

Olympics. Bush sent a note early on thanking her for "recommending our man Conan" but then turned the details of the relatively unimportant appointment over to his chief of staff, John Sununu. In July, hearing no response to her campaign, Eunice suggested that they might want to consider appointing the tennis legend Chris Evert as Arnold's co-chair. But still there was no response. After Sununu ignored her one more time, in November, she appears to have gone over his head, using her contacts to get a message to Bush himself asking why the White House was stalling. This time, according to Mathews, the president personally intervened and Arnold was finally appointed chairman on January 22, 1990, thirteen months after he had first expressed his interest in the job.

It wasn't the last time the Kennedy family— America's most famous Democrats—would rise to serve Arnold's Republican political ends.

In announcing the appointment, Bush declared Arnold "uniquely qualified to address and influence national health and fitness issues, especially among our youth." But many people were naturally skeptical. *Time* magazine sounded the first cynical note a week after the appointment, mentioning that Arnold had publicly admitted using steroids. "As a role model, Conan still has a long way to go," *Time* chided. The nation's phys ed teachers were also less than enamored of Arnold, reportedly mocking his antiquated ideas about physical fitness, and noting that his exercise books contained advice—such as deep knee lunges—that had long ago been discredited in exercise science circles. But not for the last time, his critics had underestimated Arnold, believing he was interested in the position merely as an excuse to attend White House dinners as Stallone had done during the Reagan years.

It didn't take him long to prove those critics wrong. Almost immediately, he contacted a number of experts in the field to determine where the White House could do the most good. Most of the ideas, however, included initiatives that would be impossible to achieve on the council's tiny budget, almost all of which went to administrative and personnel expenses. In his research, Arnold had repeatedly come across the name of John Cates, a professor of physical education at the University of California San Diego and an expert in fitness policy. Cates had long lamented the decline in fitness standards for American children, noting studies showing American children at risk of heart disease as early as elementary school. For years, he had lobbied unsuccessfully for legislation requiring phys ed in California's schools, since phys ed had been among the first

casualties of budget cuts, along with music and arts programs. "All the adults are buying their workout books
and joining their fancy clubs, but nobody's paying any
attention to the kids," he complained. That jibed with
Arnold's own views and he was determined to hear
what the professor had to say about nationwide fitness
standards. Cates, who was initially one of the skeptics,
later recalled the first time he met with Arnold to discuss priorities.

"It was supposed to be a half-hour meeting," he recalled. "Three hours later, we were still there, and he
was all over the room, all fired up about what we could
do. All of a sudden, his secretary tells him he's only
got a half hour before the christening of his daughter,
Katherine. I thought, 'The guy's really into this. I've
really got to get involved with this.'"

Arnold was determined to hire Cates as his assistant, but his budget was maxed out. He had already
chosen to forgo a salary himself. Now he offered to
pay Cates—who was on a two-year leave from the
university—a sizable salary out of his own pocket to
work for the council. Cates would later jokingly describe
this as becoming "Arnold Schwarzenegger's flunky."

Cates had recommended that in order to be effective, the council would have to reach out to all fifty
states, because education was under state, not federal,

jurisdiction and state programs were the only way to get anything accomplished. But there was no money at all for travel, and it seemed that phone calls would have to replace face-to-face meetings. Once again, Arnold stepped up, offering to finance an ambitious nation-wide tour, which would take him to all fifty states to promote his agenda.

For the next two years, Arnold barnstormed the country, meeting with governors and lobbying for a nationwide fitness standard. The only governor he failed to meet during this period, notes the *Los Angeles Times* reporter Joe Mathews, was Bill Clinton, who was too busy running for president to sit down with Arnold. And yet Clinton himself didn't travel to as many states during his successful campaign.

The grueling and remarkably ambitious effort had many observers wondering if Arnold was consider-ing his own run for political office. But Arnold always denied it. "I'm doing it for the kids," he insisted. In any case, the results were impressive, as was his ability to navigate a wide range of complex policy issues while bringing together people with competing interests and political agendas. Not the least of those impressed by what they saw was President Bush, who had believed he was simply granting a routine patronage appoint-ment when he gave Arnold the post. The president soon discovered how seriously Arnold was taking the position, and he took notice of a man he admitted he had severely underestimated. Ignoring the objections of the family-values crowd who made up a good portion of his Republican base, Bush was all too glad to embrace his appointee in public—even inviting Arnold to vacation at Camp David on two separate occasions—and lend the presidency to Arnold's newfound cause, although the council was not without its share of controversy.

Eyebrows—and the ire of White House counsel—were raised more than once after Arnold pursued corporate sponsorship for some of his events to make up for the lack of government funding.

When he organized a high-profile event, the Great American Workout, on the White House lawn, in 1991, he was forced to remove the Planet Hollywood logo from the event's T-shirts and return a $250,000 donation from Reebok, which wanted its logo emblazoned on the workout suits worn by the event's celebrity participants.

After Arnold forged a remarkable agreement with the National Teachers' Alliance to administer a single nationwide fitness test in American schools, he agreed to let the alliance use the seal of his presidential council on brochures and other promotional products to help offset the cost of running the tests. "That bit of marketing went a step too far," notes Joe Mathews in his book *The People's Machine*. "He had licensed the use of the President's name to physical education teachers."

Still, Bush was happy to show up with his wife at the first Great American Workout, held at the White House, and to participate in all fifteen fitness stations, including horseshoe throwing, the president's personal specialty. "You know, Arnold's stronger than I thought he was," Bush told the assembled crowd as he declared "war" on couch potatoes. "He bench-pressed the federal budget. I told my grandson Sam, who is visiting us this weekend: 'If he can do that, why can't you pick up your socks?'"

It was around this time that Bush was said to have suggested to Republican party leaders that Arnold might be a good candidate for office. "Too many skeletons," was the prophetic reply from his chief of staff.

"Everything [Arnold] did was a stepping stone to something else, and the chairmanship was a shrewd choice for his first position in American political life," noted the biographer Laurence Leamer. It was only the beginning.

23.

A Big Comeuppance

By the time his chairmanship of the Council on Physical Fitness expired at the end of 1992, Arnold was only forty-five years old. If political office fitted into his ambitions, it was not yet time, according to "the plan." His old friend from Munich, Albert Busek, claims to have always known that Arnold would enter politics but that it would happen only after he turned fifty-five. Besides, with the recent election of Bill Clinton, the tide had turned against the Republicans, at least temporarily. And Arnold was not yet through with Hollywood: he was still the number one box office draw in the world.

As befitted that status, he had just been offered a new movie, which its producers believed had megahit written all over it. Conceived by a couple of unknowns just out of college, Zak Penn and Adam Leff, *The Last Action Hero* was the story of a boy who is magically transported into the movie screen to join his fictional idol, Jack Slater, a larger-than-life action hero. Columbia Tri Star had high hopes for the project if it could sign Arnold to play Slater. The screenplay was written with him in mind, and the character Slater was based on his own life—but the studio didn't know if it could afford his price. It was trying to keep spiraling production budgets under control, and it had vowed to bring in this film for less than $100 million.

Arnold was looking for his next project, and there was no shortage of possibilities. Among the scripts he was considering were a remake of the Dumas novel *The Count of Monte Cristo;* a live-action version of *Curious George* in which he would portray the man in the yellow hat; and a comedy called *Sweet Tooth,* in which he would play a marine asked by his dying father to take over the family business as tooth fairy (a film rewritten two decades later for Dwayne "The Rock" Johnson and retitled *Tooth Fairy*). Each of these projects had appeal, especially since Arnold had vowed to start taking his film career in a different direction. The success of his two blockbuster comedies had convinced him that it might be time to stop doing action films, not because he was worried about being typecast but because of a growing concern about the conservative backlash that had nearly prevented his White House appointment two years earlier. If he wanted a political future, he could no longer afford to shrug off such concerns. "The country is going in an anti-violence direction. I think America has seen enough of what violence has done in the cities," he told *Premiere* magazine.

He had also done his part to combat real-world violence by lending his name and fund-raising clout to a Los Angeles sporting competition, the Inner-City Games, which aimed to give youth at risk an alternative to gangs, drugs, and violence, especially after the Rodney King episode and the ensuing riots devastated the city in 1992. It appeared that Arnold was attempting to soften his image, and for a time action films no longer appeared to fit into his plans.

But Columbia wanted him for its film and was clearly willing to pay dearly for him, offering a $15 million salary, generous merchandising rights, profit points, and a credit as executive producer. It was thought to be the richest deal any actor had ever received to that point, and there was no way Arnold could turn it down—not if his agent Lou Pitt had anything to say about it.

Announcing that he had signed on, Arnold downplayed the violence, emphasizing that the film was a

A BIG COMEUPPANCE · 431

child's fantasy with "great messages and an emotional ride." The studio, meanwhile, promised "the extensive action, special effects and comic brilliance that Arnold's movies have become world-famous for delivering."

By the eve of its 1993 release, the advance hype for *Last Action Hero* had reached fever pitch. At Cannes that year, Arnold had promised that the film would be "huge, large. It's monstrous. It's gigantic." So high were the studio's hopes that it announced it had reached a deal with NASA to place an ad for the film on the side of an unmanned rocket scheduled to be launched into space in May. Arnold's career, it seemed, was truly about to reach the stratosphere.

However, the first signs of trouble had begun to emerge even before production, when the studio was forced to bring in a number of people for extensive rewrites. This is never a good sign in Hollywood. Then word leaked out from the first sneak previews that the film was an unintelligible mess. After the *Los Angeles Times* reported that one test audience in Pasadena had almost unanimously panned the film, a Columbia executive denied that the preview had even taken place and the studio charged that the film was the victim of an orchestrated "smear campaign." This accusation may not have been entirely paranoid, as it was discovered that someone had indeed deliberately misled the *Los Angeles Times*. However, at another test screening—this one quite real—an audience member reportedly stood up and yelled, "This film has cancer!" The studio could see the writing on the wall. Plans for the rocket ad were quietly scrapped, and one studio executive later told the *Chicago Tribune*, "It's so embarrassing. It's like a joke. It's like putting *Howard the Duck* on the side of your rocket." Meanwhile, the director, John McTiernan, tried to recut the film into something a little more palatable before its official June release.

But nothing could save the film. From its first weekend, both the critics and the fans were harsh and unforgiving. The *New York Times* started the ball rolling by describing it as a "two-hour *Saturday Night Live*" sketch, and that was charitable compared with some of the other assessments. The *Seattle Post-Intelligencer* complained that the film was "so loud, so overproduced, so poorly developed and confusing as narrative that only very young teenagers are likely to take to it." The Los Angeles film critic Gary Franklin gave the picture a negative 5 on a scale of 1 to 10 and suggested that the film's $80 million budget would have been better spent "to feed thousands of the homeless or provide free psychiatric care for studio executives gone mad." Carol Buckland of CNN called it a "movie on steroids. It's totally artificial and it parodies something that's almost a parody anyway. So, just not a good movie."

Not all critics hated it. Some enjoyed the parody elements, such as a scene in which Arnold, playing himself, shows up with Maria Shriver for a premiere of the film within a film that is *Hero*'s premise. But such praise was sparse.

At the box office, the returns were disastrous. The film took in less than $15 million on the opening weekend and then fell off an unusual 47 percent the following weekend. In the industry, this fiasco clearly didn't bode well; and it didn't help that *Jurassic Park* opened a week later and went on to become the highest-grossing film of all time up until that point.

"It's the worst I've seen since *Heaven's Gate*," one studio executive told the *Los Angeles Times*. "This is as bad for the business as *Jurassic Park* is good. It creates a groundswell of negativity." Another executive suggested that the film's title could be prophetic. "*Last Action Hero* could dictate Hollywood's course for the rest of the decade," he said. "It could be the last of its kind."

A number of critics implied that Arnold deserved his comeuppance, given the almost nonstop orgy of hype and self-promotion he had participated in. "It is conventional wisdom that studio executives and stars who become arrogant and overconfident invite the wrath of the entire community," wrote Jack Matthews in *Newsday*. "Everybody knows that nobody knows what audiences want to see, and to claim otherwise is pure folly. But that is exactly what Columbia's chief executive Mark Canton and *Last Action Hero* star Arnold Schwarzenegger have been doing for the past year."

Matthews argued that Arnold had turned bluster into an art form and had become the victim of his own shameless self-promotion, though it had served him well in the past.

"But there is ego, and there is ego," Matthews wrote. "When Schwarzenegger was promoting himself as a celebrity his brashness had a certain charm, and to film mavens he was simply enhancing himself as a product. Since he was delivering the goods, with one hit after another, no one even begrudged him his bulging fees. With *Last Action Hero*, however, he crossed into new territory. It is one thing for him to claim to be the most popular person on Earth, it's another to base a movie on the assumption that everyone agrees with him. Since Schwarzenegger was the principal driving force behind the production, and since his $15-million fee was largely responsible for its elephantine budget, his braggadocio suddenly didn't seem so cute."

The Associated Press appeared to agree, opining that "the cocky, cigar-chomping bodybuilder had never flown higher and was ripe for a fall."

Meanwhile, Arnold was blaming all the negativity on Hollywood politics, telling the *London Daily Mail*, "Everyone in this town is jealous of the next guy. They're all a bunch of jealous bitches sitting around saying, 'I hope he takes a dive.' "

Although the movie wasn't quite the financial fiasco that had been feared, thanks to better-than-expected foreign box office receipts, it still ended up losing more than $25 million. More important, Arnold appeared to have lost his sheen of invincibility.

Arnold later admitted to a reporter that he was slightly disappointed in the film's reception "because I do have an ego," but that he had lots of other things going on in his life and that he had managed to keep his spirits up, even calling Columbia and the director, John McTiernan, to tell them they had done a great job.

"There is no blame. It was no one's fault. There is only one thing—the movie didn't work as well as I thought it would. And the press and the industry saw a little vulnerable spot there, and they hammered away at it."

Behind the scenes, however, he was not quite so philosophical about the first major failure of his career. His agent, Lou Pitt, and his publicist, Charlotte Parker, both told Laurence Leamer that they had never seen Arnold so depressed. The biographer describes a scene in the green room at *The Tonight Show* when Arnold was preparing to go on to promote *Last Action Hero* and Parker handed him a batch of the first negative reviews. Maria turned to the publicist and said, "You upset Arnold. I never want you to upset Arnold again."

Arnold later explained Maria's reaction, telling Leamer, "Maria is unbelievably protective. She will destroy if she feels someone is trying to do harm to me."

Indeed, Maria had by this point acquired a reputation as a control freak like her husband, attempting to micromanage every facet of his life and career. In fact, many people were already blaming her for advising her husband to take *Last Action Hero* in the first place even though the screenplay was clearly substandard.

"Creatively, she's a complete wash," one insider told Leamer, revealing that Maria had "tin ears" for the nuances of filmmaking. "And yet she inserts herself in a way that asserts, 'I know what I'm doing.' And she doesn't."

Maria would reject such criticism, putting it down to sexism, and she insisted that she was also unfairly blamed whenever Arnold rejected a script for a film that later turned out to be successful.

Whoever advised Arnold to take on *True Lies*, however, looked like a prophet. Just when he seemed to have hit bottom, an old friend came to his rescue. Before *Last Action Hero* was released, Arnold had already completed filming an action comedy with the director of *The Terminator*, James Cameron, about a mild-mannered computer salesman who leads a double life as a U.S. government counterterrorist agent. Some people consider the film, which costarred Jamie Lee Curtis, Arnold's best ever, and it garnered mostly positive reviews when it was released in 1999. It also performed fairly well at the box office, grossing more than $200 million worldwide, though its production budget was also prohibitively high, minimizing the profits. Still, it was a respectable comeback. More important, it partially erased the lingering stain of *Last Action Hero*.

However, it was clear that the name Schwarzenegger no longer carried the same aura or clout as it once had. A cover story in *Entertainment Weekly* had already declared Arnold a symbol of the 1980s, "as much an archetype of the decade as junk bonds, Republican presidents and Madonna."

He was clearly anxious to erase that impression and thought that he could revive his formerly exalted status by starring in an epic befitting it. He believed he had found the ideal project, *Crusade*, about an eleventh-century knight who participates in a crusade to take the Holy Land from the Muslim infidels. When Carolco Pictures, which had optioned the project, ran into financial difficulties, Arnold himself purchased the rights, but he was having trouble getting the project off the ground, clearly no longer possessing the power he once had in Hollywood.

At one point, when he attended a fund-raiser—the Environmental Media Association's annual dinner in August 1994—he found himself sitting with the CNN mogul Ted Turner and the former president of the Soviet Union, Mikhail Gorbachev. When he told the two men about the trouble he was having getting *Crusade* made, Gorbachev mentioned that he was a lawyer and that he would be glad to negotiate the deal without a fee. Although the Russian statesman was obviously joking, Arnold later told the *Los Angeles Times* that Gorbachev "saw the film in a higher way. That it would show people the danger in crusades, in that kind of fanaticism, and not to do them again."

On the domestic front, things were going a little more smoothly than his film career. Maria had given birth to another girl, Christina, in 1991; and to the couple's first son, Patrick, in 1993. In between her new maternal obligations, she continued to work for NBC, where she was a contributing anchor for the network's newsmagazine show, *Dateline NBC*, and also worked as a semi-regular correspondent on the nightly news.

In interviews, Arnold regularly portrayed himself as a typical dad, and although he was anything but typical, he clearly enjoyed the parenthood, doting on his three young children. Asked by a reporter what he was going to do when his older daughter started bringing home boys, he quipped, "Katherine has already brought home dates. Play dates. The other day, she came up to me and said, 'He's really hot for me, Daddy. I think he has a crush on me because he wants to kiss me on the mouth.' I said, 'This is it. I'm going to meet this little boy.' I'm always threatening everyone."

He also made it clear that his children were not going to be spoiled like many other celebrity kids he knew. Cracking a whip, he would wake the kids up every morning at seven, insisting they do their chores. And he declared to one reporter that they would associate with normal people to keep their "feet on the ground."

"They have the gardener's children over one day and then kids they met on the beach—you know, ordinary people," he revealed.

Every summer, Aurelia would come to visit for two months, a visit that Arnold cherished but Maria was said to dread. Her dour Austrian mother-in-law had never particularly approved of her son's choice of a wife, reputedly because she thought the Kennedys considered themselves better than her and felt Maria had married down. About all the two had in common was their strict Catholic upbringing, but even that wasn't enough to forge a bond, especially since Aurelia's English was limited.

In 1998, Aurelia died in Graz at the age of seventy-six, after suffering a stroke three weeks earlier while visiting Gustav's grave. Arnold had shown little emotion when his father died years before, or when his brother, Meinhard, was killed in a car accident while driving drunk in 1971. "He spoke of his father's death with no emotion and never talked about his brother," recalled his ex-girlfriend Barbara Outland. He chose not to attend either funeral, probably because of his antipathy for both Gustav and Meinhard—the abusive father and the bullying brother. But Aurelia's death left him devastated, according to those who knew him best.

"I think for him the deepest, saddest moment of his life was when his mother passed away in August 1998," recalled Albert Busek. "He didn't show it too much on the outside, but inside he was suffering. As a lifelong friend, I could see that his mother's death really got to him on a deep level."

A year earlier, Arnold had his own health scare, when it was suddenly announced that he had chosen to undergo "elective" heart surgery. His publicist announced that he needed an aortic valve replaced to fix a congenital heart problem that had troubled both his mother and his grandmother. The surgery was described as routine.

"I've never felt sick or had any symptoms at all, but I knew I'd have to take care of this condition sooner or later," Arnold said in a statement before being wheeled into the four-hour surgery. "I said to the doctors, 'Let's do it now, while I'm young and healthy.'"

But there were those who questioned whether his heart problems were really congenital. His steroid abuse was widely known, and he had even admitted it by this point. Many wondered if the heart disease was more related to that.

His publicist immediately denied that the condition was linked to his past use of performance-enhancing substances. "Steroids have nothing to do with this," said Catherine Olim. "This is a congenital condition that's existed in his family. We expect a very short recovery period."

But according to the medical correspondent for the *Times* of London, Dr. Thomas Stuttaford, it was not entirely accurate to say that steroids hadn't contributed to the condition. "Schwarzenegger has said that his problem is congenital, but with the lifestyle he has enjoyed it is highly probable that other, acquired, causes will have contributed," wrote Dr. Stuttaford. "As well as being an actor, he owns a chain of restaurants. Apparently he has been told to resist temptation and refrain from rich, fat-laden meals, and smoking. His admitted misuse of anabolic steroids is just as likely to have produced high levels of the pernicious low-density lipoprotein cholesterol and low levels of the cardio-protective high-density cholesterol, which will have contributed to his condition, as years of eating steaks and fried potatoes."

Other medical experts were not quite so circumspect. When a doctor in Berlin predicted on a radio show that Arnold would end up dying of heart disease, he sued the doctor for slander and was awarded a token judgment of about $4,700 by a Berlin court, which ruled that the doctor had never examined him and so it was unfair to make such a statement. Arnold also threatened to sue the supermarket tabloid *Globe* for printing a story headlined "Arnie's Got Ticking Time Bomb in His Chest," claiming that Schwarzenegger was "living in fear that after back-to-back operations on a defective valve, his heart will suddenly quit." The paper later retracted its story and agreed to donate a sum of money to a charity of Arnold's choice.

Meanwhile, Arnold didn't appear to be suffering any lingering side effects from the surgery, as he was up and about in only a few days, ready to start work on his next film, *Batman and Robin*, in which he had signed on to play the villain "Mr. Freeze." His salary was reported to be almost $25 million, proving that he could still command huge sums, despite a film career that appeared to be flatlining. Two of his previous three films, the comedies *Junior* and *Jingle All the Way*, had bombed domestically, bringing in far less than $100 million. Only the 1996 science fiction thriller *Eraser*, in which he returned to action, had performed respectably. But studios were inexplicably still willing to shell out huge sums to secure Arnold's participation.

The secret, according to industry insiders, was his continuing immense popularity with foreign moviegoers, who now accounted for a substantial portion of Hollywood's profits. Even a film that performed poorly in the United States could recoup its losses in the burgeoning overseas market. Sure enough, *Batman and Robin* was a flop, receiving execrable reviews. "Pointless, plodding plotting; asinine action; clueless, comatose characterization; and dumb dialogue," wrote one reviewer, echoing the opinion of most of his colleagues. Compared with those of its predecessors, its box office returns were also a tremendous disappointment, but once again it managed to keep its grosses respectable with a booming foreign box office.

Even the continued willingness of foreign filmgoers to see him in action, however, couldn't save his next film, *End of Days*, directed by Peter Hyams, from being declared a low point in his career. Some critics believed it sounded a death knell worse even than that of *Last Action Hero.*

"You'll walk out of *End of Days* wanting to pick a fight with Arnold Schwarzenegger. That's how bad this flick is," declared the *Dallas Morning News.* Salon. com believed the film was symbolic of Arnold's faltering career: "*End of Days* keeps asking whether faith or force will save the human race, before hedging its bets and insisting on both. Neither will be enough to save relics like Hyams and Schwarzenegger from their long, affluent drift into irrelevance." The *Chicago Tribune* summed it up best: "*End of Days* is an overblown, overspectacular, oversold movie without an original idea in its head."

As the new millennium dawned, Arnold had long since given up the mantle of world's top box office star. Offers were drying up, and the entertainment press was already beginning to refer to him as a has-been. But he didn't appear to share that assessment, at least publicly.

John Wayne, Arnold told one reporter, was still doing action movies well into his sixties. There was no reason why he himself couldn't do the same. Well, maybe there was one. "If all of a sudden my movies are not believable to people, then they will let me know," he declared. "Right now there is no indication of that."

He may have spoken too soon. His newest film, *The 6th Day*—in which he played a man who is cloned against his will—was released in November 2000, and from the outset, the scorn poured in. *Newsday* described the film as "cretinous," and the *Los Angeles Times* complained about the "half-hearted dialogue and acting." More significantly, the film opened weakly, coming in only at number four on its first weekend and grossing less than $100 million worldwide—his poorest showing since the fiasco of *Red Sonja* fifteen years earlier.

By the time *The 6th Day* was released, Arnold was fifty-three years old—only two years shy of the age Albert Busek claimed he had set for entering politics. And there just happened to be an election scheduled for 2002, shortly after he celebrated his fity-fifth birthday.

As far back as October 1999, Arnold had already given a hint of his intentions, though few took him seriously at the time. In an interview with *Talk* magazine, he said that he had often contemplated running for high office.

"The possibility is there, because I feel it inside," he revealed. "I feel there are a lot of people in politics that are standing still and not doing enough. And there's a vacuum. Therefore I can move in." Picking up on the hint, the magazine's Ian Parker asked Arnold if he might be considering a run for governor of California in 2002, when the Democratic incumbent, Gray Davis, would be up for reelection. "I could be," he replied coyly.

Asked what he thought of the prospect of Arnold Schwarzenegger as an opponent, an aide to Davis quipped, "That's fine. The governor is thinking about starring in *Terminator 3.* "

Describing himself as a "compassionate conservative," Arnold did admit to one indiscretion that had become something of an issue for politicians since Bill Clinton admitted a few years earlier that he had once smoked marijuana, but that he didn't inhale. "What it is is what it is," Arnold confessed. "I inhaled. Exhaled. Everything."

Questioned about *Talk*'s article, a spokesperson for Arnold was noncommittal, saying only that he was "not a candidate at this time."

Two years later, the political columnist George Skelton of the *Los Angeles Times* was sitting at his desk when he received an unusual phone call. He had just written a column about Gray Davis's reelection prospects, declaring that the governor had lost his aura of invincibility in recent months because of a state crisis involving the energy companies. The column ended with an observation that the capitol "longs for a General Patton."

Now on the other end of the line was Arnold Schwarzenegger, who claimed to be calling from a trailer on the set of his new film, *Collateral Damage*. He had read Skelton's column and liked the observation about Patton. "That's a really good line," Arnold said.

Although he claimed he had no political agenda—"it's just a personal call"—he spent the rest of the phone call bashing Davis.

"It comes down to leadership," he told Skelton. "You have to take risks and be able to just say, 'I've taken my best shot.' And that is what is lacking. . . . It's upsetting to everyone right now. . . . People are taking their companies out of state because they're worried [about electricity]. . . . And then someone cannot make up their mind what they really want to do. . . . You cannot make great decisions if you're just worried about your reelection."

Skelton knew that there was more to the call than a movie star's random musings. He asked Arnold whether he was considering a run against Davis the following year.

"I've thought about it many times because I love politics" came the reply. "I get such great satisfaction out of helping people. I saw in the last ten years that I'm getting much more pleasure out of that than making money and making movies. And it's increasing my desire to do that. It can lead—and will lead, probably—to some political office. I haven't really said this is the time. But, you know, the bottom line is if Davis goes on the way he is . . . then eventually there will be a vacuum in a year and I could . . . I just leave it open. . . . If he doesn't keep his promises on all those issues—energy, environment, schools, health care—then you've got to say, 'OK, there's room for someone else.'"

He ended the call by saying that he had movie commitments through 2004 but that he would be willing to sacrifice his salary of $20 million a picture to "step in." If he did run, he vowed, he wouldn't take campaign money from "special interests." He was wealthy enough to finance his own campaign.

There was at least one surprise in the phone call, considering his movie image as a gun-toting action figure, and his affiliations with a party that included another Hollywood actor, Charlton Heston, whose views on the subject were well known. Arnold believed in "sensible gun control." Weighing in on a bill then before Congress, he declared, "Definitely, I'm against assault weapons." He also offered another decidedly un-Republican stance, admitting that he believed in abortion rights.

"I'm a strong believer in social programs that work," he told Skelton. "I call myself quite liberal on those issues. But I'm conservative fiscally."

What would Maria and the Kennedy family think of him running as a Republican against a Democratic incumbent? he was asked.

"My wife is a strong believer in all the things that I do," Arnold replied, "and she will be 100 percent behind me. Family's family."

In his column the next day, Skelton joked that Arnold Schwarzenegger would face at least one obstacle if he ran: "That name won't fit on a bumper sticker."

However, for the aides who were already planning Gray Davis's reelection campaign, Arnold's interview was no laughing matter. They knew that he would be a formidable opponent if he decided to run, especially if the energy crisis got worse before the election. It was still winter, but there was a lot of sweat in Sacramento on the February day when Skelton's column ran—especially running down the brow of Davis's chief political strategist, Garry South, who had already done polling about the effect of Schwarzenegger's possible candidacy.

"If we did not provide instant and very powerful blowback on this guy, he could get started and we could never stop him," South later told Joe Mathews of the *Los Angeles Times*.

The problem for South was that, according to his polling, Californians had a generally favorable opinion of Arnold. There weren't a lot of negatives out there.

In his 1988 interview with *Playboy*, Joan Goodman had asked Arnold whether he had any interest in running for office, considering the family he had married into. At the time, he denied that he had any political ambitions, saying that he loved the job he already had. Besides, he added, being in politics means one is supposed to serve the public, "and then you have to clean up your act." Goodman asked him if his reluctance to do that was what kept him from running.

"No. I don't have anything to clean up," he insisted. "I don't live the kind of life that will backfire."

But to Garry South's delight, he was about to have some ammunition handed to him, which suggested Arnold Schwarzenegger did indeed live that kind of life.

24.

Austrian Gigolo

While Arnold was teasing Californians about a possible run for governor, *Premiere* magazine was putting the finishing touches on a story. But when the March 2001 issue of the magazine hit the stands a week later, its reverberations could be measured on the Richter scale. The story, headlined "Arnold the Barbarian," set off nothing less than a political earthquake.

Written by a former police officer turned journalist, John Connolly, it gave detailed examples of "boorish behavior" reputedly perpetrated by Schwarzenegger over the years as he rose to the top ranks of Hollywood's A-list.

Although critics would later charge that Connolly had relied on mostly anonymous sources, the article begins with three cases of alleged sexual harassment perpetrated by Arnold while he was in London a year earlier on a press junket for *The 6th Day*. In one day alone, he supposedly attempted to "cop a feel" of three female talk show hosts, each of whom was named. In one incident, he squeezed the rib cage of the celebrity interviewer Melanie Sykes, directly under her right breast. The same week, Anna Richardson of ITV's movie review program *Big Screen*, charged that after the cameras stopped rolling on its own interview, Arnold tried to determine if her breasts were real, tweaked her nipple, and then laughed when she objected. "I left the room quite shaken," she told Connolly, complaining that she was most upset because "his people rushed to protect him and scapegoated me, and not one person came to apologize afterward." The second he walked into the room, Richardson adds, Schwarzenegger was "like a dog in heat." On Channel 4's *Big Breakfast*, where Denise van Outen invites guests to climb into a big bed with her to be interviewed, Arnold was photographed grabbing her butt, though Connolly downplays the incident and van Outen later denied that Arnold had done anything inappropriate, saying she had "provoked" him, inviting him to grope her.

"You don't get it," a producer who has worked with Arnold in the past told the magazine matter-of-factly. "That's the way he always behaves."

Also, a former employee of Arnold recalled a disturbing incident he witnessed during the filming of *Terminator 2* years earlier. The director, James Cameron, was married at the time but, as it later emerged, he was having an affair with Arnold's costar, Linda Hamilton. While they were riding back from the set to the hotel one evening in a limo, the employee claims Arnold lifted Hamilton onto his lap and began fondling her breasts through her thin blouse. "I couldn't believe Cameron didn't have the balls to tell Arnold to get off his girl. The whole thing made me sick," he told Connolly.

Regarding another incident, Connolly interviewed a female producer on one of Arnold's films who recalled a time when the man who was then her husband came to visit the set. When she introduced the star of the film, Arnold asked, "Is this guy the reason why you didn't come up to my hotel room last night and suck my cock?"

In the passage most often quoted from the article, a woman recalls visiting a crew member on the set of Arnold's 1996 film, *Eraser.* "He asked me if I wanted to meet Arnold, and I said sure. When we opened the door to his trailer, Arnold was giving oral sex to a woman. He looked up and, with that accent, said very slowly, 'Eating is not cheating.' I met him again about a year later and asked him, in German, whether or not eating was cheating, and he just laughed."

Connolly interviews two witnesses who were present at an early-morning tennis game between Arnold and Maria at a hotel court, during the shooting of *Total Recall*. Suddenly Maria stopped playing and began throwing up as Arnold berated her for interrupting the match and then stormed off. A few hours later, the couple announced that Maria was pregnant. Connolly also quotes a journalist who told him Arnold had carried on an affair with his costar in *Total Recall*, Rachel Ticotin, who was herself married at the time.

"The three of us had gone to dinner, where the two of them were all lovey-dovey. We then went to a nightclub, but I left to go back to the Hotel Nikko Mexico soon thereafter. When I left them, they were making out and were all over each other on a banquette. The next day, I saw Arnold and Maria strolling out of the elevator. Maria gave me the look a married woman does when she knows that you know her husband is cheating on her. I felt terrible for her."

Arnold had fired his legendary pit bull publicist, Charlotte Parker, a few years earlier, along with his agent, Lou Pitt. It was generally assumed that he had made the changes because of the downward trajectory of his film career. But Connolly quotes a source close to Parker who told him the supposed real story: "When Charlotte couldn't kill a story about one of Arnold's infidelities, he canned her. Parker had done her best. The story was originally slated to be a feature on a television entertainment-news show; it wound up as a small gossip-column item that didn't make many waves."

The article also goes into considerable detail about Arnold's steroid use and his allegedly misleading stories about the frequency of that use. It quotes George Butler and the wife of Lou Ferrigno, who reveal that Arnold had been fitted with a pig valve during his surgery, a story that he and his doctors later denied.

But it was the stories of his behavior with women that threatened to do the most damage, especially for somebody who was considering running for political office under the banner of the "family values" party. And if not a lot of political reporters read *Premiere* magazine, Garry South was all too happy to bring it to their attention.

The day the March issue hit the newsstands, South faxed the article to every reporter he could think of around the state with little personal notes. He wrote to some, "This piece lays out a real 'touching' story—if you know what I mean." To others, he wrote, "Arnold's piggish behavior with women—is it because of the pig valve?" He later described the fax as a turd that could be thrown into Schwarzenegger's punch bowl, and this is exactly how it was received. Arnold refused to comment publicly on the allegations. Instead, he did what he usually did when something threatened his powerful position. He sicced his lawyer, Marty "Mad Dog" Singer, attorney to the stars, on his opponents. Singer had represented Arnold since 1990 and had for years kept the negative coverage to a minimum, reportedly using the tactics for which he had become famous and which had made him the favorite go-to guy for celebs like Jim Carrey, Roseanne, Bruce Willis, and other A-listers when they got into trouble.

"Marty Singer is a very nice man who loves his family," one client, Priscilla Presley, said of Singer. "But if he thinks someone has done me harm, he is a stealth rottweiler." Richard Johnson, editor of the *New York Post*'s gossip column, "Page Six," concurs. "I'll make one call to a publicist to check out a tip and pretty soon I get a hand-delivered letter from Singer threatening all sorts of disasters and financial damages," he recalls.

That's exactly what happened to Garry South within hours after he faxed *Premiere*'s article to reporters.

"Marty Singer sent me a five-page letter, threatening to sue me," South would later tell *Los Angeles* magazine. "This was sent to my office, by the way, in person, and they demanded that somebody sign for the letter. Not only did he threaten to sue me for libel—for e-mailing out an article that anyone could have bought on any newsstand—the last paragraph said, 'Oh, and by the way, this letter is in itself copyrighted, and if you release any part of this letter to the press, I will further sue you for copyright infringement.' Now, I've got to tell you, in my 32 years in politics, I had never gotten a letter like that from anybody."

South immediately sent out another fax to political reporters around the state, letting them know that he had just received a five-page threatening letter from Marty Singer on behalf of Arnold Schwarzenegger. "I would love to be able to share the letter with you, but he also said he would sue me for copyright infringement if I did so, so if you have questions about the letter, please call Marty Singer," South addded.

They did, and pretty soon the article in *Premiere* and Arnold's litigious reaction were big news. Something had to be done to contain the damage and Arnold knew just what was needed. He immediately enlisted the "Arnia"—the group of friends and loyalists he could always count on to serve his interests. First up were four of his female costars who each vouched for his impeccable behavior toward women over the years, in letters to the editor of *Premiere*. Arnold's office made sure these letters also found their way to the *Los Angeles Times*.

"I'm so upset," wrote Jamie Lee Curtis, costar with Arnold in *True Lies*. "I think he's a terrific guy, and I'm sorry he's being slammed. Does he have a ribald sense of humor? Yes. Is there a sense of playfulness to him? Yes. Do I love that side of him? Yes. I just find it really disgraceful that they would do a hatchet job on somebody who has just given so much to so many people."

Ironically, a day earlier, Curtis, a staunch Democrat, had presented Arnold with an award at an industry dinner, introducing him as "the next governor from the state of California."

"What was the point of that article?" asked Rita Wilson, who costarred in *Jingle All the Way*. "What was I supposed to learn from that?"

Kelly Preston, wife of John Travolta, echoed the sentiments of the others. "I have known Arnold since I worked with him on *Twins* and have never known him to be anything but kind, respectful and a true gentleman," she wrote to the paper.

But it was Linda Hamilton who was clearly most upset by the article, vigorously denying the groping incident detailed in Connolly's article.

"The alleged 'disgusting' incident you describe is made all the more disgusting by its never having happened," Hamilton wrote. "Let me be perfectly clear. In my near 20 years of friendship with Arnold Schwarzenegger, I have never witnessed any hint of the behavior you so carelessly ascribe to him."

James Cameron also denied the incident. "Have you guys lost it over there? This stuff is pure fiction," he wrote. "The occurrence you describe did not happen, in a limo or anywhere else . . . and though I object in principle to your printing of pure fabrication like some cheesy tabloid, I particularly object to the unfair and absurdly off-the-mark picture it paints of Arnold, who is as good a man and human being as I have known."

In addition, *Eraser*'s producer, Arnold Kopelson, wrote to refute the story about somebody's walking in on Arnold performing oral sex on an unnamed woman in his trailer, because "no one is permitted to enter a star's trailer without being announced."

When the *Los Angeles Times* asked Garry South why he had circulated the article, he was dismissive. "That's what I do," he said. "I don't understand your question. Arnie Schwarzenegger has raised his head . . . and we're responding to it." He was also generally dismissive of the denials that had begun to pour in, saying that where there's smoke there tends to be fire and he had every intention of fanning the flames. His mission had been accomplished for now.

When I began researching the life and career of Arnold Schwarzenegger a few years after the incidents detailed in *Premiere* allegedly took place, the magazine's portrayal of the way he treats women in particular tended to jibe with the kind of stories that I was being told repeatedly by those who had known him for years—bodybuilders, movie personnel, and others, none of whom appeared to have any particular vendetta against him or any political motivation. But of all the stories I heard over the years, none was so telling as my encounter with a hairdresser who had known Arnold and Maria for decades.

I was put in touch with Francesca Guerrera by an old friend of mine, Judge Larry Seidlin, who had presided over the controversial hearing on the custody of the body of Anna Nicole Smith after her death in 2007. Guerrera had recently moved to Fort Lauderdale from Cape Cod, Massachussetts, where she ran a well-known day spa and cosmetic boutique, Vista Del Mar Spa. Among her many celebrity clients were Maria Shriver and Arnold Schwarzenegger, along with other members of the Kennedy family. She frequently worked on Maria's hair and makeup as well as Arnold's hair whenever the couple visited the Kennedy compound.

"I did her wedding when I was nineteen," she told me. "I did all her family's hair and makeup when she got married at Saint Francis Xavier in Hyannis. I did Rose's hair. I knew them for more than twenty years. I used to do Ethel's hair. I beautified them, and let me tell you it was a lot of work. They were a family who let themselves go. They needed a lot of work. They only talked about politics when I was at the Kennedy house—never at the spa. At the Kennedys' house it was always about politics. That's obviously where Arnold got the idea to run for governor."

Francesca is clearly an admirer of both Arnold and Maria; she said they were like family to her. "They used to come in together and get haircuts together. Arnold would always make jokes. I never felt tension between them. Arnold would call up my ex-husband who owned a gym and rave about the haircut I gave." Maria even gave permission for her name to be used to endorse a cosmetics product line Guerrera launched at Barneys a few years ago.

This was not somebody intent on making Arnold look bad or seeking attention for herself, so I find a story Guerrera casually told me one day all the more revealing.

"Arnold talked about being young all the time," she told me. "After his open heart surgery when he was fifty he changed a lot. He said how pissed off he was that he took youth for granted. He was a good tipper.

One time I wouldn't accept a tip, so he put the money down my top. I told him, 'This is not a strip place.' Maria was embarrassed. She said, 'Thank God we know each other.'"

Years later, writing an analysis piece about Arnold for *The New Yorker*, Connie Bruck addressed Connolly's allegations, noting that many people who know Schwarzenegger have told her that the general behavior portrayed in the article sounds familiar to them. Some women, she reveals, have been pleased by the star's attentions while others have been "repelled." Schwarzenegger, however is "impervious" to the difference. She then quotes a guest who was present at the home of the famous Mexican artist Francisco Zuniga when Arnold visited there while filming in Mexico.

At a lunch served by Zuniga's wife, the guest recalls, Arnold was seated next to the attractive young girlfriend of the artist's son. Suddenly, he began stroking her arm and then loudly remarked, "You know, the thing I love about Mexican women is how furry their pussies are."

Were these incidents simply an example of Arnold's often inappropriate—but mostly harmless—behavior toward women, the kind of behavior that Arnold's friends and costars would dismiss as "flirting"? Or was there something else at play, an almost pathological sexual compulsion much like the condition ascribed to a number of prominent members of his wife's family?

Although no doubt grossly inappropriate and the type of behavior that many people would find unacceptable under any circumstances, it is easy to see how these and most of the incidents described in *Premiere*'s article can perhaps be put down to what Ben Weider described to me as "just Arnold being Arnold." But as it turned out, John Connolly wasn't the only reporter who had been looking into Arnold's past.

As a number of people suspected, Arnold's seemingly impromptu call to George Skelton that morning in February 2001 had not come out of the blue. A month earlier, at the beginning of January, he had quietly signed on with a political consultant, George Gorton, who had been a close adviser of California's former Republican governor Pete Wilson—whom Arnold had known and liked for years. Gorton worked as the national college director for Richard Nixon's 1972 campaign and was perhaps best known as the consultant who had flown to Moscow in 1995 to manage a reelection campaign for Boris Yeltsin—a mission later dramatized in the HBO movie *Spinning Boris*, in which Gorton was played by Jeff Goldblum. Gorton had been introduced to Arnold by Bob White,

Wilson's former chief of staff, who had long considered Arnold a viable political candidate, with the right advisers behind him to shape his image.

A week after signing on as Arnold's political consultant, Gorton claimed he was sitting chatting with Arnold when the actor received a call from Nelson Mandela, whom he had met while working on the Special Olympics. That's when Gorton realized Arnold Schwarzenegger was different from any other candidate he had ever encountered. He also knew that this difference would have both advantages and drawbacks. By early April, a 2002 bid for governor was a strong possibility.

"I urged him to make the race," Pete Wilson told Joe Mathews, "but I said to him and to Maria, 'Look, I have no doubt whatever about your ability as a campaigner. To the contrary, I think you may have the greatest natural gifts as a campaigner that I've ever seen, but before you make the decision, you need to understand that you're going to be under scrutiny of a kind that you've never seen before.'" His advice proved prophetic.

George Gorton had already commissioned extensive polling about the revelations in *Premiere*, to determine how damaging such stories would be to Arnold's political prospects. He found that more than 45 percent of

Californians believed California was going in the wrong direction, and this boded well for an effort to unseat an incumbent. The poll also showed that the allegations in *Premiere* had hurt Arnold but not enough to drastically lower the public's favorable perception of him, which ran 60 percent positive with only 18 percent of respondents expressing an unfavorable opinion. At the same time, one poll question asked of respondents gave a good indication of the strategy Gorton and his people were putting together:

> During his career as a movie star, like most movie stars, he was flamboyant and not always a perfect gentleman, but he and his wife are happily married, most of the accusations are either made up or greatly exaggerated, and he and his wife agree they shouldn't discuss their private life any further than that. Do you agree or disagree?

Gorton was very pleased with the results. He had all but decided to recommend a 2002 run. In short order, he arranged for Arnold to meet with a number of key political figures, including California's secretary of state, Bill Jones: the state party chairman, Shawn Steel; and Steel's deputy, Tim Clark. Each was excited about the prospective candidate. Their enthusiasm was short-lived, however. They were about to receive some unwelcome news that would all but derail their carefully laid plans.

In early April, just as Arnold had signed off on a 2002 candidacy, the *National Enquirer* announced it had uncovered a "world exclusive." Headlined "Arnold's Shocking 7-Year Affair," the story revealed his alleged affair with a former child actress, Gigi Goyette. The publication even ran photos of Goyette in a thong bikini posing with Arnold. The affair had apparently begun in 1975 and ended in 1996, with a large interval in the middle. According to the article, he had even "made love to her in the very same hotel where he was staying with *Dateline* star Maria."

The most damaging part of the story was an allegation that Goyette had first had sex with him while she was an actress on the TV show *Little House on the Prairie* and was only sixteen. If the story was true, her sexual relationship with Arnold in 1975 would have constituted statutory rape under Section 261.5 of the California penal code, which holds that sex with a minor—anybody under eighteen years of age—constitutes a misdemeanor.

Although Arnold wasn't married to Maria when he began his relationship with Goyette, the couple had already been married three years when the relationship resumed in 1989. Out of deference to his marriage, however, Goyette claimed they never actually had sexual intercourse when they got together for their annual trysts. Instead, she invented a term she called "outercourse," because "it's like foreplay." It was reminiscent of Bill Clinton's infamous relationship with Monica Lewinsky, which was, apparently, limited to oral sex because the president didn't believe that this act constituted adultery or violated his marital vows.

"I was his avenue of relaxation," Goyette later explained, dismissing this and Arnold's other dalliances over the years as harmless.

"All this stuff that he did with all these women, these good-looking women, women he worked with," she said, "he grabbed their ass and said, 'Oh, you've got a nice ass, you've got a nice body,' you know it's his way of making them feel comfortable, of complimenting them, because every woman thinks she's shoddy or she's looking bad or something's not right. When you've got a guy like that, saying something like that, it makes them feel so good."

Although the mainstream press had picked up on the article in *Premiere*, hardly any media outlets followed up on the story of Arnold's relationship with Gigi Goyette, probably owing to Marty Singer's aggressive threats.

But the men who had been huddling with Arnold for almost three months knew that the words "statutory rape" wouldn't play well in the living rooms of California voters. Singer had so far limited the damage, warning members of the mainstream press not to risk legal action by running with the *Enquirer*'s allegations, even though Arnold never sued the tabloid itself. For the most part, his trademark attack-dog tactics were successful, but George Gorton knew that a high-profile gubernatorial campaign would revive the charges in a very public way.

With little fanfare, Arnold's 2002 run was aborted before it began. Each member of his political inner circle, however, already had an eye on 2006, when Gray Davis's second term would expire. They had five years to get Arnold into shape, and this time they would be better prepared against potential turds in the punch bowl. None could have anticipated at the time that their moment would come much sooner than they expected.

25.

California Political Circus

My relationship to power and authority is that I'm all for it. People need somebody to watch over them. Ninety-five percent of the people in the world need to be told what to do and how to behave.

—Arnold Schwarzenegger, to
U.S. News & World Report, November 1990

Before Arnold abandoned his 2002 bid, George Gorton devised the perfect vehicle for him to introduce himself to the voters of California and establish his political credibility. It involved a unique quirk of the California electoral system: since 1911, voters had been allowed to rewrite the state laws by obtaining enough signatures on a petition to trigger a referendum and circumvent the state legislature. It was a form of direct democracy that was, paradoxically, California's biggest strength and at the same time almost certainly its greatest weakness. Many of the referenda have contradicted other laws on the books and have helped create the perception that California is pretty much ungovernable. In 1978, extreme right-wingers—led by Howard Jarvis—succeeded in initiating a referendum, Proposition 13, amending the state constitution to cap the property tax rate at 1 percent of 1975 values and severely restrict legislators from raising taxes in the future by requiring a two-thirds majority in both legislative houses. The proposition has haunted California ever since. Almost immediately, it resulted in a decimation of government services and severe cutbacks to the state's educational system—once considered the best in the country—as well as numerous other far-reaching detrimental effects. Most important, it sparked an almost fanatical antitax mentality that has dominated statewide politics ever since.

There were few greater fans of the ballot initiative process, however, than George Gorton, who with Governor Pete Wilson made great use of it. Wilson would later brag that he used the initiative to hammer through right-wing reforms that he knew he could never have achieved through the legislative process. Among those reforms was a controversial measure to deny illegal immigrants access to public schools and other government services, as well as a tough "three strikes" law regarding crime.

Gorton knew that association with such initiatives helped define their sponsors, and he believed Arnold could benefit greatly by spearheading one of his own. They needed something that would introduce Arnold as a compassionate conservative, an outsider who could get things done. Gorton's polling told him that while Arnold remained popular in California, many Republicans still associated him with violent films that were considered "antifamily." He was looking for something that would counter this image, perhaps something that would benefit children. They kicked around the idea of a children's health care initiative but soon abandoned it when they realized that they would have to wade through a minefield of special interests. As Hillary Clinton had learned not long before, it isn't a good idea to take on the health care lobby.

Now Arnold had an idea of his own. As part of his work with the Inner-City Games, he was involved in a pilot project to introduce after-school programs at four Los Angeles middle schools. He had already donated tens of thousands of dollars out of his own pocket to establish such programs around the country. It was clearly a cause close to his heart.

"The hours after school are when kids are most susceptible to negative influences and I have seen firsthand the unbelievable difference it makes when a child has a safe place to go after the school day ends." It seemed the perfect choice for a ballot initiative, which would soften his image and present Arnold as a viable leader.

When Arnold had first assembled his advisers in February 2001, he made it clear that he wasn't a typical Republican. According to Joe Mathews, he had told the state party chairman, Shawn Steel, at their first meeting, "Well, Shawn, you should know that I'm pro-gay, pro-lesbian, pro-transgender, pro-bisexual, pro–reasonable gun control, and pro-choice."

Steel made it clear that those were all surmountable positions as long as he took a strong stand against tax increases—the only issue that would be anathema to voters. The Christian right had never really established a stronghold in California the way it had in some other states, where social issues dominated Republican Party politics. But taxes were another matter.

A few years earlier, Arnold had watched as his longtime Hollywood friend Rob Reiner—a staunch Democrat and liberal—sponsored a successful initiative, Proposition 10, in 1998 to raise state tobacco taxes by 50 cents a pack in order to fund early childhood education programs.

School programs definitely fit the bill as an issue that could showcase Arnold's political strengths, but such programs cost money. How would they be financed without taking the funds out of the pockets of taxpayers? Huddling with experienced strategists and lawyers who had helped draft other ballot initiatives, Groton came up with a plan for Arnold, which would become known as Proposition 49. The initiative would provide $550 million for after-school programs to be taken out of the state budget, but only if the state was running a surplus. It was a wishy-washy scheme, with no guarantee that the programs would ever be implemented, but it would appease the antitax fanatics and appeal to women voters at the same time. It accomplished Gorton's goals perfectly, presenting Arnold as a social progressive and a fiscal conservative.

By the time they settled on an initiative, Arnold had already bowed out of the 2002 governor's race, but the Republicans close to Pete Wilson decided to press on, using the ballot campaign to help launch Arnold's political career. In June, two months after the bombshell in the *Enquirer*, George Gorton drafted a memo, later obtained by the *Los Angeles Times*, describing the goals of the "Schwarzenegger Initiative," leaving no doubt about the hidden agenda for a 2006 run.

The initiative, he wrote, would begin to "brand" Arnold politically, to create a massive fund-raising base that Arnold could tap for a future run; and "to create a team of top professionals loyal to Arnold."

Meanwhile, Arnold had signed on to appear in *Terminator 3*—again directed by James Cameron— which, despite his flagging film career, was all but guaranteed to be a hit and, most important, a huge moneymaker. If Arnold intended the film to be his last before he entered the political arena, as many have suggested, he could claim that he went out on top, having secured $30 million to appear in *T3*, even though his career had long since evaporated and he was making this kind of salary only for appearing in a franchise he had started when he was still a major star. Gorton and his other political advisers gave him the green light to appear in the film, hoping its success would erase the stench of failure attached to his last few projects. It was important to present him as a "winner" when they went to the voters, not as an over-the-hill actor whose glory days were long behind him.

The money he was making from his new film project would come in handy because he was personally committed to financing a substantial portion of the $10 million needed to pass the Schwarzenegger Initiative, lobbying teachers' associations and voters across the state.

In April 2002, Arnold made a public appearance to announce that he had received 750,000 signatures to place his After School Education and Safety Program Act on the November ballot.

"There are millions of kids home alone, and when kids are home alone, I don't have to tell you what that produces—problems, lot of problems," he told a gathering of parents and county workers, noting that he had obtained twice the required number of signatures needed to get an initiative on the ballot. This wasn't, however the grassroots groundswell it was portrayed as. With Arnold's money, Gorton had hired two signature-gathering firms—one affiliated with Democrats and one with Republicans—to get the required names.

Before Arnold barnstormed the state campaigning for his plan, Gorton assembled a team of consultants to draft more than forty questions and answers he might be asked during the course of the campaign. What better way to prepare an actor who is used to reading from a script? The most important of these questions was meant to dispel suspicion that this initiative had been crafted merely as an excuse to launch a future run for political office, as of course it had. Arnold learned to deftly deflect such queries, almost as if the questioner were casting doubt on his sincerity about helping children.

Meanwhile, Governor Gray Davis of California was campaigning for his political life, involved in a tight re-election campaign even without Arnold to battle. He was up against a largely unknown right-wing business-man, Bill Simon, who had snatched the Republican nomination from the more moderate former mayor of Los Angeles, Richard Riordan. Davis had once been popular but was beginning to plunge in the polls, thanks to a growing energy crisis which was not of his making but which he had been slow to address.

Although the full details were not yet known, the crisis had been precipitated by a gradual deregulation of electricity in the previous decade, which would have far-reaching implications for California in particu-lar. When the Republican Pete Wilson was governor during the 1990s, he presided over a complicated series of changes to the state's electricity guidelines that had actually been proposed by the Democratic chair of the state energy committee, Steve Peace. In the summer's of 2000 and 2001, the state was hit by a severe electric-ity shortage that necessitated a series of rolling black-outs and increased residents' energy bills significantly, some to as much as triple their previous level. At first Californians were told simply that two unusually hot summers had increased demand beyond normal capacity. Gray Davis was widely blamed for not anticipating the shortage. In Washington, President Bush appeared to inexplicably pin the crisis on the state's strict environmental standards, many of which had been introduced by the incumbent governor.

It wasn't until a few years later that the real truth emerged. A number of large energy companies had deliberately and illegally conspired to manipulate the energy markets for their own profit. At one point, two of these companies secretly blocked the flow of natural gas into California to keep the price up and rake in billions of dollars in profits made possible by the newly deregulated markets. The most notorious of the companies was Enron, which was later exposed and brought down in one of the greatest corporate scandals in American history. On a day when California experienced a "stage 3" power emergency, for example, Enron actually conspired to take power plants offline, in order to keep prices artificially inflated. At another point, when a forest fire shut down an important transmission line into California, cutting power and raising prices, Enron's energy traders celebrated. Their comments were caught on a tape that was later uncovered. "Burn, baby, burn. That's a beautiful thing," one trader is heard calling out on the tape, which was later obtained by the U.S. Justice Department as part of its investigation into the price gouging.

When Gray Davis attempted to address the problem by proposing new regulations at the beginning of the crisis, in fact, Enron's CEO, Kenneth Lay —a long-time backer and adviser to George W. Bush and Bush's brother Jeb—told the chairman of the California Power Authority, "In the final analysis, it doesn't matter what you crazy people in California do, because I got smart guys who can always figure out how to make money."

The role of Enron and other major energy companies, however, would not be exposed until years later. For now, many voters were blaming Gray Davis for their rising energy bills, the inconvenience of the blackouts, and a skyrocketing budget deficit resulting in part from the energy crisis. The fact is that during Davis's term, thirty-seven new power plants had been licensed, and more were on their way; but not a single new plant had been licensed between 1994 and 1998, when Pete Wilson was governor. Only his good luck in running against a Republican, much farther to the right than the majority of Californians could accept, allowed Davis to pull out a narrow reelection victory in November, 47.4 percent to 42.4 percent.

Arnold's Proposition 49, in contrast, fared much better, winning the approval of more than 56 percent of the state's voters. As Arnold took the stage at the Hollenbeck Center to celebrate the victory on election night, he was flanked by two dozen children who made a convenient prop. After introducing his in-laws Sargent and Eunice Shriver, he thanked Maria for taking care of his own children's after-school activities and spoke about his own longtime dedication to the cause. He ended his speech with a fitting line from *The Terminator:* "I'll be back." A reporter couldn't help asking whether that meant he planned to run for governor in 2006. "I haven't made up my mind," he replied. "But as I always say: If you can take the heat, stay in the kitchen. If you can't take the heat, get out of the kitchen."

And although the election was still a full four years away, Democratic leaders in California couldn't resist offering a preview of what might happen if he did decide to run. "He just might be the Republicans' choice in 2006 if the tabloids don't destroy him," Bob Mulholland, a campaign strategist for the state Democratic Party, told the *New York Times.* "Look at the press a year ago—women and trailers and what-not. It was like pigs who hadn't eaten in a week. I have no idea where the stories came from, but I saw a lot of people in the supermarkets looking at them."

But the *Times'* reporter, who had followed Arnold on the campaign trail, couldn't help observing that he might indeed be a formidable campaigner if he did decide to throw his hat in and that his celebrity status could be a considerable asset.

"Mr. Schwarzenegger seems to be a quick study in the role of political candidate. Speaking recently at a town hall meeting at the Beverly Hilton hotel, Mr. Schwarzenegger acknowledged that he paled next to other speakers who had occupied the same stage: presidents, secretaries of state and religious leaders. 'It could be very intimidating,' he told the lunch crowd. 'But I said to myself: "Hey, which of those guys ever won Mr. Universe? Who had Danny DeVito as a twin brother? Who did a movie with Sharon Stone? Who is married to Maria Shriver?"' Me, so there you go."

As the deficit continued to climb and a recession took hold in California, the newly elected Gray Davis's popularity continued to plunge. He was meeting daily with Republican and Democratic legislators in Sacramento to forge a bipartisan plan to resolve the crisis and get the state back on its feet. But as Davis's approval rating moved downward, a number of forces sensed an opportunity.

It's still a matter of debate who started the idea of a recall—the act of voting to remove the governor— but Arnold sure as heck benefited from the eventual tidal wave. There had been thirty-one previous efforts to recall California governors, yet none had succeeded in getting the required signatures necessary to put the recall to a vote. The California constitution requires 12 percent of the number of ballots that were cast in the last gubernatorial election. In California, unlike other states where a recall is an option, its backers do not have to show grounds why a politician should be yanked, though the spirit of the law is clear: it was meant to replace corrupt politicians guilty of high crimes in office. In 2003, 12 percent would have meant almost 900,000 signatures—a formidable, almost unobtainable number.

So when a right-wing talk show host, Melanie Morgan, mentioned the idea of a recall in December 2002, few people took the prospect seriously. When a political consultant in Sacramento started a Web site a month later to fuel the effort, it still looked like a bunch of cranks blowing steam. When a far-right Christian assemblyman took up the cause, nobody was paying any attention. A few more ears pricked up in February when the leader of an antitax movement, Ted Costa, took to the airwaves to announce his support for the recall and started gathering signatures and encouraging his followers to organize. This is roughly how previous recall efforts had been started. Each eventually fizzled. Still, Costa gathered the signatures necessary to certify the recall effort according to state law. Once he submitted his "Notice of Recall" to the secretary of state on March 25, he had 160 days to gather the 867,158 signatures required to recall a sitting governor.

However, this particular recall effort started with something that previous efforts didn't have—the Internet. Two separate recall committees set up Web sites and soon announced that more than 1 million copies of their petition had been downloaded. Still, the signatures were coming in at a relative trickle, and they didn't have much time.

Meanwhile, right-wing radio talk shows had begun to pay attention, thinking maybe there was something to this recall. The drumbeat started getting louder, and a grassroots movement began. Californians couldn't enter their local supermarket without passing a table with workers collecting signatures for the recall effort. Democrats labeled the recall leaders "nutballs" and the mainstream media had still barely registered what was happening. Indeed, observers—watching the signatures come in slowly—concluded that the recall didn't have a chance. The Republican Party had been reluctant to get involved, and there were no high-profile backers yet.

But the tide suddenly began to shift in May, when Darrell Issa, a right-wing businessman turned congressman, suddenly announced that he was supporting the recall effort and that he was willing to put a portion of his vast automotive electronics fortune—estimated at $250 million—behind it. For the first time, the proponents of the recall could afford to hire professional signature-gatherers. By July, the recall effort had gathered 1,356,408 signatures on its petitions, nearly 500,000 more than were needed. As per state law, the lieutenant governor set the date of the recall election for October 7.

But with three months to go, it was anybody's guess who would run to replace Davis if he was recalled. Media speculation reached fever pitch, and the biggest question on everybody's mind was whether Arnold would run. Conveniently, he was in the process of promoting the recently released *Terminator 3* as speculation continued to mount and the deadline for declaring approached. During Arnold's appearance on *The Tonight Show* in late June, the host, Jay Leno, asked, to rapturous applause, whether he was going to run for governor.

His response was typical: "In a few days from now, I do have to make a very, very—probably one of the most difficult—decisions of my life . . . what to wear on my opening day of *Terminator 3*."

As the guessing games continued and Arnold continued to be coy, however, he had all but made up his mind. And ultimately it may have been a recent media acquisition that got him there.

In 2002 AMI—probably best known for the businesses it owns, which include virtually every major celebrity tabloid in the United States, such as the *National Enquirer, Globe,* and *Star*—wanted to diversify its publication base. David Pecker, the president and CEO, heard that Joe Weider was looking to sell his highly successful company, Weider Publications. Well into his eighties, Weider no longer had the stamina to run his increasingly complex web of businesses, which included a range of bodybuilding magazines, nutritional supplements, and fitness products. The two men's business operations were already, in fact, inextricably linked because Weider relied almost exclusively on Pecker's tabloids to advertise his nutritional products—especially the controversial diet supplement ephedra—which accounted for as much as 30 percent of the papers' advertising revenue. It seemed a natural fit.

By November, AMI had won control of Weider Publications in a silent auction, paying $350 million in cash and stock, and beating out Pecker's old company, Hachette. A month later, just as the recall effort in California was getting under way, Pecker met with Joe and Betty Weider at Beverly Hills' Peninsula Hotel to celebrate the acquisition.

Pecker later revealed that at this dinner, Weider broached the subject of how he intended to "handle the bodybuilding world," pointing out that this subject was close to his heart.

Pecker knew of Weider's concern. "I said, 'Yes, I understand that. I know that you have a very close relationship with Arnold Schwarzenegger,'" he would later tell Ann Louise Bardach, a reporter for *Los Angeles* magazine, who revealed that at this same dinner, Weider recommended that Schwarzenegger be given a 10 percent share in the company as a "publicist."

As Pecker knew from his due diligence, Arnold had been an integral component of the company's success, appearing on the cover of Weider's publications more than fifty times over the years and endorsing Weider's many products. At this point in the conversation, Weider cut to the chase, worrying that Arnold might be reluctant to sign on because of "all the scandal" in AMI's tabloids.

Weider, like his protégé, was acutely aware that the *National Enquirer* had gleefully taken credit for Arnold's deciding not to run in 2001 and had vowed that as soon as he entered the race, there would be what

Laurence Leamer describes as a "Krakatoa of tabloid eruptions spewing the lava of supposed dalliances and untoward conduct."

Pecker immediately caught the gist of what he was being asked. He assured the aging publishing mogul that Arnold would no longer be a target of AMI's negative reporting.

"I said, 'There is one thing that I can tell you. We don't, as a company, rehash old stuff,'" Pecker told Bardach during her thoroughly researched investigation into the transaction, later published as "Taming the Hydra-Headed Carnivorous Beast."

As the recall effort gathered steam, the *New York Daily News* reported that Pecker had assured Joe Weider that the tabloids would "lay off" Schwarzenegger. The *News* quoted Weider talking about Pecker's assurance. At the time, Pecker denied he had given such a guarantee, but when Bardach analyzed the contents of AMI's papers, she discovered something interesting. "The tabloids suddenly became Arnold free." Four separate sources at AMI told Bardach this was no coincidence. "When Weider was being bought," said one senior AMI staffer, "the edict came down: No more Arnold stories."

On July 11, Pecker personally flew to Los Angeles to meet with Arnold and arrange for him to stay on with

Weider publications in an official capacity. It was the first time he had met the man whose political career had been derailed by one of his publications two years before. But the meeting got off on a good footing, as Pecker mentioned that when his former company, Hachette, published *George,* he had been friends with John Kennedy Jr. He also knew Maria's brother Bobby. Arnold said he had checked up and heard good things about Pecker, who claims that never once did the star mention any of the lurid tabloid stories about his affairs. At this meeting, they appear to have discussed a deal through which Arnold would stay on, become an editor at both *Muscle and Fitness* and *Flex,* and be paid more than $1 million annually for his participation. This would all benefit AMI. It would soon become apparent how the company would return the favor.

Three weeks after meeting with Pecker, Arnold had still not publicly declared his intentions, although the field of candidates to succeed Davis—if he lost the recall—was getting crowded. California law allowed anybody willing to pay $3,500 and collect sixty-five signatures to appear on the ballot. Sure enough, the kooks started coming out of the woodwork announcing their intention to run; they included one woman who sold thong underwear, and the pornography publisher Larry Flynt of *Hustler* magazine, whose slogan was "Vote for a Smut-Peddler Who Cares."

Davis's people liked the prospect of a hundred fringe candidates. The muddier the waters, they reasoned, the more likely California voters would be to decide to stick with the governor. There were also some serious candidates pondering a run, however, including the Republican businessman Peter Ueberroth, a former commissioner of major league baseball, who had presided over the successful 1984 Los Angeles Olympics. Ueberroth was loudly hinting that he would run as an independent. The highest-profile Republican considering a run was former mayor of Los Angeles Richard Riordan, a moderate who polls showed was a popular choice among California voters. The Democrats, in contrast, were in disarray. They feared that running their own candidate would signal that they assumed Davis would be recalled, creating a self-fulfilling prophecy. But if they didn't run a candidate to replace him, they might be stuck with a Republican. The popular Democratic senator Dianne Feinstein was being urged to run, but she was still publicly on the fence, as was Lieutenant Governor Cruz Bustamante, who was a logical successor.

Meanwhile, Arnold kept his cards close to his vest, huddling with Gorton, former governor Wilson, and other close advisers. Then in early August rumors began to leak from this circle that Arnold had decided against running. He would instead endorse Richard Riordan for governor.

Hearing these rumors, Dianne Feinstein announced on August 6 that she had decided not to run. Polls showed that she would probably have beaten Arnold Schwarzenegger in an election but that she would have a much tougher time against Riordan.

With Feinstein out, Arnold called the booker of *The Tonight Show* and asked to appear the following night. He had an announcement he wanted to share with Leno's viewers. There was a sense of excitement at NBC at the prospect that Arnold would use the show to announce his candidacy. But it was tempered by rumors that he would instead use the opportunity to announce his decision not to run.

When Arnold showed up by limo for the taping at NBC studios in Burbank on the afternoon of August 6, he was greeted in the parking lot by Jay Leno, then ushered into the greenroom with his advisers, George Gorton, Mitch Mulanix, and Sean Walsh. All were tight-lipped about the planned announcement, although some people wondered why Arnold would bring along three political advisers if he had decided not to run.

The taping began. After Jay's monologue, as Arnold strode onto the stage, dressed casually, there was palpable excitement in the studio. Leno wasted no time getting right to the point. "Let me ask you about this now. I know it's been weeks and people go back and forth, and it's taken you a while and you said you would come here tonight and tell us your decision. So what is your decision?"

"Well, Jay, after thinking about this for a long time, my decision is . . ." A sudden censor's beep seemed to drown out his announcement, to the delight of the audience members, who laughed uproariously at the surprise. It was a planned bit that he and Leno had discussed backstage before the show.

"We've joked about this and thank you," continued Leno, returning to the question at hand. "It's been in my monologue. It's been a slow workweek. It's been good for like a thousand jokes. But seriously, what are you going to do? You said you were going to come here tonight and tell us. What are you going to do?"

The response was trademark Arnold and had been partially crafted in the greenroom with the help of one of Leno's comedy writers. "My decision is a very difficult decision to make. It was the most difficult decision to make in my entire life except the one in 1978 when I decided to get a bikini wax."

Turning serious, he declared that California was in a very serious situation. When he moved to the state in 1968, he continued, Califonia had been a fantastic place. There were countless opportunities for everybody. Now the situation has changed. The atmosphere was "disastrous." There was a disconnect between the people of California and its politicians, he lamented.

"The politicians are fiddling and fumbling and failing," he declared, finding his rhythm now. "And the man that is failing the people more than anyone is Gray Davis. He's failing them terribly and this is why he needs to be recalled and this is why I am going to run for governor of the state of California." The studio audience went crazy, drowning out the end of his announcement. Television stations across the state immediately broke into their programming to announce the news, which wouldn't actually be broadcast until several hours later when *The Tonight Show* appeared on the East Coast.

George Gorton would later claim that Arnold had in fact decided not to run. He had arrived at Leno's studios with an announcement in his pocket to that effect, and this is what he was supposed to reveal on the show. It wasn't until he was sitting on Leno's couch, Gorton claims, that Arnold changed his mind and decided to run after all. The news of his candidacy was just as much a surprise to Gorton as it was to the people of California, he claimed. Arnold himself appeared to go along with that story, when Leno asked him what changed his mind, implying that the 1.6 million signatures on the recall petition had persuaded him to say to Davis: "*Hasta la vista*, baby."

But in late 2009, a former associate of Gorton told me that the entire appearance had been scripted from beginning to end.

"Arnold went in there fully prepared to run, although I don't think Jay knew it. There was never any question about that. It had been decided a long time before. George stage-managed the whole *Tonight Show* appearance to heighten the drama and also to draw out Dianne Feinstein. We quietly let it be known to some key people that Arnold wouldn't be running, in hopes that Senator Feinstein would go public with her intentions. It worked beautifully. Nothing George does is seat of the pants. He knew exactly how it would play out and he loved the impression that it created that Arnold was his own man, not some actor having his strings pulled by professionals."

Indeed, years later Arnold told the Associated Press that he had informed Maria about his decision to run while the two were in their backyard Jacuzzi—lending credence to my source's version and contradicting Gorton's official account.

The rest of America, however, was stunned by the political theater it had just witnessed. Most people assumed that Arnold Schwarzenegger had about as much a chance of being elected governor as Gary Coleman—the diminutive actor from *Diff'rent Strokes*—who had also recently entered the race. But Californians knew something the rest of the country did not. They had recently witnessed Arnold run a deft, intelligent, skillfully crafted yearlong campaign for his after-school initiative. They had gotten to know Arnold the person instead of the tough-guy caricature most had seen on the big screen, the guy with the funny accent who liked to blow away bad guys.

So while the world watched the circus unfolding in California, shocked at the developments, it came as little surprise to Californians when they awoke a few days after the announcement on *The Tonight Show* to discover polls showing Arnold Schwarzenegger as the front-runner to replace Gray Davis. Richard Riordan announced his own decision not to run, which left Arnold as the top Republican contender.

It appeared that they would also be waking up in less than two months to a state headed by Governor Arnold Schwarzenegger. But Arnold himself was keenly aware that there were still a few bumps in his path. He alluded to these almost as soon as the applause had died down following his surprise announcement before the *Tonight Show* audience. "I know that they're going to throw everything at me and they're going, you know, to say that I have no experience and that I'm a womanizer and that I'm a terrible guy and all this kind of things that are going to come my way."

Again, Gorton had prepared him well, cleverly anticipating the kind of questions that he knew would rear their head during the ugly two-month campaign to come. This time, however, they would be prepared for whatever was thrown their way. Or so they believed.

26.

"Arnold, the American Dream"

Arnold's campaign got off to a rough start when George Gorton trotted him out to make the rounds of the morning talk shows the day after his announcement, and it quickly became evident that he had no concrete plans to address the serious issues plaguing the state. On question after question, he either stonewalled, obfuscated, or winged it as frustrated interviewers attempted to discover exactly where he stood.

On family leave: "I would have to get into that."

On gay marriage: "Well, I don't want to get into that right now because . . ."

And on state versus federal budget deficits: "You know, I don't mix apples with oranges."

When Matt Lauer asked on the *Today* show whether Arnold would make his tax returns available to the public, he put his hand to his ear mic: "Say again."

LAUER: Are you going to make your tax returns for the past several years available . . .

ARNOLD: I don't hear anything.

LAUER: . . . to the press?

ARNOLD: I—I didn't hear you.

A spokesman for the California Democratic Party immediately pointed to this poor performance, saying, "He's not ready for prime time, and California doesn't need an on-the-job training program for the executive of the fifth largest economy in the world."

The exchange with Lauer reminded many observers of another actor turned governor of California, Ronald Reagan, who frequently pretended he couldn't hear a question whenever he didn't want to answer it. The *Today* show's technicians noted that they could find no audio problems.

According to Joe Mathews's behind-the-scenes account of the recall campaign, which he was covering for the *Los Angeles Times*, this is approximately when Maria Shriver stepped in to head off disaster, furious that Gorton had put her husband in the line of fire so soon.

To Gorton, she shot off a series of rapid-fire questions: "What is your plan? Where is the staff? What is your message? What was the point of these

TV appearances? What direction is the campaign going in?"

Arnold would later admit that Maria had cried when he initially told her he was planning to run for governor. Although politics was in her family's blood, she had also seen the potentially devastating consequences of political life. The invasion of privacy was bad enough, but she had also seen two beloved uncles shot and killed in the service of a political career. She hadn't approved of her husband's candidacy, but now that he was in it, she would damn well make sure it was done right. The first thing she insisted on was bringing in somebody other than Gorton to run the campaign. Wilson's loyalist Bob White was her first choice, and he was quickly enlisted while Maria met with the rest of the quickly assembled team and gave people their marching orders: open a campaign headquarters; assemble a campaign coalition; come up with a budget. She also quietly asked Bonnie Reiss, a liberal Democrat who had worked with Arnold at the Inner City Games Foundation, to be an adviser.

Taking charge, Maria also came up with a slogan for Arnold: "The People's Governor." She decided that in the short term, she would keep him away from the press to minimize any potential damage. He could be of better use raising funds. He was immediately dispatched 3,000 miles away to meet with the advisers and fund-raisers of another moderate Republican governor, George Pataki of New York.

Meanwhile, Maria tapped her own connections to bring in a figure who was more closely associated with Democrats than with Republicans—the billionaire fund manager Warren Buffett, whose Berkshire Hathaway was one of the world's most successful financial funds. Buffett agreed to become co-chair of Arnold's economic campaign team. He set off a political tsunami almost immediately, when he gave an interview to the *Wall Street Journal* suggesting that the state's sacred cow, Proposition 13, was a mistake and should be "revisited." Property taxes, Buffett said, were too low. Arnold was quickly forced to distance himself from these remarks, and emphasize his own belief that Californians are in fact overtaxed. Conservatives were suspicious enough of his Democratic-sounding views on social issues, and of his wife's family. He couldn't afford to take on the tax issue.

To counter fears that Arnold would alienate the Republican base, he was immediately booked on conservative talk radio shows all over the state, and he was ordered to stay far away from social issues and keep hammering at the state's overspending and overtaxation. The strategy paid off: starstruck hosts were afraid to ask any hard-hitting questions, and Arnold's popularity among Republican voters began to soar.

One conservative who wasn't afraid to ask Arnold to account for his liberal views was the fiery right-wing rising star on the Fox News Channel, Sean Hannity. But Arnold had been well coached to reiterate his opposition to partial-birth abortion, which, though he was still pro-choice, was supposed to distinguish him from liberal Democrats. It was during his interview with Hannity that he made his most famous gaffe of the campaign, though voters appeared to find it charming. Asked whether he supported gay marriage, Arnold replied, "No, I think gay marriage is something that should be between a man and a woman."

Meanwhile, lieutenant governor Cruz Bustamante had emerged as the leading Democratic candidate, and Arnold merely had to tar him for his association with Gray Davis to win points with disaffected independents and moderate Democrats. In early September, Bustamante held a five-point lead over Arnold, but that began to shift as Arnold and his team began skillfully targeting crucial demographics—women, Latinos, and independents who were once firmly in the lieutenant governor's camp. Arnold had also raised millions of dollars for crucial TV advertising, much of which he spent attacking his Democratic opponent. He had actually supplied a great deal of these funds from his own vast personal wealth, deftly skirting California's campaign financing laws by "lending" his campaign millions of dollars—a major advantage he had over Bustamante in a state so large that TV advertising was the only way to reach most voters. It was also a way to keep Arnold on message and avoid the gaffes that Maria and others feared would trip up his campaign, mindful of his embarrassing performance on the TV talk shows the day after he announced. As the campaign progressed, reporters complained constantly that they were being kept away from the candidate and were unable to ask him any serious questions. He was simply coasting on his popularity, they fretted.

By the last week of the campaign, the polls showed Arnold with a comfortable eight-point lead over Bustamante, mostly as a result of increasing public support for the recall. It appeared that Arnold was cruising to an easy victory. And then the storm hit.

When California's voters—most of whom had already made up their minds—picked up their newspapers on October 2, five days before the election, they saw a huge banner headline that would cause them to rethink their position: "Women Say Schwarzenegger Groped, Humiliated Them; the Acts Allegedly Took

Place over Three Decades; a Campaign Aide Denies the Accusations."

The story in the *Los Angeles Times* followed up on the earlier piece in *Premiere* magazine and went on to detail the stories of six women who came into contact with Arnold on movie sets, in studio offices, and in other settings who claimed he had touched them in a sexual manner without their consent. Three of them described incidents in which he grabbed their breasts; another said he once reached under her skirt and grabbed her ass; a fifth claimed he had groped her and attempted to remove her bathing suit in a hotel elevator; the sixth said he had pulled her onto his lap and asked whether a certain sexual act had ever been performed on her.

"Did he rape me?" said one woman who claimed he grabbed her breast. "No. Did he humiliate me? You bet he did."

Four of the six women asked that their names not be mentioned, because they worked in Hollywood, where Arnold was still a powerful figure. In each case, the reporter spoke to friends or relatives of the women who confirmed that they had complained about the incidents long before Arnold decided to run for governor.

One of the two women named was Anna Richardson, the British TV personality who had told her story to *Premiere* in 2001. The other was E. Laine Stockton, who was married at the time to a former friend of Arnold's, the bodybuilder Robby Robinson. Nineteen years old at the time of the alleged incident, she said she encountered Arnold at Gold's Gym in 1975 when she was working out. She claims that as she sat on an exercise bench, Arnold walked up behind her, reached under her T-shirt, and touched her bare breast. "The gym is full of bodybuilders and Arnold comes and he gropes my breast—actually touches my breast with his left hand," Stockton told the *Los Angeles Times*. She said he then walked away without saying a word.

Arnold's campaign spokesman, Sean Walsh, immediately denied the charges, claiming that "Democrats and others are using this to try to hurt Arnold Schwarzenegger." But the newspaper claimed that it had discovered the women's stories on its own during the course of a seven-week investigation and that none of the women had contacted it.

Behind the scenes of the campaign, strategists were scrambling to address the crisis, at the same time wondering if there was more to come. Arnold was scheduled to address a campaign rally in San Diego, and he used the opportunity to attempt damage control. He began the rally by appearing to dismiss the women's stories as politically motivated. "You know, when you get into politics, they try to tear down your character, and as you know this morning, they have begun with the tearing down. But I know that the people of California can see through this trash politics," he said, prompting wild cheering from the 2,000 supporters inside the convention center.

But his next words stunned the crowd into silence, as he appeared to acknowledge unspecified wrongdoing. "I always say that wherever there is smoke, there is fire," he said. "So I want to say to you, yes, I have behaved badly sometimes. Yes, it is true that I was on rowdy movie sets, and I have done things that were not right, which I thought then was playful. But I now recognize that I have offended people. And to those people that I have offended, I want to say to them, I am deeply sorry about that, and I apologize."

Later, on CNN, he said, "I don't remember so many of the things that I was accused of having done" and then, when pressed, claimed that "most of it is not true." To another reporter, he appeared to echo his campaign spokesman, who was already calling the accusations an orchestrated "smear campaign."

"One wonders what the motivation is," Arnold asked a reporter. "Why am I getting all this stuff thrown at me now? No one complained. If someone comes to me and says to me, 'How dare you say this? How dare you do this?' I can apologize right then."

The accusations appeared to throw the entire race into chaos, and with only four days to go, nobody could predict the fallout. "The *Times* story is very graphic, very specific and well-documented," Barbara O'Connor, a political scientist at California State University Sacramento, told CNN. "Anyone who reads it will have severe reservations about Mr. Schwarzenegger's treatment of women, as recently as two years ago. I think it does hurt him. When you're running on a platform of moral superiority . . . anything that goes to your character can be damning."

Bruce Cain, a political scientist at the University of California, Berkeley, believed the nature of the accusations could be extremely damaging to Arnold's chances.

"This is not just philandering or adultery," he said. "This is stuff that people get fired for pretty regularly,"

Meanwhile, Maria—who had taken a leave of absence from NBC to campaign with her husband—hadn't been heard from since the allegations emerged, and political analysts were predicting that her reaction would determine if Arnold could weather the storm. When Hillary Clinton sat beside her husband on *60 Minutes* during the 1992 campaign after the first reports had emerged about his womanizing, her steadfast support was thought to be the turning point of the campaign.

Instead of appearing at her husband's side, however, Maria visited a Republican women's club in ultraconservative Orange County to address the allegations. "In the end, in these final 48, 72 hours, you can make a decision—you can listen to all the negativity and you can listen to people who have never met Arnold, or who met him for five seconds 30 years ago," she told the small gathering of women. "Or you can listen to me. I wouldn't be standing here if this man weren't an A-plus human being." To observers, she appeared shaken.

The first polls after the allegations were published showed that Arnold's support had narrowed considerably among women voters. The accusations were clearly taking a toll. The situation got worse when more women stepped forward the next day, claiming that they too had been victims of Arnold's bad behavior. A forty-one-year-old wife, mother, and waitress—Gail Escobar—appeared at a Schwarzenegger rally in Costa Mesa and told reporters that when she was a sixteen-year-old student, Schwarzenegger had rolled down the passenger window of a car driven by someone else and told Escobar and her friend, "We are going to rape you tonight." Schwarzenegger's spokesman, however, called Escobar's story a "political hit" because she belonged to a union that supported Bustamante. "We believe this is an obvious coordinated attack by Democratic operatives," he said. "But it's nothing we didn't expect."

But the accusations just kept on coming, as three more women stepped forward with similar stories, including two who claimed that Arnold had harassed them on the set of his 1988 film *Twins*. One, an assistant director, told the *Los Angeles Times* that he used to undress in front of her when she was in his trailer and that once he had pulled her down with him on his bed. Another woman who had been on the same set claimed he once pressed up against her and forced his tongue into her mouth.

And a stuntwoman, Rhonda Miller, called a press conference at the office of her attorney, Gloria Allred, to claim that the star had once accosted her in a makeup trailer during the filming of *Terminator 2* in 1991. "Arnold suddenly pulled my T-shirt up and snapped a Polaroid photo of my breasts," she said. "He lifted my shirt up further and began to suck on my breasts. I was horrified."

This was the first of the allegations that Arnold chose to address specifically, telling reporters, "The statement made today by Rhonda Miller is not factually correct. I recall seeing photographs of crew members in the makeup trailer during the filming of *T2*, and on numerous occasions made crude comments when a nude photo would be added to the ceiling. If my crude comments offended anyone, I apologize," he said.

Meanwhile, less than half an hour after Rhonda Miller had completed her press conference, Schwarzenegger's campaign aides had sent an e-mail to hundreds of reporters alerting them to the fact that Miller had a history of arrests for prostitution, having been arrested for soliciting seven times and convicted six times. Unfortunately, that was the wrong Rhonda Miller and the stuntwoman eventually filed a libel suit over the defamatory accusations.

The timing of these women's accusations seemed suspicious to many people. I too wondered, even knowing about *Premiere* magazine's earlier accusations, if this was all a smear campaign.

I wanted to see if there was indeed fire behind all the smoke. I had come across countless stories about crude behavior and inappropriate conduct with women, and rumors of womanizing. But none quite rose to the level of reliability—other than my conversation with his hairdresser—and many were merely secondhand. Eventually, though, my digging produced results. A longtime producer and film investor, who had encountered Arnold numerous times over the years, told me that in 2006 she and a friend, a Los Angeles real estate agent, dined at Arnold's old restaurant, Schatzi on Main, in Santa Monica. Having finished dinner, the two decided to go for a drink in a nearby cigar bar, where Arnold was hosting a cigar party. Almost from the moment they entered the bar, he was all over both of them, she claims.

"He's a male whore," she told me. "I was shocked because I knew he was married. Arnold was all over us, trying to get us to go home with him. He plied us with alcohol and kept making the moves on us all night. It was as if he thought he was entitled to take one of us home with him. He came across as a big pervert."

A few months later, the same producer attended a party at the Playboy Mansion, which Arnold also attended. She told me that during this party, she and other guests saw him go into a private room with a Playboy model for almost two hours. "There's a rumor that Hef has video, for security purposes, of everything that goes on in those rooms. I hope that tape comes out so his wife can see what kind of a pig he is."

Whether or not Arnold Schwarzenegger is a serial womanizer, however—and from my own investigations I no longer have any doubts that he is—the voters of California didn't seem to care. Americans had just been through the scandal involving Monica Lewinsky, and had seen Bill Clinton's popularity actually rise during the subsequent impeachment process. Either Americans—much like Europeans—had come to expect this kind of behavior from their leaders or they felt it didn't reflect on the ability of a politician to do his job. Still, the first polls after the *Los Angeles Times*' story showed that Arnold had taken a hit with women voters. His lead had narrowed, though he was still comfortably ahead.

His aides had very skillfully deflected the political fallout by demonizing the *Times* for the last-minute "smears." By brilliantly casting the barrage of stories as a dirty trick by a liberal-leaning newspaper, they managed to bring a considerable number of conservatives into Arnold's camp, even though such voters had always been suspicious of him in the past because of his liberal social policies.

The editor of the *Times*, John Carroll, a respected veteran newspaperman considered one of the finest in the business, was undaunted by the attacks on his paper's integrity. "We're in the business of publishing, not concealing," he protested. "We had information we felt was significant. How could we justify not providing it to voters?" Carroll strongly believed his paper had a duty to its readers to expose the truth about the man they were about to put into office. Ben Bradlee, who withstood withering criticism directed at his paper during the Watergate crisis, felt the same way about his own role; and Carroll would later invoke Watergate and Bradlee as a cautionary tale.

When Nixon was a politician in California during the 1940s and 1950s, Carroll explained, "he showed all the traits of character that later came out in Watergate." But the *Los Angeles Times* during that era was not a particularly good newspaper, he explained. "It was promoting Nixon, and was basically not interested in writing any of this stuff." The paper, he argues, failed to do its job at that time and, as a result, an oblivious nation later elected a corrupt president who destroyed the fabric of the Constitution. That would not be allowed to happen again on Carroll's watch.

Ironically, it may have helped Arnold that a slew of other damaging stories happened to emerge around the same time as these women came forward—including the first revelation about George Butler's book proposal, in which Arnold was said to have "admired" Hitler. This was followed shortly afterward by the *Los Angeles Times'* investigation revealing that Gustav Schwarzenegger had voluntarily enlisted in Hitler's Brown Shirts. Voters found it hard to keep track of the seemingly never-ending barrage of negative stories about Arnold, which lent credence to charges by his campaign that he was the victim of an organized smear.

Arnold had also defused the bomb that had knocked him out of the earlier race. In 2005, the *Los Angeles Times* would reveal that Gigi Goyette had signed a hush-hush confidentiality agreement with the publisher of the *National Enquirer* American Media (AMI), two days after Arnold announced his candidacy for governor. Goyette was paid $20,000 for her story by AMI, which never ran it. This is the company whose CEO, David Pecker, had assured Joe Weider during the same month that he would "lay off" Arnold Schwarzenegger in an effort to persuade him to stay on at Weider's publications. Laurence Leamer, who broke the story, later asked, "Does American Media have the right to have that impact in the election? The big question with Gigi is: Was the *National Enquirer* legitimately buying her story intending to run it? Or were they essentially bribing her during the campaign?"

It appeared to be the latter. As it turned out, David Pecker kept his promise to Weider. Instead of running the Goyette story or other revelations that might have damaged Arnold's election chances, American Media published a glossy, 120-page preelection magazine titled "Arnold, the American Dream."

One former AMI staffer told *Los Angeles* magazine that "Pecker ordered [*National Enquirer*'s editor] David Perel to commission a series of brownnosing stories on Arnold" that would hit the stands during the campaign. Perel denied it. But in August, shortly after Arnold declared, the *Star*—another AMI paper—ran a full-page story headlined "Vote Schwarzenegger!" accompanied by six flattering photos.

Mission accomplished.

When the dust cleared, Gray Davis became the first governor ever recalled in United States history, with 55 percent of voters opting to remove him from office. And, despite the potentially devastating accusations during the last week of the campaign, Arnold Schwarzenegger beat Cruz Bustamante by almost 1.5 million votes to become California's thirty-eighth governor.

27.

Chastened by Defeat

When one has money, one day it becomes less interesting. And when one is the best in film, what can be more interesting? Perhaps power. Then one moves into politics and becomes governor or president or something.

—Arnold Schwarzenegger, interview
with *Stern* magazine, 1977

In 1966, soon after Ronald Reagan unseated California's liberal governor Edmund (Pat) Brown by a 1-million-vote landslide, a reporter asked the winner what kind of a governor he would be. "Gee, I don't know" came the response. "I've never played a governor."

Now another actor had captured the governorship, and the comparisons were already coming fast and furiously. As far back as 1962, a small cabal of wealthy California businessmen had an idea after they heard the B-list actor Reagan mention that he happened to be a Republican. In Hollywood back then, members of the GOP were as rare as they would be four decades later; and the group, led by a used-car salesman, Holmes Tuttle, thought Reagan could be useful. They visited him at his home and asked him if he would consider running for a U.S. Senate seat vacated by a retiring Republican, but Reagan politely declined. He was reluctant to make the financial sacrifice of giving up his Hollywood career for a comparatively paltry politician's salary. Two years later, he gave a nationally televised speech at the Republican convention in support of the archconservative presidential candidate Barry Goldwater. Overnight, Reagan became the new star of the party's right wing, which was anxious for a standard-bearer after the moderate policies of Republicans like Dwight D. Eisenhower and Nelson Rockefeller.

A year before Reagan's convention speech, a public relations executive transplanted from New Jersey, dedicated to establishing a far-right ideology in the United States, had founded the United Republicans of California (UCO) to take back the conservative movement—in effect, to hijack the Republican Party.

Although they weren't affiliated, UCO drew many of its members from the John Birch Society, an extremist right-wing organization founded in California five years earlier and dedicated to anticommunism, free markets, Christian morals, and limited government. The UCO was looking for somebody to carry its torch, and when members saw Reagan give a fiery speech in favor of their candidate, Goldwater, they knew they had found their man.

They immediately set their sights on the 1966 governor's race in California, hoping to unseat the incumbent, Pat Brown, whose liberal policies were anathema to them. Although few took Reagan's candidacy seriously at first, he proved to be a genial campaigner, conveying the kind of optimism and clichés that would become very familiar to the rest of the country two decades later. Meanwhile, Brown ran a negative campaign centered on Reagan's lack of qualifications for the job. In one infamous TV ad, he asks a group of schoolchildren, "I'm running against an actor, and you know who killed Abe Lincoln, don't you?"

Reagan pulled out a surprise landslide victory, and the men who got him elected had a willing pawn. As they well knew, Reagan was easily controllable and perfectly content to do their bidding while they made countless millions from his free-market-friendly policies. In deference to their ideology, the new governor also cut spending, taunted antiwar protesters, and cut back many of California's vaunted social programs, as well as its respected public university system, considered the jewel of the nation.

The men who were pulling Reagan's strings already knew what the American people would learn many years later. He wasn't particularly bright. His aides would later tell stories about how disengaged their boss was, spending most of his time watching movies at the residence while the professionals ran the government. Years later, his close friend and ideological soul mate Margaret Thatcher would be heard commenting about Reagan, "Poor dear. There's nothing between his ears." In 1980, many of the California businessmen who had made Reagan governor persuaded him to run for president so that he could impose the same conservative ideology and free-market policies on the entire nation. These men later became known as the "kitchen cabinet," and their plan was more successful than they could ever have imagined

When Arnold Schwarzenegger was enlisted to run for governor, the men who approached him couldn't possibly have imagined that he would become a standard-bearer for conservative ideology like Reagan. His liberal social views were already fairly well known.

But these men did count on one thing that was just as good: Schwarzenegger, like Reagan, was an unabashed fan of the economist Milton Friedman.

Friedman was a Nobel Prize–winning economist who taught at the University of Chicago from 1946 to 1976 and who had firmly rejected Keynesian economics in favor of a complex system he called monetarism. He believed that regulation was the bane of society and favored a virtually unfettered free enterprise system. This made him the darling of conservatives and libertarians, and he found favor with a number of right wing governments around the world during the 1980s. The most notorious of these was Chile, where the dictator Augusto Pinochet implemented Friedman's theories as part of his "shock" program to end the hyperinflation that had racked his country for years, importing Friedman's disciples from the University of Chicago—nicknamed the "Chicago boys"—to undo the reforms of his predecessor, Salvador Allende. The program substituted severe austerity measures for tax increases, cutting government spending on social programs as a means to cure the economic ills of the nation. Although Friedman was widely criticized for overlooking Pinochet's brutal practices—which included torture, jailing dissidents, and murdering political opponents—his economic theories appeared to work at first, and Friedman was celebrated as a genius by neoconservatives such as Ronald Reagan and Margaret Thatcher. His ideas were used for years to justify their own free-market economic policies. But in later years, as its debt mounted and financial corruption paralyzed the country, Chile was forced to nationalize many of the deregulated financial institutions that were at the heart of the crisis. Years later, George W. Bush used Friedman's theories to justify his own deregulation, which many economists now blame for the catastrophic financial crisis of 2008.

Arnold Schwarzenegger claims that he first came across Friedman's theories while studying business at the University of Wisconsin. He says that when he saw the economist's documentary series, "Free to Choose," it "opened his eyes" and "changed his life." Arnold would talk frequently of his admiration for Friedman and for Friedman's policies, even before he entered politics, though it's unlikely he could have grasped Friedman's complex macroeconomics, which even many experienced economists find hard to understand.

It may have been Arnold's frequent public references to Friedman, in fact, that first brought him to the attention of the California Republican Party, whose leaders cared more about free markets than about Christian morals. It is even conceivable that Enron's

CEO, Ken Lay, knew about Arnold's loyalty to Friedman when he invited the would-be candidate for governor to a secret meeting at the Peninsula Hotel in Beverly Hills on May 17, 2001, during the energy crisis in California. Also present was the notorious stock swindler Michael Milken, who had been convicted of insider trading a decade earlier.

To this day, nobody except Milken, Arnold, and Ken Lay—who died in 2006 after being convicted of ten counts of securities fraud—knows what the three men talked about on May 17. We do know, however, that the meeting took place only two weeks after California's Democratic lieutenant governor Cruz Bustamante had filed a $9 billion civil suit against five power producers implicated in deliberately precipitating California's energy crisis. "They are an energy cartel, which has scammed California taxpayers out of billions of dollars by manipulating the energy market," Bustamante said as he announced the lawsuit on behalf of the taxpayers of California. The meeting had to be more than a coincidence. The energy companies were nervous. They knew that they were vulnerable. The Justice Department had enough evidence to build a strong case against them. A multibillion-dollar civil judgment would put many of them out of business. They needed to settle the suit, but a Democratic administration was in no mood for conciliation. Enron and the other companies needed somebody more friendly to business in the governor's office.

The role of the energy companies in the subsequent recall effort is still murky. But when Arnold took office in October 2003, the members of the energy cartel were among many entities that undoubtedly assumed he would do their bidding, as another actor turned neophyte politician—Ronald Reagan—had done for the forces of free enterprise four decades earlier. They were to be sorely disappointed. To the chagrin of many, Arnold Schwarzenegger was no Ronald Reagan.

Republicans were overjoyed at the cataclysmic turn of events. Could Schwarzenegger's landslide portend an end to the Democratic domination of the nation's largest state? If the Democrats lost California, with its fifty-five electoral votes, it would virtually guarantee Republicans in the White House for generations. Was Arnold the party's new savior? George W. Bush seemed to think so, arriving in California nine days after the recall election to bask in the glow of Arnold's victory. "I understand there have been a couple of changes in California since I was here last time," Bush purred. During a fifteen-minute ride from Riverside to San Bernardino, where Arnold was to introduce the president before a talk on terrorism, the governor-elect used the opportunity to press for more federal funding, having been briefed on Washington's indifference to the state during the recent energy crisis. But the president was noncommittal. He hadn't traveled all the way to California to talk substantively. It was merely a "courtesy call," his people said. A statehouse aide close to Arnold during his first term later told me that Arnold wasn't at all impressed with the president.

"He practically revered the father, George Bush Sr., but he kept saying that he couldn't believe he had produced a son like this. The governor was a shrewd judge of character and he just couldn't fathom how the American people had elected a guy like this as their president. I think he eventually convinced himself that he could find common ground on terrorism. He liked the way Bush had handled 9/11 and he decided that's where he could speak well of him without sounding like a hypocrite." Publicly, however, Arnold told the media that "the White House will be helping us."

As he prepared for his transition, he needed to choose a chief of staff who could guide him through the tangled web of California politics, aiding him with navigating in an overwhelmingly Democratic state legislature. Wilson's loyalists who had helped get him elected wanted one of their own. He owed them for their role in vaulting him into Sacramento. They still assumed that Schwarzenegger's administration would merely be a continuation of Pete Wilson's—so rudely interrupted by Gray Davis for five years. Arnold would be a proxy for Wilson, who was still a major force behind the scenes, and for Wilson's conservative, pro-business policies, meant to reward wealthy friends and allies.

Maria had other ideas. She suggested her brother, Tim Shriver, for chief of staff. Arnold's brother-in-law had taken the mantle from Eunice as head of the Special Olympics years before and had deftly managed it into a powerful international force. Arnold would later admit that he considered Tim for the position because Tim "would cover my back." For her part, Maria was unapologetic about the role she played in attempting to shape Arnold's agenda. "There would be something wrong if I didn't weigh in with my husband, wouldn't there?" she told *Vanity Fair.* "We are a team." But the Republicans managing the transition effort were nearly apoplectic at such an idea. They knew the Shrivers were fiercely partisan Democrats who would ensure that Wilson's people would be shut off from access to the governor's office. Maria proceeded to try a different tactic. What about co-chiefs of staff, one Democrat and one Republican? Her choice for the Democratic position was the former speaker of the state assembly, Bob Hertzberg, an old family friend and a close friend of *Terminator*'s producer, Gale Ann Hurd.

For Hertzberg, who had publicly urged Arnold to adopt a bipartisan approach to governing, the idea fitted well with his idea of getting things done in Sacramento. The Republican post was then offered to Pete Wilson's former deputy chief of staff, Pat Clarey, who had been suggested by Congressman David Dreier, head of Arnold's transition team. Clarey wasn't at all keen on the idea, and neither were the other Republicans involved in the transition, nervous that Arnold was already distancing himself from the GOP. That's when Dreier and Bob White put their foot down. With Maria kept out of the discussion, they told Arnold to appoint Clarey and stop pussyfooting around with the Democrats. He reluctantly agreed, and the idea of bipartisan cooperation was quickly scrapped along with Hertzberg.

The next day, he announced the appointment of Clarey as his chief of staff. Together, they would reform Sacramento and clean the mess left behind by the Democrats. "Action, action, action, action," he vowed. "That's what people voted me into this office for. They wanted a governor that is filled with action—that performs and represents the people."

When the governor's new team was announced, Democrats were all but shut out. Maria quietly accepted defeat in her efforts to steer her husband toward a bipartisan approach.

"He all but ignored the people, not just Maria, but others who were telling him to surround himself with Democrats and Republicans if they wanted to get things done," a former aide told me. "He was very cocky; he thought he could handle the Democrats. He got a rude awakening in a hurry."

In short order, Arnold announced that he would tackle the state's growing economic crisis by calling a special session of the state legislature and getting a budget deal done. As a symbol of his commitment to cut spending and eliminate the deficit, he would forgo the governor's annual $175,000 salary. He could afford to do this. But nobody was sure the state could afford the measures he soon proposed to tackle the crisis.

With guns blazing and declaring that "failure is not an option," the new governor demanded the legislature approve a plan to refinance past debt and place a cap on government spending. Democrats balked, however, fearing that his proposed cap could lead to billions of dollars in cuts to health and social programs. In a nod to conservative Republicans who had helped elect him, he also promised to repeal a new law granting driver's licenses to illegal immigrants; this law had been introduced by Gray Davis and was widely unpopular in some circles.

"That driver's license thing was an embarrassment. Governor Schwarzenegger was basically pandering to racists," the aide told me. "The California economy is dependent on undocumented workers. Anybody who understands California understands that. The Governor definitely understood it. But every once in a while some politician will come up with a scheme to take away rights from illegal immigrants to appeal to the knuckle-dragging rednecks. I'm a Republican and even I was embarrassed by that."

But the budget, not immigration, was at the core of the battle. When the two sides met to iron out their differences, partisanism quickly took hold. It was soon apparent, to everybody but Arnold, that the Democratic leader of the Senate, John Burton, was not going to cave in to his bluster. A midnight deadline for an agreement came and went, and the new governor had suffered his first defeat.

The influential *Sacramento Bee* blamed both sides for the impasse, but made it clear that Arnold's style would have to change if he was going to get anything accomplished with a Democratic-controlled legislature.

"Arnold Schwarzenegger, with characteristic self-confidence bordering on swagger, declared that 'failure is no option, it just doesn't exist' in his quest for a solution to California's very severe budget crisis—but his first foray into the Capitol's fiscal swamp has gone poorly, and he must shoulder at least some of the responsibility," wrote the *Bee.*

He appeared to take the criticism to heart. Chastened by the defeat, he spent the next week hammering out a compromise with Democratic leaders: a $15 billion bond issue would be put to the voters as a temporary budget fix. He had already established a cigar tent to skirt the state's strict antismoking laws, and it is there that he liked to meet with Democratic leaders and smooth out their differences over cigars while attempting to charm his opponents onside. The bond issue was a quick fix but was hardly a solution to the state's long-term woes. By the following July, Democrats and Republicans were once again locked in a fierce battle, with Democrats vowing to stand in the way of a new $103 billion budget Arnold had put forward, which contained provisions unacceptable to most of them, and also to some Republicans. This time, instead of brokering a compromise, he decided to go over the head of the unpopular legislature directly to the people. Speaking at a rally in a shopping center, he fired the first salvo at his Democratic opponents, invoking the popular sketch "Pumping Up with Hans and Franz" on *Saturday Night Live*—a sketch that, ironically, was inspired by Arnold.

"If they don't have the guts to come up here in front of you and say, 'I don't want to represent you, I want to represent those special interests, the unions, the trial lawyers, and I want them to make millions of dollars'—if they don't have the guts, I call them girlie men," he shouted, calling on voters to "terminate them at the polls" if they didn't pass his budget.

Such sound bites were undeniably popular—Arnold's approval rating soared. But this was no way to get things done, and the Democrats dug in their heels even further, determined not to be bullied into accepting devastating cuts that would tear apart the social safety net.

At the Republican national convention the following month, Arnold had been offered a prime-time speaking spot so that Americans could meet the party's newest star. But he was at first reluctant to accept. He had been a longtime friend of the Democratic nominee, John Kerry, who had helped him raise money to produce *Pumping Iron* three decades earlier, and he had even briefly flirted with the idea of endorsing his friend.

Maria advised him not to accept the convention slot—and not just because she was a loyal Democrat. She knew he despised the GOP nominee, George W. Bush, who represented everything about Republicans that Arnold believed was destroying the party—a rigid, moralistic, conservative ideology beholden to the Christian right. Still, the opportunity to showcase himself on national television before tens of millions of people was simply too tempting to pass up. It was here that he told the story of how he had first become a Republican and invoked his always inspirational tale about the poor immigrant boy who had come to the United States and made good. Americans loved it. For most, it was their first opportunity to meet Arnold the politician, instead of Arnold the cartoonish tough guy.

Following his masterful performance, his approval ratings rose to new heights, and Californians were clearly proud of their governor's national stature. Arnold Schwarzenegger was seemingly on top of the world. The Democrats wouldn't dare to mess with him now, he appeared to believe.

The swagger was evident as he huddled with his Republican advisers, virtually shutting Maria out of the process and leaving her to tackle various low-level initiatives such as a Women's History Museum, the

Military Family Initiative, and the Governor's Office of Protocol.

When he emerged, they had come up with a bold plan to circumvent the Democratic legislature by again going over its head to ask the voters to usher in new referenda. In early January 2005, Arnold used his annual state of the state address to propose a series of radical reforms challenging the legislature to tackle a number of sacred cows. It was a marked turn to the right for a politician who called himself a moderate and who had vowed to govern in a bipartisan style. One measure he proposed was a scheme to privatize the pensions of public employees; another was to peg teachers' salaries to performance and restrict tenure; a third, separate plan was to redistrict the state's congressional districts to make them less secure for incumbents, paving the way for Republicans to make future gains in the legislature.

If Democrats didn't go along with his reforms, he warned, he would go over their heads to the people and call a special election.

The proposals attracted immediate scorn from a wide variety of interest groups, including teachers' unions, firefighters, and nurses. And Democrats vowed to oppose the reforms with all their might, as Arnold knew they would. The idea behind the reforms was clearly to reshape the state and neuter his opponents in one fell swoop. But if he thought the people would go along with his agenda, he had clearly miscalculated.

His once soaring approval ratings began to plunge as more and more Californians cottoned to the antidemocratic intent behind the reforms.

But the protests didn't seem to bother Arnold in the least as he marched confidently ahead toward the special election he was sure he could win, mustering the kind of rhetoric that he employed in his old action films and pronouncing the election "judgment day."

On November 8, 2005, Californians delivered their verdict—a resounding rejection of each one of Arnold's proposed reforms. It was probably the greatest defeat he had ever suffered, personally or politically. The *Los Angeles Times* announced that the governor had finally met the limits of his celebrity.

In the weeks that followed, his approval ratings plummeted to new lows. With an election looming in 2006, only 35 percent of Californians told pollsters they would vote to reelect their governor. His political career appeared to be over. The Terminator had finally met his match.

However, the conservative *American Spectator* offered the governor some unsolicited advice about how

he could still salvage his political career and win reelection, advising him not to abandon the right wing of
his party. The Democrats, warned the magazine, were
not his real friends.

"They may be next to him in the cigar tent but
not in the back rooms where the real deals happen.
Regardless of the disagreements Republicans have had
with him, Arnold remains the most reform-oriented
candidate on the ballot.

"And, while he failed to get support for his reforms,
he needs to show that he will continue to work for a
conservative agenda. Finally, the governor needs to
mobilize his Republican base. He must regain the trust
of his party and prove that he is the strong leader they
elected."

Maria Shriver, however, had other ideas.

28.

Political Hummer

Maria was not happy. She had been shuffled off to the sidelines long enough. She had gone along with the whole bit: lighting the Christmas tree, being the gracious hostess. That's what a first lady is supposed to do, they told her. "I feel that the whole job of being the first lady is so stagnant. . . . You should cut a ribbon and then go sit in the corner? It is archaic in its concept," she complained to a reporter in early 2005. To make matters worse, since arriving in Sacramento, the couple had been living out of an unglamorous hotel suite at the Hyatt, a far cry from her ritzy Brentwood mansion, and from the American ambassador's residence, overlooking the Eiffel Tower, where she had spent her youth. And as she watched her husband eviscerated in the media and his approval ratings plunge for listening to the Republicans who had forced him to the right, Maria was no longer content to sit around and play the smiling wife.

It was bad enough that she had been forced to leave the job she loved at NBC shortly after her husband was elected governor. She had been determined to stay on and had even contributed two reports to *Dateline NBC* after the 2003 recall election. But in early 2004, Maria was abruptly informed that she had been "relieved of her duties at NBC News," owing to a potential conflict of interest between her role as first lady of California and her status as a journalist. In the summer of 2009, shortly after I appeared on the *Today* show, a long-time NBC staffer revealed what she had heard about Shriver's severance from the network.

"She was not well liked in the last few years," the staffer told me. "She had a very strong sense of entitlement. People respected her talent; they just couldn't take her attitude. I never worked closely with her, but I heard the stories and I witnessed her in action a few times. She thought she was the queen bee. When one of my colleagues heard she wasn't coming back, he said, 'Ding dong, the witch is dead.' I think if she was nicer, they would have found a way to keep her on. I mean, how often was she going to cover stories about California politics. The whole thing didn't ring true."

Maria had become a confidante of another first lady of California, Nancy Reagan, and she had recently asked Nancy what she should do. "Do whatever you want," Reagan reportedly told her, "because whatever you do, they'll criticize you for it." Maria knew exactly what she wanted to do. Now she had to get her husband to go along with it.

Arnold Schwarzenegger never liked to lose, and the special election had been his most public trouncing ever. He also wasn't comfortable with the Republicans he had been forced to cozy up to to get his feet into Sacramento. He believed they had a "schnitzel up their ass," as he put it to one aide after he was taken to task for supporting a Democratic bill. In contrast, he often found himself enjoying the company of his political opponents as they smoked cigars and negotiated agreements together under the canvas tent he had set up in a private courtyard of the state capitol. So far, political life had been like a straitjacket. He wasn't having any fun. He wasn't being himself. He had let himself be talked into a radical shift to the right, which he never really agreed with and which had backfired in a very public manner.

Maria couldn't stand the Republican strategists, who she believed had hijacked her husband's agenda and

turned him into somebody she didn't recognize anymore. She knew from the beginning that the special
election was political folly, but she had been shut out
of the loop repeatedly. Now it was time to exorcise the
men who she believed were bringing her husband down
in an idiotic power game they couldn't possibly win.

"One hundred percent of her agenda is Arnold," her
older brother, Bobby Shriver, once said about Maria.
"You cross Arnold, and Maria will cut your head off.
She's a tough customer. The people who have taken
Maria on and won—well, it's a very very short list."

Now, with the next election less than twelve months
away and his reelection prospects dim, Arnold knew
his wife was right. It was time for a change.

After being elected governor, he had once been
described as "a Trojan horse with Kennedy string
pullers." If he was going to be accused of that anyway,
he might as well follow his instincts.

The announcement arrived like a ton of bricks in
the capitol, with stunned Republicans doing a double take upon hearing the news. On November 30,
2005, only three weeks after the debacle of the special election, Arnold appointed a longtime Democratic
Party activist, Susan Kennedy, as his chief of staff.
"It's like George W. Bush appointing Hillary Clinton

to be in charge of his administration," lamented one conservative.

Those Republicans unfamiliar with the forty-five-year-old Kennedy incorrectly assumed that she must be a member of Maria's family. But they were in for an even ruder shock when they discovered her true pedigree. Kennedy was a veteran Democratic political operative. She had previously served as cabinet secretary and later deputy chief of staff to Gray Davis during his term as governor and was respected as a workhorse who knew her way around the capitol. She had also served as executive director of the California Democratic Party and executive director of the California Abortion Rights Action League. The clincher was her domestic situation. She was a longtime lesbian activist who had married her partner, Vicki Marti, in Hawaii in 1999.

"I think the Kennedy thing was just the last straw," an exasperated Mike Spence, president of the California Republican Assembly, complained to the *Los Angeles Times.* "There's not even one Republican in the state to be qualified as chief of staff?" Acccording to Spence, Kennedy "embodies everything I have spent my life opposing. . . . There is a list of things now where it appears we would have been better off if Gray Davis were governor." Indeed, some Republicans could even be heard to grumble about recalling Arnold.

Kennedy's appointment did not, in fact, come out of the blue. In preparation for a more prominent political role in her husband's administration, Maria had recently hired her own chief of staff, Daniel Zingale, who had also been a secretary in Gray Davis's cabinet and was, like Kennedy, openly gay. Zingale was already advising Maria how to put her plan into action.

In announcing the appointment of his new chief of staff, Arnold declared the birth of a new era he called "post-partisanship." He now had two Kennedys to help him achieve this goal: Susan and his wife, Maria, who going forward would play a huge role in molding his political agenda without Republican gatekeepers closing the door.

Before long, Democrats had filled a number of key posts and were playing a vital role in guiding state policy. Many of the old Republicans were still around, but their role was greatly diminished.

"The Republicans would watch these Democrats with a free run of the governor's office and it's like they knew they were licked. They would call the Democrats surrounding Arnold 'the posse,' " one statehouse staffer told me.

One of the first orders of business was mending fences with Democratic leaders in the legislature. Maria counseled Arnold to make friends, telling him,

"It shouldn't be too hard to get into bed with the Democrats. You sleep with me every night"—a joke he would later recycle at rallies.

Indeed, it was easier for Arnold to adopt a conciliatory approach than it would have been for a truly partisan Republican, but there was no love lost between him and the Democratic speaker of the state assembly, Fabian Núñez, who in late 2003 had declared "political war" on the new governor after Arnold promised to "blow up" the state bureaucracy and go over the heads of the legislature to do it. In the two years since then, it was clear Núñez had won the war. It was up to Arnold to offer an olive branch. He served up the next best thing, the $25 cigars that he kept in one of his many humidors (I'm told that these cigars frequently violated the long-standing U.S. embargo against Cuban imports).

In the early 1970s, Núñez's parents—a gardener and a maid—had moved the family from a rough section of Tijuana, Mexico, to San Diego in order to provide a better life for their children. Fabian had taken full advantage of the opportunity, walking miles every day, past drug dealers and junkyards, to a decent school—while many of his friends ended up dead or in prison. Somehow, he would claim, he "slipped through the cracks," and he was now the most powerful Mexican-

POLITICAL HUMMER • 539

American in a state where Latinos were, for the first time, starting to be taken seriously as a political force.

Known for his considerable charm and the negotiating skills he had cultivated working as a union organizer, Núñez was at first unimpressed with the new governor, as he saw Arnold pandering to the anti-immigrant sentiments that had caused his people to be victimized for generations and supporting the plan to keep undocumented immigrants from applying for driver's licenses. After Arnold's notorious comment about "girlie men," Núñez came back with a riposte that received considerably less attention: "I don't know that he wears lifts—I know that's the rumor. I don't even know that he wears makeup—I know that's the rumor." During the special election, the speaker publicly accused Arnold of seeking "the power to be king." Núñez vowed to stop him in his tracks, and succeeded. But now he recognized a new opportunity. Arnold, humbled, finally seemed willing to get things done while giving Núñez and his Democratic majority the respect due them.

The Democrats, including many of the speaker's principal advisers, wanted to use Arnold's flagging popularity to take back the governorship in November, when he would be up for reelection. If they continued to block his agenda, a Democrat would be likely to sweep back into office. But Núñez sensed an opportunity to get things done, and besides, he feared a backlash from voters if he wasted a year on pointless political gamesmanship. The new Arnold, and his talk of post-partisanship, was somebody Núñez could work with.

The results were astonishing, especially considering the bridges that had been burned in the previous year. Over Cohibas, the two men developed an ambitious agenda. "I am a results-oriented person," Arnold declared. "So is the speaker." Some of the items were pet projects of Núñez. Some belonged to the governor—or, more accurately, to the governor's wife.

Maria Shriver had long since lost interest in her women's history museum and the other low-level initiatives she had pretended to passionately embrace in her role as first lady. With the appointment of Susan Kennedy as chief of staff in November 2005, she finally heard her destiny calling.

For Maria's family, unlike most of their friends and neighbors—East Coast, Ivy League, American aristocrats—it wasn't blue blood that ran through the veins. It was power. But unlike some who seek power for its own sake—and many believe Arnold Schwarzenegger fits into that category—they appeared to regard power as a sacred trust, to be used in pursuit of the common good. That's what distinguishes us

from Republicans, Maria was often told when she was
growing up. And yet, despite her family's status as an
illustrious political dynasty, their own opportunities for
real power had been rare and fleeting. Her grandmother's father, "Honey Fitz" Fitzgerald, started the tradition when he served as a reform mayor of Boston at the
beginning of the twentieth century, championing the
cause of poor immigrants. He was allied, in the Boston
political scene, with another reformer, P. J. Kennedy.
When P. J.'s son Joseph married Fitzgerald's daughter,
Rose, the fabled political dynasty began. But although
the offspring of this dynasty would spend much of the
next century in a quest for power there was surprisingly little to show for their efforts.

Joseph Kennedy thought big. He believed the surefire route to power was the White House, and he vowed
to use his vast fortune, accumulated as a bootlegger
during Prohibition, to make his golden child—his
firstborn son, Joseph Jr.—president. When Joseph was
killed in action during World War II, the mantle was
passed to his next eldest son, John Fitzgerald Kennedy.
When JFK achieved his father's ambition in 1960, it
appeared that the Kennedy destiny had been fulfilled.
But before the young president could achieve his bold
agenda for the nation, an assassin's bullet ended the
dream and, it appeared, the family's quest to shape

history. Five years later, the next chosen one, Bobby, took up his slain brother's torch, promising an even bolder and farther-reaching transformation of the American dream, only to have it seized from his grasp in the kitchen of L.A.'s Ambassador Hotel four months before he would almost certainly have assumed his brother's position in the Oval Office.

It was, ironically, the youngest brother, Teddy—of whom nothing had been expected—who ended up partially realizing his family's political potential. Having taken over his brother John's vacated seat in the Senate in 1962, Ted had become a remarkably effective power broker on Capitol Hill, achieving a mountain of progressive legislation. If not for the curse of the Kennedys and an ill-fated car ride over a bridge at Chappaquiddick on the night of the Apollo moon landing, he would probably have had a chance to achieve genuine power and take up where his brother Jack left off.

Like her mother's family, Maria's father had been brought up to believe power should be used to serve the people. And yet Sargent Shriver never really had that opportunity; he was fated instead to serve as an acolyte of the Kennedys while shelving his own political ambitions for most of his career. And by 2005, even Uncle Ted's once vaunted ability to influence events had been virtually neutered, with a Republican majority in Congress and George W. Bush in the White House.

But now there was a family member or at least an in-law in charge of the world's fifth-largest economy, with enormous power to effect change. During the recall effort, neither the Kennedys nor the Shrivers publicly endorsed Arnold's effort. Officially, they had to remain loyal to their party and make clucking noises of disapproval about the effort to unseat a Democratic governor.

Asked before the election whether he supported Gray Davis or his niece's husband, Ted Kennedy hardly offered a ringing endorsement. "I like and respect Arnold," he told a reporter. "I've been impressed with his efforts to promote after-school education in California, and his willingness to come to Congress and the administration to fight for that program. But, I'm a Democrat, and I don't support the recall effort." Behind the scenes, however, the family members could barely conceal their glee at the prospect of Arnold in office with Maria exercising the same kind of influence she had exerted throughout his career and their marriage, which the couple always referred to as a "partnership."

Immediately after Arnold's victory, Ted Kennedy weighed in again, saying that the family had its own "big tent" and that he was pleased by Arnold's victory.

"I look forward very much to working with him on the many issues where we agree, especially in improving the quality of education and expanding opportunities for all our people," the senator said. "What better proof could there be that America really is a nation of immigrants?"

Maria's cousin Christopher Kennedy Lawford later told me that his clan had great respect for Arnold almost from the beginning, despite his political affiliations. "We'd all make jokes about him being a Republican, but he was never really that kind of Republican, if you know what I mean." Lawford believes Arnold's affiliation with the Kennedy and Shriver families had had an enormous influence on his thinking. "I think he learned about what was truly involved with public service and having the vision and compassion to be a public servant from his time spent with Eunice and Sergeant Shriver and the others," he told me.

A lesser-known Kennedy, Bobby Jr., was even more effusive about his in-law's potential for great accomplishments, telling reporters that Arnold had made him an important political promise. At the time, however, few paid attention.

Now, a little more than two years later, Schwarzenegger and the powerful Democratic speaker were about to embark on an ambitious agenda that all the members of Maria's family on both sides would approve of. And well they should, because many of them had a hand in shaping, even writing, it.

"After Susan Kennedy arrived on the scene, neither Maria nor the governor even bothered to hide her influence anymore," one member of the communications staff told me. "There were so many Shrivers and Kennedys running around here that it looked like a family reunion."

Indeed, Arnold's careful efforts to distance himself from his wife and her family, for fear of alienating suspicious Republicans, had all but evaporated by the beginning of 2006. Her brother Bobby Shriver had just won a seat on the Santa Monica city council, making housing and homelessness his priorities. Now he had a sympathetic ear in the governor's office, where such issues can be addressed—though not usually by a Republican administration.

Meanwhile, before long the speaker and the newly progressive governor had agreed to deals on a wide variety of Democratic-sounding initiatives, including Arnold's surprising support for gradually raising the state minimum wage from $6.75 an hour to $8, the highest rate in the country, despite his two previous vetoes of the measure during his first years in office.

The announcement drew a withering attack from one of his biggest supporters, the California Chamber of Commerce, which argued that it would hurt business, but Arnold disregarded the criticism, saying that the increase was "the right thing to do."

Next up was a bill to provide health care to all children throughout the state. It soon ran into a number of obstacles—thanks in large part to the drug companies, which had provided hundreds of thousands of dollars to Arnold's election campaign and retained considerable influence, despite his vow not to cater to "special interests." Health care reform would be an albatross throughout his governorship, yet in September Arnold forged an impressive deal with the Democrats to provide discount drugs to 6 million low-income Californians. It was a bill he himself had blocked for nearly three years and another sign of the post-partisan era—along with many smaller measures he signed into law with the votes of the Democratic majority.

Giving another sign that he was moving to the center, or even the left, he finally apologized for his earlier anti-immigrant stance. During the recall campaign, he told reporters that in 1994 he had voted for Proposition 187—the measure that prevented undocumented immigrants from obtaining public services, including education and health care. Now, in an interview with a Spanish-language newspaper, he apologized for that vote: "I think, looking back, it was the wrong decision."

Nothing symbolized Schwarzenegger's new attitude, however, more than the legislation that would be likely to define his legacy. In his first election campaign, Arnold had promised an environmental agenda, vowing to protect California's "air, water and landscape." In a state that valued its natural beauty, such commitments were not particularly unusual, even for a Republican. Ronald Reagan had also introduced some environmental initiatives, though he is better known for saying, "A tree is a tree. How many more do you have to look at?" when he opposed the expansion of Redwoood National Park.

Few paid attention to Arnold's promises, and those who did couldn't help being skeptical. In 1992, he had become the first civilian to purchase a Hummer—a giant military vehicle—after persuading the U.S. Army's supplier, General Motors, to sell him one for his personal use. Not only was the vehicle known as a gas guzzler, but Hummers emit three times more carbon dioxide than regular cars. It was hard to take a candidate seriously when he talked about the environment, knowing he drove such a polluter in one of the most polluted cities in the United States, which was known for smog so thick you could cut it with a knife. After his election, despite his strong environmental commitment to create a "zero emissions state," he hadn't followed through on the tough green legislation he had promised—except for a largely symbolic measure, when he announced that his Hummer would be converted to run on hydrogen.

He had made one important concession, though it had not yet borne fruit. Shortly before the recall election, when he was coming up with his platform, Arnold flew to Hyannis to ask for advice about his environmental agenda from Maria's cousin Robert Kennedy Jr., one of the most important and influential environmentalists in the country. A specialist in environmental law, Kennedy had founded an umbrella organization, Waterkeeper, to protect and clean up America's rivers. When Arnold asked for advice on protecting California's environment, RFK's eldest son was all too glad to oblige. He also had a recommendation for the position of secretary of the California Environmental Protection Agency: a well-known Democratic environmentalist, Terry Tamminen, founder of the group Santa Monica Baykeeper. The Republicans heading the transition team wanted Pete Wilson's former secretary of agriculture for the post, but they bowed to Arnold on the appointment of Tamminen, one of the few Democrats who received an important position in the new administration. Since 2003 Tamminen's hands had been tied, but they were about to be loosened.

In the summer of 2006, Arnold and the speaker suddenly announced that they had agreed to introduce a new bill, the Global Warming Solutions Act, to cut greenhouse pollutants and other harmful emissions 25 percent, to 1990 levels, by 2020. The legislation also included some of the world's strictest vehicle emission standards, which angered Detroit. It was perhaps the farthest-reaching and most progressive environmental legislation in U.S. history, and environmentalists couldn't believe it had come from a Republican. Arnold's own party, needless to say, was firmly opposed to the legislation; Republicans believed it was a betrayal of the people who had gotten him into office. If they had known who was really responsible, it would have confirmed their worst suspicions.

Robert Kennedy Jr. would later admit his direct role in crafting the legislation, "which Arnold read and then adopted." He also believed it was even stronger than the policy of Al Gore, who had emerged as one of the world's most respected advocates against global warming.

Environmentalists, who had once mocked Arnold—as the driver of a Hummer, he could not have much commitment to greenness—now appeared to agree: they gushed with praise for the new policy. "California is the model," said Daniel Esty, director of the Yale Center for Environmental Law and Policy.

But California's businesses were not as enthusiastic, complaining that it would cost them millions to comply with the new act. The governor was accused by his own supporters of being antibusiness. Gone was the politician who once preached the virtues of his antiregulation hero, Milton Friedman. In September, Arnold followed through on his commitment to address global warming by authorizing his attorney general to sue six carmakers—General Motors, Toyota, Ford, Honda, Chrysler, and Nissan—regarding their vehicles' greenhouse gas emissions, which, he charged, accounted for 30 percent of all carbon dioxide emissions in the state. The state sought hundreds of millions of dollars for damages to the "health, economy, and environment" of Californians. At the same time, he announced he was giving up his own fleet of Hummers to underscore his commitment.

California's strong stand soon prompted twelve other states to adopt their own vehicle emission standards, although the White House had already called

California's standards illegal. The Environmental Protection Agency (EPA), which, under George W. Bush, had become a tool of polluters and corporate interests, argued that California would need a waiver in order to implement standards tougher than those of the federal government. No such waiver was forthcoming, however, and Arnold would have to wait until there was a Democrat in the White House before he could finally put his landmark legislation into effect. Indeed, President Obama granted the EPA waiver shortly after taking office, and California's standards have now been adopted by thirteen states as well as governments all over the world, making Arnold Schwarzenegger an unlikely environmental hero.

As Arnold worked on these and other measures, sharing credit with Speaker Fabian Núñez, the unprecedented bipartisan cooperation between the two men—once sworn political enemies—was hailed by the media as a model.

Cynics charged that Arnold moved to the center simply in order to win reelection. Indeed, as he introduced and passed one progressive measure after another, his approval ratings soared, much to the chagrin of Democrats, who charged that Núñez had been *too* cooperative, denying them a chance to retake the governor's office in November. Their fears were justified.

Written off as dead only a year earlier, Arnold won re-election by a landslide in 2006, capping a remarkable political comeback.

Maria Shriver should have been on top of the world. Thanks to her bold intervention after the 2005 special election, her husband's career had been salvaged. More important, her efforts—and her family's direct influence—had moved Arnold significantly to the left and had prompted historical legislation that could help change the world. And yet something was wrong.

The whispers had started years before. When Maria Shriver first became a television personality in the 1980s, she was described by one magazine as "Rubenesque." This never seemed to bother her. She had her first child in 1989, followed by three more over the next eight years. Under normal circumstances, women gain weight after having children, but over the years she inexplicably got thinner. For television and movie personalities, weight is often an ongoing concern. The camera does, after all, add pounds. But after she retired from television and followed her husband into politics, her dramatic weight loss continued.

"Maria's absolutely skeletal," a photographer for the *Los Angeles Times* told me in 2009. "She keeps losing more and more weight every time I see her. It's a little disconcerting."

As I began my research in Los Angeles and Sacramento, talking to people who know her and who have followed her career, this was a constant refrain. Each person had the same explanation, or rather a variation on the same theme. Some people have told me they believe the first lady suffers from anorexia—the eating disorder that killed Karen Carpenter and that plagues hundreds of thousands of American women. Others believe it's bulimia—the disorder suffered by Princess Diana, characterized by binge eating, followed by deliberate vomiting to avoid gaining weight. "There's something terribly wrong with her," said one capitol staffer. "There's a lot of gossip about it, but no facts."

One woman who has known her since 1999 told me that Maria is a fan of fad diets. "She tries every diet out there. She's tried them all. She's obsessive about her weight. These days it's the Beverly Hills Diet; tomorrow it will probably be some concoction involving raisins and kale."

A former colleague of Maria's at NBC News had her own story related to anorexia. "I remember years ago, when she was still here, there was a tabloid—I think it was the *Enquirer*—that ran a story claiming Maria had anorexia. Instead of being upset, she said how she was thrilled, how flattered she was that they thought she was so thin. She said she was going to hang up the clipping and send them a thank-you note or something. It was creepy. She was already thin as a rail. I don't know why she would have reacted like that."

People I've talked to who know her tell me roughly the same thing. The wife of a reporter in Sacramento told me, "Arnold likes his women thin." She said she once saw him "slap Maria's butt and say something to the effect of how she's getting a little chunky. I couldn't believe it because there's not much there, to be frank. She's like a signpost."

Could it really be Arnold's aesthetic preferences that have caused Maria to shrink so rapidly? Surely such a strong-willed woman wouldn't risk her health just to please her husband. And yet there are a number of incidents on the record over the years suggesting that Arnold may have inherited Gustav's old-fashioned Austrian views about women.

In his 1988 interview with *Playboy*, for example, Arnold admits that he won't allow Maria to wear pants in public. "I hate pants," he reveals. "This is something I have inherited from my father. He despised pants, and my mother was never allowed to wear them at home. We're talking about a different time period now, when the man was much more the ruler of the house. But I still feel that way, and neither my mother nor Maria is allowed to go out with me in pants. . . . In general, I still like the old-fashioned way. A dress represents the opposite sex. It's more feminine and it's sexier. There are times when I can understand that a woman would want to wear pants. A stewardess doesn't want anyone looking up her dress. Maria would never wear pants, believe me."

An even more revealing episode came from the mouth of Maria herself in 1996, when she was conducting an interview for *Dateline NBC* with Karen Pomer, a woman who had been kidnapped and raped at gunpoint. Pomer later claimed that after the cameras were turned off, Maria turned to her and said, "Karen, I can't believe your boyfriend stayed with you. My husband wouldn't go near me again. He would leave me, because I would be damaged goods."

When Pomer first revealed the story years later, a spokesman for Schwarzenegger denied it, saying that the crew had heard no such statement. But a woman who had accompanied Pomer to the interview told the *New York Daily News* that she was present. "Everyone sort of gasped," said the eyewitness, "because that was sort of an odd thing to say about your husband, and plus we all knew who her husband was."

Arnold's macho image was reinforced a few years later when he bizarrely told *TV Guide* that kids watch too much TV because of "women's equal rights."

Many observers in California insist it was the groping scandal uncovered by the *Los Angeles Times* that pushed Maria over the edge and caused her rapid weight loss and her skeletal appearance of recent years. The toll the 2003 recall campaign took on Maria was undeniable, especially after the first stories began to emerge of inappropriate conduct involving women. She later admitted that it was "very difficult," but never once maintained her belief in her husband's innocence.

"You think she didn't know what was going on," one of Maria's former colleagues told me. "Come on, she's a Kennedy. That's how they're raised."

Indeed, Maria's beloved grandmother Rose was famous for standing by stoically as she watched her husband publicly parade one mistress after another, once even traveling on a transatlantic cruise with him and his mistress at the time, the movie star Gloria Swanson.

The New York society columnist Doris Lilly, author of *How to Marry a Millionaire*, claimed that one of Joe's mistresses confided to her that "Rose didn't care how many women Joe kept, as long as she had her family." Rose's sons JFK, Bobby, and Ted were equally notorious while their wives smiled and played the adoring political hostess. And yet Maria was also a Shriver, and her father was thought to be loyal to Eunice throughout their strong fifty-year marriage, which Maria always claimed would be the model for her own.

For months, as I pursued the story, I assumed, like many who knew her, that an eating disorder was responsible for Maria's rapidly worsening appearance and weight loss, though such a condition is impossible to verify without access to medical records—which I requested to no avail from the office of the first lady.

However, while I was eating at one of Shriver's favorite restaurants last year, I heard another plausible explanation. I was anxious to get details of her eating habits in order to determine whether she does, in fact, have an eating disorder as many claim. But when, after work, I asked an employee whom I had befriended during a number of previous visits, I was told that her eating habits are quite normal. "She doesn't have anorexia," the employee told me matter-of-factly. "She has Addison's."

"How do you know?" I asked.

"You hear a lot of stuff working at a restaurant frequented by the high and mighty," the employee replied. "I think she'll talk about it after Arnold leaves office."

While I have come up with no evidence to prove that this employee's claim is anything other than rumor or sheer speculation, I knew that President Kennedy, Maria's uncle, was believed to suffer from Addison's disease, but I had no idea what it was or whether it was genetic. When I consulted the medical literature, I discovered that the disease is a relatively rare disorder of the adrenal glands, with a number of symptoms, one of which is indeed weight loss. Addison's can strike at any age and usually develops gradually over time. Interestingly, I discovered that Maria's mother, Eunice, also suffered from the disease, as did Eunice's brother JFK. Multiple cases of Addison's disease in the same family occur only 1 percent of the time.

The disease, once fatal, is now treatable with cortisone, though the severity of the symptoms varies from case to case. One of the common symptoms is severe lethargy, which could account for Maria's diminished public role during her husband's second term. Though many people expected her to resume her journalistic career once her husband leaves office in 2010—and indeed, she had always vowed to do so—she inexplicably announced that this was no longer her intention. Following the death of Anna Nicole Smith in 2007, Maria publicly vowed that she was so fed up with the media circus that she wouldn't be returning to her old job. "It was then that I knew that the TV news business had changed and so had I," she said at the time.

"I called NBC News and told them I'm not coming back." Many people I've spoken with considered this explanation disingenuous and few bought her explanation, but most were at a loss over why she would turn her back on the work she professed to love. Could her medical prognosis be the real reason? Only time will tell if it is Addison's disease that accounts for Maria's condition or if some other factor is at play.

By the time I started my on-the-ground research about Arnold Schwarzenegger, he was already well into his second term as governor. I spent considerable time in both Sacramento and Los Angeles—flying coast to coast a number of times for interviews with important players. For much of this period, I was simply a reporter or a filmmaker asking the kinds of questions necessary to fill in the blanks and gain insights into Arnold's unique and multifaceted personality. But at some point I realized that something was missing, something I couldn't figure out. I wondered: Why is Arnold Schwarzenegger a Republican?

Full disclosure: Like most people from Canada, where our political system is far different from the American model, and where things like socialized medicine, gay marriage, and a strong social safety net are sacred cows, I had always regarded Republican politics as vaguely Neanderthal and politicians such as George W. Bush as downright odious. But Arnold Schwarzenegger seemed different. Does the Republican Party, as it claims, really have a "big tent" policy, so that diverse views are welcome, even encouraged? I needed to find out in order to make sense of my subject. I had already interviewed a number of Republicans, but these were political operatives, not the members of the party's grassroots who had elected him.

For my previous book and film projects, I had gone undercover as a male model, an actor, and a paparazzo, and had infiltrated the bizarre and mysterious Church of Scientology. But now I decided to embark on my most frightening assignment of all. I would go undercover as a Republican.

The venue I chose for my first foray into the strange world of California Republican politics was a Tea Party rally, a gathering of disaffected conservatives and "patriots" in Yorba Linda, the birthplace of Richard Nixon, located about forty-five minutes southeast of Los Angeles. I had no idea what to wear to look like a Republican, but I chose the most appropriate attire I could muster—a Sarah Palin T-shirt featuring a smiling photo of Ronald Reagan giving Palin a thumbs-up. As it turned out, this was the perfect choice: three people complimented me on the shirt and asked where they could get one.

The crowd that greeted me at a local community center was smaller than I expected, maybe 750 people in all, and older than I expected. But it was exactly as white as I expected. I counted one Latino in the crowd and no blacks whatsoever. The people were, however, less extreme than I had anticipated. The event was billed as a "Tax Day party" because it was held on the day by which Americans are required to file their tax returns. And taxes seemed to be the theme, with speaker after speaker complaining about how Americans are taxed to death and how President Obama wants to take more of their hard-earned money from their pockets. But I wasn't there to hear about Obama. I was anxious to hear what these people, presumably all Republicans, thought of their governor. When I broached the subject with a number of them, I received an earful about how Schwarzenegger had "let us down." Two people referred to him as a "rhino," which at first I assumed was a California expression, like "dinosaur." But when a third person, a woman in her sixties who complained about Schwarzenegger's support for stem cell research, used the term, I had to ask, "What's a rhino?" As it turns out, this is an acronym: RINO.

"Republican in name only," she replied, seemingly surprised at my ignorance. "He's got that Maria Shriver telling him what to do up there." When I asked if she had voted for him, she told me she had not, even though she's been a Republican all her life. She had ended up voting for one of the other 134 candidates, "a Christian," the first time around and didn't vote at all in 2006.

"Isn't Arnold Schwarzenegger a Christian?" I asked. "Yeah," she scoffed, "he's a Christian like he's a Republican. Don't get me started."

These Tea Party patriots weren't quite the extremists I had expected when I decided to attend the rally, but they were hardly mainstream Republicans either. This was, after all, Orange County, home of the original "Reagan revolution" as well as the John Birch Society. It was time for me to become a card-carrying member of the Republican Party.

Two weeks later, I made my way to the California GOP headquarters in Burbank, not far from the NBC studios where Arnold had announced his candidacy seven years earlier. After being greeted by a woman on the first floor, I told her my name was Isaac Moses Jacobs, and that I was the son of a Holocaust survivor. She brought me upstairs and introduced me to a woman who sat at the front desk and was intrigued that I was the son of a survivor, telling me she was from a family of survivors from Poland—my father's country. This immediately established something of a bond between us, at least until she opened her mouth again. "Obama's administration is like Europe in the 1930s," she declared with a straight face. "It's the most frightening thing we've ever seen." I had noticed huge photos of Ronald Reagan all over the office and, changing the subject before I blew my cover, pointed to them. "This is where he started when he campaigned to be governor," she told me. "He was the greatest. He was a president who got things done, unlike what we have in office representing the country today."

Picking up on the theme and remembering why I had come, I told her I was upset with Obama and thought the country would soon end up in "a ditch" if we didn't take action. I told her I was breaking a long family tradition by joining the Republican Party but that I could no longer sit by and watch what was happening to the country.

"I used to be a Democrat too, back in the Clinton days," she said. "Today they're a scary bunch. They have no idea what they're doing. They have killed the role of small businesses. There's no place for them anymore. We're dominated now by Walmart and Target.

Small businesses have been run into the ground, with no chance of being resurrected."

She praised me for my courage in coming to join the party. "You made the best decision of your life. Every vote counts." She handed me a party registration form and asked me to fill it out. I was about to do so until I noticed a fraud warning prominently displayed in red. I told her I'd fill it out at home.

It was at that point that I finally broached the subject I had come to discuss, the governor of the state. I told her I had heard that Arnold might run for president in 2012. "Do you think he'd be a good candidate?" I asked.

"Are you kidding me?" she replied. "Arnold supports Obama; we'd never support him. He just came out today and supported Obama's health care plan, which last week was proved with documentation to be a terrible plan. Trust me, Schwarzenegger will never head this party. He's not well liked or respected here. It's not the path we're seeking now. I guarantee you that he does not have even a tiny chance."

As she was talking, I couldn't help noticing the portrait of Schwarzenegger that hung on the wall. I was astonished at how openly contemptuous a Republican Party employee (though she may have been a volunteer) spoke about the head of her party in front of a total stranger. It was a very revealing visit. I had gotten what I had come for.

As this somewhat traitorous party employee had noted, Schwarzenegger had that morning come out in support of Obamacare—all the more remarkable considering that the president's health care plan had become a lightning rod throughout the nation and especially at the grassroots level of the Republican Party. "I'm not a party servant; I'm a public servant," he told a group of health care workers in supporting the plan, which he had strongly criticized just a few months earlier.

The economic crisis of 2008 had not been kind to California or its economy, which—because of its dysfunctional tax system—does very well when times are good and abominably when times are bad. When the country suffered its worst recession since the Great Depression, this had a devastating effect on California, and the deficit exploded. This time, simple bipartisan cooperation would not solve the crisis—not in a state where tax increases must be approved by a two-thirds majority of legislators. Unable to reach a deal with Democrats to solve the crisis, Arnold once again proposed a series of bold moves to address the state's fiscal woes. In 2005, Arnold had called a special election to subvert democracy, but this time he genuinely believed it was the best chance, maybe the last chance, to rescue the state's economy and avert disaster. Among the measures he took to the people were a spending cap, a scheme to borrow against lottery revenues, and, surprisingly, a number of tax increases.

And, although his motives were different this time around, the results were much the same as in 2005: all but one relatively minor measure were defeated resoundingly by more than 60 percent of the electorate.

"Arnold's governorship was supposed to be an action movie. Now it's a disaster movie," the political scientist John Pitney declared the next day.

As Arnold headed into his last year as governor, a lame duck, his approval ratings dropped even lower than Gray Davis's, his second-term accomplishments were decidedly mixed, and the pundits were writing him off once again. But he has spent much of the year huddled with Democrats forging a compromise solution to the state's quagmire, and the economy is slowly beginning to fight its way back, though not without severe and unpopular austerity measures. It will be up to the next governor to attempt to find the seemingly impossible long-term solution that Arnold Schwarzenegger repeatedly tried but failed to pull from his political bag of tricks.

As the 2010 race takes shape, it is hardly a surprise that the GOP front-runner, the former CEO of eBay,

Meg Whitman, has been rapidly distancing herself from Schwarzenegger's legacy even though Arnold's old political mentor Pete Wilson is her campaign chair. Meanwhile, the Democratic favorite, the former governor Jerry Brown, occasionally talks about carrying on Arnold's environmental policies instead of running against his record as would be expected. It is an odd spectacle, and it illustrates how Arnold has turned California politics on its head during his seven years in office.

It is said that there are no second acts in American politics, but the Governator has already proved this adage wrong.

And as many of Arnold's friends and foes alike contemplate what retirement has in store for him when term limits force him out of office in November 2010, there just may be a third act.

29.

Planning the Next Act

In May 1977, just after the release of *Pumping Iron*, Arnold attended the Cannes Film Festival to promote the documentary that was about to make him a star. As he was walking along the beach one day, the Belgian publicist Yanou Collart spotted him and asked if she could photograph him for a Laura Ashley campaign she was coordinating. After he happily posed with four girls hanging on him, and the shoot wrapped up, Collart invited him to lunch. Midway through the meal, she asked him about his ambitions.

"I will be the top actor in America," he declared with typical confidence. "Well, you are going to have to erase your accent," Collart told him. Without missing a beat, Arnold responded, "I will. And one day I will be president of the United States." As unlikely as the prospect may have seemed, she believed him.

More than three decades later, he has achieved virtually every other goal that he set for himself after arriving in America in 1968—what he has always called "the plan." But there is still one thing holding him back from the last item on his list: Article 2, Section 1, Clause 5 of the United States Constitution.

When the founding fathers assembled in 1787 to propose a series of checks and balances to guard against what they called an "oppressive government," they inserted a clause that declared, "No person except a natural born citizen . . . shall be eligible to the office of president." The reasons behind the clause are murky. The only document historians have ever uncovered about discussion of such a passage is a letter of July 25, 1787, written by John Jay—former president of the Continental Congress—to George Washington, who was presiding over the Constitutional Convention at the time.

"Permit me to hint, whether it would not be wise & seasonable to provide a strong check to the admission of Foreigners into the administration of our national Government," Jay wrote to the future president, "and to declare expressly that the Command in chief of the American army shall not be given to, nor devolve on, any but a natural *born* citizen," he wrote.

Historians are divided about the reasoning behind the letter. One theory had it that Jay was suspicious about the loyalty of Baron von Steuben, a Prussian aristocrat who served as inspector general of the Continental Army and who had expressed political ambitions. Another theory has to do with a rumor that the convention was concocting a monarchy, to be ruled by a foreigner. Whatever the motivation, this obscure clause is preventing Arnold Schwarzenegger from fulfilling what he believes is his destiny.

In 1994, shortly after Arnold climbed the first rung of the political ladder—when excitement about his election was still frenzied and his approval ratings were hovering around 70 percent—a Republican senator from Utah, Orrin Hatch, proposed what he hoped would be the twenty-eighth amendment to the Constitution. Hatch was the powerful chairman of the Senate Judiciary Committee, where such amendments originate. His amendment read:

A person who is a citizen of the United States, who has been for 20 years a citizen of the United States, and who is otherwise eligible to the Office of President, is not ineligible to that Office by reason of not being a native born citizen of the United States.

It was not by coincidence that Hatch added the twenty-year requirement. He claimed, "I didn't bring it up with Arnold in mind. I just thought it was the right thing to do now"; but his denial seemed disingenuous because his amendment just happened to come almost exactly twenty years after Arnold Schwarzenegger became a naturalized citizen of the United States. According to Hatch's hometown newspaper, the *Deseret News*, Arnold was both a "pal" and a "fundraising helper" of the influential senator at the time.

Asked about the intentions of the founding fathers who imposed the original requirement of being a natural-born citizen, Hatch claimed that their reasons no longer applied. "I think they were quite concerned about, you know, some outsiders coming in and taking over just because they had the money or the power to do so. Well, now we're way beyond that," he said. "And, frankly, if you're a U.S. citizen—let's say you were born to an American family serving the State Department and you spent your first thirty-five years outside of the country—you could run for president even though you don't even understand the slightest bit about the country."

At first, when millions of Americans were enamored of the Republican Party's new star politician, there was considerable enthusiasm for the amendment. Editorials in a number of influential newspapers called the prohibition against foreign-born presidents "archaic" and "appropriate for another era."

"This issue needs a poster child, and Schwarzenegger is an excellent one," opined one newspaper, the *Tennessean*. "Hatch is right. This is the land of opportunity. There are no valid reasons to deny a long-time citizen—someone who worked hard to become an American—the right to serve in the nation's highest office. And while this newspaper traditionally is reluctant to support constitutional amendments, the elimination of the native born requirement can be achieved only through an amendment. Would Schwarzenegger be a good president, or even a good candidate? Who knows? His worthiness to serve in the Oval Office isn't the point. The point is that in America, he should have the chance."

Many people thought that in a nation of immigrants, the constitutional prohibition smacked of racism, and there appeared to be a groundswell of support that would give Arnold his opportunity. The title of a Web site set up to promote the amendment made no secret of its goal—"Amend for Arnold." It received 4 million hits in its first three days. But as Arnold's star fell during the debacle of the 2005 special election, so too did the amendment's chances. Hatch allowed it to die a slow death.

But if Orrin Hatch and others had given up on the idea of Arnold as president, there was at least one person who hadn't.

As Arnold Schwarzenegger's second and last term rolls toward its end in January 2011, speculation about his future plans has become a cottage industry. Will he return to making movies? Will he take over Weider's publications, as some people have theorized, or put his considerable business acumen to work running Weider's fitness empire when Joe, now in his nineties, dies? Will he simply fade into the sunset to spend his golden years with Maria?

"Don't sit around waiting for Arnold to star in *Terminator 4*," a former gubernatorial aide told me in the winter of 2009. "It ain't going to happen." That's hardly a surprise. It would be unseemly for somebody of Arnold's new stature as a statesman and politician to return full-time to the tawdriness of Hollywood, though he will undoubtedly appear in the occasional cameo. What is unusual is what he has planned instead, according to the aide and three other sources who have filled me in on an audacious plan that would be hard to believe if it involved anybody but Arnold Schwarzenegger.

"The governor fully believes he is going to be president of the United States and he is going to devote every waking moment and every penny of his fortune to see that it happens," said one insider who has been peripherally involved in these discussions.

This did not come as a particular shock when I was first apprised of it midway through my research. Arnold has made no secret of the fact that he would like to attain the Oval Office. When *60 Minutes* asked him whether he wanted to be president, shortly after Hatch introduced his amendment, he was unequivocal. "Yes. Absolutely," he said. "I think, you know, because why not? Like with my way of thinking, you always shoot for the top." At the time, however, he claimed he wasn't preoccupied with the idea, because he was too busy attending to the business of running California.

But, according to one strategist who was initially involved in the plan but has since decided the logistics are unworkable, Arnold's fiasco in the 2005 special election was in fact a result of his presidential ambitions.

"After Senator Hatch proposed what people were calling the 'Schwarzenegger Amendment' in 2004, Hatch and others were telling him that he has to start sounding like a 'real' Republican if he was going to have any chance of getting party support for a future run," this strategist revealed. "At the time, they were talking about 2008. We didn't think it could happen that fast, but they were talking about Arnold as a successor to Bush. So what happened is they advised him to move to the right to get the GOP on board. They even sent in some so-called advisers to teach him how to satisfy the party faithful. He listened to them and he got burned badly, though to give him credit, he rejected a lot of their ideas. At one point, they wanted him and Maria to start talking about their 'faith' to attract the religious right who never trusted him. They had focus groups, private polling, and everything. They spent some real money at the time. I'm not sure how much, but it wasn't cheap."

The initial strategy, he reveals, was to "get people excited" about changing the constitution. "Arnold and his people never had any doubt that he would win the presidency. It was all about the amendment. They believed that was the only thing holding him back."

As part of this strategy, the people around Arnold quietly enlisted a prominent California green-energy executive, Lissa Morgenthaler-Jones of LiveFuels—a former mutual fund manager who had helped finance and organize the 2003 recall effort—to generate spontaneous "grassroots support." It was, in fact, Morgenthaler-Jones who set up the Amend for Arnold Web site and the accompanying fund-raising organization. The group ran a series of advertisements featuring her declaring, "You cannot choose the land of your birth. You can choose the land you love. Twelve million people have chosen America. Help us to amend the constitution. Help us to amend for Arnold."

Although he publicly maintained that he wasn't focused on a presidential run, Arnold barely tried to conceal his involvement in the movement. Nor did Morgenthaler-Jones deny his support when asked.

"Arnold had done everything but sent up smoke signals that he wanted this," she said at the time, admitting that he had "authorized" his name and likeness for her site as well as for the merchandise being sold to finance the effort.

In November 2004, CBS News declared that "Arnold was popular, so popular, reason some analysts, that the amendment process, requiring two-thirds approval of both houses of Congress and passage by three-quarters of the states, could be accomplished in time for Schwarzenegger to run in 2012."

A decade earlier, Arnold's onetime rival in action movies appeared to have prophesied exactly the scenario that was now playing out. In his 1984 film *Demolition Man*, Sylvester Stallone played a Los Angeles police officer who is cryogenically frozen and then thawed out three decades later to catch his criminal nemesis, who has also been frozen. When he awakes to chase the similarly thawed-out criminal, he partners with Sandra Bullock's character, a police officer of the future. As she is showing him around Los Angeles circa 2032, she casually mentions the "Schwarzenegger Presidential Library." Stallone looks at her in shock, until she explains that Arnold Schwarzenegger had became so popular that the American people waived the "native-born requirement" to make him their leader.

But as that popularity rapidly waned with Arnold's polarizing special election in 2005, the once plausible scenario now seemed like something out of a Hollywood movie. The Amend for Arnold Web site was quietly put on "hiatus," as was the movement.

It was after his reelection in 2006, I'm told, that Arnold began to rethink his strategy for attaining ultimate power, envisioning a bold plan that could unalterably change the American political landscape.

In 2004, at the height of the campaign to amend the constitution, Arnold suddenly began to pledge his unwavering support for President Bush, saying the country was in "good hands" and calling Bush a leader who "doesn't flinch, doesn't waver, does not back down." He even called Democrats who criticized the president's handling of the economy "economic girlie men." But in 2006, after his dramatic move to the center, Arnold's tone also changed dramatically and he began to openly criticize the leader of his party. That same year, he attacked the president for failing to declare a preemptive federal disaster, freeing up funds to protect California's fragile levees a year after

Hurricane Katrina showed that such a failure could be catastrophic. A year later, he attacked the president for his inaction on climate change and said Bush's continued stalling on the issue "borders on malfeasance." In 2008, he launched another salvo, criticizing Bush's economic bailout plan. The same year, he attacked Bush for his "failure of leadership" over the environment. After Barack Obama took office and Republicans attempted to block Obama's stimulus package, Arnold criticized members of his own party for their intransigence and inexplicably called Obama's plan "terrific." What was going on? asked his old GOP allies. Had Arnold Schwarzenegger secretly joined his wife's party after sleeping with the enemy for all those years? Had he gone over to the dark side?

But the reality was that he had not become a Democrat. Instead, as I have recently learned from a series of insiders, he had devised a bold new strategy for his campaign to take the Oval Office. Arnold and his loyalists have devised a startling plan in which he would run for office not as a Republican, not as a Democrat, but as an independent.

"He won't actually call himself an independent," says one consultant familiar with the discussions. "They're looking at a new term. They're already focus-grouping a number of options. One of the ideas was 'the Third

Wave' but that was rejected. In essence, they believe they can generate an entire new political movement. It will involve Reagan Democrats, moderate Republicans disgusted by the hijacking of the party by the religious and radical right, and especially independents. They have polling to show this could be a massive force. They've done their homework."

Indeed, the United States has seen some high-profile independent presidential movements in its recent history, including the candidacy of the segregationist George Wallace in 1968 as the American Independent Party candidate and the remarkable rise of H. Ross Perot and his Reform Party in 1992. But each of these movements was merely a spoiler and eventually fizzled. Why does Arnold believe his movement would be any different?

"Governor Schwarzenegger has no doubt he would win a presidential election. No doubt whatsoever. He has it all figured it out," said the consultant. "He believes the American people will call on him to end the inaction and bickering in Washington as the only figure who has proved he can truly put aside petty partisanship to get things done. Post-partisanship will be his mantra."

I asked whether there was a chance he could still run as a Republican. "No, he says he's been told outright that he can never get the nomination. Not with his stand on abortion, gay marriage, the hot-button issues. That's why he abandoned the Republican Party in the first place: he says he didn't turn his back on the party; they turned their back on him. He thinks that's the same reason why Colin Powell never ran even though he'd have been a shoo-in."

The plan, though still in its formative stages, has already hit a number of obstacles, not the least of which is Arnold's precipitous decline in popularity during his second term as governor. Another obstacle, I'm told, is the rise in skepticism about global warming. A cornerstone of Arnold's branding is his environmental credentials. Yet, with the growth of this skepticism—a movement funded and fueled largely by corporate polluters but alarmingly successful—battling global warming may not have the appeal it once did.

"After *An Inconvenient Truth* came out, Arnold believed it was his ticket. He was even talking about enlisting Al Gore in his movement. But now they're starting to rethink that," said a Los Angeles communications consultant involved in the discussions. He also believes that Schwarzenegger's failure to sign comprehensive health care reform is a result of his presidential ambitions.

"I never heard anybody say so directly, but I'm convinced that he vetoed a single-payer system because he feared being targeted by the drug companies in a future race," this consultant explains. "Health care reform could have been his greatest legacy, but I think he anticipated the kind of stuff that happened to Obama when he proposed a similar system for the whole country a few years later. I suspect he was warned by Big Pharma not to go there, but that's just speculation on my part. I do know that he supported it, then suddenly changed his mind." During his governorship, Arnold repeatedly vetoed bills approved by the legislature to create a state universal health insurance system, claiming that "socialized medicine" is not the solution.

Another potential obstacle is Arnold's age. He will be sixty-three years old when he leaves office in 2010. "Age is the only thing that Arnold admits could stop him before he reaches his goal," the consultant reveals. "He constantly talks about Reagan. He's obsessed with Reagan. He always says that Reagan did it. Reagan was sixty-nine when he became president. That was Arnold's goal, become president by sixty-nine, which is 2016. But that doesn't leave a lot of time. He can't go much beyond that before he's seen as an old man. The clock is ticking."

Indeed, that ticking clock and the seemingly impossible task of amending the constitution in time have prompted Maria Shriver to say she believes the presidency is a futile goal. Asked by *Vanity Fair* in 2005 about her husband's presidential prospects, Maria said she would support his candidacy but emphatically declared, "It is not going to happen. The process takes years, and this is as far as it goes."

The process of amending the constitution is not an easy one. It requires a two-thirds majority in the House and Senate, followed by ratification by at least thirty-eight states. It is a process that can take years.

"It's true that amending the constitution can be a very long process," said a former strategist for Arnold's presidential efforts. "Just look at the Equal Rights Amendment. But they've got it all figured out. Whenever that comes up, they immediately point to the Twenty-sixth Amendment, the voting age amendment. That took less than a year to get passed. That's the benchmark for Arnold. I really don't know where Maria stands on this. I can't imagine he would do something like this without Maria, but she hasn't been visible at all in this stuff; she doesn't seem to be calling the shots. It's possible she genuinely opposes the idea or thinks it's unrealistic. I don't blame her. I do as well." In response to student activism and the reality that an eighteen-year-old in the United States could be drafted into the army to fight in the Vietnam War but couldn't vote, a constitutional amendment was proposed in 1971 lowering the voting age from twenty-one to eighteen. On March 10, 1971, the U.S. Senate voted unanimously for the amendment. Thirteen days later, the House approved it overwhelmingly, sending it to the states for ratification. Within seven months, the required three-quarters of state legislatures had approved it and the Twenty-sixth Amendment was passed.

"The way they plan to do it is they are going to use immigration as their wedge issue," explains the former strategist. "Keep in mind that most of this is only going to happen when Arnold leaves office next November. But they're already poring over the electoral maps and figuring out which states have the most immigrants, especially Latinos. They're going to use those populations to get them over the top. They'll be counting on the legislatures not to risk alienating these voting blocs. They've already counted those states in their plus column. They've done the math and it's not as daunting as it might look, especially with Arnold's money. He's said he has half a billion to spend and he'll spend it all if necessary. That's the figure he uses—I guess that's how much money he has in his personal fortune. There's apparently no real financial controls on how much somebody can spend to amend the constitution."

I've been told that Arnold will not be directly involved in these efforts in the beginning. Instead he will wait for an opportune time to join what appears to be a spontaneous grassroots effort.

To determine the extent of her own involvement in this movement, I contacted Lissa Morgenthaler-Jones in the spring of 2010—as an interested party, not as a reporter—and asked her the status of her Amend for Arnold organization. Intriguingly, the LiveFuels CEO responded that the site is currently in "hibernation" but that she is just waiting for the signal to revive it.

As recently as April 2010, when Arnold appeared on *The Tonight Show*, Jay Leno asked Arnold whether he would run for president if the Constitution was amended.

"Without a doubt," Arnold responded. "There's no two ways about that."

Meanwhile, there has been no decision yet on where Arnold will position himself while he's waiting for destiny to call.

"They've been kicking around all sorts of possibilities. Nothing's been decided yet. At one point they were talking about him running for the Senate, but he's not terribly popular in California at the moment and there's some doubt he could win," reveals a communications strategist who has been involved on the margins of the campaign. "I think they'll find something with some gravitas, maybe an environmental foundation, or he's talked about perhaps being the champion of the electric car, but they need to first make sure it's not a dud before attaching him to that. I think they'll wait for the dust to clear on his governorship awhile, wait for people to forget some of the unpopular budget stuff of the last couple of years and then emphasize all the stuff he's accomplished," says the strategist.

Posing as a chiropractic patient, I asked Arnold's best friend and confidant, Franco Columbu, whether he thinks Arnold has presidential plans. "Nah, never," he replied. "He's too busy to be president. And I don't think he wants to be away from his family and friends. He has many other things he wants to pursue. He'll do business, consulting, and advising for major corporations. Arnold's great at business."

Although I had been apprised for months that the Arnold for President movement was a go, one strategist recently revealed what could be the first sign that even Arnold might be having second thoughts.

"I heard the governor talking about it last week, and for the first time he mentioned somebody other than himself who could lead this movement, somebody who he said he could 'get behind.' That's Mike Bloomberg, the mayor of New York. He made a joke about how Bloomberg has more money than even him and that with their money put together they could just buy the

White House. Then he began to sort of ruminate about how Bloomberg would make a great president, how great the job he's doing as mayor, how they could go to Washington together and be the real 'twins.' "

Schwarzenegger has, in fact, been known to refer to Bloomberg, the billionaire moderate mayor of New York, as his political soul mate, so such an alliance is certainly not outside the realm of possibility and could be a powerful political force if Arnold were to put his efforts behind an independent Bloomberg candidacy. Arnold refused to follow suit when Bloomberg left the Republican Party and declared himself an independent in 2007. Yet they have made many appearances together in the years since then. However, another insider familiar with Arnold's presidential ambitions assures me that he has not backtracked on his plan at all, though she acknowledges that she could see Arnold backing Bloomberg as a "last resort."

"No, Arnold has one single-minded goal and that's to be president. I don't think he'd be content to take a backseat to anyone. In fact, I can't even see him settling for vice president. For Arnold that would be like kissing your sister."

Despite the elaborate efforts and political machinations behind the scenes, most pundits remain skeptical that Arnold could ever succeed in amending the

Constitution while he is still young enough to run. The odds against him, constitutional experts claim, are astronomical.

But George Butler, who has known him for almost four decades and played a larger role than almost anyone else in launching him into the public arena, has his own revealing assessment of his friend's chances.

"If you think Arnold can be stopped by a few phrases on a piece of parchment—well, you just don't know Arnold."

Afterword

When I first set out to tell the story of Arnold Schwarzenegger, I wasn't sure what I was expecting to find, or what I thought of a man whom I once dismissed as a cartoonish figure.

As I began my research into his life and career, I found myself torn between disdain for the brashness, arrogance, and bullying that characterized his early years and grudging admiration for the remarkable drive and determination that set him apart from most of his peers in the world of bodybuilding and show business. I had always been cynical about the Horatio Alger elements of his story—poor immigrant boy comes to America and makes good. It sounded like something scripted by the same Hollywood writers and publicists who transformed a musclebound, language-challenged cliché into a superstar.

But a funny thing happened on my way to making sense of his improbable rise to the corridors of power. I found myself discovering what many Americans, not to mention the Kennedy and Shriver families, have always found appealing about my subject, and I started to like him in spite of myself. I even started to be inspired by his larger-than-life story and his undeniable success in almost every endeavor he has undertaken over the years.

I was under no illusions about his tenure as governor, which was marked by equal measures of political opportunism, cowardice, and truly impressive accomplishments, including some of the boldest and farthest-reaching environmental legislation in history. Despite his remarkable game-changing ability to work with his political opponents in what he calls a post-partisan approach, his governorship was also marked by a number of glaring failures. I am not thinking of his inability to solve the state's financial woes. That is a nearly impossible task, the fault not of Schwarzenegger but of a shortsighted antitax mentality that long ago doomed California and its once shining system of public services and education to generations of decline.

Instead, his most disappointing legacy is his failure to sign a series of health care reforms far more progressive than those eventually introduced by Barack

Obama—a single-payer system that would have provided the kind of universal health coverage that I and
other Canadians have always taken for granted and that,
despite the myths perpetuated by its opponents, works
remarkably well and is a cornerstone of a just society.
His repeated roadblocks to approving such a system
have been an affront to the legacy of his wife's uncle
Ted Kennedy, who fought during most of his career
for these health reforms. Worse still, Arnold Schwarzenegger knows this, and he knows that the arguments
of the opponents of health reform are as odious as the
smoke from his own expensive cigars. Still, we have
come to expect exactly this sort of realpolitik from our
leaders—especially ones who aspire to higher office
and must by necessity bow to forces far more powerful
than the people they swear to serve.

I found myself convinced by his friend Franco
Columbu's assurance that Arnold has evolved considerably from the arrogant, insensitive bully that he once
was. Indeed, his continuing maturity was on display
during his seven-year governorship, as he slowly transformed himself from a politician who attempted to
browbeat and insult his opponents to one who gradually learned to find common ground and achieve great
legislation in a display of genuine bipartisanship that
has become a model for politicians everywhere. I am

A Note on Sources

During the course of my research, I interviewed more than 250 people in Austria, Canada, New York, Los Angeles, and Sacramento. Not all of them knew what I was writing about. I am grateful to those who were brave enough to speak to me on the record, but I understand the reasons why many did not. Shortly before I went to press, one of my sources at the statehouse in Sacramento contacted me and begged me not to use her name, even though she had previously given me permission to do so. "His tentacles just extend too far," she explained, reflecting the fears of many others familiar with Arnold Schwarzenegger's history of taking vengeance on his imagined enemies and with his enormous power in both Hollywood and political circles. A former colleague of Maria Shriver at CBS News told me almost exactly the same thing about her.

I am especially grateful to the late Ben Weider for his insights into his friend and protégé, as well as for inspiring me to write this book.

I owe a special debt to the biographers who came before me: Wendy Leigh for her remarkable research into Schwarzenegger's early life and career—greatly aided by something I lacked, a fluent command of German—which resulted in her excellent "warts and all" 1990 book, *Arnold: An Unauthorized Biography;* Laurence Leamer for his thorough and objective 2006 account, *Fantastic,* which had an advantage that I could only dream of, the cooperation of Arnold and Maria, who sat down with Leamer on numerous occasions; and the British biographer Nigel Andrews for his well-sourced 2003 account, *True Myths.* I am also grateful to the *Los Angeles Times* reporter Joe Mathews for his mesmerizing account of the 2003 recall effort, *The People's Machine,* published in 2006.

I am indebted to the remarkable 2004 investigation undertaken by Louise Bardach for *Los Angeles* magazine, which resulted in her fascinating exposé of the deal to suppress negative tabloid coverage of Schwarzenegger, "Taming the Hydra-Headed Carnivorous Beast."

Some readers may have qualms about the methods I sometimes use to obtain my interviews. As a journalist who specializes in undercover investigations, I often struggle with such questions myself. But any ethical reservations I may have are balanced by the fairness I owe to my subject, which requires interviewing people who would otherwise not be free to speak to me. My approach often ends up providing a more objective account, allowing friends and colleagues to tell their side of the story, and I strive to ensure that my techniques never result in ambush journalism.

Acknowledgments

This book is the result of the guidance and constant motivation of several individuals. First and foremost, I am especially indebted to my agent/manager/ close friend, Jarred Weisfeld, for his unwavering support and enormous faith in this project.

I will be forever grateful to my editor, Matthew Benjamin, for his impeccable guidance. Special thanks to Mac Mackie for his generous assistance improving the manuscript and to Lynn Grady for her enthusiasm about the project.

Any attempt to credit everyone would be futile. Nonetheless, with apologies to others, I thank Max Wallace and Christopher Heard for assisting in research and leads to sources connected to Arnold. I thank Ron Deckelbaum, David Gavrilchuk, Laurent

Medelgi, Annie Dixon, George Thwaites, Noah Levy, Aldon James, Diane Bender, Jeffrey Feldman, Olivier Mahoney, Chris Grant, Charles Small, Greg Smith, Lynn Crosbie, Mike Cohen, Stuart Nulman, Paul Carvalho, Howard Stern, Jerry Horowitz, Elise Lagace, Elvin Robinson, Andrew Walker, Clover Sky, and Tyler Walsh. And everybody at *The Insider* and *ET*, and Judith Regan.

Above all, thanks to the brave individuals who spoke on the record and to those who preferred anonymity. This book could have not been possible without your support.